Lecture Notes in Computer Scie

Commenced Publication in 1973
Founding and Former Series Editors:
Gerhard Goos, Juris Hartmanis, and Jan van Leeuwen

Rogério de Lemos
Felicita Di Giandomenico   Cristina Gacek
Henry Muccini   Marlon Vieira (Eds.)

Architecting Dependable Systems V

Volume Editors

Rogério de Lemos
University of Kent, Computing Laboratory
Canterbury, Kent CT2 7NF, UK
E-mail: r.delemos@kent.ac.uk

Felicita Di Giandomenico
ISTI-CNR, Area della Ricerca CNR
Via G. Moruzzi 1, 56124 Pisa, Italy
E-mail: felicita.digiandomenico@isti.cnr.it

Cristina Gacek
University of Newcastle upon Tyne, School of Computing Science
Newcastle upon Tyne, NE1 7RU, UK
E-mail: cristina.gacek@ncl.ac.uk

Henry Muccini
Università dell'Aquila, Dipartimento di Informatica
Via Vetoio, 1, 67010 L'Aquila, Italy
E-mail: muccini@di.univaq.it

Marlon Vieira
Siemens Corporate Research
755 College Road East, Princeton, NJ 08540, USA
E-mail: marlon.vieira@siemens.com

Library of Congress Control Number: Applied for

CR Subject Classification (1998): D.2, D.4, B.8, E.1

LNCS Sublibrary: SL 2 – Programming and Software Engineering

ISSN   0302-9743
ISBN-10   3-540-85570-X Springer Berlin Heidelberg New York
ISBN-13   978-3-540-85570-5 Springer Berlin Heidelberg New York

Springer is a part of Springer Science+Business Media

springer.com

© Springer-Verlag Berlin Heidelberg 2008
Printed in Germany

Typesetting: Camera-ready by author, data conversion by Scientific Publishing Services, Chennai, India
Printed on acid-free paper   SPIN: 12446032   06/3180   5 4 3 2 1 0

Foreword

Innovative, high-impact research results in the sciences and engineering may seem to an outsider to have sprung forth from a vacuum, but in truth, they are the result of novel combinations of known ideas. The right conditions to produce such results are often created through the intentional mixing of different communities, each with its own point of view.

For six years now, the Workshop on Architecting Dependable Systems (WADS) has brought together two distinct and very different communities, the software architecture and dependability communities, in order to provide a seedbed for the growth of new ideas concerning the design, construction, and validation of large-scale software-based systems that must be dependable. The importance of bringing together these communities has steadily grown during this period, as our society's dependence on information-technology-based systems continues to grow and as the amount of software in such systems increases.

This volume in the series focuses on methods for designing and validating critical infrastructures, both from an application-driven, top-down perspective and from a bottom-up, technology-driven perspective. In both cases, the authors include people from both the dependability and security community and the software architecture community. The discussion at the associated workshop at the IEEE/IFIP Dependable Systems and Networks meeting was lively, and the revised and expanded papers presented in this volume capture the results of those discussions, and some of the excitement of the exchanges that day.

I applaud Rogério de Lemos, Felicita Di Giandomenico, Cristina Gacek, Henry Muccini, and Marlon Vieira for their work in putting together this volume, and in their long-standing organization of the WADS series. In bringing together people from both the software architecture and dependability communities in a sustained way each year, they are engaging in a community-building effort that could have a significant payoff: the creation of the ability to architect software-based systems that are dependable by design, and remain dependable when configured in different ways throughout their range of use and lifecycle.

Such community-building is hard work, but its value is immense. I look forward to seeing the ongoing efforts that are reflected in this volume bear fruit for many years to come.

June 2008   William H. Sanders

Preface

This is the fifth book in a series on Architecting Dependable Systems we started six years ago that brings together issues related to software architectures and the dependability of systems. This book includes expanded and peer-reviewed papers based on the selected contributions to two workshops, and a number of invited papers written by recognized experts in the area. The two workshops were: the Workshop on Architecting Dependable Systems (WADS) organized at the 2007 International Conference on Dependable Systems and Networks (DSN 2007), and the Third Workshop on the Role of Software Architecture for Testing and Analysis organized as part of a federated conference on Component-Based Software Engineering and Software Architecture (CompArch 2007).

Identification of the system structure (i.e., architecture) early in its development process makes it easier for the developers to make crucial decisions about system properties and to justify them before moving to the design or implementation stages. Moreover, the architectural level views support abstracting away from details of the system, thus facilitating the understanding of broader system concerns. One of the benefits of a well-structured system is the reduction of its overall complexity, which in turn leads to a more dependable system. System dependability is defined as the reliance that can be justifiably placed on the service delivered by the system. It has become an essential aspect of computer systems as everyday life increasingly depends on software. It is therefore a matter for concern that dependability issues are usually left until too late in the process of system development.

Making decisions and reasoning about structure happen at different levels of abstraction throughout the software development cycle. Reasoning about dependability at the architectural level has recently been in the focus of researchers and practitioners because of the complexity of emerging applications. From the perspective of software engineering, traditionally striving to build software systems that are fault-free, architectural consideration of dependability requires the acceptance of the fact that system models need to reflect that it is impossible to avoid or foresee all faults. This requires novel notations, methods and techniques providing the necessary support for reasoning about faults (including fault avoidance, fault tolerance, fault removal and fault forecasting) at the architectural level.

This book comes as a result of bringing together research communities of software architectures and dependability, and addresses issues that are currently relevant to improving the state of the art in architecting dependable systems. The book consists of three parts: "Critical Infrastructures," "Rigorous Design and Fault Tolerance," and "Verification and Validation."

The first part entitled "Critical Infrastructures" includes six papers focusing on various aspects of architecting critical infrastructures. The structuring of software systems at the architectural level is especially fundamental for the development of critical infrastructures. Nowadays, public health, economy, security and quality of life heavily depend on the resiliency of a number of critical infrastructures, including energy, telecommunications, transportation, emergency services and many others. The technological advances and the necessity for improved efficiency resulted in increasingly automated and interlinked infrastructures, with consequences on increased vulnerabilities to accidental and human-made faults. Addressing the development of such systems with rigorous methodologies and evolutionary approaches at an architectural level has high potential to enhance dependability and resiliency in these critical sectors. In recognition of this emerging necessity, this book includes a specific part on architecting critical infrastructures. The six contributions grouped in this section focus on architecting critical infrastructures at both the system design level, where intrusion tolerant architectures, virtualization, improved middleware technologies and efficient communication infrastructures are addressed, and at the verification and validation level, where the problem of modeling and understanding interdependencies among interlinked critical infrastructures is tackled.

The first paper in this part, "The CRUTIAL Architecture for Critical Information Infrastructures," is by P. Verissimo, N. Neves, M. Correia, Y. Deswarte, A. Abou El Kalam, A. Bondavalli and A. Daidone. In this paper the authors highlight the susceptibility of critical information infrastructures to computer-borne attacks and faults. They discuss how to overcome these problems and propose a generic architecture as well as a set of techniques and algorithms aiming at achieving resilience of critical information infrastructures to faults and attacks in an automatic way.

The paper "A Middleware Improved Technology (MIT) to Mitigate Interdependencies Between Critical Infrastructures" by C. Balducelli, A. Di Pietro, L. Lavalle and G. Vicoli deals with new middleware technologies (MIT) to support co-ordination among different large complex critical infrastructures (LCCI). The objective is to mitigate interdependency effects so as to enhance the resilience and survivability of LCCIs. The features provided by the MIT technology, as well as the adopted reference architecture and an experimental environment for testing purposes, are overviewed. The paper is developed in the framework of the EU IRRIIS project, which aims at protecting critical infrastructures in the energy and telecommunication domains.

S. Chiaradonna, F. Di Giandomenico and P. Lollini contribute to the book with the paper "Evaluation of Critical Infrastructures: Challenges and Viable Approaches." This paper introduces critical infrastructures with a focus on the challenges for evaluation. Furthermore, it provides initial results from a Moebius modeling framework to evaluate failures in the ICT infrastructure of an electric power system. The experience gained by the authors in a European project is reported and discussed.

The fourth paper, written by A. Daidone, S. Chiaradonna, A. Bondavalli and P. Verissimo is entitled "Analysis of a Redundant Architecture for Critical Infrastructure Protection." In the CRUTIAL reference architecture each LAN is connected to the WAN through a special interconnection and filtering device. Replica rejuvenation strategy applied to these devices is based on both periodic (proactive) recoveries and on event-triggered (reactive) recoveries, seeking perpetual unattended correct operation. This paper analyzes the redundant architecture of these devices by evaluating how effective the trade-off between proactive and reactive recoveries is, identifying the relevant parameters of the architecture and finding the best parameter setup.

The fifth paper in this part, "A Robust Semantic Overlay Network for Microgrid Control Applications," is by G. Deconinck, T. Rigole, H. Beitollahi, R. Duan, B. Nauwelaers, E. Van Lil, J. Driesen, R. Belmans and G. Dondossola. In this paper the authors present Agora, which is a semantic overlay network that allows one to efficiently route queries in overlay networks. The routing is related to microgrid control, and the semantics is based on an XML description of the static and dynamic characteristics of the intelligent electronic devices. It is robust against changes, and provides graceful degradation in case of unrecovered failures.

The paper "Architecting Dependable and Secure Systems Using Virtualization" by B. Jansen, H. V. Ramasamy, M. Schunter and A. Tanner explores the emerging virtualzation approach, through which the real hardware system configuration is abstracted from, to enhance systems dependability and security. A practical realization of a subset of the proposed enhancements, namely, intrusion detection and protection, using the Xen open-source virtual machine monitor (VMM) is detailed. In such a context, the impact of virtualization on node reliability is quantified using combinatorial modeling. The results of these analyses constitute useful guidelines on design options to effective leveraging of virtualization to system dependability purposes. They also triggered further improvements by the authors on the VMM design.

The second part of this book is entitled "Rigorous Design and Fault Tolerance" and contains three papers.

The paper "Model-Based Approaches for Dependability in Ad-Hoc Mobile Networks and Services" by G. Pinter, Z. Micskei, A. Kovi, Z. Egel, I. Kocsis, G. Huszerl and A. Pataricza reports the authors' research activity to architect dependable, distributed systems through a model-driven design approach. The ad-hoc mobile networks context adopted by the EU Hidenets project is specifically addressed. Contributions include the construction of the UML model of the Hidenets platform, the construction of a metamodel of the applications running on the platform, the UML profile for the metamodel as well as the definition of a set of design patterns to support the implementation of applications built for the Hidenets platform using the defined profile.

In the paper "Design, Implementation and Deployment of State Machines Using a Generative Approach", G. N.C. Kirby, A. Dearle and S.J. Norcross present an approach to designing and implementing a distributed system as a family of related finite state machines, generated from a single abstract model. The state machine family formalizes the interactions between the components of the distributed system, allowing increased confidence in correctness. The feasibility of the proposed approach was demonstrated in the context of a Byzantine fault-tolerant commit protocol used in a distributed storage system.

The third paper in this part, "Handling Emergent Nondeterminism in Replicated Services," is written by J. Slember and P. Narasimhan. This paper presents Midas, an approach to identifying and addressing multiple sources of nondeterminism in a multi-service replicated distributed architecture. Midas involves a combination of compile-time dependency, concurrency and nondeterminism analyses, followed by the performance-sensitive compensation of nondeterminism at runtime.

Part three of the book is on "Verification and Validation" and includes five papers focusing on approaches to architecture level verification, validation, analysis and evaluation.

This part starts with a paper by M. H. Diallo, L. Naslavsky, T. A. Alspaugh, H. Ziv and D. J. Richardson that is entitled "Toward Architecture Evaluation Through Ontology-Based Requirements-Level Scenario." The paper describes an approach for evaluating whether a candidate architecture dependably satisfies stakeholder requirements expressed in requirements-level scenarios. The approach maps scenarios expressing both functional requirements and quality attributes of the system, to architectural elements through an ontology of requirements-level event classes and domain entities. This in turn provides a clear connection between stakeholder requirements and architectural solutions to address them.

In their paper entitled "Combining Formal Verification and Testing for Correct Legacy Component Integration in Mechatronic UML," H. Giese, S. Henkler and M. Hirsch present a combined use of testing and formal verification for verifying complex real-time component-based systems that include legacy components. The approach is motivated by the need of sufficiently validating the integration of real-time, embedded, and legacy components, and by the claim that a testing phase alone, when applied to such a domain, cannot provide enough guarantees. Thus, the approach proposed here is composed of many steps: a behavioral model of embedded legacy components is derived from the existing interface description; then, such an initial model is submitted to formal verification; if the verification step identifies a failure, the produced counterexample is used to test the legacy component; the execution information is used for refining the behavioral model of the legacy components; the new synthesized behavior is then the starting point for the next iteration. In summary, while formal verification is used for verifying components interactions, local testing of the legacy components is used to refine the behavioral model.

S. Wang, G. S. Avrunin and L. A. Clarke, in their paper "Plug-and-Play Architectural Design and Verification," focus on software plug-and-play architectural design. They propose an approach that allows designers to experiment with alternative design choices of component interactions in a plug-and-play manner. The paper describes how to design and present plug-in-play components using a set of notations to show classified component interactions; furthermore it provides details of how reusable formal models can be created for the connector building blocks. This approach is particularly useful to specify and present different component connection relationships.

In the fourth paper, entitled "Data Flow-based Validation of Web Services Compositions: Perspectives and Examples," C. Bartolini, A. Bertolino, E. Marchetti and I. Parissis describe the use of data flow modeling for testing composite Web services (WSs). The central problem on testing WSs is that the dynamic binding of services makes it impractical to test in advance all the concrete service combinations that can be involved in a workflow. By considering in an explicit way a model of how data are expected to be exchanged between the combined services, it is possible to check whether desired properties are satisfied or also to test whether the implemented Web services composition (WSCs) complies with that model. The authors discuss ways in which, depending on the information available, the flow of data in WSCs can be usefully referred to for verification and validation purposes.

The fifth paper, by T. Kettu, E. Kruse, M. Larsson and G. Mustapic, is entitled "Using Architecture Analysis to Evolve Complex Industrial Systems." This paper from industry provides practical advice on how to reconstruct the architecture of existing software systems by combining the use of tools and the existing knowledge within the organization. The authors claim that to obtain an up-to-date view of the system and prevent expensive mistakes during system evolution, it is fundamental to obtain an up-to-date view of the architecture of the system. The paper is based on experiences from two cases related to industrial automation.

Architecting dependable systems is now a well-recognized area, attracting interest and contributions from many researchers. We are certain that this book will prove valuable for both developers designing complex applications and researchers building techniques supporting this. We are grateful to many people that made this book possible. Our thanks go to the authors of the contributions for their excellent work, the DSN 2007 WADS and CompArch 2007 ROSATEA participants for their active participation in the discussions, and Alfred Hofmann from Springer for believing in the idea of a book series on this important topic and for helping us to get it published. Last but not least, we appreciate very much the efforts of our reviewers who helped us in ensuring the high quality of the contributions. They are Sascha Konrad, Tao Xie, Graham Kirby, Rick Kazman, Simona Bernardi, Istvan Majzik, Bedir Tekinerdogan, Miguel Correia, Gergely Pinter, Silvano Chiaradonna, Stephan Storck, Sandro Bologna, Santosh Shrivastava, Paolo Lollini, Alan Hartman, Giovanna Dondossola, Nuno Neves, Sasikumar Punnekkat, Mauro Gaspari, Holger Giese, Eda Marchetti, Kristina Lundqvist, Paris Avgeriou, Luciano Baresi, Andrea Polini, Joseph Slember, Andreas Ulrich, Andrea Bondavalli, Suzanne Embury, Jerry Gao, Roberto Baldoni, Daniel Paulish, Stephan Storck, and several anonymous reviewers.

June 2008

Rogério de Lemos
Felicita Di Giandomenico
Cristina Gacek
Henry Muccini
Marlon Vieira

Table of Contents

Part 3. Verification and Validation

The CRUTIAL Architecture
for Critical Information Infrastructures*

Paulo Veríssimo[1], Nuno F. Neves[1], Miguel Correia[1], Yves Deswarte[2],
A. Abou El Kalam[3], Andrea Bondavalli[4], and Alessandro Daidone[4]

[1]Universidade de Lisboa, FCUL
Lisboa, Portugal
[2]LAAS-CNRS [3]IRIT, ENSEEIHT-INPT, Université de Toulouse
[4]University of Florence
Florence, Italy
{pjv,nuno,mpc}@di.fc.ul.pt, yves.deswarte@laas.fr,
anas.abouelkalam@enseeiht.fr, bondavalli@unifi.it,
daidone@dsi.unifi.it

Abstract. In this chapter we discuss the susceptibility of critical information infrastructures to computer-borne attacks and faults, mainly due to their largely computerized nature, and to the pervasive interconnection of systems all over the world. We discuss how to overcome these problems and achieve resilience of critical information infrastructures, through adequate architectural constructs. The architecture we propose is generic and may come to be useful as a reference for modern critical information infrastructures. We discuss four main aspects: trusted components which induce prevention; middleware devices that achieve runtime automatic tolerance and protection; trustworthiness monitoring mechanisms detecting and adapting to non-predicted situations; organization-level security policies and access control models capable of securing global information flows.

1 Introduction

The largely computerized nature of critical infrastructures on the one hand, and the pervasive interconnection of systems all over the world, on the other hand, have generated one of the most fascinating current problems of computer science and control engineering: how to achieve resilience of critical information infrastructures. In this chapter, we are concerned with the susceptibility of the latter to computer-borne attacks and faults, i.e., with the protection of these infrastructures.

We propose an architecture and a set of techniques and algorithms aiming at achieving resilience to faults and attacks in an automatic way. Although we focus on the computer systems behind electrical utility infrastructures as an example, the architecture we propose is generic and may come to be useful as a reference for modern critical information infrastructures.

---

* This work was mainly supported by the EC, through project IST-FP6-STREP 027513 (CRUTIAL) and NoE IST-4-026764-NOE (ReSIST), by the FCT through the Large-Scale Informatic Systems Laboratory (LaSIGE) and the CMU-Portugal partnership.

R. de Lemos et al. (Eds.): Architecting Dependable Systems V, LNCS 5135, pp. 1–27, 2008.
© Springer-Verlag Berlin Heidelberg 2008

It is worthwhile recapitulating some of the reasoning behind the blueprint of this architecture, recently published [23]. Although inspired by previous intrusion-tolerant system architectures, the CRUTIAL architecture was largely influenced by two facts. Firstly, the fact that Critical Information Infrastructures (CII) feature a lot of legacy subsystems (controllers, sensors, actuators, etc.). Secondly, the fact that conventional security and protection techniques can bring serious problems, when directly applied to CII controlling devices, by preventing their effective operation. Although they are very practical problems, we will show ahead that they yielded in fact very interesting research challenges.

Another relevant fact was that our belief that the crucial problems in critical information infrastructures lie with the forest, not the trees, has been confirmed everyday as new incidents have occurred. That is, the problem is mostly created by the generic and non-structured network interconnection of CIIs, which bring several facets of exposure impossible to address at individual level. Whilst it seems today non-controversial that such a status quo brings a considerable level of threat, to our knowledge there had been no previous attempt at addressing the problem through the definition of a reference model of a *critical information infrastructure distributed systems architecture*. One which, by construction, would lay the basic foundations for the necessary global resilience against abnormal situations. Our conjecture was that such a model would be highly constructive, for it would form a structured framework for (1) conceiving the right balance between prevention and removal of vulnerabilities and attacks; (2) achieving tolerance of remaining potential intrusions and designed-in faults; and (3) enabling adaptation and self-awareness mechanisms to overcome unforeseen situations. In this chapter, we will report some advances in this area.

Finally, and in a related manner, we conjectured that any solution, to be effective, has to involve automatic control of macroscopic command and information flows, occurring essentially between the several realms composing the critical information infrastructure architecture (both intra- and inter-organizations), with the purpose of securing appropriate system-level properties, at organizational level. This has to be addressed, in an automatic way, through innovative access control models that understand the organizational reality, and are thus capable of translating the related high-level security policies into the adequate technical mechanisms such as access control matrices and firewall filter rule-sets.

The chapter is organized as follows: Section 2 does the Architecture Description. Then, the Protection Strategies and Services are introduced in Section 3, followed by the Trustworthiness Monitoring Services in Section 4. The chapter concludes with a discussion on Access Control for Critical Information Infrastructures, in Section 5.

2 Architecture Description

The CRUTIAL architecture encompasses four aspects. (i) Architectural configurations featuring trusted components in key places, which a priori induce prevention of some faults, and of certain attack and vulnerability combinations. (ii) Middleware devices that achieve runtime automatic tolerance of remaining faults and intrusions, supplying trusted services out of non-trustworthy components. (iii) Trustworthiness monitoring mechanisms detecting situations not predicted and/or beyond assumptions made, and adaptation mechanisms to survive those situations. (iv) organization-level security policies and access control models capable of securing information flows with different criticality within/in/out of a CII. It is important to point out that the notion of CII is hard to formalize. The generic idea is that the CII is the computer systems (or ICT) part of a critical infrastructure, which is the working definition that we use in this chapter.

Intrusion tolerance mechanisms are selectively used in the CRUTIAL architecture, to build layers of progressively more trusted components and middleware subsystems, from baseline untrusted components (nodes, networks). This leads to an automation of the process of building trust: for example, at lower layers, basic intrusion tolerance mechanisms are used to construct a trustworthy communication subsystem, which can then be trusted by upper layers to securely communicate amongst participants without bothering about network intrusion threats. Middleware services and protocols in the architecture use distinct techniques that address different levels of criticality of the architecture, such as randomization and wormholes, software or hardware implementations, and support a diverse set of requirements from the applications: dynamic and static groups; synchronous, partially-synchronous, and asynchronous execution; tolerance from benign accidental faults to malicious coordinated attacks.

CRUTIAL Information Switches (CIS) route the information to and from LANs with different criticality levels, wherever they are in the infrastructure: intranet, SCADA, Internet gateway. In fact, a lot of the protection and intrusion resilience reside in this class of components that interconnect the several LANs comprising a CRUTIAL architecture. But they are more than mere TCP/IP routers: in a simplistic way they could be seen as sophisticated circuit or application level firewalls combined with equally sophisticated intrusion detectors, connected by distributed protocols. Collectively they act as a set of servers providing distributed services relevant to solving our problem: achieving control of the command and information flow, and securing a set of system-level properties.

Monitoring and diagnosis can be performed at several levels, through diverse mechanisms: CIS self-diagnosis, the diagnosis inside the CIS as part of the fault tolerance policy of the CIS itself; diagnosis on other components in the system (making assumptions on the security policy applied inside the CIS); diagnosis on the LANs and their nodes; diagnostic information gained by processing the security policy decisions, interpreting them as error detections. The collected information may be used in order both to take local decisions and to coordinate CIS activities.

Access control is a key issue. Although several organizations are normally involved and have to cooperate in the operation of a CII, from the access control point of view, each organization in a CII should keep its independence and responsibility on its assets and personnel. We propose that: each organization defines its own security policy (according to the OrBAC model), and enforce it with its own authentication and authorization means; the organizations cooperate through web services, and for each web service, a contract is signed between the provider and the client; this contract is translated in security rules (expressed within the Poly-OrBAC model), these rules being implemented with the involved CIS, and enforced at each step of web service interaction; the interactions are recorded into logs by each involved CIS, and these logs can serve as evidence in case of dispute: each organization stay liable of all actions initiated by its own personnel.

2.1 Key Architecture Aspects

The CRUTIAL architecture, despite inspired by previous intrusion-tolerant reference architectures like MAFTIA [22], extends them significantly to attend the specific challenges of the critical information infrastructure problem, for example, legacy, global access control, and above all non-stop operation and resilience.

Given the severity of threats expected, some key components are built using architectural hybridization methods in order to achieve extremely high robustness:

– *Trusted-trustworthy* operation [22] is an architectural paradigm whereby components prevent the occurrence of some failure modes *by construction*, so that their resistance to faults and hackers can justifiably be trusted. In other words, some special-purpose components are constructed in such a way that we can argue that they are always secure, so that they can provide a small set of services useful to support intrusion tolerance in the rest of the system. This concept is in line with, but richer than, recent technological concepts like trusted computing or trusted platform modules.

Another interesting aspect of this work is related with the mechanisms that we had to develop, to preserve the large legacy composition of CII and keep changes to a minimum:

– *Fully-transparent intrusion tolerance* aims at preserving the complete illusion of a standard system to legacy components. It is implemented by innovative replica control and communication algorithms. Any SCADA and corporate network technologies stay unchanged, the only modification foreseen being the requirement of IPsec at communication level, but this is considered a trend anyway [4].

Another innovative aspect of this work is our approach to achieve resilience. This goes further to mere intrusion tolerance, and can be seen as a specialization of this kind of architecture to critical infrastructures. The problem is addressed through two paradigms:

– *Proactive-resilience* to achieve exhaustion-safety [20], and ensure perpetual, non-stop operation despite the continuous production of faults and intrusions. This is not a requirement of many intrusion-tolerant systems, but it is definitely of importance for unattended operation, as is desired of the control part of CII.
– *Trustworthiness monitoring* to perform surveillance of the coverage stability of the system, that is, of whether it is still performing inside the assumed fault envelope or beyond assumptions made [2]. In the latter case, dependable adaptation mechanisms are triggered to stabilize coverage and thus, the operational guarantees. This is of extreme importance for situations of instability, either caused by accidental events or malicious attacks, and we believe it can be a key to lower the risk of cascading and/or escalating failures.

Finally, the desired control of the information flows is partly performed through advanced protection mechanisms:

– the *OrBAC firewall* is an adaptation of the classical firewall rule-set operation to enforce an organization-based access control model (OrBAC) [11] for implementing global-level security policies. OrBAC allows the expression of security policy rules as high level abstractions, and it is of importance for homogenizing the diverse security policies of organizations involved in a CII into one policy that controls the global information flow.

In summary, the mechanisms and algorithms in place achieve system-level properties of the following classes: trustworthiness or resistance to faults and intrusions (i.e., security and dependability); timeliness, in the sense of meeting timing constraints raised by real world control and supervision; coverage stability, to ensure that variation or degradation of assumptions remains within a bounded envelope; dependable adaptability, to achieve predictability in uncertain conditions; resilience, read as correctness and continuity of service even beyond assumptions made.

2.2 Main Building Blocks

The overall picture of a CRUTIAL system, shown in Figure 1, was detailed in [23].

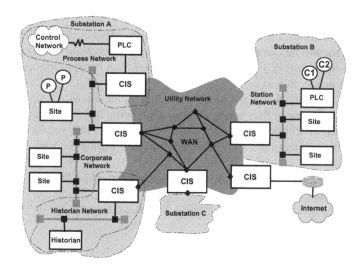

Fig. 1. CRUTIAL overall architecture (WAN-of-LANs connected by CIS)

We view the system as a WAN-of-LANs. There is a global interconnection network, the WAN, that switches packets through generic devices that we call *CRUTIAL Information Switches (CIS)*, which in a simplistic way could be seen as sophisticated circuit or application level firewalls combined with equally sophisticated intrusion detectors, connected by distributed protocols. The WAN is a logical entity operated by the CII operator companies, which may or may not use parts of public network as physical support. A LAN is a logical unit that may or may not have physical reality (e.g., LAN segments vs. Virtual LANs (VLANs)). More than one LAN can be connected by the same CIS. All traffic originates from and goes to a LAN. As example LANs, the reader can envision: the administrative clients and the servers LANs; the operational (SCADA) clients and servers LANs; the engineering clients and servers LANs; the PSTN modem access LANs; the Internet and extranet access LANs; an historian network (to store monitoring data); etc.

CIS collectively act as a set of servers providing distributed services relevant to solving our problem: *achieving control of the command and information flow, and securing a set of necessary system-level properties.* In consequence, no traffic set to enjoy CRUTIAL-level protection can go from one LAN to another without crossing a CIS.

3   Protection Strategies and Services

We now discuss the failure assumptions underpinning the architecture design, concerning the main architectural devices: WAN, LAN, CIS. Shadowing in the figure symbolizes untrusted areas:

- The WAN interconnect (heavily shadowed) is assumed to have arbitrary behavior, which is akin to saying it can be totally compromised.
- The CII facilities (lightly shadowed) are assumed to have varying faulty behavior, from arbitrary to crash failure.
- Inside the facilities, the LAN is the unit of failure. This is akin to assuming that some LANs will be completely trusted (e.g., by construction, or by recursive use of intrusion tolerance), whereas other LANs may even be arbitrary (e.g., in consequence of insider threats).
- Overall, we assume that faults (accidental, attacks, intrusions) continuously occur during the life-time of the system, the only limit being that a maximum number of f malicious (or arbitrary) faults can occur within a given interval. Note that this is weaker than assuming that only f faults may occur during the whole life-time of the system.
- CIS components are trusted to securely switch information flows as a service to edge LANs as clients.
- LANs trust the services provided by the CIS, but are not necessarily trusted by the latter.

The assumptions described above have a few implications on the protection strategies chosen. Let us start by the CIS construction:

- The CIS is a main target to any hacker having understood the CRUTIAL architecture, since the CIS is supposed to be a trusted component. We recognize this threat by assuming that a number of CIS or components thereof can be corrupted.
- In order to be trusted, the CIS must be trustworthy. As such, the CIS itself must be made intrusion-tolerant, prevent resource exhaustion providing perpetual operation (i.e., can not stop), and be resilient against assumption coverage uncertainty, providing survivability.
- The CIS is thus implemented as a set of redundant units (multiple-box physically replicated hardware units, or single-box logically replicated software units), depending on the level of resilience to attain.

- Given the nature of malicious faults, which can be made common-mode, CIS construction and or reconfiguration may be based on diversity techniques (ex. n-version programming, obfuscation, etc.).
- The CIS also has proactive recovery mechanisms, so that each component is periodically rejuvenated in such a way that if it suffered an intrusion, then the intrusion is no longer present after the rejuvenation process.
- The CIS is further monitored by special run-time trustworthiness monitoring mechanisms, which make sophisticated sanity checks. Reactive recovery may for example be triggered immediately an successful attack or failure is detected. Adaptation mechanisms may also be parameterized by these monitors.

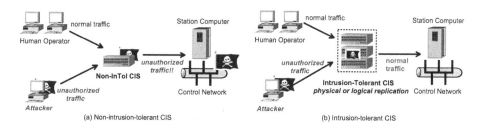

Fig. 2. Building trust in CRUTIAL (CIS level)

As exemplified in Figure 2a, a simplex (i.e., non intrusion-tolerant) CIS, once attacked, becomes under the control of the attacker and can fail. In the figure, attack traffic will go through the compromised CIS and hit the station computer and control networks in the CII. On the other hand, an intrusion-tolerant CIS (Figure 2b) despite corruption of one or more components, will continue providing correct service, as long as not more than a quorum f of component failures occur. CIS can be physically or logically replicated, examples of this incremental intrusion tolerance strategy are discussed in [1]. The figure shows a triple with a corrupted replica ($f = 1$): despite attacked by unauthorized traffic, voting between all replicas discards these messages, only letting normal traffic through to the station computer.

Let us look at the services running in or among CIS:

- The local services implemented on the CIS servers enjoy the CIS intrusion tolerance to secure the desired properties in the presence of malicious traffic and/or commands.
- The distributed services implemented on sets of CIS servers are subject to possibly Byzantine attacks. In consequence, cooperating CIS must be interconnected with intrusion-tolerant protocols, in order to correctly implement the desired services.

Consider that the CIS boxes in the next figures represent intrusion-tolerant logical CIS. That is, to any services running locally on top of a logical CIS, the latter appears as being fail-controlled, in a good example of recursive use of intrusion-tolerance featured by this architecture. As exemplified in Figure 3a, services running on an intrusion-tolerant CIS are trusted to run correctly, despite faults or attacks. As such, these services are trusted-trustworthy, that is, trusted because they are trustworthy.

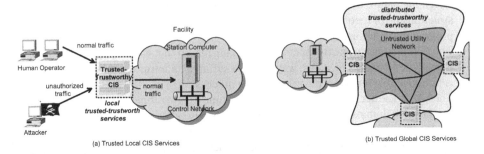

Fig. 3. Building trust in CRUTIAL (WAN level): a) Trusted Local CIS Services; b) Trusted Global CIS Services

On the other hand, some services may need to be run cooperatively amongst CIS, and thus be subject to attacks at the WAN interconnect level. If one generalizes the distributed intrusion tolerance concept to CIS interconnection, one will run specialized intrusion-tolerant algorithms amongst CIS, which end-up achieving what is portrayed in Figure 3b: a trusted-trustworthy communication fabric amongst CIS, overcoming the initial untrusted basic WAN interconnect.

4 Trustworthiness Monitoring Services

The main diagnostic problems that can be found in a modern power grid distributed infrastructure as CRUTIAL are the following:

– The use of SCADA sub-systems which were not designed to be widely distributed and remotely accessed, and that do not cover security issues (they grew-up as stand-alone systems). SCADA systems are not going to be redesigned or rebuilt, so they cannot be modified in order to comply with the information infrastructure needs.
– Some of the components/sub-systems used within the infrastructure already implement monitoring and/or recovery techniques that could in some way work "against" the needs of the infrastructure itself. It is hence necessary to coordinate all the monitoring and/or recovery activities in order to favor the infrastructure needs (sometimes despite of component/sub-system needs).
– The use of large grained components: there are many interactions among sub-components, so it is difficult to link a single error with a well focused fault. Two kind of actions may follow: i) if the detected error is severe enough to require immediate action, then determine the set of all components that could harbor the originating fault, as well as the specific commands able to bring each component to a correct, consistent state; ii) otherwise, if it is not beneficial, as soon as an error (or deviation) is observed, to immediately declare an entire component "failed" and to proceed to repairing or replacing it; it is thus better to collect streams of data about error symptoms and deviation detection, and proceed to fault assessment by observing component behavior over time.

– The heterogeneity of the environment where diagnosis is performed: many different entities will coexist in the system, so each component needs specific diagnostic solutions (station sub-systems need to exchange values in order to perform the secondary power control, whilst the substation web service provides visibility of selected information over internet).
– The goodness of a component could be related to the quality of the service provided, rather than on the absence of faults.
– The infrastructure has to be distributed by its very nature, so it is exposed to communication and coordination problems, as well as to those caused by hardware or operating system ones; it is not possible to manage these problems at the component level, but it is necessary to do that at middleware level (or at least at application level). In order to provide fault tolerance to distributed component based applications, it is necessary to implement mechanisms which take into account the fault tolerance policies implemented by the different components within the system, and to add the necessary coordination support for the management of fault tolerance at application level.

4.1   The Diagnosis Framework

The diagnosis framework adopted to tackle these challenges involves the following actors (see Figure 4):

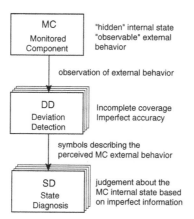

Fig. 4. The diagnosis framework

Monitored Component (MC). It is the system component under diagnosis. The monitored component, when first introduced in the system, works properly; during system lifetime, the monitored component could be affected by some faults that might compromise its functional behavior. The internal healthy state[1] of the component

---

[1] The "internal state" is something related to the component situation with respect to faults; there is no relationship between the above "internal state" and the possible component states related with the work performed by the component itself.

is therefore "hidden", whilst the external behavior is "observable". Since the same observed incorrect behavior could be caused by different faults, it is an ambiguous indicator of the healthy internal health state of the component itself.

Deviation Detection (DD). It is the entity introduced in the system in order to observe the monitored component external behavior and to judge whether it is suitable or not. Unsuitable component behavior could be the result of the manifestation of an internal or external fault affecting the monitored component or it could be determined by a change in the requirements of the application that is using the component monitored services. In the literature on fault tolerance, a wide variety of error detection mechanisms are available, which are classified in different categories according to several criteria, among which the type of checks they perform, the implementation support (hw or sw), the system components they are tailored to, the applicability time (on-line or off-line) [19]. The deviation detection mechanism has indeed incomplete coverage and imperfect accuracy, so it can raise false positives (when it detects an inexistent deviation) and false negatives (when it does not detect an existent deviation). In critical systems both false positives and false negatives are undesired: false positives led to an early depletion of system resources, while false negatives drastically decrease the system dependability.

State Diagnosis (SD). Basing on information coming from the deviation detection mechanism, the state diagnosis mechanism has to guess the internal state of the component. Deviation detection information is an imperfect judgment describing the instantaneous external behavior of the monitored component; the state diagnosis mechanism has to trace the monitored component deviations over time in order to decide whether the monitored component services continue to be beneficial or not for the rest of the system, deviations notwithstanding.

The diagnosis framework requires two information flows:

- MC↔DD: the deviation detection mechanism has to observe the monitored component.
- DD↔SD: the state diagnosis mechanism has to collect deviation detections performed by the deviation detection mechanism.

Each of the above information flows could be managed following a proactive or a reactive schema: in the proactive schema, the entity interested in fresh information has to ask for it, whilst in the reactive schema the entity that generates information has to send it to the entity interested in it. More interaction patterns can be found in [17].

The above solutions have different balances in terms of QoS vs. cost of the data fed to the SD mechanism: continuous monitoring is very costly and probably too aggressive in terms of the overhead it induces on the system; buffered asynchronous monitoring is cheaper then the continuous monitoring for the interaction cost, but requires storing capabilities in the DD mechanism and negatively affect the promptness of the SD; the failure triggered synchronous monitoring combines the advantages of the continuous monitoring (timeliness of the input data and no need for storage) and of the buffered asynchronous monitoring (reduction in communication cost), but can be impaired by omission faults in the DD.

The traditional diagnostic problem is the identification of failed components in a usually large set of homogeneous ones; fine grained components are the target of diagnosis, therefore, one-shot diagnosis of a collected syndrome[2] is performed. Literature shows that many over-time diagnostic mechanisms are available; each approach can be mapped on the schema presented earlier and described involving only one component and its deviation detection mechanisms. Two approaches are relevant:

Heuristic diagnosis. Heuristics are typically simple mechanisms suggested by intuitive reasoning and then validated by experiments or models. Most heuristic diagnosis solution are based on a count-and-threshold approach [14], as exemplified by alpha-count [3] a heuristic designed to discriminate whether a monitored component is affected by a transient fault (the component is healthy but is temporally behaving bad) or by a permanent fault (the component is physically damaged and need maintenance). The idea behind the alpha-count heuristic consists in counting error signals collected over time, raising an alarm when the counter passes a predefine threshold. When non-error signals are collected, the counter is decreased using a decreasing factor. Suppose $J(t)$ is a Boolean error signal coming from the deviation detection mechanism at time t ("0" means no-error detected, "1" means error detected) and suppose that K is the internal parameter that decreases the counter value when a "no-error" signal is collected; the alpha counter $\alpha(t)$ is formally defined as follow:

$$\alpha(0) = 0$$
$$\alpha(t) = \begin{cases} \alpha(t-1) \cdot K & \text{if } J(t) = 0 \\ \alpha(t-1) + 1 & \text{if } J(t) = 1 \end{cases} \quad (0 \leq K \leq 1)$$

Every time the counter is evaluated, it is also compared with a predefined threshold value α_t in order to discriminate if an alarm has to be raised ($\alpha(t) \geq \alpha_t$) or not ($\alpha(t) < \alpha_t$). Extended analyzes about parameter tuning are available in [3] while applications and variants are described in [2] [18].

Probabilistic diagnosis. Probabilistic diagnosis mechanisms (e.g. [6] based on HMM - Hidden Markov Models and [16] based on Bayesian inference) are tailored to evaluate the probabilities of the monitored component being in each of the "internal" state envisioned in the fault model, based on symbols coming from the deviation detection mechanism. Probabilistic diagnostic mechanisms compute a state occupancy probability vector $f(t)$ at time t, using the symbols coming from the deviation detection mechanism at time t and the state occupancy probability vector $f(t-1)$ at time $t-1$. The idea behind probabilistic diagnosis is to use the Bayesian inference. Suppose to have a conjecture x on which we are uncertain (we believe in x being true with probability $p(x)$); we aim to update our belief in x when some new, relevant evidence is observed. Both evidence and conjecture are described as events, that is, subsets of the set of all the possible outcomes of some experiment. Using the Bayes' theorem we can write that in general:

$$p(x|evidence) \cdot p(evidence) = p(evidence|x) \cdot p(x)$$

---

[2] A syndrome is a vector of Boolean deviation detection results.

Interpreting the left-most probability in the above equation as the "posterior" probability of conjecture x (taking into account the observed evidence) and the right-most probability as the "prior" probability of conjecture x, we can write

$$p_{posterior}(x \,|\, evidence) = \frac{p_{prior}(x) \cdot p(evidence \,|\, x)}{p(evidence)}$$

Given a set C of mutually exclusive conjectures such that their union has probability 1 (e.g. healthy states of a monitored component), the above formula allows us to update the posterior probability of conjecture x given some evidence (e.g. the outcome of deviation detection) using the following formula:

$$p_{posterior}(x \,|\, evidence) = \frac{p_{prior}(x) \cdot p(evidence \,|\, x)}{\sum_{cong \in C} p_{prior}(cong) \cdot p(evidence \,|\, cong)}$$

Both approaches solve the problem with the same computational cost, but diagnosis based on HMM accounts for higher modularity and relies on a richer framework to solve diagnostic problems (e.g., helps in case of incomplete information on the involved parameters).

Diagnosis activity has to be performed at different granularity levels (Fault Replacement Unit), depending on the controllability of control on the monitored component (e.g., when dealing with COTS and legacy subsystems) and on the cost/efficacy ratio of the detection/diagnosis/reconfiguration operations. On one side, fine grained diagnosis is very helpful since it allows replacement of smaller parts of the system, avoiding wasting still useful subparts of the components under diagnosis. However, fine grained diagnosis incurs in higher costs from the point of view of setting up diagnosis activities. Opposite trends are instead shown by a coarse grained approach.

When diagnosis needs to be performed in a large system it is not practical to have a centralized SD entity that has to gather and analyze all the deviation detections in order to diagnose the system; this kind of centralized state diagnosis should be ultra-reliable and communication links to all the parts of the system should be guaranteed. Therefore, methods for distributed diagnosis are mandatory in which every system node decides independently about the system (e.g. which are the healthy nodes and which the faulty ones).

Considering a distributed system comprised by completely connected nodes, the Hybrid Fault-Effect Model [28] can be assumed, so that all fault classification is based on a local classification of fault-effects (to the extent permitted by the deviation detection mechanism of the sub-system itself) and on a global classification, thus developing a global opinion on the fault-effect. Diagnosis is thus performed using a two-phase approach on a concurrent, on-line and continual basis:

1. Local detection and diagnosis, aiming to diagnose the sub-system itself.
2. Global information collection and global diagnosis, obtained through exchange of local diagnosis. Since each sub-system may have a different perception of the errors observed on the remote sub-systems, each node has some private values (the results of private diagnosis on remote sub-systems) and the goal is to ensure consistent information exchange and agreement against Byzantine behavior. An agreement (or consensus) algorithm is thus needed in order to solve the problem.

In the general case, the necessary conditions to achieve consensus in spite of up to f arbitrarily faulty nodes are:

– at least $3f + 1$ nodes in the system.
– at least $f + 1$ rounds of message exchange.

Under the assumption of authenticated messages [8], which can be copied and forwarded but not altered without detection, the condition on the minimal number of nodes can be relaxed to $f + 2$.

4.2 Diagnosis in CRUTIAL

The CRUTIAL infrastructure is organized as a WAN-of-LANs (see Section 2.2), where each LAN is connected to the WAN by a CIS. Given that the computers inside the LANs cannot be modified/updated, all the diagnosis activity has to be performed inside the CIS. The following diagnosis scenarios arise:

– CIS self-diagnosis (local view): CIS monitors both itself (e.g. to diagnose hardware or software faults) and its LAN (e.g. to "measure" its level of trustworthiness).
– CIS distributed diagnosis (global view): CISes construct a common view about the "state" of a certain CIS in the infrastructure (e.g. related to the liveness and trustworthiness of a specific CIS)

CIS Self-Diagnosis. From a local viewpoint the CIS is a sophisticated application level firewall (combined with equally sophisticated intrusion detectors) which is required to:

– be intrusion-tolerant;
– prevent resource exhaustion providing perpetual operation;
– be resilient against fault assumption coverage uncertainty providing survivability.

In order to comply with the above requirements, the CIS has a hybrid architecture and is replicated (with diversity) in n replicas. Each CIS replica is built using a synchronous and secure local wormhole and an asynchronous and insecure payload.

Two monitoring/failure detection scenarios arise:

1. internal monitoring: monitoring performed inside a single replica, trying to detect local failures;
2. external monitoring: monitoring performed on the perceived behavior of the other replicas.

The internal monitoring has to be performed on the following components/services (so far, components/services that need to be monitored were not definitely identified):

– Hardware components (e.g. network interfaces, processing units, memory modules...) which are supporting the replica. The monitoring activity on these components makes sense only when physical replication is used; in case of logical replication, these components need to be monitored in the host system running the replicas.

- Software components belonging to several architectural levels in the payload or in the operating system.

Several signals coming from many architectural levels are collected and processed over time: an example of signal coming from low architectural levels (O.S.) is related to a CPU fan that is working too slow or a temperature sensor that is signaling the CPU is too warm. An example of signal coming from a higher architectural level is an application-generated exceptions or error return code.

The internal monitoring activity has hence to identify compound system conditions which could require diverse corrective actions; for example, repeated application errors could be interpreted as manifestation of software aging requiring rejuvenation, or could be correlated with lower level signals (the CPU is too warm because the CPU fan is working too slow), requiring another kind of reconfiguration (e.g. replacing the CPU fan). The rationale behind internal monitoring and failure detection is to try to stop the replica before it starts to behave incorrectly.

The external monitoring is performed by each replica on the perceived behavior of the other replicas, given that a replica is not guaranteed to always behave correctly. The monitoring activity is performed at service level, so that each service is in charge of detecting whether its peers running in the other replicas seem correct or not. An example of middleware service monitoring its peers on other replicas is the Protection Service.

CIS LAN Diagnosis. The CIS monitors over time the nodes in its protected LAN to evaluate their trustworthiness. The evaluated trustworthiness level is used to request maintenance actions on the protected node (e.g. replacing hardware, refreshing the software, changing passwords...).

A trustworthiness indicator for each protected node N is defined (it could be multi-dimensional) and modified based on the following events:

- the instance of the security policy applied within the CIS itself to the outgoing traffic detects that N is trying to violate the security policy (e.g. trying to send something without being allowed to do it);
- the instance of the security policy running on a remote CIS detects that a message sent by N to one of its protected nodes was rejected. The CIS distinguishes whether an incoming packet really comes from a station computer (instead from an hacker in the WAN) using the LAN Traffic Labeling service (the CIS protecting the source node signs the label). The signed label is hence a proof of the source of the packet.

The LAN Diagnosis service collects over time the above detections in order to evaluate the trustworthiness indicator of each protected node. If protected trustworthiness indicator of node N goes over a given threshold, the LAN Diagnosis service alerts its peers about N being un-trustable (so that they can possibly take adequate countermeasures).

CIS Distributed Diagnosis. The several replicas that made up a single CIS are required to perform the same operations; this simplifies somewhat the task of checking their correctness on the run. Each single CIS, as seen from the WAN, is a different logical entity, in terms of actions, services and requests toward other CISes. In the ordinary information flow there is no simple comparison rule check that can be performed, to catch on the fly a mischievous partner. On the other hand, if a CIS becomes compromised, internal redundancy and resilient architecture notwithstanding, then necessarily the basic hypothesis on the fault occurrence has been broken: more than f replicas are out of order together. Of course, this is the catastrophic case, whose probability has to be lowered down to a target level by choosing proper redundancy figures. However, a local catastrophe (regarding a single LAN controlled by a compromised CIS) not necessarily should imply the downing of the entire system. In fact, on the WAN side, all CISes attempt to maintain a common view of two parametric descriptors its partners' health: Liveness and Trustworthiness.

Liveness is checked in two ways: i) passively, by monitoring normal network traffic from the target; ii) if the former is not frequent enough, exert a form of resilient ping, by means of a simple challenge/response protocol. Trustworthiness is built up by checking the formal correctness of the messages coming from the target, as well from any access violation detected by the Protection Service.

5 Access Control for Critical Information Infrastructures

Because Critical Information Infrastructures (CII) become more and more complex and accessible via the Internet, they are more and more vulnerable to security threats. Moreover, due to the interdependencies between CIIs, simple failures can have dramatic consequences. In this context, security issues in CIIs become obvious and serious. Several works was dedicated to study the causes; the results have shown that one of the most common problems is the lack of specific security policies, in particular in modern SCADA environments [12].

Basically, a security policy is defined by the Common Criteria as *the set of laws, rules, and practices that regulate how an organization manages, protects, and distributes sensitive information* [15]. In this respect, a security policy is specified through: the security *objectives* that must be satisfied, e.g., "*classified information must not be disclosed to a competing organization*"; and the *rules* expressing how the system may evolve in a secure way, e.g., "*the owner of an information is allowed to grant a read access right on its data to other organizations*".

Nevertheless, by itself, the security policy does not guarantee a secure and correct functioning of the system. The security policy can indeed be badly designed or intentionally / accidentally violated. Consequently, it is important to express the policy according to a security model; a model helps to: abstract the policy and handle its complexity; represent the secure states of a system (i.e., states that satisfies the security objectives) as well as the way in which the system may evolve; verify the consistency of the security policy and detect the possible conflicting situations; etc.

Addressing these issues, this work progressively derives an access control model, a secure architecture and applies our approach to secure CIIs. To do so, we first identify the security requirements of a CII and we confront them to existing access control models. Note that even if we take our examples from electric power grid, the same approach and results can be applied to any kind of CII.

Globally, a CII can be seen as a WAN connecting several organizations involving different actors and stakeholders (e.g., power generation companies, substations, energy authorities, maintenance service providers, transmission and distribution system operators) and various LANs. LANs are composed of one or more logical and physical systems and are interconnected through specific Switches, called CIS (*CRUTIAL Information Switches*). The general architecture is presented in Section 2.

In this respect, we can identify some security-related requirements such as:

1. *Secure cooperation* between different organizations, possibly mutually suspicious, with different features, functioning rules and policies.
2. *Loosely coupled organizations*: each organization controls its own security policy, applications, etc., while respecting the global functioning of the whole system. In other words, we need a global security policy that manages the communication between partner organizations while keeping each CII responsible for its own assets and users.
3. *Coherence and consistency*: as no SCADA system operates in isolation, the global as well as local security policies should be compatible.
4. *Decentralization*: it is desirable that the enforcement and administration of the security policies be decentralized. Actually, a centralized approach is not interesting since CIIs involve the cooperation between independent organizations. Inversely, handling the collaboration between the organization subsystems while keeping some local self-determination seems more interesting.
5. *Heterogeneity*: the different CII organizations have their own structure, services, OS, and local objects. These entities' structures may be different from an organization to another.
6. *Granularity vs. scalability*: on the one hand, security rules must be extensible in size, structure, and number of organizations; on the other hand, internal authentication as well as local access controls should be managed by each organization separately.
7. *Fine-grained access control*: access decisions should take the context (e.g., specific situations, time and location constraints) into account. Moreover, as the context may change often and as certain reactivity is required in these systems, organizations should support dynamic access rights.
8. *Users-friendliness and easiness of rules administration*: as the global system links several organizations geographically distributed and as it handles a large amount of information and a big number of user, the access right management should be sufficiently user-friendly to manage this complexity without introducing errors.
9. *Remote accesses*: as organizations control large installations, the security policy should define if and how outsiders and users from a partner organization can connect to the automation system and to resources belonging to each organization. For example, it is important to define how vendors can access the system remotely for off-site maintenance and product upgrades, but also how other organizations participating in the CII can access local resources.
10. *Compliance with the specific regulation*: for example, in the United-States, NERC 1200 [5] specifies requirements for cyber-security related to electric utilities.
11. *Confidentiality, integrity and availability*: contrarily to other systems where mostly confidentiality (military systems), integrity (financial systems) or availability is

needed, in the organization we often need these three properties (confidentiality of each organization's data, e.g., invitation of tenders, but also integrity and availability of data such as the voltage/frequency measurements).

12. *Enforcement of permissions, explicit interdictions as well as obligation rules.* In fact, explicit prohibitions can be particularly useful as we have decentralized policies where each administrator does not have details about the other parts of the system. Moreover, explicit prohibitions can also specify exceptions or limits the propagation of permissions in case of hierarchies. Similarly, obligations can be useful to impose some internal / external, manual / automatic actions that should be carried out by users or automatically by the system itself.

13. *The security policy must be vendor- and manufacturer-independent.* As technologies change and new acquisitions occur, the policy must remain effective. When vendor- or technology-specific statements are used, the maintenance burden for the policy increases. Then, the policy would be changed any time there is a new purchase or an advance in technology. If the security policy is not updated, it becomes obsolete, which would not be acceptable in such systems.

14. *Audit and assessment:* the security policy will define the logging requirements such as what will be logged, when, where, etc. In particular, an audit will determine if the protections which are detailed in the policy are being correctly put in practice on the system; it also checks if the contracts / agreements established by the partner organizations are well-respected.

To satisfy these requirements, we propose a secure architecture where each organization defines its own security policy and enforces it into its CISs (see Section 2). CISs are thus responsible for checking if local actions are in accordance with internal security policies, but also if inter-organization flows are done according to the global policy and to the contracts established by partner organization. Finally, CISs keep log files as evidence in case of abuse or conflict. In this respect, the first question that arises is how the security policies will be specified and what security model will be adapted to organizations?

An analysis of classical access control policies and models shows that unfortunately, none of these policies and models satisfies the CIIs security-related requirements. For instance, HRU represents the relationships between the subjects, the objects and the actions by a matrix M [9]. $M(s, o)$ represents the action that s is allowed to carry out on o. It is thus necessary to enumerate all the triples (s, o, a) that correspond to permissions defined by the policy, which is very complex in large systems. Moreover, when new entities are added to or removed from the system, it is necessary to update the policy, still adding to the complexity. Consequently, models associated to discretionary access control policies (including HRU) are not capable of managing huge, multi-organizational and decentralized systems such as CIIs.

Role Based-Access Control (RBAC) is more flexible: roles are assigned to users, permissions are assigned to roles and users acquire permissions by playing roles [7]. Even if RBAC is suitable for a large range of organizations, it does not cover all the requirements of a CII, in particular it does not define how users of an organization can play roles in another organization.

5.1 OrBAC

In [11] we have defined the OrBAC (*Organization-based Access Control*) model as an extension of RBAC that details permissions while remaining implementation independent. Our first goal was to express the security policy with abstract entities only, and thus to separate the representation of the security policy from its implementation. Indeed, OrBAC is based on roles as the abstraction of users (like in RBAC [7]), views as the abstraction of objects (like in VBAC [24]), and activities as the abstraction of actions (like in TBAC [21]).

Actually, in OrBAC, an organization is a structured group of active entities, in which subjects play specific roles; an activity is a group of one or more actions; a view is a group of one or more objects; and a context is a specific situation that conditions the validity of a rule.

As a user can play several roles in several organizations, the *Role* entity is used to structure the link between the subjects and the organizations. In fact, contrarily to RBAC that considers a binary relation between roles and subjects, OrBAC consider the ternary relationship *Empower (org, r, s)*: it means that *org* employs subject *s* in role *r*. In the same way, the objects that satisfy a common property in a certain organization are specified through views (the *Use(org, view, object)* relationship), and activities are used to abstract actions in organizations (the *Consider (org, activity, action)* relationship) (Figure 5).

Now, once the relationships between the different system' entities are defined, we can specify the security rules. Actually, an OrBAC security rules have the *Permission (org, r, v, a, c)* form: in the context *c*, organization *org* grants role *r* the permission to perform activity *a* on view *v*. *Obligation* and *Prohibition* are defined similarly (*Obligation (org; r; v; a; c)* and *Prohibition (org, r, v, a, c)*).

Actually, two security levels can be distinguished in OrBAC (Figure 5):

- *Abstract level*: the security administrator defines security rules through abstract entities (roles, activities, views) without worrying about how each organization implements these entities.
- *Concrete level*: when a user requests an access, concrete authorizations are granted (or not) to him according to the concerned rules, the organization, the played role, the instantiated view / activity, and the current parameters (e.g., the context).

The derivation of permissions (i.e., runtime instantiation of security rules) can be formally expressed as indicated in (Figure 5):

$\forall org \in Organization, \forall s \in Subject, \forall \alpha \in Action, \forall o \in Object, \forall r \in Role, \forall a \in Activity,$ $\forall v \in View, \forall c \in Context$
Permission(org, r, v, a, c) ∧   // **a security rule in its abstract form**
Empower(org, s, r) ∧   // in *org*, the role *r* is played by a subject *s*
Consider(org, α, a) ∧   // in *org*, the activity *a* correspond to an action *α*
Use(org, o, v) ∧   // in *org*, the view *w* corresponds to an object *o*
Hold(org, s, α, o, c)   // in *org*, the context *c* is true for *s*, *α* and *o*
→ *is-permitted(s, α, o)*   // **runtime decision allowing *s* carrying out *α* on *o***

This rule means: *if* in a certain organization, a security rule specifies that "role *r* can carry out the activity *a* on the *v* when the context *c* is True"; *if* "*r* is assigned to subject

Fig. 5. The ORBAC model

s"; *if* "action α is a part of a"; *if* "object o is part of v" and, *if* "the context c is True; *Then* s is allowed to carry out α on o.

As rules are expressed only through abstract entities, OrBAC is able to specify the security policies of several collaborating and heterogeneous organizations (e.g., in a CII), if they are considered as "sub-organizations" of a "global organization" with a single OrBAC policy. In fact, the same role, e.g., *"operator"*, can be played by several users belonging to different sub-organizations; the same view, e.g., *"TechnicalFile"*, can designate a *TF-Table* or a *TF1.xml*; and the same activity *"read"* could correspond in a particular sub-organization to a *"SELECT"* action (if the sub-organization has a database system) while in another sub-organization it may specify an *OpenXMLfile()* action.

In our context, OrBAC present several benefits and satisfies several security requirements of CIIs:

- *Rules expressiveness:* OrBAC defines permissions, interdictions, obligations, and constraints (by means of contextual conditions).
- *Abstraction of the security policy:* OrBAC has a structured expression of the policy; it separates the specification of the policy from its implementation. Consequently, OrBAC greatly reduces the cost of administering security policies as well as making the process less error-prone.
- *Scalability:* thanks to its abstraction levels, OrBAC has no limitation in size or capacity. It can define an extensible and huge policy. It is then easily applicable to large-scale environments.
- *Loose coupling:* each sub-system can manage its own local OrBAC security policy, as far as it respects the global policy.
- *Evolvable:* a local policy in OrBAC is evolvable. It easily handles changes in organizations.
- *User-friendly:* the specification and update of a local OrBAC security policy is easily managed at the local organization level.
- *Standardized:* OrBAC has a growing community. Many research tracks are being conducted (see www.orbac.org).

However, OrBAC is centralized and does not handle collaborations between organizations, while these aspects are very important in CIIs. In fact, as OrBAC security rules have the *Permission(org, r, v, a, c)* form, it is not possible to represent rules that involve several independent organizations, or even, autonomous sub-organizations of a particular collaborative system. Moreover, it is impossible (for the same reason) to associate permissions to users belonging to other partner-organizations. As a result, if we can assume that OrBAC provides a framework for expressing the security policies of several organizations, it is unfortunately only adapted to centralized structures and does not cover the distribution, collaboration and interoperability needs of current CIIs.

Moreover, the enforcement of the policy to access control mechanisms is not treated in OrBAC. It is thus necessary to describe suitable architecture and implementation of the studied system's security.

To cover these limitations, we suggest enhancing OrBAC with new concepts and calling on some mechanisms of the Web Services (WS) technology [10]. In fact, WS is a set of technologies that provide platform-independent protocols and standards used for exchanging heterogeneous interoperable data services. Software applications written in various programming languages and running on various platforms can use WS to exchange data over computer networks in a manner similar to inter-process communication on a single computer. WS also provide a common infrastructure and services (e.g., middleware) for data access, integration, provisioning, cataloging and security. These functionalities are made possible through the use of open standards, such as: XML for exchanging heterogeneous data in a common information format [26]; SOAP acts as a data transport mechanism to send data between applications in one or several operating systems [25]; WSDL is used to describe the services that an organization (e.g., a CII) offers and to provide a way for individuals and other organizations to access those services [27]; UDDI is an XML-based registry/directory for businesses worldwide, which enables businesses to list themselves and their services on the Internet and discover each other [13].

Web services (WS) have several benefits that could be interesting in our context:

- *Interoperability and heterogeneity*: WS support data exchanges between different platforms.
- *Resources sharing*: WS are adapted to applications where organizations share their resources.
- *Standardized mechanisms*: WS use open protocols and standards (e.g., HTTP, XML).
- *Easiness*: a small amount of code and resources is necessary to develop and carry out a WS.
- *Compatibility with OrBAC*: it is easy to couple web services with OrBAC.

5.2 PolyOrBAC

At this stage, we have demonstrated that OrBAC as well as WS could be suitable for CIIs. The question that takes place is: how adapting OrBAC as well as WS mechanisms to specify and enforce secure collaboration between CIIs. To answer this question, we have defined the PolyOrBAC [10], a global access control model that can be perfectly applied to CIIs.

Actually, PolyOrBAC distinguishes two phases:

First phase *publication and negotiation of collaboration rules as well as the corresponding access control rules.* First, each organization determines which resources it will offer to external partners. Web services are then developed on application servers, and referenced on the Web Interface to be accessible to external users.

Second, when an organization publishes its WS at the UDDI registry, the other organizations can contact it to express their wish to use the WS. To highlight the PolyOrBAC concepts, let us take a simple example where organization *B* offers *WS1*, and organization *A* is interested in using *WS1* (Figure 6).

Third, *A* and *B* negotiate and come to an agreement concerning the use of *WS1*. Then, *A* and *B* establish a contract and jointly define security rules concerning the access to *WS1*. These security rules are registered – according to an OrBAC format – in a database (connected to the *A* and *B*'s CIS) containing the Security policy. For instance, if the agreement between *A* and *B* is *"users from A have the permission to consult B's measurements in the emergency context"*, *B* should:

- have (or create) a rule that grants the permission to a certain role (e.g., *Operator*) to consult its measurements: *Permission(B, Operator, Measurements, Consulting, Emergency)*; note that every user playing the Operator role will have this permission
- create a "virtual user" *PartnerA* that represents *A* for its use of *WS1*
- add the *Empower(B, PartnerA, Operator)* association to its rule base.

In parallel, *A* creates locally a "virtual object" *WS1_image* which represents *WS1*, and adds a rule in its OrBAC base to define which of *A*'s roles can invoke *WS1_image* to use *WS1*.

Second phase: *runtime access to remote services.*

Let us first precise that we use an *AAA (Authentication, Authorization and Accounting)* architecture: we separate authentication from authorization; we distinguish access control decision from permissions enforcement; and we keep access logs in CISs. Basically, if a user from *A* (let us note it *Alice*) wants to carry out an activity, *she* is first authenticated by *A*. Then, protection mechanisms of *A* check if the OrBAC security policy (of *A*) allows this activity. We suppose that this activity contains local as well as external accesses (e.g., invocation of *B*'s *WS1*). Local accesses should be controlled according to *A*'s policy, while the *WS1*'s invocation is both controlled by *A*'s policy (Alice must play a role that is permitted to invoke *WS1_image*), and by *B*'s CIS, according to the contract established between *A* and *B*. If both controls grant the invocation, the execution of *WS1* is executed under the control of *B*'s OrBAC policy (in *B*, *PartnerA* plays role *Operator* that is permitted to consult measurements).

More precisely, when *Alice* is authenticated and authorized (by *A*'s policy) to invoke *WS1*, an XML-based authorization ticket "*T1*" is generated (based on the positive decision) and granted to *Alice*.

T1 contains the access-related information such as: the virtual user played by *Alice*: "*PartnerA*"; *Alice*'s organization: "*A*"; the contract ID; the requested service: "*WS1*"; the invoked method, e.g., "*Select*"; and a timestamp to prevent replay attacks.

Note that $T1$ is delivered to any user (from A) allowed to access to *WS1* (e.g., *Jean, Alice*). When *Alice* presents its request as well as $T1$ (as a proof) to B, B's CIS extracts the $T1$'s parameters, and processes the request. By consulting its security rules, B associates the *Operator* role to the virtual user "*PartnerA*" according to *Empower(B, PartnerA, Operator)*[3]. Finally, the access decision is done according to *Permission(B, Operator, Measurements, Consulting, Emergency)* $\wedge$*mpower(B, PartnerA, Operator)*.

PolyOrBAC offers several benefits:

- *Peer to peer approach*: we use a decentralized architecture where organizations mutually negotiate their common rules; each organization is responsible for its users authentication and is liable for their use of other organizations' services; it also controls the access to its own resources and services.
- *Independence*: all security rules are specified in OrBAC independently by each organization, and the organizations remain loosely coupled (through jointly agreed rules, expressed by contracts).
- *Information non-disclosure*: the WS technology allows communications between organizations without intimate knowledge of each other's IT systems; moreover, even if remote accesses are possible, it is not necessary to know the internal structure of the other organizations.
- *Extensible structure*: the OrBAC extensibility and the WS standards facilitate the management and the integration of new organizations (with their users, data, services, policy, etc.).

5.3 A Scenario

Let us now apply PolyOrBAC to a real electric power grid scenario: in emergency conditions, the TS CC (*Transmission System Control Center*) can trigger load shedding on the DS (*Distribution System*) to activate defense plan actions (e.g., load shedding activities) on the Distribution Grid. More precisely, the TS CC (*Transmission System Control Center*) monitors the Electric Power System and elaborates some potentially emergency conditions that could be remedied with opportune load shedding commands applied to particular areas of the Grid.

Actually, as indicated in Figure 6, during normal operation, the Distribution Substations (DSS) send signals and measurements (voltage, Frequency, etc.) to the Transmission System Control Center TS CC (via the Distribution System Control Center DS CC); in the same way, the Transmission Substations (TSS) send signals and measurements (voltage, frequency, etc.) to the TS CC (steps 1, 2 and 3 in Figure 6).

At the TS CC level, when the TSO (*Transmission System Operator*) detects that a load shedding may be needed in the near future, it sends an arming request to the Distribution System CC (step 4 in Figure 6).

Consequently, the DSO (*Distribution System Operator*) selects which distribution substations (DSS) must be armed (these substations are those on which the load shedding will apply if a load shedding is necessary), and then sends arming commands to

---

[3] Let us recall that *Empower(B, PartnerA, Operator)* has been added after the negotiation phase (phase 1).

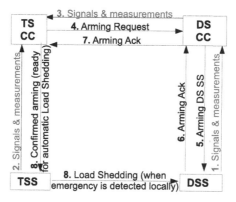

Fig. 6. The exchanged commands and signals

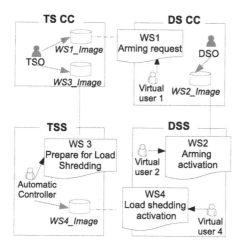

Fig. 7. The different WS invocations

those DSS. The DSO has naturally the permission to arm or disarm any DSS in the depending area of the DS CC.

If a Transmission SS (TSS) detects an emergency, it triggers (sends) a load shedding command to all the distribution substations (DSS) of its area. Of course, only the DSS already armed will execute the load shedding command.

In this scenario, we distinguish four organizations (TS CC, a TSS, DS CC and a DSS), two roles (TSO and DSO) and four web services (Figure 7): *Arming Request, Arming Activation, Confirmed Arming* and *Load Shedding Activation*.

Basically, when negotiating the provision/use of *WS1* between TS CC and DS CC, on the one hand, TS CC locally stores the WSDL description file and creates a new object as a local image of WS1 (whose actions correspond to WS1 invocations), and on the other hand, DS CC creates a virtual user (playing a role authorized to invoke *WS1*) to represent TS CC.

Table 1. The different WS of our scenario

WS1-Arming Request	Provider: DS CC
	Client: a user (TSO) or a process at TS CC
WS2-Arming Activation	Provider: DSS
	Client: DSO or a virtual user at DS CC
WS3-Confirmed Arming	Provider: TSS
	Client: a virtual user at TS CC
WS4-Load Shedding Activation	Provider: DSS
	Client: a user (automatic controller) at TSS

Moreover, TS CC adds local rules allowing Alice, a user playing the role TSO, to invoke *WS1_image*: *Empower(TS CC, Alice, TSO)*, and *Permission(TS CC, TSO, Access, TSO Distribution Circuits, Emergency)*. In this respect, when Alice requests the access to *WS1*, the access decision is done according to the following rule:

> *Permission(TS CC, TSO, Access, TSO Distribution Circuits, Emergency)* ∧
> *Empower(TS CC, Alice, TSO)* ∧
> *Consider(TS CC, rwx, Access)* ∧
> *Use(TS CC, WS1-Image, TSO Distribution Circuits)* ∧
> *Hold(TS CC, Alice, rwx, WS1_Image, emergency)* ∧
> → *is-permitted(Alice, rwx, WS1_Image)*

Besides, at the DS CC side, two rules are added: *Empower(DS CC, Virtual_User1, Operator)* and *Permission(DS CC, Operator, Access, DSO Distribution Circuits, emergency)*. Consequently, when Alice invokes WS1_Image, this invocation is transmitted to the DS CC by activating a process (running for Virtual_User1) which invokes *WS1*. This access is checked according to DS CC's policy and is granted according to the rule:

> *Permission(DS CC, Operator, Access, DSO Distribution Circuits, Emergency)* ∧
> *Empower(DS CC, Virtual_User1, Operator)* ∧
> *Consider(DS CC, rwx, Access)* ∧
> *Use(DS CC, WS1, TSO Distribution Circuits)* ∧
> *Hold(DS CC, Virtual_User1, rwx, WS1, emergency)* ∧
> → *is-permitted(Alice, Virtual_User1, WS1)*

The other Web Services are negotiated and activated in the same way. This example shows that PolyOrBAC is a convenient framework for the security of Critical Information Infrastructures.

6 Conclusion

The chapter presented a distributed systems architecture for resilient critical information infrastructures, with respect to both accidental faults and malicious attacks and intrusions. Several aspects, such as design decisions and innovative mechanisms, were discussed and explained, in order to guide the reader through the making of such architectures.

The rationale for this work was based on three fundamental propositions: classical security and/or safety techniques alone will not be enough to solve the problem; any effective solution has to involve automatic control of macroscopic command and information flows between the LANs composing the CII; and, the unifying paradigm should be a reference architecture of "resilient critical information infrastructures" performing the integration of the different realms of a CII system.

The proposed solution encompasses a range of mechanisms of incremental effectiveness, to address from the lower to the highest criticality operations in a CII. Architectural configurations with trusted components in key places induce prevention of some attacks. Middleware software attains automatic tolerance of the remaining faults and intrusions. Trustworthiness enforcing and monitoring mechanisms allow unforeseen adaptation to extremely critical, not predicted situations, beyond the initial assumptions made.

Functionally, the information flow is controlled by basic mechanisms of the firewall and intrusion detection type, complemented and parameterized by organization-level security policies and access control models, capable of securing information flows with different criticality within a CII and in/out of it.

Some of the services running in CIS may require some degree of timeliness, given that SCADA implies synchrony, and this is a hard problem with malicious faults, so we plan to do research in this issue. We also take into account that these systems should operate non-stop, a hard problem with resource exhaustion, since the continued production of faults during the life-time of a perpetual execution system leads to the inevitable exhaustion of the quorum of nodes needed for correct operation.

Acknowledgements

CRUTIAL is a project of the IST programme of the European Commission. Several institutions participate to the project: CESI RICERCA (Italy), FCUL (Portugal), CNR-ISTI (Italy), LAAS-CNRS (France), K.U.Leuven-ELECTA (Belgium), CNIT (Italy). Details about the project can be found at: http://crutial.cesiricerca.it/. We warmly thank our partners at the project for many discussions on the topics of the chapter. We also thank our colleagues and students in our research groups for their collaboration and feedback on this work.

References

1. Bessani, A.N., Sousa, P., Correia, M., Neves, N.F., Verissimo, P.: Intrusion-tolerant protection for critical infrastructures. DI/FCUL TR 07–8, Department of Informatics, University of Lisbon (April 2007)
2. Bondavalli, A., Chiaradonna, S., Cotroneo, D., Romano, L.: Effective fault treatment for improving the dependability of COTS- and legacy-based applications. IEEE Transactions on Dependable and Secure Computing 1(4), 223–237 (2004)

3. Bondavalli, A., Chiaradonna, S., Di Giandomenico, F., Grandoni, F.: Threshold-based mechanisms to discriminate transient from intermittent faults. IEEE Transactions on Computers 49(3), 230–245 (2000)
4. Byres, E., Karsch, J., Carter, J.: NISCC good practice guide on firewall deployment for SCADA and process control networks. Technical report, NISCC, Revision 1.4 (February 2005)
5. North American Electric Reliability Council. Urgent action standard 1200 (2003)
6. Daidone, A., Di Giandomenico, F., Bondavalli, A., Chiaradonna, S.: Hidden Markov models as a support for diagnosis: Formalization of the problem and synthesis of the solution. In: 25th IEEE Symposium on Reliable Distributed Systems (SRDS 2006), pp. 245–256 (October 2006)
7. Ferraiolo, D., Sandhu, R., Gavrila, S., Kuhn, D., Chandramouli, R.: A proposed standard for role-based access control. ACM Transactions on Information and System Security 4(3) (2001)
8. Gong, L., Lincoln, P., Rushby, J.: Byzantine agreement with authentication: Observations and applications in tolerating hybrid and link faults. Dependable Computing for Critical Applications, IFIP WG 10.4, preliminary proceedings 5, 79–90 (1995)
9. Harrison, M.A., Ruzzo, W.L., Ullman, J.D.: Protection in operating systems. Communications of the ACM 19(8), 461–471 (1976)
10. El Kalam, A.A., Deswarte, Y., Baina, A., Kaaniche, M.: Access control for collaborative systems: A web services based approach. In: Proceedings of the IEEE International Conference on Web Services, pp. 1064–1071 (2007)
11. El Kalam, A.A., Elbaida, R., Balbiani, P., Benferhat, S., Cuppens, F., Deswarte, Y., Miége, A., Saurel, C., Trouessin, G.: Organization-based access control. In: IEEE 4th International Workshop on Policies for Distributed Systems and Networks, pp. 277–288 (June 2003)
12. Kilman, D., Stamp, J.: Framework for SCADA security policy. Technical report, Sandia Corporation (2005)
13. Lala, J.H. (ed.): Foundations of Intrusion Tolerant Systems. IEEE Computer Society Press, Los Alamitos (2003)
14. Mongardi, G.: Dependable computing for railway control systems. In: Proceedings of the International Conference on Dependable Computing for Critical Applications, pp. 255–277 (1993)
15. International Standards Organization. ISO/IEC Standard 15408-1, Common Criteria for Information Technology Security Evaluation, Part 1: Introduction and general model 3 (July 2005)
16. Pizza, M., Strigini, L., Bondavalli, A., Di Giandomenico, F.: Optimal discrimination between transient and permanent faults. In: Proceedings of the 3rd IEEE High Assurance System Engineering Symposium, pp. 214–223 (1998)
17. Romano, L., Bondavalli, A., Chiaradonna, S., Cotroneo, D.: Implementation of threshold-based diagnostic mechanisms for COTS-based applications. In: Proceedings of the 21st IEEE Symposium on Reliable Distributed Systems, pp. 296–303, October 13-16 (2002)
18. Serafini, M., Bondavalli, A., Suri, N.: Online diagnosis and recovery: On the choice and impact of tuning parameters. IEEE Transactions on Dependable and Secure Computing 4(4), 295–312 (2007)
19. Siewiorek, D.P., Swartz, R.S.: Reliable Computer Systems: Design and Evaluation. A.K. Peters (1998)
20. Sousa, P., Neves, N.F., Verissimo, P.: How resilient are distributed f fault/intrusion-tolerant systems? In: Proceedings of the IEEE International Conference on Dependable Systems and Networks (June 2005)
21. Thomas, R., Sandhu, R.: Task-based authorization controls. In: Proceedings of the 11th IFIP Working Conference on Database Security, pp. 166–181 (1997)

22. Verissimo, P., Neves, N.F., Cachin, C., Poritz, J., Powell, D., Deswarte, Y., Stroud, R., Welch, I.: Intrusion-tolerant middleware: The road to automatic security. IEEE Security & Privacy 4(4), 54–62 (2006)
23. Verissimo, P., Neves, N.F., Correia, M.: The CRUTIAL reference critical information infrastructure architecture: A blueprint. International Journal of System of Systems Engineering (to appear, 2008)
24. Vitek, J., Jensen, C.: A view-based access control model for CORBA. In: Vitek, J. (ed.) Secure Internet Programming. LNCS, vol. 1603. Springer, Heidelberg (1999)
25. W3C. SOAP, version 1.2. W3C Recommendation (June 2003)
26. W3C. Extensible markup language (XML). W3C Recommendation (February 2004)
27. W3C. WSDL, version 2.0. W3C Candidate Recommendation (March 2006)
28. Walter, C.J., Lincoln, P., Suri, N.: Formally verified on-line diagnosis. IEEE Transactions Software Engineering 23(11), 684–721 (1997)

A Middleware Improved Technology (MIT) to Mitigate Interdependencies between Critical Infrastructures

Claudio Balducelli, Antonio Di Pietro, Luisa Lavalle,
and Giordano Vicoli

ENEA (Italian National Agency for New Technologies, Energy and the Environment)
Via Anguillarese 301, 00060 Rome, Italy

Abstract. Public life, economy and society as a whole depend to a very large extend on the proper functioning of critical infrastructures (CIs) like energy supply or telecommunication. The extensive use of information and communication technologies (ICT) has pervaded the critical infrastructures, rendering them more intelligent but even increasingly interconnected, complex, interdependent, and therefore more vulnerable. In this paper a new technology (MIT - Middleware Improvement Technology) is proposed: it is based on a collection of software components aiming at enhancing the dependability, the survivability and the resilience of LCCIs (Large Complex Critical Infrastructures) by mitigating dependency and interdependency effects. It should prevent and limit cascading effects and/or support automated (if possible) recovery and service continuity in critical situations. The research activities and results described in the paper have been developed inside EU/FP6 Integrated Project IRRIIS - Integrated Risk Reduction of Information-based Infrastructure Systems.

Keywords: interdependencies, critical infrastructure, information sharing, middleware technology, situation awareness, risk assessment, soap, ejb, jms, java, application server.

1 Introduction

Every artificial system is composed by a set of interconnected *elementary components,* every one with a certain role inside the system; the complete functionality of the whole system depends on the proper functioning of the single components.

If a system is *simple* (it is formed by a small amount of elementary components), the failure of a single component may generate a general failure of the whole system.

If a system is *complex* (it is formed by a large amount of elementary components), it can in general survive in presence the failure of a single component, because its functionality may be replaced by some other components. This is the so called "N-1" property of a complex system: it normally contains N components working, but it can also survive with N-1 components working when a single component fails.

In general, more a system is complex, more such *self-healing* capacity is strong. But this intrinsic self-healing capacity could decrease when the system has the necessity to be interfaced by some other external systems from which it receive some

R. de Lemos et al. (Eds.): Architecting Dependable Systems V, LNCS 5135, pp. 28–51, 2008.

critical services. In this case the survivability of the system is not preserved only by its internal components but also by the resources received by other external systems; this resources cannot be furnished by the internal system components.

In the last years it was recognized that Large Complex Critical Infrastructures (LCCIs) [1], are complex systems that suffer of major instability problem today respect to the past. This problem is increasing today because the degree of *connectivity* between LCCIs is also increasing.

2 The Interdependency Problem

The *interdependency* problem is considered by the emergency management institutions and communities, and its significance has increased since governments and citizens became aware that services furnished by power distribution networks, telecommunication networks, transport infrastructures and other key resources are actually more critical, and these LCCIs are today more interconnected respect than in the past. To maintain their style of living, modern societies are more dependent on their critical infrastructures; but, ironically, the actual ICT advances do not reduce the critical infrastructures instability problem. Some new types of emerging vulnerabilities are producing a strong impact in the future emergency management practices and in the social security strategies.

The need for protecting critical infrastructures becomes more important also as a consequence of the so-called 'cascading effect', caused by mutual *interdependencies* [1] of the networks. There are different causes and external conditions that contribute to augment such type of interdependency. When we consider critical infrastructures, we have to take into account that they are not simply 'physical' plants and networks. In fact, they contain not only a physical layer, but are also made of 'cyber' components and systems, and include human organisations that manage and supervise the daily operations of the infrastructure.

2.1 Interdependencies in the Physical Layer

If we look at physical layer only, as the example of fig 1 for an electricity network, it is possible to understand some "intrinsic" instability problems.

Fig. 1 shows a simple electrical transport network, as it is described in the IEEE Transaction paper [2]. The basic elements in the network are:

o the "generators", that are different types of power production plants (Oil/Steam, Coal/Steam, Hydro, Nuclear etc.) and represent the points in which energy is produced,

o the "loads" that represent the points in which power is consumed (by a city distribution network, by an industry or by a railway energy substation),

o the "nodes" that represent the points where power flow coming from the generators is dispatched to the loads,

o the "lines" that represent the electrical cables used to transport energy between different nodes .

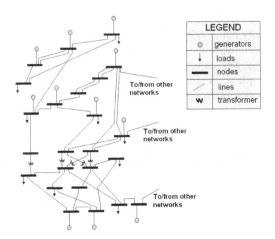

Fig. 1. A simple electrical transport network

Different portions of the network generally work at different voltage levels, and are interfaced with "transformers".

The stable working condition of such system may be easily explained in the same way as the stability of a tandem bike on which more cyclists are pedalling[3].

Every cyclists on the bike have to pedal at the same frequency since all sprockets are connected with same chain. Also in the electrical network all generators (turbines) have to rotate at the same frequency to maintain constant (50 hertz) the electrical power frequency.

If some cyclists are simply sitting on the bike and do not pedal they could be compared to the loads of the electrical network; in fact they are points in which the energy produced by the other cyclists is consumed. To keep constant the speed of the bike the total force of the active cyclists (total generation) has to be the same as the total power absorbed by the passive cyclists (total loads).

It could be noted that the chain between the cyclists may be slightly elastic; it means that an *angle difference* may exist between the pedals positions of the different cyclists. The same phenomena happens in the electrical network when a *phase angle* exists between active and reactive generated power, and all the generators have to work in such way to reduce as much as possible these phase angles differences. For the bike system a great angle difference indicates that some cyclist pedals too slowly and some other too fast. In the electrical transmission network the angle difference indicates an insufficient power production in some part of the network and a surplus of production in some other parts. In such situation, for the bike and for the network system as well, some instability conditions could arise.

It is interesting to note that, in the previous condition, the instability level of the tandem bike system increases much if the bike speed is low (bike oscillations can arise), and, on the contrary, decreases when the speed of the bike increases.

In the same way, also the electrical network system results more vulnerable, due to such instability problem, when the electrical production and consumption is low. The Italian electrical black-out of September 2003, mainly determined by the too high power imported flow from foreign countries, happened during the night, the period in which the internal energy production (and consumption) is low; in such occasion the Italian energy operator (GRTN) said that the same black out may be avoided during the day, when the production and consumption are higher.

From the above considerations we can learn the following lesson: to work in a safe condition, whatever the considered system is, the system operator have to maintain its parameters near the nominal working states.

But the electrical networks are not managed by a single operator; the electrical system operators have no possibility to control in a single place the complete working status of the network, because more portions of such network are distributed on different countries that could have different management strategies. In addition, the recent globalisation of the energy markets makes more complex the management of such type of interconnected networks.

Generally the electrical system operator of a certain nation have to decides or plan the day before what generators (production plants) will be used the day after to satisfy the internal energy consumption and the external requests. This is imposed by the fact that it is not possible to execute rapid start-ups or shut-downs of the production plants. Depending on the plant typologies these procedures may require long times (hours) for the execution.

In the energy field new possibilities were recently introduced for distributed generation of renewable energy like solar energy or wind. But the power transmission networks and their control and supervisory systems are not ready to manage these new autonomous energy producers that introduce additional instability inside the electrical system. In fact is not always possible to forecast with sufficient accuracy where and when the weather conditions requested by the renewable energy production plants will be available. This types of plants have a "degree of autonomy" that is not always compatible with the need to maintain the whole system in a safe condition (far from the instability zones).

The consequence of the serious incident, which originated in the North German electrical grid during the night of 6 November 2006 was simply the European grid separation in three large islands; but, during this contingency, Europe risked a very large blackout, involving a lot of countries. One of the reasons of this incident was attributed to voltage instabilities caused by the wind energy production plants, installed in the North of Germany by autonomous energy providers.

The free energy market imposes today also the necessity to sell and acquire energy from different countries during some time periods that are determined by economical reasons, but that do not take in account the systems instability constraints.

2.2 Interdependencies in the Cyber Layer

When we speak about Critical Infrastructure instabilities we have consider not only faults that arise in the physical layer of the infrastructure but also anomalies that could happen on the cyber and the organisational layers [4].

In the fig. 2 is illustrated a situation in which an interdependency problem occurs between an electrical and a telecom infrastructure, caused by some loss of the services that this two infrastructures exchange each other. Some substations of the electrical infrastructure furnish the power (services 1 and 2) necessary for some telecom gateway switching devices that control the voice and data traffic in a regional area. Failures or anomalies of these devices may have some consequences, as a decreasing of data transport services (service 3) of switching devices of an urban area that are utilised by the Control Centres of the electrical company.

Also if this may not cause immediate consequences on the electrical network, due to the impossibility for the electrical operator to supervise and tele-control the network, any other fault event on the electrical grid will not detected and properly managed, so that a general cascading failure of the grid will be possible.

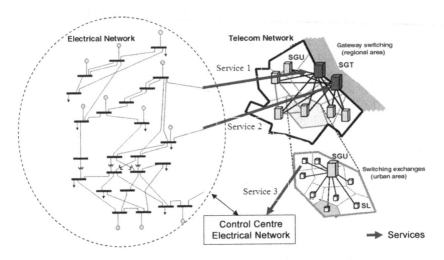

Fig. 2. Interdependencies caused by mutual services exchange

The above example describes as the control and supervisory system functionalities, designed to allow the operators to maintain the physical network far from well known instability zones, can be indirectly attacked by the effects of interdependencies between LCCIs.

New instabilities appear today also in the human organisations managing infrastructures. In the global world this is generated by the necessity to reduce the organisational and industrial costs, that for a company are determined by the competition with other companies.

The globalisation of the markets and the competition make both computer systems and human organisations more vulnerable and exposed to external threats.

Sources of instabilities in the cyber layers of LCCIs are also caused by loss of employers or industry operators with critical skills. The introduction of a new generation of information/control systems often requires more knowledge/expertise about these new technologies. But frequently, the companies are afraid about the introduction of new technologies, and at the same time, the oldest ones are not competitive anymore.

To reduce personnel cost, many energy distribution companies promote the utilisation of 'remote' maintenance of devices and cyber components utilising the internet connectivity. But this new type of connectivity can be used also by malicious users or cyber-terrorists to damage the network functionality.

2.3 How to Solve the Interdependency Problem

For these reasons the LCCIs SCADA[1] systems have been improved with additional components able to reduce/mitigate the interdependency effects caused by failures at physical, cyber or organisational level, generated also by external attacks.

In this paper we propose to reduce such systems instabilities with additional tools aimed to improve the *coordination* between the different organisations that manage critical networks and infrastructures.

It is well known that inside every infrastructure many procedures, tools and resources are available for the operators to prevent and manage crisis or instability events. But every infrastructure operator normally looks only inside his own infrastructure and has the primary goal to protect it against failures and disruptions. Anyway actually the infrastructures are more and more interconnected; they produce *services* and *materials* that are utilised by other infrastructures; as illustrated in the above section the lack of a certain service inside a local infrastructure may produce failure inside remote one that, if consequently fails, could produce additional damage inside the local one. While for the instability problems encountered inside single plants, the local operators are generally trained to maintain the system inside the operative zones, far from well known instability regions, interdependency is a *new instability phenomena*, affecting sets of coupled infrastructure, for which the operators have not sufficient information and knowledge.

To front this new type of instability is necessary to improve the co-operation and the information sharing between different infrastructure owners about the status of critical services that are essential for the survival of the coupled infrastructures.

There are two main types of information that have to be exchanged to mitigate the possible instabilities arising from interdependency problems:

1. *Info about quality and continuity of services*: the infrastructure that acts as service provider informs the service consumer about the quality and the continuity of the service delivery. Information can not only be related to actual service delivery but also to "future service delivery". Information related to future service delivery may be accompanied with a probability of occurrence. One purpose is that the service provider can inform the service consumer of possible future problems to give the service consumer sufficient time to take mitigation measures.

2. *Negotiation info*: in this case the service provider and the service consumer negotiate the terms of possible service degradations. One party sends a proposal to the other one. Proposals contain suggestions concerning the minimum quality of service levels for certain services, time spans and locations. The other partner can then accept or reject each proposal. Negotiation messages are always exchanged in both ways. There are different possibilities how negotiation can start. For example, an electricity distributor has to disconnect a certain area for some time but he is flexible with the exact time. He can suggest possible times for the disconnection and a telecommunication provider can choose one of the options. Another possibility is that a service consumer sends, as a reaction to an information about quality of certain services for the next future, a preference list with the most important services. These preferences can be considered during recovery crisis and recovery phases.

3 The MIT Technology

3.1 General Overview

The MIT Technology, we are going to present in this paragraph, has been proposed inside the EU Integrated Project IRRIIS [5] which aims at protecting of critical infrastructures (CIs) like energy supply or telecommunication system.

This project will provide a technological system named MIT (*Middleware Improved Technology*) which is composed of a collection of software components that facilitates IT-based communication between different infrastructures and different infrastructure providers. By supporting recovery actions and increasing service stability in case of critical situations, MIT components will substantially enhance the security of large complex critical infrastructures. MIT system will be able to:

- Reduce the chance that failures spread (prevention),
- Limit cascading effect (mitigation),
- Improve situational awareness (prevention and response and recovery).

Prevention, by detecting and mitigating threats, is without any doubt the first and the best way to avoid disasters or minimise their impact by accelerated reaction capabilities. Mitigation will try to reduce the impact and extend of failures as soon as they occur. Response after critical situation should be both automatic and manual.

Recovery is a very important topic to reduce failure/outage time and thus increase security. Recovery actions shall be done as fast as possible and using an effective order. This requires situational awareness of the availability of other infrastructure capabilities and the status of one's own. The Recovery functions of the MIT system should give an estimation of time to return in stable phase.

There are a lot of dependencies and interdependencies also within some LCCIs. For example, within Electricity LCCI, data transmission to and from control centre needs communication and this, as it has been said, will be even more crucial in distributed generation. Anyway, prevention of failures caused by (inter)dependency effects would benefit also from improved resilience of each LCCIs, i.e., reducing risk of failures within an LCCI. To some extent, cross-sector technology and tools which clearly provide other CI sectors with better resilience are subject for MIT as well, while focus will be set on dependencies and interdependencies between *different* infrastructures.

Moreover, MIT aims at providing a valuable solution; thus all existing tools and processes which are implemented within an LCCI to reduce risk will be at the base for further MIT to improve resilience.

3.2 MIT Architecture

The starting point to define an architecture for MIT System is the following picture:

The small box in the picture represents the MIT System installed in each LCCI. Each MIT System is composed by the following components:

- o Communication Components (light circles in Figure 3)
- o Add-On Components (black circles in Figure 3)

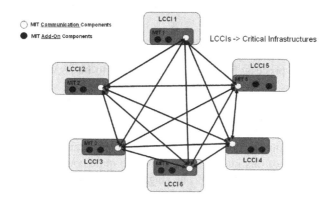

Fig. 3. Interdependencies caused by mutual services exchange

o   Database, files (log files, configuration files), GUI (not represented in Figure 3)
o   Other resources as Run-Time Environments, Servers (not represented in Figure 3)

The communications in the above MIT general architecture should be implemented making use of a client-server paradigm without a centralized server. This means that each MIT System will communicate with other MIT Systems sending and/or receiving information through the client server paradigm. A MIT System that start the communication sending an information or a request assumes the role of *Client*. The MIT System that receives an information or a request assumes the role of *Server*. Each MIT System can assume *Client* or *Server* role depending on the operation it has to execute.

The above picture shows an example of six LCCIs. Each LCCI has its own MIT System (small box). Each MIT System is composed by Add-On Components and by Communications Components. The black bidirectional arrows means that the communications can happen in both directions: for example MIT 1 of LCCI 1 can send an information to MIT 2 of LCCI 2 or MIT 2 of LCCI 2 can send information to MIT 1 of LCCI 1. Following the previous example, in the first case MIT 1 has a Client role and MIT 2 has a Server role while in the second case MIT 2 has a Client role and MIT 1 has a Server role.

The advantages of this solution are: there is not a central server so there is not a node of this network to maintain in terms of software/hardware maintenance and in terms of authority. The central solution introduces a new node in the network so it potentially introduces an additional vulnerability.

The drawbacks of these solutions are: introducing and removing MIT Systems in this network is not simple and each MIT System should be updated and re-configured. Since each MIT System contains all the logic of MIT Communication System, each MIT software upgrade will cause the upgrade of each MIT System.

After the description of the general architecture of MIT, the following paragraph will focus on a brief introduction of each MIT Add-On Component.

3.3 MIT Add-On Components

It has been already stated that MIT aims at reducing the risk of failures due to dependency and interdependency, by preventing or at least by mitigating them and supporting the recovery process. But what are the threats to be prevented or mitigated? And what actions have to be taken to cope with them?

According to earlier studies [6][7], the most likely reasons for severe incidents are extraordinary natural conditions (for example, earthquakes, floods or hurricanes), malicious attacks, and human errors.

In effective mitigation against natural disasters, very often, the keyword is "collaboration". Incidents of this kind lead very often to quite complex situations, where most likely a failure storm, instead of one single failure, happens. Despite how good recovery and continuity plans in place be, mutual support between critical infrastructures is always needed to take care of people's safety and homeland security. So, helpful add-on components should support consultation and co-ordinated actions between neighbouring infrastructure systems for the establishment of effective mitigation measures, as well as early warning notification of coming threat, whenever possible.

Against malicious attacks, which include both cyber attacks and malicious operation, add-on MIT components shall improve security by preventing or at least detecting them as early as possible. Security weaknesses in one infrastructure decrease security of all the dependent LCCIs, so it is both a dependability and dependency issue. Of course, basic cyber security administration (like closing open ports) is not task of MIT.

Against human errors, there is a need for supporting the operator with situational awareness and emergency handling, especially about the state of neighbouring systems his own LCCI is dependent on and about consequences of these dependencies.

To sum up, the following general actions are needed to prevent or mitigate disrupt of operation in home LCCI and neighbouring ones:

- PREVENT, if possible, the incident to avoid its impact on dependent infrastructures;
- PROVIDE EARLY WARNING of deteriorating system conditions to the operator, so that he can take corrective actions;
- DETECT AS EARLY AS POSSIBLE the incident and NOTIFY it to the dependent infrastructures so that neighbouring operators can take pre-emptive action to limit the cascading effect of disturbances;
- ESTIMATE the probability of disrupt of his own LCCI operation due to internal causes and NOTIFY, if requested, to the dependent infrastructures;
- ASSESS THE own infrastructure RISK due to information about neighbouring status so that operator can take pre-emptive action to limit the cascading effect of disturbances;
- HANDLE THE EMERGENCY, if needed by negotiating co-ordinated actions;
- RECOVERY support/awareness.

The mentioned functionalities have been developed into particular components. Figure 3 shows MIT Communication Components and MIT Add-On Components.

The following general classes of functions (Figure 4) have been identified for MIT Add-On Components:

- **Internal assessment** (situation awareness about home LCCI) to build situational information based on internal LCCI.
- **Risk assessment** (situation awareness about home LCCI and neighbouring LCCIs) to correlate the internal status of the LCCI with the statuses of the neighbouring LCCIs to estimate the probability of occurrence of undesirable event based on both internal and neighbouring status.
- **Emergency management** (computer supported systems to manage the contingencies) to support the operator while handling the emergency, both by decision support and by recovery support; to support the local LCCI operator in the negotiation process with operators or the neighbouring LCCIs during an emergency.
- **Information sharing** to ensure that information will be efficiently shared, and that LCCIs authorized procedures are considered to filter information, to be shared, to publish filtered information and to subscribe and read the published information.
- **Risk Management** (additional off-line tools to improve risk management situations).

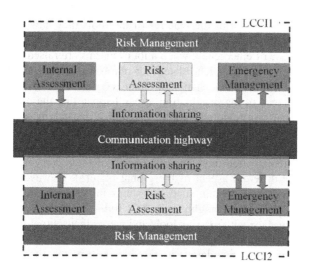

Fig. 4. MIT Add-On Components functional architecture

For each class of functions the following Add-On Components have been identified in Table 1:

Information Publisher (IPU) and Information Subscriber and Reader (ISR) just support communication among neighbouring LCCIs. As they use commercial technologies, their description is out of the scope of this paper.

Table 1. List of the Add-on components

Tools to Extract LCCI Functional Status – **TEFS** (Internal Assessment)
Risk Estimator – **RE** (Risk Assessment)
Incident Knoledge Database –**IKA** (Risk Assessment)
Assessment of Cascading/Escalating Effects – **ACEE** (Emergency Management)
Display of Emergency Management Procedures – **DEMP** (Emergency Management)
NEGotiator – **NEG** (Emergency Management)
Information **PU**blisher – **IPU** (Information Sharing)
Information Filtering – **IFI** (Information Sharing)
Information Subscriber and Reader – **ISR** (Information Sharing)

The following sections go into detail of the other add-on components rationale and requirements.

Tool to Extract LCCI Functional Status (TEFS)

LCCIs are interested in being informed about some parameters of the neighbouring LCCIs status, actually both known status and foreseen one in a reasonable lapse of time. On the other side, operators often claim to be overwhelmed by a large amount of information and disable most of the features of the tools they have in order to have manageable information, but in this way they underutilise them. Moreover, this is extremely true in case of emergency, when a lot of alarms are raised by tools in place and it gets challenging to extract/correlate/filter relevant information. In that case, an operator has to confirm simultaneously more than 100 different alarms. As there is no filter on the importance of the information, it can happen that the operator also confirms "the" important information without realising it and taking appropriate countermeasures.

In many sectors, most of the required information is already available as it is provided by existing tools (often more than one, each of them carrying out a different analysis to cover a different aspect of the global picture). However, it needs to be collected and aggregated to obtain state and status information, as well as planned maintenance work, required by neighbouring LCCI(s).

A tool able to interface with existing tools and merge their output in order to have a clear and complete picture taking into account various functional statuses is needed. This add-on component is mandatory to provide information to dependent LCCIs after being filtered to fulfil privacy and security requirements as well as bi-lateral agreements and run-time requests.

This tool will carry out data fusion of cross-sector/multi-analysis already available data in order to identify relevant current functional statuses (in service/out of service and/or quality of service if relevant) and expected ones in the near future. Depending on the requested reaction time of the operator, data of different time ranges may be required. Functional status should also take into account scheduled and on-going maintenance, as well as expected restoration time, as dependent LCCIs could make proper arrangement to cope with the loss of service, if any.

Information to be provided may include:

- LCCI part (line etc) details: Name and Location
- Confidence about information: this field states if information provided is Known / Estimated
- Severity: Warning/Alert/Alarm
- Functional Status: InService/OutOfService/QoS (if relevant, to say that agreed service level is not fully available)
- Risk of service reduction
- Cause of the declared Functional Status (in case of OutOfService or QoS less than expected/agreed) and expected time needed for it
- Expected Restoration Time

Information from different sources will be correlated and filtered, if needed, in order to have just one picture.

For the electrical power sector and whenever else it applies, the CIM (Common Information Model) IEC 61970 standard shall be used as output format.

It's worth noting that as it can contain sensitive information, the output of this tool must be filtered according to bilateral agreements before being notified to legitimate LCCIs. Moreover, it must be not accessible by unauthorised people.

Two versions of this tool, one for electrical power sector and one for telecommunication sector, shall be provided, as different LCCIs have different parameters to be monitored to get the global picture and different tools available.

Risk Estimator (RE)

The key assumption in the rationale of this add-on component is that sometimes a specific condition itself is not critical, but it becomes critical if some coincidences happen. For example, SCADA requires some network traffic for tele-monitoring and supervisory telecontrol, which grows significantly in case of failures as a lot amount of alarms will be sent by the remote control units. If a Telco operator, for maintenance reasons, halves the available bandwidth for a power grid SCADA, power operation will not be impacted in case of normal operation, but that reduction may be a big issue in case of a failure situation, especially for communication with IPP in distribution

This add-on component will estimate immediate risk and potential cascading and/or escalating effects. Estimation could take into account:

- real-time info (internal assessment)
- status information from other LCCI(s)
- planning information
- scheduled maintenance
- information from the web (weather forecast, strikes, events…)
- other information resources.

To provide an added value, it may need to query/interface to existing tools. To accomplish its job, estimation could be based on:

- correlation rules - for example, it could check if some values (or trends) coming from neighbouring LCCIs are higher than threshold or if an outage is possible and backup batteries are not available

o   findings or algorithms aimed at identifying, for example, the arcs who dis-
        connect the network
o   co-ordinating inputs/output of existing tools, if possible - for example, it
        could feed the state estimator with trends/projections of coming situation or
        it could start any simulation tool running an extended model, i.e, taking val-
        ues).

Moreover, it will subscribe for needed frequency/threshold sensitivity to other
LCCIs Internal Assessment MIT Add-on components. The required sensitivity may
vary according to operating conditions and on-going risk assessment analysis.

As some progress can be made in risk assessment understanding, especially about
dependency, new correlation rules have to be fast implemented and/or modified.

It's worth noting that risk of screwing down must be avoided, so usually risk identified by Risk Estimator will not be notified to neighbouring. A clear state expectation
and state status should be derived from internal data, not from internal expectation...
as one will mitigate the problem (first).

Incident Knowledge Analyser (IKA)

Based on public incidents, some incidents databases have been built to store knowledge and experience, to trace common trends among similar classes of failures and to
get clues about dependencies and interdependencies and failure propagation patterns.
The database on Critical Infrastructure outages established by the IRRIIS consortium
and the one built by British Columbia University of Technology about SCADA failures are examples of those. Moreover, most LCCIs have also their own incident database.

It could be useful to exploit stored experience and identify whether the current
situation has some similarity with one of the preconditions which led to a disruption
of operations in the past.

This tool has the following added values:

o   As a LCCI incident database contains sensitive information and it therefore
        would not be available at large, a public database can be useful. Of course, if
        interested, LCCI stakeholders can apply the same approach to their own in-
        cident database.
o   Not all the LCCIs must have experienced the same failures (and then the re-
        lated disruptions) but it could be useful to warn the operator if an on-going
        failure already happened in the past and led to disruption of operation (so
        LCCIs can exploit the knowledge about all the known disruptions)
o   This tool could be very useful if in the future all the LCCIs will be forced to
        report incidents by an independent regulatory authority. Such a process is
        already on-going in the USA for the power and telecom industry, and for the
        power industry in several European nations.

This tool shall check in real-time if an on-going identified failure is contained in
the incident database as leading (or symptom) to a major disruption of operations in
the past. For electricity, failure of equipment such as line, substation, transformer,
switchgear etc is detected very fast by probes in place.

As an optional feature, this tool shall be able store new occurred incidents in the
database, at least the starting failure and the sequence of occurred events. Anyway, a

database administrator must validate them. Not validated incidents must be clearly identifiable and if this tool uses them for future reference, it shall show a lower confidence of result.

However, as an additional module, a tracer for failures could be useful and could also give a clue for self-awareness. In fact, after a good test phase, the internal assessment should be reliable as it relies on the existing tool. Therefore, if the risk estimator gives a wrong forecast for a while or if it is not working properly (may be because the situation is not manageable with given algorithms) it shall be disabled.

Display of Tailored to the Situation Emergency Management Procedures (DEMP)

Emergency management plans are already in place at each utility as pre-planned decisions. Some of them are legally binding, some others are not. They should be followed if the on-going contingency is provided in one of them, but sometimes the operator fails to recognise the right procedure, especially if abnormal conditions appear such as outage of several lines and if he/she needs to take into account, for example, financial decision. Existing emergency management plans do not cover new threats, for example the ones related to dependency. If no pre-planned decisions exist for the on-going contingency, decision options should be suggested.

This tool shall identify if the on-going identified contingency has any match in the preconditions of any procedure. If so, it shall prompt the relevant procedure and check the progress. Any deviation and the reason thereof shall be logged. If no match is found this tool shall work out emergency management plans by intelligent adaptation of procedures from all the available and relevant sources (for example, mitigation policies for single failures, existing "Incident and Crisis Centre" DB, topology analysis).

The tool shall provide the operator one or more solutions to resolve an abnormal event with all the consequences of these solutions. This tool could benefit from the Negotiator (see later in this section) to take into account non-technical constraints (financial issues, political issues etc).

Tracking of decisions taken (with reason - especially when neglecting best proposal) with time tracking alarms on issued actions to third parties / people shall be implemented. As a guideline is to relieve the operator from duties unrelated to preserving his/hers LCCI, reasons for actions shall be stored, but are not mandatory to be filled in during the emergency. If the adapted emergency plan succeeds, it shall be stored for future reference.

Assess Cascading/Escalating Effects of Decision Options (ACEE)

Even if the primary goal of LCCI is to maintain proper "own" state, actions for emergency handling can impact dependent LCCIs and then even turn on his own LCCI by interdependency. Support to decision-making taking into account dependency structures shall be implemented.

This tool shall:

o Show the direct and indirect effects (cascading effects) of actions taken.
o Evaluate cascading/escalating effects in own and dependent LCCI(s). To be useful, assessment of cascading/escalating effects shall be performed in near real-time and predictive way.

Action can be extracted by official policies, for example, if emergency involves two neighbouring TSOs, by UCTE Policy 5 Procedure P2.6 or similar.

As this tool requires system knowledge of infrastructure and consequences, the Negotiator (see later on this section) or an interdependency simulator may be of help.

Negotiate Emergency Management Plans with Dependent LCCIs (NEG)

Sometimes it is possible or convenient to agree or negotiate contingency plans. This is specially true in normal conditions, when healthy LCCIs can support the ones in danger. It has been verified, for example, that in many conditions the operator has to solve a N-1 situation and he usually has several ways to proceed, allowing room for negotiation. For example, in order to negotiate, if possible, power outage to impact the delivery of telecommunication services as less as possible, the following information could be shared:

- o   off-line list of critical sites on power delivery point of view,
- o   on-line (real time during a power supply failure) list of sites on which it is recommended a faster re-establish of power supply, due for example to remaining battery-life or available gasoline for auxiliary power supply, or air conditioning, heating, or humidity problems.

Negotiation should be used to agree remedial actions when required (for example by UCTE Policy 5 Procedure P2.6).

Negotiation should also be used to verify some assumptions about neighbouring LCCI status.

In the electrical power sector, decisions to manage some outages are taken by simulating all the possible disconnection options, and then by choosing amongst the set of best solutions. If more than one solution exists, neighbouring LCCIs could ask to take into account additional constraints (for example, Telco LCCI will ask to not disconnect a particular site) in order to limit the impact on their own LCCI. The same function can be useful for Telco operators, because in case of failure in one node they are in charge to choose an additional path and they usually have more than one option. Negotiation shall also take into account which action could benefit more the whole system (because of interdependency, all the LCCIs are interconnected as part of one system).

This tool shall inquire neighbouring LCCIs for additional ongoing activities, constraints-like general needs (some sites are more important than others) and authoritative contingency information (for example, Rome is as important as Milan, but in Milan snowing is expected, so do not disconnect Milan). Constraints must be prioritised.

This tool shall also provide a feedback to neighbouring LCCIs to make them informed if their request will be satisfied or not.

Request format should be based on the ISO/IEC 61970 standard "CIM", in order to be easily fed in proper simulation tools.

During incident, a 1-1 link with Negotiation of other LCCIs shall be established for clarification of state and expectation of recovery.

Like all the other add-on components, if relevant, decision-support MIT add-on components shall interface to DSS tools already in place.

Information Filtering (IFI)

Internal assessment information are relevant both for internal use and for neighbouring LCCIs. Similar information could be shared with different neighbours. A tool in charge of filtering relevant internal assessment output to be shared with interested LCCIs according to established agreements and privacy policies is needed.

Information to be shared by LCCIs will be a subset of the internal assessment data. For example, to mitigate problems on telecommunication networks due to its dependency of the power grid, the following information is needed:

- o   When a planned power outage will happen (time and date)
- o   When a potential power outage may happen (time and date)
- o   When an power outage occurred (time and date)
- o   Expected power outage duration
- o   Where the power interruption will happen, in order to detect both main Telco's objects (exchanges; NOC, masts, gateways, ..) involved and service area involved.

In case of unplanned outage, it could be important, in order to plan countermeasures, to be notified about conditions and restoration plans.

Each LCCI will be responsible for filtering his own information.

3.4   Implemented Technology

In order to describe the technology used to implement the MIT we need to consider the problem of communications between MIT Systems. Receiving and sending information can be done considering an **Application Server** (AS). Such technology provides all the infrastructure to receive and send information through a network. This means that we don't have to worry about multiple request and don't have to manage server and client processes. We only have to develop the right components which define the *"business logic"* of the problem. Such components (Application Server components) must be deployed into the Application Server in order to work. Another consideration is that Application Server technology is strictly related to **Java** technology, more in detail to Java Enterprise technology. This means that Java will be the main language for MIT but it could not be the only language.

Now it is clear that some MIT Components we have discussed in the previous paragraphs such as IPU, ISR, NEG and IFI, can be developed and deployed as Application Server Components (for example making use of **EJB** technology).

Fig. 5 shows an UML Component Diagram representing a single MIT System where each box represents a MIT Component; the grey box is the Application Server. The meaning of this figure is that some MIT Components are deployed in the Application Server and other ones are external to the Application Server. MIT Components deployed in the Application Server are also managed by the Application Server so they access all the services provided by the Application Server. The figure also shows that some external MIT Components must communicate with MIT Components in the AS.

About the communication process among different MIT systems, each Application Server with its MIT Communication Components represents the front-end side in regard to other MIT Systems. Two different MIT systems are connected through the network using TCP/IP as communication protocol at transport level.

A different approach should be used to exchange information at application level: usually inside an organization (a LCCI in our case) there is only a limited number of open ports (often only port 80) in order to allow http traffic; this must be taken in

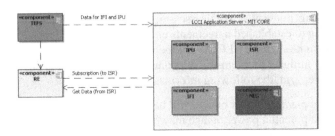

Fig. 5. UML Component Diagram of MIT

account for the design of MIT. For that reason, we have chosen **SOAP** as protocol at application level which is a protocol that makes use of XML to serialize the data to transfer and of HTTP as transport protocol. XML is a textual format, http is a protocol to transfer textual contents, the web protocol that, by default, makes use of port 80. This way, two applications residing on different sites can communicate each other without opening further ports.

Communication between external components and internal components can be bidirectional. This means that an external component can send an information to internal components or an internal component can send an information to external components. In the first case the communication can be synchronous or asynchronous. Synchronous communication means that the external component first must obtain a reference to the component inside the AS (remote component), then it can send the information to the remote component (executing the method of remote component). Asynchronous communication means that the external component sends information (as a message) to an internal service (Java Message Service – **JMS**), in particular to a Queue or a Topic. This message will be delivered to the right MIT Component by the AS. In both cases the utilized protocol is AS proprietary (RMI – IIOP).

In the second case (the internal component send the information to external component) the communication can only be asynchronous because the components deployed in the AS can't obtain a reference to external components.

4 An Experimentation Environment to Test MIT Technology

The architecture of a complex hardware and/or software system, like a car or like the above described MIT system, is generally formed by a set of interconnected components, every one having a specific role inside the whole system. As illustrated in fig 5, a development and a stand-alone testing phase of every component must be followed by the "experimentation" phase of the whole system.

To produce a good experimentation is necessary the presence of the "environment" in which the system have to realise the designed functionalities.

The environment in which MIT system works are very complex infrastructures composed by hardware, software and human organisations. These infrastructures offer their critical services to citizens, industries and other infrastructures. The production of these services cannot be stopped or reduced during the time necessary for

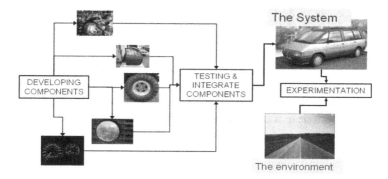

Fig. 6. Development, testing and experimentation of a complex system

experimentation. Interfacing a not experimented MIT system to such infrastructures may be not acceptable for safety and security reasons.

To address the experimentation problem properly, the infrastructures behaviour must be simulated in an "artificial" environment suitable for an exhaustive test of MIT. In the field of Critical Infrastructures protection, and more in particular for SCADA and control systems security, some scientific Institutions already developed complex test beds for experimentation able to produce real and simulated test data [4][8][9].

In such test beds the role of simulators for experimentation consists mainly in the "on demand" production of the data and information, normally produced by the LCCIs during normal and in anomaly conditions; such data are the necessary inputs to analyse the interdependency problems and to test the candidate solutions.

Depending on the types of considered scenarios, more simulators may be necessary to model and generate operative data relative to different physical and cyber layers of a same LCCI.

As evidenced in fig 7 a single interdependency scenario between two or more LCCIs is produced by a certain set of exchanged services. To reproduce the dynamic

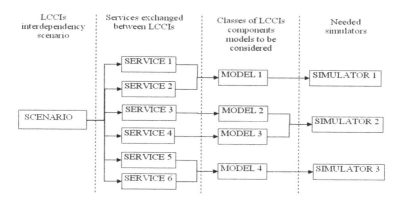

Fig. 7. Scenario/simulators relations schema

behaviour of such services some subsets of LCCI components have to be considered and modelled; these models could be used by a set of simulators to reproduce the considered scenario and all its possible variations.

Looking, for example, at the telecom and electricity distribution infrastructures the following set of simulators may be necessary to have a complete coverage of the various situations.

A data packets exchange simulator is needed to emulate the congestion of data transfer across the Telecom communication network due to the loss of some Telco critical component.

An event based simulator is also necessary to emulate the (event-based) behaviour of the power backup systems supporting the telecom devices in case of electrical power blackouts.

It is also necessary to consider a power-flow simulator to produce load-flow and other electrical data generated in the substations and in the electricity lines.

Finally, also an emulator of the SCADA system is necessary. SCADA systems, in fact, support operators for remote control operations and at the same time collect electrical data from the remote substations and send them through the communication network to the Control Centres operators to make them aware about the status of the power network. This simulator has to simulate the data collection and transfer process from the peripheral components of the electricity network and the electrical system operators activities like the management of remote tele-operations. It may be considered as a special interface between the previous electrical simulator and the telecom network simulator.

4.1 Relationship and Dependencies between the Various Simulators

Taking in account characteristics of the considered scenario it is possible to define the relationships between the different simulators.

Consider for example the scenario illustrated in the fig 7:

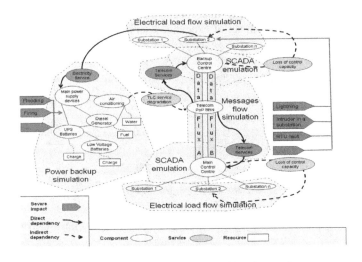

Fig. 8. Characteristics of the considered scenario

A Telecom building contains routers and servers belonging to the back bone of the national telecommunication network (PoP BBN in the figure). In the figure if two components are linked by the a normal line they have a *direct dependency* (a failure of on a component has an immediate physical effect on the second). It they are linked by a dotted line they have an *indirect dependency* (a failure in the first one generates only an increasing risk of producing some effects on the second).

A flooding event, caused by a leakage in the water transport network that serves the air conditioning system of the building, is one of the first causes of this emergency scenario. The flooding produced some failures in the components (diesel generator, UPS system, batteries) belonging to the power backup systems of the building. For such reason, in presence of loss of the main power supply from the electrical network, the data fluxes A and B could be interrupted; if such event occours the main Control Centres of the electrical distribution network losses the data visibility and the remote operability of all the substations connected through a backup Control Centre. As one of these substations (substation 2 in the figure), furnishes the electricity service to the same telecom building affected by the flooding, it produces an "interdependency effect" that augments the emergency problem on the telecom side.

The figure evidences how many other events, on the telecom or on the electrical LCCI could produce consequent cascading effects between LCCIs. The components are grouped into different (grey) zones; every zone evidences a sets of components that may be simulated by a certain type of simulator.

The *electrical load flow simulator* has to produce (cyclically) data that will be collected by the *SCADA emulator* of the control centres. The same route, in the opposite direction, is used for sending commands, asked by the control centres operators. Commands produce a change in the network status that will be considered by the load flow simulator that executes a new calculation and updates the electrical data sets. The data flow between two control centres is managed by a *Telecom message flow simulator*.

The status of the electricity services is considered by the *TELCO power backup simulator*; in case of lack of electrical service it actuates the available backup strategies and, if some of such strategies fails, it communicates to the Telecom message flow simulator the eventual degradation level of the telecom services.

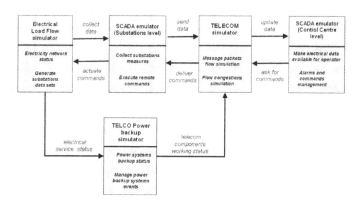

Fig. 9. Simulators relationship for mini-Telco scenario case

The degradation level may be determined not only by an immediate failure but also by a more slow changing in the *resources* status, until that the continuity of the service is no more guaranteed. The residual charge of a backup battery is an example of such resources; other examples may be the availability of fuel for the diesel backup generators or the availability of the water pressure necessary for the air conditioning systems of the Telecom building.

The data relationships between the considered simulators are shown in fig. 9.

4.2 The Architecture of Experimentation Environment

The general architecture visualized in fig. 10 is adopted as experimentation environment of the MIT components:

Here follow the main characteristics of the experimentation environment components:

The Simulators: in the left part of the figure are evidenced the set of simulators that are interfaced to the SimCIP (Simulation for Critical Infrastructure Protection) environment by a set of dedicated interfaces. In the figure is also evidenced with different colors the classes of layers (physical, cyber and service) containing the simulated components. In this case the electrical load flow simulator and the TELCO power back-up simulator are dedicated to simulate the status of physical components, while the SCADA emulator and the telecom simulator emulate the cyber functionalities necessary for messages exchanging and remote network controlling. The inner parts of SimCIP, utilize data and information coming from the simulator, to emulate the service exchanging between LCCIs.

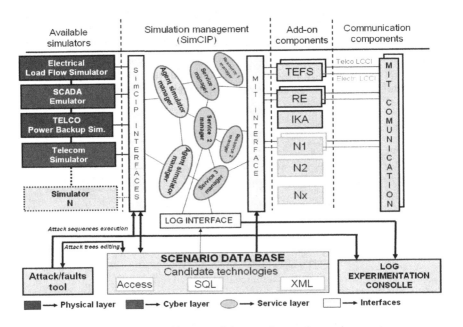

Fig. 10. Generic architecture of the experimentation environment

Simulator management agents: SimCIP is a *discrete event simulation system* which is built upon an agent-based modelling paradigm called LAMPS which combines various concepts, such as agent-based modelling, iteration of differential equations, rescaling of models in time, function and space, service oriented realisation and modelling. Each simulated agent is dedicated to the management of a certain simulator using the previous dedicated interface. These agents are in charge of "operating" the simulator, requesting the operations that are normally requested by the simulator users (load models into the simulator, start simulation, stop simulation, execute commands, read produced data etc.).

Services management agents: from all data produced by each simulators the Service management agents are in charge to extract only those that are related to the "services" that the LCCI produce for the other LCCIs and that must be made available for the current experimentation scenario. Examples of such services may be the energy supplied by a certain substation to the power backup system of a telecom device or the availability of a certain communication link furnished by that a telecom router device for data exchanging between two critical nodes (like two control centres) of the SCADA system. Service agents have to produce not only the "current" status of such services but also <u>the trends of the services during a certain period of time</u>. In fact the current status of the services may be acquired also from the scenario Data Base where all the on line data are stored; but for the experimentation of MIT components (like TEFS) may be necessary to consider also the trends of the critical LCCIs parameters, that generally are stored inside the "archive systems" of the EMS (Energy Management Systems).

Resources management agents: The necessity to consider the "trends" is required also by the "Resources management agents" that works as a support of the Service agents. Resources agents store the information relative to the resources necessary to produce a certain service. An examples of resources are the "water" resource that is needed to support the functioning of air conditioning systems inside the telecom node (SGT) or inside substations and Control Centres; it support the services produced by such nodes; a "degradation" in the availability of such resource generates an higher risk level of the relative service. Another example is the availability of fuel for diesel generators of electrical charge for backup batteries. It is obvious the availability of "trends" about resources statuses is very important to make the service risk level estimation. Resource agents have to maintain the history of such trends during the experimentation phases.

SimCIP interfaces: depending on the type of simulators and on their roles SimCIP interfaces may be more or less sophisticate; some simulators may be interfaced simply through some tables of Scenario Data Base or XML files; some other simulators may utilise API (Application Processes Interfaces) libraries to realise a more "interactive" interface. Some simulators could be used as a single entity but other ones may also be interfaced together by a dedicated data channel. For example in the figure the SCADA emulator receive and send data to and from the electrical Load Flow Simulator so that these two simulator must be used together as they are dependent each other.

Scenario Data Base: as it is shown in the figure, a scenario Data Base contains all the current LCCIs data at components or at service/resource level. Some parts of this Data Base will contain the actual variables state, other parts may contain also the trends of such variable during the time. Different technologies may be used for this

Data Base. SQL or Access technologies may be more useful for these sets of data on which queries may be executed by external applications. The XML format may be more useful to build a Data Base structure based on files that may by utilised for communication and information sharing between different machines. A mixed utilisation of SQL and XML formats may be also considered.

MIT interface: MIT interface have to realise an interface with MIT add-on components more similar as possible with the interfaces that are available in the real LCCIs. From the Scenario Data Base TEFS add-on components could retrieve the trends of the most critical LCCIs parameters, normally stored into the EMS archive systems of the (electrical) LCCIs. Service management agents use the MIT interface to inform add-on components when some operative alarms (network change of status or values out of limits) or some diagnostic alarms (tele-operations problems) occurs.

MIT components: different instances of some add-on components, like TEFS and RE, are installed for every LCCIs considered in the exercise. Other add-on components, like IKA, have the same instance for every LCCIs. As in the figure only two infrastructures are considered (Telco and Electricity), only two instances of a single add-on component are considered. On the contrary, the same instances of communication components will be present on every LCCIs, but the process of subscribing and reading information could be different for the two LCCIs.

Attack/fault tool: an attack/fault tool utilises the scenario Data Base to retrieve and store sets of attack or fault sequences defined by the experts. These sequences must be executed into the experimentation environment, are sent to the SimCIP interface. The same sequences are also communicated to the log experimentation console where the experimenter may visualise and archive the time-log of attack and fault actions as they are sent to the simulation environment.

Log interface: a log interface is the component that can be used by the experimenter, to select the data and information he like to monitor and log on the log experimentation console. Every data present inside the Scenario data base may be selected for log and on the experimentation console trends and graphics about such data could be visualised during and after an experimentation phase. Data about the current status of services availability can be also acquired by the log interface from the services management agents. On the Log Experimentation Interface such data logs may be put in correlation with the logs of the (eventual) sequence of faults and the attacks, so that a comparison may be executed about the case in which a certain faults sequence is introduced respect to the same case if no faults sequence is introduced.

5   Conclusions

Actually complex networked systems are the core of many critical infrastructures, that are coupled together and that exchange critical services each other. Instabilities of a specific physical system are often well known by the systems operators and they have sufficient knowledge to avoid intra-system cascading failures.

But, when the risk of cascading failure involves components and systems belonging to different infrastructures, the operators are not sufficiently prepared to manage the situation, in which a not usual co-ordination strategy is needed.

We hope that the experimentation of MIT technology, that is undertaken inside the EU IRRIIS integrated project, could confirm that this system may be used as mutual co-ordination support for the different infrastructures operators.

Also if these first sets of tests will take under consideration incident scenarios involving only a distribution electrical LCCI and a telecom LCCI, the developed experimentation environment could be reconfigured for the additional inclusion of other LCCIs like transportation, health care, water distribution and other types of LCCIs

We hope also that the results of such experimentation, that will be available in the first months of 2009 could address and solve, almost in part, the increasing instability of coupled critical infrastructures.

References

1. Rinaldi, S.M., Peerenboom, J.P., Kelly, T.K.: Identify Understanding and Analysing Critical Infrastructures Interdependencies. IEEE Control System Magazine, 11–25 (December 2001)
2. The IEEE Reliability Test System – 1996. IEEE Transaction on Power Systems, 14(3) (August 1999)
3. Soder, L.: Explaining Power System Operation to Nonengineers. IEEE Power Engineering Review, 25–27 (April 2002)
4. Balducelli, C., Bologna, S., Lavalle, L., Vicoli, L.G.: Safeguarding information intensive critical infrastructures against novel types of emerging failures. Reliability Engineering and System Safety 92(9), 1218–1229 (2007)
5. IRRIIS - Integrated Risk Reduction of Information-based Infrastructure Systems – EU FP6 project (2006), http://www.irriis.org
6. http://www.cert.org/insider_threat/
7. http://ww3.psepc-sppcc.gc.ca/opsprods/other/TA03-001_e.asp
8. Dondossola, G., Szanto, J., Masera, M., Fovino, I.N.: Evaluation of the Effects of Intentional Threats to Power Substation Control System. In: Proceedings of CNIP 2006 – Complex Network & Infrastructure Protection, Rome, Italy, March 28-29 (2006)
9. Kuipers, D.G.: US CERT Control System Centers Input/Ourput I/O conceptual Design., Idaho National Laboratory, INL/EXT-05-00810 (February 2005), http://www.inl.gov/technicalpublications/Documents/3562864.pdf

Evaluation of Critical Infrastructures: Challenges and Viable Approaches

Silvano Chiaradonna[1], Felicita Di Giandomenico[1], and Paolo Lollini[2]

[1] Italian National Research Council, ISTI Dept., via Moruzzi 1, I-56124, Italy
{chiaradonna,digiandomenico}@isti.cnr.it
[2] University of Firenze, Dip. Sistemi e Informatica,
Viale Morgagni, 65, I-50134, Italy
lollini@dsi.unifi.it

Abstract. Critical Infrastructures (CI) are complex and highly inter-dependent systems, networks and assets that provide essential services in our daily life. Given the increasing dependence upon such critical infrastructures, research and investments in identifying their vulnerabil-ities and devising survivability enhancements are recognized paramount by many countries. Understanding and analyzing interdependencies and interoperabilities between different critical infrastructures and between the several heterogeneous subsystems each infrastructure is composed of, are among the most challenging aspects faced today by designers, developers and operators in these critical sectors. Assessing the impact of interdependencies on the ability of the system to provide resilient and secure services is of primarily importance; following this analysis, steps can be taken to mitigate vulnerabilities revealed in critical assets. This paper addresses the analysis of CI, with focus on interdependencies be-tween the involved subsystems. In particular, the experience gained by the authors in an on-going European project is reported and discussed, both in terms of identified challenges and in viable approaches under investigation.

ACRONYMS

ATC	Area Tele-control Center
CI	Critical Infrastructure
DG	Distribution Grid
DTOS	Tele-Operation System for the Distribution grid
EI	Electric Infrastructure
EPS	Electric Power System
ITCS	Information-Technology based Control System
LCC	Local Control Center
LCS	Local Control System
NTS	National Tele-control System
RTS	Regional Tele-control System
TG	Transmission Grid
TTOS	Tele-Operation System for the Transmission grid

R. de Lemos et al. (Eds.): Architecting Dependable Systems V, LNCS 5135, pp. 52–77, 2008.

1   Introduction

Critical Infrastructures (CI) are complex and highly interdependent systems, networks and assets that provide essential services in our daily life. They span a number of key sectors, including energy, finance, authorities, hazardous materials, telecommunications, information technology, supply services and many others. With our increasing dependence upon such critical infrastructures, an unavoidable expansion in complexity is observed since these sectors are continuously called to provide new services and products to a growing population. Moreover, the framework conditions under which these infrastructures operate are continuously evolving. In fact, while in the past they were used to provide services mostly in isolation, with very limited interconnections with each other, so they could only be impaired locally, nowadays several infrastructures cooperate in the provision of services. This implies that strong networking within and between sectors mainly trough information technology means is in place, whose dimension may also go beyond the national borders. The future trend is even more alarming since, among the others: i) disturbance phenomena will more and more affect large portions of critical infrastructures, ii) the variety and sophistication of threats is increasing, iii) incidents abroad are increasingly becoming a problem for the availability/security of the services provided by internal critical infrastructures.

Critical infrastructure protection is therefore a priority for most of the countries and several initiatives are in place to identify open issues and research viable solutions in this highly challenging area, especially to identify vulnerabilities and devise survivability enhancements on critical areas. This paper addresses the evaluation of CI, focusing on interdependencies in presence of malfunctions/attacks and assessing the impact of such interdependencies on dependability and security related measures. The offered contribution is twofold. First, the difficulties in carrying on this crucial task are pointed out and an overview of major approaches to accomplish is presented. Then, the evaluation framework set up in the ongoing European project CRUTIAL is discussed, as a concrete research direction tailored to the electric power systems.

The paper is organized as follows. Section 2 discusses the threats undermining the critical infrastructures, namely the interdependencies and types of failures, and overviews some international programs to CI protection. The challenges when approaching the evaluation of critical infrastructures and the major approaches to accomplish this evaluation task are presented in Sect. 3, with reference to ongoing initiatives. The experience of the authors in understanding and evaluating the effects of interdependencies in electric power systems, among the major representative of critical infrastructures, is outlined in Sect. 4. This activity is currently on-going in the context of the European project CRUTIAL. Final conclusions are drawn in Sect. 5.

2   Critical Infrastructures: Peculiarities and Related Activities

The systems that support our daily activities are clearly complex and vulnerable; therefore it is paramount that they be reliable and resilient to continue providing their essential services. Hence, there is the need to: i) build such critical infrastructures following sound engineering design principles; ii) to protect them against both accidental and malicious faults, and iii) to evaluate them to assess their degree of resilience/trustworthiness.

These needs, and the difficulties in their accomplishment, have triggered a number of research initiatives. An overview of major peculiarities of CI and research efforts dealing with them is provided in the rest of this section.

2.1   Interdependencies and Types of Failures

There is a consensus in the literature on critical infrastructures that interdependency analyses are of primarily importance to improve the resilience, survivability and security of these vital systems. An interdependency is a bidirectional relationship between two infrastructures through which the state of each infrastructure influences or is correlated to the state of the other [1]. Infrastructure interdependencies can be categorized according to various dimensions in order to facilitate their identification, understanding and analysis. Six dimensions have been identified in [1], which include: a) the couplings among the infrastructures and their effects on their response behavior (loose or tight, inflexible or adaptive), b) the state of operation (normal, stressed, emergency, repair), and c) the type of failure affecting the infrastructures (common-cause, cascading, escalating).

Interdependencies increase the vulnerability of the corresponding infrastructures as they give rise to multiple error propagation channels from one infrastructure to another that increase their exposure to accidental as well as to malicious threats. Consequently, the impact of infrastructure components failures and their severity can be exacerbated and are generally much higher and more difficult to foresee, compared to failures confined to single infrastructures. As reported in [2], typically blackouts can be caused by the outage of a single transmission (or generation) element, which is not properly managed by automatic control actions or operator intervention, so gradually leading to cascading outages and eventually to the collapse of the entire system. Three types of failures are of particular interest when analyzing interdependent infrastructures: 1) cascading failures, 2) escalating failures, and 3) common cause failures. Cascading failures occur when a failure in one infrastructure causes the failure of one or more component(s) in a second infrastructure. Escalating failures occur when an existing failure in one infrastructure exacerbates an independent failure in another infrastructure, increasing its severity or the time for recovery and restoration from this failure. Finally, common cause failures occur when two or more infrastructures are affected simultaneously because of some common cause. Of course, besides analyzing the types of failures, it is important to understand the different causes that might lead to the occurrence of such failures. As discussed in [3], faults and their sources are very diverse. They can be classified according to different criteria: the phase of creation (development vs. operational faults), the system boundaries (internal vs. external faults), their phenomenological cause (natural vs. human-made faults), the dimension (hardware vs. software faults), the persistence (permanent vs. transient faults), the objective of the developer or the humans interacting with the system (malicious vs. accidental faults), their intent (deliberate vs. non-deliberate faults), or their capability (accidental vs. incompetence faults). Knowing the cause of the failure, proper measures could be taken at level of the system controlling the infrastructure so as to prevent future occurrence of the same fault or at least mitigate its effects on the system.

In previous decades, accidental threats were basically the only real threats facing infrastructure, especially natural disasters, which tend to be localized to one region and have a fixed and, at times, predictable duration. Until the bombing of the Murrah Federal Building in Oklahoma City in 1994, low attention was devoted to malicious acts targeting these critical components. In more recent years, preparation for Y2K (2000), fall-out from post-9/11 events, and a series of blackouts of the power systems experienced both in US and Europe have all reinforced the evidence of how vulnerable these systems are or can become. This awareness has promoted many initiatives, on both national and international scales, to protect critical infrastructures from all hazards, both natural and man-made disasters and cyber-attacks.

2.2   Related Activities

The two volumes of the International CIIP Handbook 2006 [4,5] are a comprehensive collection of information about the various initiatives undertaken by the different countries on the theme of Critical Information Infrastructure Protection (CIIP), mainly at governmental level. The CIIP Handbook underlies the need of developing methodologies for analyzing interdependencies and guiding the protection of critical information infrastructures. In the Unites States many research initiatives and activities related to the protection of critical infrastructures have been undertaken since nineties. Just to mention a few, the North American Electric Reliability Corporation (NERC) has promoted standards and initiatives that are deemed essential for cybersecurity, ranging from security management controls, to the identification and definition of critical assets, controls, personnel and functions such as training, systems security management, incident response and recovery plans. NERC also works closely with the U.S. Department of Homeland Security and Public Safety Canada to ensure that the critical infrastructure protection functions are fully integrated and coordinated with the governments of the United States and Canada. In the specific field of the electric power sector, the Electric Power Research Institute (EPRI) started the Infrastructure Security Initiative addressing power system security at both electrical and cyber levels. The Department of Energy (DOE) published the 21 Steps to Improve Cyber Security of SCADA Networks, whilst the Sandia National Laboratories developed a research program on SCADA electronic security. The Critical Infrastructure Protection Modeling and Analysis Program (CIPMA), launched by the Australian

Government in 2006, examines the relationships and dependencies between critical infrastructure systems and shows how a failure in one sector can greatly affect the operations of other critical infrastructure sectors.

Also in Europe the need of setting up research programs on critical infrastructures has been recognized since several years, both at national and at cross-national levels. The ACIP (Analysis & Assessment for Critical Infrastructure Protection) and the AMSD (A Dependability Roadmap for the Information Society in Europe) projects were accompanying measures in the FP5-IST program that produced a roadmap about R&D activities to be performed on the CI and in the area of information system dependability, respectively. The FP5-IST research project SAFEGUARD (Intelligent Agents Organization to Enhance Dependability and Survivability of Large Complex Critical Infrastructure) proposed an agent-based architecture for the supervision and decision support systems in critical infrastructural domains. The recently concluded FP6-IST co-ordination project CI2RCO on Critical Information Infrastructure Research Co-ordination has developed a research agenda that provides important insights in research and development topics that need to be funded to build resilient, self-diagnostic and self-healing Critical Information Infrastructures [6].

More recently, projects involving international efforts have been promoted, including the on-going european projects IRRIIS [7], CRUTIAL [8], GRID [9], and the NSF project TCIP [10]. Some details on these projects with reference to the specific topic of CI evaluation addressed in this paper will be given in Sect. 3.4.

Among other initiatives, the CRIS Institute[1], with presence in Europe, North America and Asia, was constituted in January 2001 as an international association to promote, encourage and develop awareness and knowledge to increase the dependability of the critical infrastructures in society, mainly the power system, communication system and the computer network. The IFIP Working Group 11.10 on Critical Infrastructure Protection[2] is an active international community of scientists, engineers and practitioners dedicated to advancing the state of the art of research and practice in the emerging field of critical infrastructure protection. The Institute for Information Infrastructure Protection I3P[3] is a Consortium that includes academic institutions, federally-funded labs and non-profit organizations. With a nationwide membership that continues to grow, the I3P brings experts together to identify and help mitigate threats aimed at the U.S. information infrastructure. Of course, the above mentioned programs are a relevant but partial subset of the initiatives undertaken in the entire world; a comprehensive review is outside the scope of this paper.

2.3   Role of CI Analysis and Evaluation

Not all infrastructures are critical and not all critical infrastructures have the same level of criticality. An analysis and evaluation process is required to

---

[1] http://www.cris-inst.com/
[2] http://www.cis.utulsa.edu/ifip1110/
[3] http://www.thei3p.org/

identify vulnerabilities, interdependencies and interoperabilities between systems, to understand what specific assets of the addressed CI are utmost critical and need to be protected the most. Following this analysis, steps can be taken to mitigate the identified vulnerabilities, in an order that reflects the assessed level of criticality.

Specifically, analyzing infrastructure and various interdependencies allows a greater understanding of the cascading effects caused by damage to a particular asset and protect that asset accordingly. Evaluating that an asset may be more critical than another, due to its effects on other infrastructure and essential services, plays a very important role when looking at CI. For example, if an electric substation is damaged leading to a blackout, complications are experienced by a number of other systems/infrastructures and by the services they provide, like railroad operations causing a decreased movement of commodities and potential complications for emergency services. Thus, that electric substation must be protected not only for the Energy Sector, but also for the safeguarding of other sectors infrastructure. Advances in technology and SCADA systems have increased these interdependencies, enhancing sector operations but creating additional vulnerabilities. Such vulnerabilities must be addressed to adequately protect critical infrastructure.

3 Approaches to CI Evaluation

Addressing the analysis and evaluation of CI poses a number of challenging issues, among which:

- complexity and scalability, because of the characteristics of CI in terms of largeness, multiplicity of interactions and types of interdependencies involved. Abstraction layers and modular, hierarchical and compositional approaches are viable directions to cope with these aspects;
- ability to integrate in the evaluation framework the effects of both accidental and malicious threats;
- ability to reproduce both structural aspects and temporal behaviors in a context where the studied infrastructures are assembled from many heterogeneous subsystems having different nature, operation phases and regimes with different configurations and behaviors;
- potential need of combining different formalisms to describe the various components of a system and their dependencies, due to their inherent heterogeneity;
- potential need of combining discrete and continuous variable into a hybrid modeling, e.g. in the case of electric systems encompassing physical electrical infrastructure and the cyber control one (see Sect. 4).

Major pursued approaches in this crucial and difficult task span both model-based evaluation and experimental techniques. Most of the initiatives mentioned in the previous section are dedicating significant effort to this purpose. In the following we briefly overview the major characteristics of these evaluation approaches, trying to point out their strength and weakness with respect to the above listed challenges.

3.1   Model-Based Evaluation

Model-based evaluation is commonly used to support the analysis of dependable computer systems in all the phases of the system life cycle [11,12,13]. During the design phase, models allow to evaluate various alternatives. In assessing an already built system, they constitute a means for providing insights into specific aspects and for suggesting solutions for future releases. The modeling also allows to analyze the effects of system maintenance options and of possible changes or upgrades of the system configuration. Moreover, sensitivity analysis of the models is very useful in performing bottleneck analysis and optimizations. Various methods and tools for evaluations have been developed which provide support to the analyst, during the phases of definition and evaluation of the models. Combinatorial methods, model checking, state-based stochastic methods and discrete-event simulation are major representative approaches in this area; an overview is provided in [11,12].

Model-based evaluation is generally cheap for manufacturers and has proven to be useful and versatile in all the phases of the system life cycle [13]. A model is an abstraction of a system "that highlights the important features of the system organization and provides ways of quantifying its properties neglecting all those details that are relevant for the actual implementation, but that are marginal for the objective of the study" [14]. Several types of models are currently used in practice. The most appropriate type of model depends upon the complexity of the system, the specific aspects to be studied, the attributes to be evaluated, the accuracy required and the resources available for the study. Simple combinatorial techniques are not adequate to deal with the complex interdependencies of CI, therefore they have limited applicability in this context. State-based stochastic methods are instead adequate to deal with complexity and interdependencies; the main disadvantage of this category is the well-known state-space explosion problem since the dimension of the state space grows exponentially with the number of parts. This problem has triggered many studies and significant results have been achieved in the last 15 years. The two general approaches for dealing with the state explosion problem are largeness avoidance and largeness tolerance [12]. Largeness avoidance techniques try to circumvent the generation of large models using, for example, state truncation methods, state lumping techniques, hierarchical model solution methods, model decomposition and approximate solution techniques. However, these techniques may not be sufficient as the resulting model may still be large. Thus, largeness tolerance techniques are needed to provide practical modeling support to facilitate the generation of large state-space models through the use of structured model composition approaches. The basic idea is to build the system model from the composition of submodels describing system components and their interactions. Generic rules are defined for the elaboration of the submodels and their interconnection. It is worth noting that the two categories of techniques (largeness avoidance and largeness tolerance) are complementary and, most of the time, both of them are used when detailed and large dependability models need to be generated and processed, putting more emphasis on one or the other. A number of modeling approaches based on largeness avoidance and largeness tolerance have appeared in the literature. They span: i) compositional modeling approaches, both at level of defining suitable composition operators to build models from a set of building blocks (particularly helpful when the modeled system exhibits symmetries), as well as defining composition rules that allow structuring the modeled system into different abstraction layers with a model associated to each level; ii) decomposition/aggregation modeling approaches, where the overall model is decoupled in simpler and more tractable sub-models, and the measures obtained from the solution of the sub-models are then aggregated to compute those concerning the overall model; iii) derivation of dependability models from high-level specification, e.g. from UML design. A quite detailed survey of major approaches to modeling based on largeness avoidance and largeness tolerance is in [15].

Rather than generate and analyze the entire state space, the simulation technique samples many paths, independently of each other, through the state space and analyzes and evaluates the system only through them. The problem in simulation is how to ensure the statistical quality of the estimates. Especially, assuring that the estimator be unbiased and have low variance are the major issues especially when the measure under analysis is a small probability, as it is for typical dependability indicators (e.g., unreliability or unavailability). In fact, in case of analysis of rare events, applying standard simulation techniques may pose the problem that the statistical significance in the estimation of the target measures becomes very poor. As for the analytical approach, the accuracy of the obtained evaluation depends on the assumptions of the analyzed system, as well as on the behavior of the environment, and on the simulation parameters. Anyway, discrete-event simulation is one of the most commonly used modeling techniques in practice, especially for highly complex systems, for which analytical solution is generally precluded (e.g., to overcome the exponential distribution for events occurrences, which is usually implied by the analytical solution).

3.2   Experimental Evaluation

Experimental measurement is an attractive option for assessing an existing system or prototype and constitutes a very effective way to assess the efficiency of fault tolerance mechanisms and to obtain the detailed characterization of the behavior of the whole system (or parts of it) in presence of faults. An overview on the experimental approaches for the evaluation of computer systems dependability is in [16]. These techniques include both evaluation based on measurements performed on real-life systems, known as field measurements, and evaluation based on controlled experiments, either based on ad hoc approaches or following well-specified dependability benchmarking approaches, known as fault injection and robustness testing. Major issues with the acceptability of the experimental evaluation consist in a) the ability to reproduce the observations and measurements, either on a deterministic or on a statistical base; b) the capability of selecting meaningful system conditions (e.g., failure events) so as to have high representativeness of the evaluated results with respect to the real operation profile of the system under evaluation (especially when based on controlled experiments); c) the ability of generalizing the results through some form of formal reasoning. The first two aspects enhance the confidence in the experimental results, while the third one allows to use the results beyond the restricted experimental set-up. Also, avoiding/minimizing intrusiveness of monitoring systems employed to perform evaluation of the target system is another relevant issue. Recently, the approach on dependability benchmarking has been proposed, aiming at quantitative dependability evaluation through standardizing the experimental procedure, in order to provide generic ways to characterize the behavior of systems/components in the presence of faults [16].

With respect to model-based approaches, experimental methods are very accurate, especially when applied to real-life systems, since they exercise the real system rather than building an abstraction of the system behavior, as the former do. As a drawback, they are costly and not always applicable, e.g., when the interest is in very rare events. So, what is usually done is to construct a proof-of-concept prototype, to test and validate design assumptions, to gain experience with the system, and to provide a vehicle for advanced development. Experimental techniques are well employed in the evaluation of CI. Typically, testbed platforms representing major functionalities/aspects of the studied CI are set-up, on which experiments are conducted to assess specific measures of interest.

3.3   Composite Evaluation Approaches

Model-based methods, as well as experimental approaches show different characteristics, which determine the suitability of the method for the analysis of a specific system aspect. The most appropriate method for quantitative assessment depends upon the complexity of the system, its development stage, the specific aspects to be studied, the attributes to be evaluated, the accuracy required and the resources available for the study. The largeness and complexity of dependability-critical infrastructures, together with the necessity of continuous verification and validation activities during all the design and development stages in order to promptly identify deviations from the requirements and critical bottleneck points, call for a composite (i.e., holistic) evaluation framework, where the synergies and complementarities among several evaluation methods can be fruitfully exploited.

The idea underlying the holistic approach follows a divide and conquer philosophy, where the original problem is decomposed into simpler sub-problems that can be solved using appropriate evaluation techniques. Then the solution of the original problem is obtained from the partial solutions of the sub-problems, exploiting their interactions. Examples of possible interactions are: i) comparison of results for a certain indicator obtained through the application of two alternative methods allows cross-validation of both; ii) feeding a system model with parameter values derived through experimental measurement is a central example of cross-fertilization among different methods; iii) applying higher level analysis may reveal which parts/behaviors of a system have major impact on the evaluated measure and therefore require deeper analysis (typically through different techniques).

3.4 On-Going Studies

Understanding the reciprocal effects of interdependencies among interacting critical infrastructures (both inside the same application domain and among several ones), as well as quantifying resiliency, security and robustness related indicators are tackled by a number of research initiatives/organizations. Pointers to a few relevant on-going studies in this challenging sector are provided in the following, although they are far from being a complete overview.

In the USA panorama, the Department of Homeland Security DHS[4] is heavily involved in programs for critical infrastructure protection with significant support from many other sectors of the government. The National Infrastructure Simulation and Analysis center (NISAC), a program under the Department of Homeland Security's Infrastructure Protection/Risk Management Division, provides advanced modeling and simulation capabilities for the analysis of critical infrastructures, their interdependencies, vulnerabilities and complexities. NISAC is a partnership between Sandia National Laboratories and Los Alamos National Laboratory. They adopt a dynamic simulation modeling approach to quantify and evaluate the effects of infrastructures and their interdependencies on supply and demand under different conditions (e.g., time of the day, time of the year, unusual event, new regulations, incentives, market structures). A recent survey of U.S. and international research on Critical Infrastructure Interdependency modeling methodologies and tools is provided in [17], mainly obtained by collecting data from open source material and, partially, through direct contact with the individuals leading the research.

TCIP's [10] research plan is focused on securing the low-level devices, communications and data systems that make up the power grid, to ensure trustworthy operation during normal conditions, cyber-attacks and/or power emergencies. One of the focus areas of the TCIP project is quantitative and qualitative validation, which explores means to model, simulate, emulate and experiment with the various subsystems in the power grid to allow for adequate quantitative and qualitative validation of the investigated solutions. A number of existing tools (namely PowerWorld, RINSE - Real-time Immersive Network Simulation Environment, formal logics, PowerWeb and APT - Access Policy Tool) are being extended/integrated to be profitably used to investigate/analyze several challenging aspects in the power sector, including: i) the impact of security and of emergency solutions on performance and power generation capability, ii) the wide-area-network communication availability, iii) the performance of a distributed control system under cyber-attack scenarios and the impact on power grid behavior, just to mention a few. Some initial results are in [18,19].

---

[4] http://www.dhs.gov/index.shtm

Two major European projects are currently in progress in the critical infrastructures sector: IRRIIS and CRUTIAL. Both devote significant effort to interdependencies analysis and modeling, to understand and quantify their effects on cascading, escalating and common-mode failures.

IRRIIS [7] is developing SimCIP (Simulation for Critical Infrastructure Protection), an agent-based simulation environment for controlled experimentation with a special focus on CIs interdependencies. The simulator is intended to be used to deepen the understanding of critical infrastructures and their interdependencies, to identify possible problems and to develop. It also intended to be used to validate and test appropriate architectural solutions aiming to enhance the dependability of large critical information infrastructures. The network model for SimCIP is based on a multi-layer simulation approach (technical, cyber, management). Among the others, the Leontief input-output economical model dedicated to the market dynamics representation is exploited and adapted to model critical infrastructures dependencies. The infrastructures addressed by IRRIIS are electricity and telecommunications; their behaviors under both normal and faulty conditions are simulated by SimCIP. Some initial results are in [20,21].

The CRUTIAL project [8] addresses new networked systems based on Information and Communication Technology (ICT) for the management of the electric power grid, in which artifacts controlling the physical process of electricity transportation need to be connected with information infrastructures, through corporate networks (intra-nets), which are in turn connected to the Internet. A major research line of the project focuses on the development of a model-based methodology for the dependability and security analysis of the power grid information infrastructures. The modeling framework, accounting for both qualitative and quantitative analysis and evaluation methods, is aimed at building generic models of interdependencies, taking into account the various forms of interactions and coupling the different systems and infrastructures to be considered in the models. Specifically, the conceptual modeling framework under development is well suited: i) to characterize and analyze the interdependencies between the information infrastructure and the controlled power infrastructure, especially the various types of failures that can occur in the presence of accidental and malicious faults, and ii) to assess their impact on the resilience of these infrastructures with respect to the occurrence of critical outages. Some initial results are in [22,23,24]. In addition, two testbeds are under development which integrate the electric power system and the information infrastructure. A first testbed consists of several power electronic converters, which are interconnected via off-the-shelf communication protocols (TCP/IP); this platform is used to execute different hierarchical and distributed control algorithms. A second testbed builds on environments that are used in industrial automation (SCADA-based) and it is based on a platform for supporting the simulation of attack scenarios. The testbeds and the modeling activities are intended to complement each other and to provide ways of cross validation and fertilization.

These initiatives are still in progress and the developments under study are not yet at a mature stage; so it is premature to attempt a comparison of the different pursued approaches in terms of methodologies and technologies developed so far.

In the next section, a more detailed overview of the work in progress in CRUTIAL on a quantitative approach to model and analyze the interdependencies is provided. An overview on the qualitative modeling approach can be found in [15,23].

4   A Modeling Framework for the Quantitative EPS Analysis under Development in the CRUTIAL Project

As already sketched in Sect. 3.4, one of the main objectives of CRUTIAL [8] is the definition of modeling approaches for understanding and mastering the various interdependencies between the information control system and the controlled electrical infrastructure, thus providing both qualitative and quantitative support for the identification, analysis and evaluation of the identified critical scenarios.

The goal of this section is to provide an overview of the quantitative modeling framework that the authors of this paper are currently developing inside CRUTIAL. The body of the modeling framework has been already introduced in [22] and a part of it is outlined here to provide a complete context overview and for better understanding the new developments presented in this paper. For this purpose, in Sects. 4.1 and 4.2 we focus on the identification of the main logical components of the two infrastructures composing the Electric Power System (EPS): the Electric Infrastructure (EI) and the information infrastructure (ITCS). The interdependencies between ITCS and EI are then discussed in Sect. 4.3, while Sect. 4.4 summarizes the main features characterizing the modeling framework.

In [22], the authors also discussed the feasibility of the proposed framework using Möbius [25], a powerful multi-formalism/multi-solution tool, and presented the implementation of a few basic modeling mechanisms adopting the Stochastic Activity Network (SAN) formalism [26], which is a generalization of the Stochastic Petri Nets formalism. The goal was not to provide a complete model representing a concrete instance of an EPS system, but just to show how some basic frameworks characteristics can be actually obtained.

The last part of this paper starts attacking this pending aspect; in particular Sect. 4.5 presents the concrete EPS system under analysis, the corresponding overall model and it provides a high-level functional description of the system's aspects captured by each submodel.

4.1   Logical Scheme of EI

EI represents the electric infrastructure necessary to produce and to transport the electric power towards the final users. It can be logically structured in different components: the transmission grid (TG, operating in very high voltage levels), the distribution grid (DG, operating in medium/low voltage levels), the high, medium and low voltage generation plants, and the high, medium and low voltage loads.

The main elements that constitute the power grid are generators, loads, substations and power lines. One or more *generators* can be situated inside the power plants. The energy produced by the generators is then adapted by transformers, to be conveyed with minimal dispersion, to the different types of end users (*loads*), through different power grids. The *power lines* are components that physically connect the substations with the power plants and the final users, and the *substations* are structured components in which the electric power is transformed and split over several lines. In the substations there are transformers and several kinds of connection components (bus-bars, protections and breakers). In particular, each substation is logically divided into different sections, which are characterized by certain voltage levels and are connected each other through transformers. Each section consists of a single or double bus-bar.

Voltage, frequency, current, angle, active and reactive power are some of the main (not independent) physical parameters associated to the electric equipments constituting EI (generators, substations, power lines and loads); their specific values are of primary importance in determining the current status of the overall EI. In fact, they affect the behavior of the electric equipments they are referred to (e.g., in terms of availability and reliability of the electric equipment), thus also influencing the evolution of the overall power grid.

Figure 1 depicts an example of high-level logical scheme corresponding to a typical physical scheme of a substation with the connected power lines. The main electric equipments (bus-bars BB, transformers TR, protections PR, breakers BR, power lines PL) have been grouped following an approach which has the advantage to simplify the logical representation. The component N_S represents the parts common to all substations (e.g., the bus-bars, the transformers, the breakers and associated protections), while breakers and protections connected to the power lines are now included in the scheme of the new logical component A_L. In Fig. 2 the corresponding high-level logical scheme for a dummy transmission grid is presented, where the components N_G and N_L represent a generation plant and a load, respectively, and the arcs connecting the different logical components have no physical meaning, but only define the current grid topology. The grid topology may dynamically change during time by opening/closing breakers.

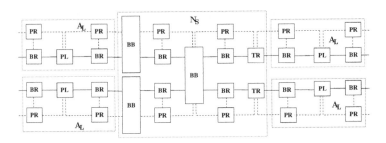

Fig. 1. Example of logical scheme for substation and connected power lines

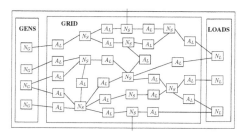

Fig. 2. Example of logical scheme for a dummy transmission grid

4.2   Logical Scheme of ITCS

ITCS (Information-Technology based Control System) implements the information control system and its main purposes are: i) reducing out of service time of generators, power lines and substations (availability); ii) enhance quality of service (through frequency and voltage regulation); iii) optimizing generators and substations management. To these aims, ITCS performs the following activities: a) remote control of the electric infrastructure (it receives data and sends commands); b) coordination of the maintenance (it plans the reconfiguration actions that can affect generators, substations, loads and lines); c) collection of the system statistics. Among the several logical components composing ITCS, we focus the attention on the tele-operation systems for the distribution grid (named *DTOS*) and for the transmission grid (named *TTOS*), since a failure of these logical components can affect a large portion of the grid, also leading to black-out phenomena.

In Fig. 3 we depict a possible logical structure of *TTOS* and *DTOS*. The components *LCS* (Local Control System), *RTS* (Regional Tele-control System) and *NTS* (National Tele-control System) of *TTOS*, and the components *LCC* (Local Control Center), and *ATC* (Area Tele-control Center) of *DTOS* differ for their criticality and for the locality of their decisions.

Different actors (like Power Exchange *PE*, Energy Authority *EA*, Network Management System *NMS*) are involved in the electric system management and there can be a necessity to exchange grid status information and control data over public or private networks (e.g., *TSOcomNet* and *DSOcomNet*). The transmission and distribution grids are divided in homogeneous regions and areas, respectively. *LCS* and *LCC* guarantee the correct operation of substation equipment and reconfigure the substation in case of breakdown of some apparatus. They include the acquisition and control equipment (sensors and actuators). *RTS* and *ATC* monitor their region and area, respectively, in order to diagnose faults on the power lines. In case of breakdowns, they choose the more suitable corrective actions to restore the functionality of the grid. Since *RTS* and *ATC* are not directly connected to the substations, the corrective actions to adopt are communicated to the *LCS* or *ATC* of reference. *NTS* has the main function of supervising the entire grid and handling the planning of medium and long term operations. *NTS* also assists *RTS* (and *ATC*) to localize breakdowns on the

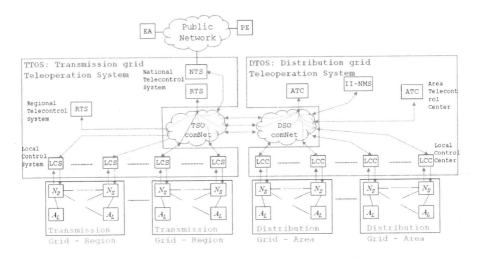

Fig. 3. Logical scheme of $TTOS$ and $DTOS$

power lines situated between two regions (two areas). LCS and LCC, such as RTS and ATC, cooperate to decide operation of load shedding.

4.3   Interdependencies

As defined in Sect. 2.1, an interdependency is a bidirectional relationship between two infrastructures through which the state of each infrastructure influences or is correlated to the state of the other. Among the possible types of interdependencies, here the focus is on the cyber and physical interdependencies. EI requires information transmitted and delivered by ITCS, for example when ITCS triggers a grid reconfiguration for economic optimization; therefore the state of EI depends on the outputs of ITCS (cyber interdependency). Vice versa, the state of ITCS could be affected by failures in EI (e.g. in case of blackout that leads to a failure or service degradation of the information infrastructure), thus revealing a physical interdependency.

Failures in ITCS impact on the state of EI, i.e. on the topology T and on the values of the physical parameters associated to each electric equipment, depending on the logical components affected by the failures and obviously by the type of the failures (cyber interdependency). For example, consequences of a failure of the component LCS associated to a component N_S, N_G or N_L (see also Fig. 3) can be:

- Omission failure of LCS, fail silent LCS. No (reconfiguration) actions are performed on N_S or A_L.
- Time failure of LCS. The above (reconfiguration) actions on N_S or A_L are performed after a certain delay (or before the instant of time they are required).

 – Value failure of LCS. Incorrect closing or opening of the power lines A_L directly connected to the failed component is performed.

The failure of the component RTS (or NTS) corresponds to an erroneous (request of) reconfiguration of the state of EI (including an unneeded reconfiguration) affecting one or more components of the controlled region. The effect of the failure of RTS (or NTS) on a component N is the same as the failure of the component LCS associated to the component N. In the case of Byzantine failure these effects can be different for each component N. In general, the failure of the components LCS, RTS and NTS may depend on the failures of the components connected to them through a network.

On the other direction (physical interdependency), failures of the EI infrastructure impact on (parts of) the ITCS system by lessening its functionalities (till complete failure in the extreme case the failure is a total blackout of the power grid).

4.4   Major Characteristics of the EPS Modeling Framework

To represent and model the behavior of EI and ITCS and their interactions, the modeling and evaluation framework should possess a number of features encompassing the following aspects : i) modeling power, i.e., the basic modeling mechanisms required to build the EPS model; ii) modeling efficiency , i.e. the advanced modeling mechanisms required to build the EPS model more efficiently; and iii) solution power, i.e., the ability to provide efficient solution methods adequate for the EPS modeling complexity and for the assessment of the specific measures of interest. These requirements are fully in line with the challenges pointed out in Sect. 3. With specific reference to the structural and behavioral aspects of EPS systems, major requirements on a suitable modeling framework include:

1. The system has a natural hierarchical structure, as shown in the examples of logical schemes of Fig. 3. Therefore, the modeling framework should support hierarchical composition of different sub-models. The model for the overall EPS could be facilitated considering replication of (anonymous and not anonymous[5]) sub-models, and the replicated and composed models should share part of the state (common state).
2. The state of EI is completely described through the physical parameters associated to each electric equipment (voltage, current, etc.) and through the topology (T) of the grid: the first set of parameters defines the current status of each EI component, while the topology defines how such components are connected together to form the overall EI. Therefore, it is crucial that the modeling framework should support the representation of a hybrid-state composed by a discrete part (the topology) and a continuous one (the electric parameters).

---

[5] Not anonymous replicas can be identified by an index.

3. The time to failures of the components N_S, N_G, N_L and A_L depends also on the value of the electric parameters associated to the components. This means that the framework should support time and probability distributions, as well as conditions enabling the time consuming events (e.g., for the activation of a local protection) that can depend both on the discrete and on the continuous state.

4. We need to consider the reconfiguration actions triggered by the ITCS components, e.g., by LCS and RTS. Moreover, the automatic evolution (auto-evolution) of the electric parameters in case of instability events, e.g. in correspondence of a power line failure, should also be considered. Therefore, the framework should support the call to the functions implementing the reconfiguration algorithms, as well as the autoevolution algorithm.

5. To manage complexity at solution level, ability to perform separate evaluation of different sub-models and combination of the obtained results should be supported.

6. Risk analysis of EPS based on a stochastic approach requires the definition of measures of performability, which is a unified measure proposed to deal simultaneously with performance and dependability. To this purpose, a reward structure should be set-up by associating proper costs/benefits to generators/loads and interruption of service supply.

4.5   The Analyzed EPS Instance

In [22] the authors demonstrated the feasibility of the depicted modeling framework showing how its major characteristics (some of those detailed in Sect. 4.4) can be concretely implemented using a specific modeling and solution tool (Möbius) and a specific modeling formalism (SAN). Here we perform a further step: with reference to the concrete instance of the EPS that is currently under study, we identify the corresponding basic models and we describe their behavior from a functional point of view, that is detailing which system's aspects they capture without showing their actual implementation. Models implementation has been performed and can be found in [27]. For the sake of simplicity, the proposed instance is limited to a homogeneous region of the transmission grid of EPS. Thus, the Local Control System (LCS) and the Regional Tele-control System (RTS) are only considered for ITCS. Some simplifying assumptions have been made to represent the power flow through the transmission grid, following the same approach used in [24,28,29,30]. Therefore, the state and the evolution of the transmission grid are described by the active power flow F on the lines and the active power P at the nodes (generators, loads or substations) which satisfy linear equations for a direct current (DC) load flow approximation of the AC system. The initial setting of the distribution of the power produced by each generator is obtained by distributing the overall power demand to each generator proportionally to the maximum power that the generator can produce.

The operations performed by ITCS on EI, to control its correct functioning and activate proper reconfiguration in case of failure of, or integration of repaired/new, EI components are not considered in detail but they are abstracted at two levels, on the basis of the locality of the EI state considered by ITCS to decide on proper reactions to disruptions [24]. Each level is characterized by an activation condition (that specifies the events that enable the ITCS reaction), a reaction delay (representing the overall computation and application time needed by ITCS to apply a reconfiguration) and a reconfiguration strategy ($\mathcal{RS}$), based on generation re-dispatch and/or load shedding. The reconfiguration strategy $\mathcal{RS}$ defines how the configuration of EI changes when ITCS reacts to a failure. For each level, a different reconfiguration function is considered:

- $\mathcal{RS}_1()$, to represent the effect on the complete transmission grid of the reactions of ITCS to an event that has compromised the electrical equilibrium[6] of EI when only the state local to the affected EI components is considered. Given the limited information necessary to issue its output, $\mathcal{RS}_1()$ is deemed to be local and fast in providing its reaction. $\mathcal{RS}_1()$ is performed by LCS (or LCC) components when they locally detect a non (electrical) equilibrium.
- $\mathcal{RS}_2()$, to represent the effect on the complete transmission grid of the reactions of ITCS to an event that has compromised the electrical equilibrium in EI when the state global to all the EI system under the control of ITCS is considered. Therefore, differently from $\mathcal{RS}_1()$, $\mathcal{RS}_2()$ is deemed to be global and slower in providing its reaction. $\mathcal{RS}_2()$ is performed by RTS.

The activation condition, the reaction delay and the definition of the functions $\mathcal{RS}_1()$ and $\mathcal{RS}_2()$ depend on the policies and algorithms adopted by $TTOS$.

An autoevolution function $\mathcal{AS}()$ is also considered to represent automatic evolution of EI when an event modifying the grid topology occurs. In this case, EI tries to find a new electrical equilibrium for the new grid topology, by changing the values of the power flow through the lines but leaving the generated and consumed power unchanged (only redirection of current flows). The autoevolution is triggered each time an event that modifies the grid topology occurs (typically, a disruption of an EI component or the integration of a repaired/new EI component in the electric grid). The new equilibrium is reached instantaneously (if any) and no ITCS actions are performed. Otherwise, LCS and RTS operations are triggered to generate the new values for P and F, modeled through evaluating reconfiguration strategy function $\mathcal{RS}_1()$ and $\mathcal{RS}_2()$. The reconfiguration strategy $\mathcal{RS}_1()$ is applied immediately, $\mathcal{RS}_2()$ is applied after a time needed to RTS to evaluate it. In the considered instance, the output values of $\mathcal{AS}()$ for active power flow F on the power lines are derived by solving a linear power flow equation system for fixed values of P. The output values of $\mathcal{RS}_1()$ and $\mathcal{RS}_2()$ for P and F are derived considering that for a given power demand, the power flow equations do not have a unique solution. The adopted definition for the function $\mathcal{RS}_1()$ is given by the solution (values for P and F) of power flow equations while minimizing a simple cost function, indicating the cost incurred in having loads not satisfied and having the generators producing more power.

---

[6] Events that impact on the electrical equilibrium are typically an EI component's failure or the insertion of a new/repaired EI component; for simplicity, in the following we will mainly refer to failures. ·

The output values of $\mathcal{RS}_2()$ for P and F are derived by solving an optimization problem to minimize the change in generation or load shedding, considering more sophisticated system constraints, as described in [24]. All these functions are based on the state of EI at the time immediately before the occurrence of the failure. When new events occur changing the status of EI during the evaluation of $\mathcal{RS}_2()$, then the evaluation of $\mathcal{RS}_2()$ is restarted based on the new topology generated by such events. As far as the measures of interest are concerned, we are interested in performability measures on the basis of a reward structure where costs and rewards are considered with respect to the point of the view of the power producers and distributors. Among them: i) the expected reward at a given instant of time or in a given time interval; ii) the expected percentages of blackouts at a given instant of time or in a given time interval; iii) the expected numbers of EI components affected by a failure at a given instant of time or in a given time interval.

4.6   The Submodels Composing the Overall EPS Model

In modeling the considered EPS, we followed a modular and compositional approach. The following atomic models (the leaves in Fig. 3) have been identified as building blocks to generate the overall EPS model.

- PL_SAN, which represents the generic power line with the connected transformers.
- PR1_SAN and PR2_SAN, which represent the generic protections and the breakers connected to the two extremities of the power line (see Fig. 1).
- N_SAN and LCS_SAN, which represent, respectively, a node of the grid (a generator, a load or a substation) and the associated Local Control System LCS (see Fig. 2).
- AUTOEV_SAN and RS_SAN, which represent, respectively, the automatic evolution of EI when an event modifying its state occurs, and the local reconfiguration strategy applied by LCS (function $\mathcal{RS}_1()$).
- RTS_SAN and COMNET_SAN, which represent, respectively the Regional Telecontrol System RTS, where the regional reconfiguration strategy $\mathcal{RS}_2()$ is modeled, and the public or private networks (e.g., $TSOcomNet$ and $DSOcomNet$ of Fig. 3).

In Fig. 4, it is shown how the atomic models are composed and replicated to obtain the composed model representing the EPS region.

The model AL represents a power line with the associated protections and it corresponds to A_L logical components of Fig. 2. This model is then replicated to obtain all the necessary non anonymous A_L components of the grid. The model N_LCS is obtained by composing the atomic models N_SAN and LCS_SAN. Then the model is replicated to obtain all the necessary non anonymous N_G, N_S and N_L components of the grid, with the associated LCS. The model Auto_Control is obtained by composing the atomic models AUTOEV_SAN and RS_SAN, so it

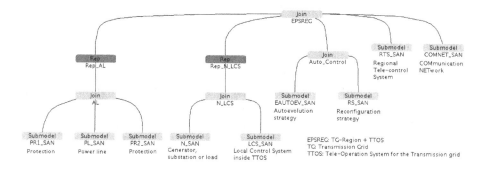

Fig. 4. Composed model for an **EPS** region

represents both the autoevolution function and the reconfiguration strategy locally applied by the *LCS* components. The overall **EPSREG** model is finally obtained through composition of the different models and it represents the EPS instance under study.

The different atomic models interact with each other sharing some places (common and extended) that represent the parameters or part of the states of the EPS, like the topology of the grid, the susceptance of each line, the initial and the current power of each node of the grid, the initial and the current power flow through each line of the grid, the status of the propagation of a failure or a lightning, the disrupted/failed components, the open lines, etc.

These models populate our modeling framework as template models, which are used to represent a large variety of specific scenarios in the EPS sector. Theoretically, all the possible EPS configurations involving (a subset of) the addressed components are representable through proper combination of the proposed models, unless some aspects have been currently not yet captured. Exercising the developed framework on several different scenarios will be useful to reveal possible aspects not included and then proceed with a refinement.

In the following we provide some more details on the system's aspects captured by each atomic model. The focus is especially on failure events and on how they propagate among interacting components/subsystems.

The Atomic Model PL_SAN

PL_SAN represents the generic power line. In particular, it models the power flow through the power line, the temperature associated to the line and the state of the power line (working correctly or affected by a permanent or transient failure).

The considered failures are: i) external failure caused by a lightning, ii) external failure not caused by a lightning, iii) internal failure caused by an overload, and iv) internal failure not caused by an overload. The rate of the internal failures are set with a function depending on the power flow of the line. In particular, the rate for the overload failure also depends on the temperature of the line, following the same approach proposed in [30] for modeling the heating.

The value of the power of the lightning is also represented and is generated randomly from an uniform distribution, when the lightning occurs. The probability that a lightning produces a permanent failure (the break down of the line) depends on the power of the lightning. If the failure is transient (the line does not break down) and the breakers do not open, the lightning can propagate to the ending nodes i and j of the power line (e.g., half power of lightning moves toward node i and half power moves toward node j). When the lightning passes through a line or a node of the grid it reduces its power. The lines, the nodes or the breakers passed through by a lightning can fail (break down) depending on the power of the lightning and on the power flow through them. The propagation ends when the protections stop the propagation, or the lightning reaches a failed line/node or an open breaker, or when the lightning exhausts its power. If the lightning produces a permanent failure of a line or a node, it exhausts and does not propagate anymore.

The failure propagation is instantaneous; it starts from the failed line or node and stops: i) when the propagation reaches an open breaker, ii) when a protection fires (thus opening a breaker), iii) when the propagation reaches a node already touched by the propagation process, or iv) when the propagation reaches a failed line or node. The effect of the propagation of a lightning or a failure is to isolate the failed component from the rest of the grid. If the propagation reaches a generator or a load (because the protections did not fire), these components are considered failed.

The Atomic Models PR1_SAN and PR2_SAN

PR1_SAN and PR2_SAN represent the states and the behavior of the generic protections and the breakers connected to the two extremes of the power line, respectively (see Fig. 1); they are similar. The following states of the breaker connecting a line and a node are modeled: i) closed (when the line and the node are connected), ii) stuck closed (when the line and the node are connected but, due to a failure, the breaker cannot open), iii) opened (when the line and the node are not connected and the power cannot flow), iv) stuck opened (when the line and the node are not connected but, due to a failure, the breaker cannot close), and v) open to repair (when the breaker is open during the repair).

When the connected line is overloaded, i.e., the power flow through the line is greater than a threshold (depending on the line), after a deterministic time, the protection fires and the breaker opens, if it is not stuck closed. When, after a failure, the variation of power required from the generator connected to the protection is greater than a threshold or the associated LCS is affected by an omission failure, after a deterministic time the protection fires and the generator is disconnected from the grid.

Propagation of a failure and of a lightning can move in input toward the model PR1_SAN from the connected line or node, i.e., from the models PL_SAN or N_SAN, respectively, and can cause the opening of the breaker, if it is not failed (stuck closed). Depending on the power of the lightning, the propagation can also probabilistically cause the stuck closed failure of the breaker, if it is closed and not already failed. If the breaker is stuck closed, the lightning continues the propagation in output toward the model N_SAN, if it comes from PL_SAN, or vice versa. The lightning propagation stops if the breaker is already opened or if it is closed but the protection fires.

The Atomic Model N_SAN

N_SAN represents the states and the behavior of the generic node of the grid (generator, substation or load). In particular, it models the states where the node works correctly or is affected by a permanent or transient failure. The considered failures are the same of PL_SAN, except for the failure caused by an overload.

The propagation of a failure and of a lightning can move in input toward the model N_SAN from a connected line; the lightning propagation can probabilistically cause the failure of the node if it is not already failed. In this case, the lightning exhausts its power, otherwise the lightning moves with a reduced power toward the models of all the connected lines (passing through the protection models PR1_SAN or PR2_SAN, depending on the logical direction of the line). The lightning propagates toward the output lines if it did not exhaust its power passing through the node. The lightning power propagated in output towards each line is proportional to the value of the susceptance of the output lines.

For the instance of the model representing a generator, when, after a failure, the variation of power required by the generator is greater than a threshold, or the associated LCS is affected by an omission failure, the protection is triggered to fire after a deterministic time and the generator fails after a deterministic time, if the protection did not fire. If the variation of power required by the generator is below a threshold, the protection is probabilistically triggered depending on the value of the variation. In this way, it is probabilistically modeled the probability that variations of the power required to a generator can cause the disconnection from the grid or the failure of the generator.

The Atomic Model LCS_SAN

LCS_SAN represents the states and the behavior of the Local Control System inside TTOS associated to a node. In particular, it models the states where LCS works correctly and the states where omission failure occurs (the only kind of failures considered at the moment for ITCS).

When LCS is affected by an omission failure, the generator or load controlled by it cannot be reconfigured by assigning proper power values. Failures can be transient or permanent. The duration of the permanent failure is equal to the deterministic time to repair the component LCS.

The Atomic Models AUTOEV_SAN and RS_SAN

AUTOEV_SAN and RS_SAN do not represent the behavior of a single component of EPS. They model, in terms of generation, re-dispatch and load shedding, the effect on the complete transmission grid of the autoevolution and of the $\mathcal{RS}_1()$ reconfiguration strategy applied by LCS components.

The Atomic Model RTS_SAN

RTS_SAN represents the states and the behavior of the Regional Tele-control System RTS, that is triggered to generate the new EI state (i.e., the new values for P and F, as described in Sect. 4.5). In particular, it models states where RTS works correctly, the states where omission failure occurs, the reconfiguration strategy $\mathcal{RS}_2()$ and the list of the LCS that are failed during the evaluation of the reconfiguration strategy $\mathcal{RS}_2()$.

When RTS is affected by an omission failure, the reconfiguration strategy $\mathcal{RS}_2()$ cannot be applied. Failures can be transient or permanent and are modeled like in LCS_SAN.

The Atomic Model COMNET_SAN

COMNET_SAN represents, in a simplified way, the states and the behavior of the public or private networks $TSOcomNet$ and $DSOcomNet$ of Fig. 3. In particular, it models states where $TSOcomNet$ and $DSOcomNet$ work correctly, the states where transient or permanent omission failure occur. The considered failures are modeled like in LCS_SAN.

The time to failures can depend on the status of the transmission grid (e.g., the failure rate could increase in case of blackout). The duration of a transient failure is exponentially distributed. The duration of the permanent failure is the deterministic time to repair the components $TSOcomNet$ and $DSOcomNet$, which can depend on the status of the transmission grid (e.g., the time to repair could depend on the blackout size).

4.7   Current Status and Next Steps

Currently, the solution of the overall model of the addressed EPS instance is in progress using the tool Möbius, adopting some simple artificial scenarios, but well representative to show the impact of interdependencies on measures related with system blackouts. These results are expected to be highly useful to better understand the dynamics of the two interacting EI and ITCS infrastructures, and to help identifying appropriate architectural mechanisms to mitigate the impact of the revealed vulnerabilities.

We plan to exercise the developed framework on a wide variety of scenarios, including realistic control scenarios offered by the CRUTIAL consortium. This way, it will be possible to understand whether and where refinements/extensions of the proposed models are necessary, to cope with missing aspects or to make them more efficient from the solution point of view. The final goal is to pursue a truly general and composable modeling framework, adequate for the interdependencies evaluation in general EPS scenarios, and possibly extendible to interdependencies analysis in other critical infrastructure systems.

5   Conclusions

This paper has addressed the evaluation of critical infrastructures with focus on the interdependencies that strongly characterize these systems. First, a general discussion on vulnerabilities of CI and necessity to analyze them to take appropriate protection actions is presented. Then, major challenges posed by the evaluation process targeted to CI have been sketched; pointers to relevant international research initiatives in this area have been also identified. In addition, major approaches to evaluating CI from the dependability and security perspective have been discussed. The second part of the paper has introduced a concrete approach to the definition of an evaluation framework tailored to electric power system, which is currently under development in the context of the European project CRUTIAL. Specifically, the identification of the logical components composing the EPS infrastructures as well as their interdependencies have been outlined, mainly reporting from a previous work by the authors. On the basis of the characteristics of the involved components and of the challenges in evaluating CI, major features to be possessed by a model-based evaluation framework for quantitative analysis of the interdependencies and their impact on the correct operation of EPS systems have been pointed out. Then, a specific instance of the EPS system has been more concretely tackled, by providing the abstract view of the models representing the several involved components and the mechanisms through which they interact. For space reasons, this description is kept at functional/behavioral level only, without detailing the implementation, which has been already performed through the SAN formalism inside the Möbius tool. Actually, the developed models are reusable template models, which can be assembled to represent a number of specific scenarios in the EPS sectors (theoretically, the proposed building block models should allow representing all the possible EPS configurations involving (a subset of) the addressed components).

An evaluation campaign is currently in progress to derive quantitative assessment of the impact of interdependencies on blackouts related indicators. The results are expected to be very useful, first to guide the possible refinement/extension of the proposed modeling framework, so as to have a solid base for a better understanding of EPS vulnerabilities, thus leading to enhanced design choices for EPS protection at architectural level. Comparison with the results obtained through the EPS simulator [24], under development by the research group the authors belong to, will be a valuable source for cross validation of the two assessment methods.

Acknowledgments. This work has been partially supported by the European Community through the IST Projects CRUTIAL [8] (Contract n. 027513).

References

1. Rinaldi, S.M., Peerenboom, J.P., Kelly, T.K.: Identifying, understanding, and analyzing critical infrastructure interdependencies. IEEE Control Systems Magazine, 11–25 (2001)
2. Pourbeik, P., Kundur, P.S., Taylor, C.W.: The anatomy of a power grid blackout. IEEE Power and Energy Magazine, 22–29 (2006)

3. Avizienis, A., Laprie, J.C., Randell, B., Landwehr, C.: Basic concepts and taxonomy of dependable and secure computing. IEEE Transactions on Dependable and Secure Computing 1, 11–33 (2004)
4. Dunn, M., Abele-Wigert, I.: International CIIP Handbook 2006 (Vol. I). An Inventory of 20 National and 6 International Critical Information Infrastructure Protection Policies. Center for Security Studies, ETH Zurich (2006)
5. Dunn, M., Mauer, V. (eds.): International CIIP Handbook 2006 (Vol. II) - Analyzing Issues, Challenges, and Prospects. Center for Security Studies, ETH Zurich (2006)
6. CI2RCO: European Project CI2RCO - Critical information infrastructure research co-ordination, http://www.ci2rco.org
7. IRRIIS: European Project IRRIIS - Integrated risk reduction of information-based infrastructure systems, http://irriis.org
8. CRUTIAL: European Project CRUTIAL - Critical utility infrastructural resilience, http://crutial.cesiricerca.it
9. GRID: European Project GRID - A coordination action on ict vulnerabilities of power systems and the relevant defence methodologies, http://grid.jrc.it
10. TCIP: Nsf Project TCIP - Trustworthy cyber infrastructure for the power grid, http://www.iti.uiuc.edu/tcip/
11. Bondavalli, A., Chiaradonna, S., Di Giandomenico, F.: Model-based evaluation as a support to the design of dependable systems. In: Diab, H.B., Zomaya, A.Y. (eds.) Dependable Computing Systems: Paradigms, Performance Issues, and Applications, pp. 57–86. Wiley, Chichester (2005)
12. Nicol, D.M., Sanders, W.H., Trivedi, K.S.: Model-based evaluation: From dependability to security. IEEE Transactions on Dependable and Secure Computing 1, 48–65 (2004)
13. Trivedi, K.S., Ciardo, G., Malhotra, M., Sahner, R.: Dependability and performability analysis. In: Donatiello, L., Nelson, R. (eds.) SIGMETRICS 1993 and Performance 1993. LNCS, vol. 729, pp. 587–612. Springer, Heidelberg (1993)
14. Balbo, G.: Introduction to stochastic Petri nets. In: Brinksma, E., Hermanns, H., Katoen, J.-P. (eds.) EEF School 2000 and FMPA 2000. LNCS, vol. 2090, pp. 84–155. Springer, Heidelberg (2001)
15. CRUTIAL Consortium: Methodologies synthesis. Technical report (2007), http://crutial.cesiricerca.it/Dissemination/DELIVERABLES-OF-THE-PROJECT
16. Silva, G.J., Madeira, H.: Experimental dependability evaluation. In: Diab, H.B., Zomaya, A.Y. (eds.) Dependable Computing Systems: Paradigms, Performance Issues, and Applications, pp. 319–347. Wiley, Chichester (2005)
17. Pederson, P., Dudenhoeffer, D., Hartley, S., Permann, M.: Critical infrastructure interdependency modeling: A survey of U.S. and international research. Technical Report INL/EXT-06-11464 (2006), http://www.pcsforum.org/library/files/1159904563-TSWG_INL_CIP_Tool_Survey_final.pdf
18. Davis, C.M., Tate, J.E., Okhravi, H., Grier, C., Overbye, T.J., Nicol, D.: Scada cyber security testbed development. In: 38th North American Power Symposium, Carbondale, IL, pp. 613–618 (2006)
19. Nicol, D.M.: Tradeoffs between model abstraction, execution speed, and accuracy. In: 2nd European Modeling and Simulation Symposium, Barcelona, Spain, pp. 13–20 (2006)
20. Schmitz, W.: Simulation and test: Instruments for Critical Infrastructure Protection (CIP). Information Security Technical Report 12, 2–15 (2007)

21. Le Grand, G., Hecker, A.: A framework for critical information infrastructure protection simulation. In: Skanata, D., Byrd, D. (eds.) Computational Models of Risks to Infrastructure. NATO Science for Peace and Security - Series D: Information and Communication Security, vol. 13, pp. 56–64. IOS Press, Amsterdam (2007)

22. Chiaradonna, S., Lollini, P., Di Giandomenico, F.: On a modeling framework for the analysis of interdependencies in electric power systems. In: IEEE/IFIP 37th Int. Conference on Dependable Systems and Networks (DSN 2007), Edinburgh, UK, pp. 185–195 (2007)

23. Laprie, J.C., Kanoun, K., Kaniche, M.: Modeling interdependencies between the electricity and information infrastructures. In: Saglietti, F., Oster, N. (eds.) SAFE-COMP 2007. LNCS, vol. 4680, pp. 54–67. Springer, Heidelberg (2007)

24. Romani, F., Chiaradonna, S., Di Giandomenico, F., Simoncini, L.: Simulation models and implementation of a simulator for the performability analysis of electric power systems considering interdependencies. In: 10th IEEE High Assurance Systems Engineering Symposium (HASE 2007), pp. 305–312 (2007)

25. Daly, D., Deavours, D.D., Doyle, J.M., Webster, P.G., Sanders, W.H.: Möbius: An extensible tool for performance and dependability modeling. In: Haverkort, B.R., Bohnenkamp, H.C., Smith, C.U. (eds.) TOOLS 2000. LNCS, vol. 1786, pp. 332–336. Springer, Heidelberg (2000)

26. Sanders, W.H., Meyer, J.F.: Stochastic activity networks: Formal definitions and concepts. In: Brinksma, E., Hermanns, H., Katoen, J.-P. (eds.) EEF School 2000 and FMPA 2000. LNCS, vol. 2090, pp. 315–343. Springer, Heidelberg (2001)

27. Chiaradonna, S., Lollini, P., Di Giandomenico, F.: Modelling framework of an instance of the electric power system: Functional description and implementation. Technical Report RCL071202, University of Florence, Dip. Sistemi Informatica, RCL group (2007),
http://dcl.isti.cnr.it/Documentation/Papers/Techreports.html

28. Dobson, I., Carreras, B.A., Lynch, V., Newman, D.E.: An initial model for complex dynamics in electric power system blackouts. In: 34th Hawaii Int. Conference on System Sciences (CD-ROM), Maui, Hawaii. IEEE, Los Alamitos (2001)

29. Chen, J., Thorp, J.S., Dobson, I.: Cascading dynamics and mitigation assessment in power system disturbances via a hidden failure model. Electrical Power and Energy Systems 27, 318–326 (2005)

30. Anghel, M., Werley, K.A., Motter, A.E.: Stochastic model for power grid dynamics. In: 40th Hawaii Int. Conference on System Sciences (CD-ROM), Waikoloa, Big Island, Hawaii. IEEE, Los Alamitos (2007)

Analysis of a Redundant Architecture for Critical Infrastructure Protection

Alessandro Daidone[1], Silvano Chiaradonna[2],
Andrea Bondavalli[1], and Paulo Veríssimo[3]

[1] University of Florence, viale Morgagni 65, I-50134, Italy
`daidone@dsi.unifi.it, bondavalli@unifi.it`
[2] ISTI-CNR, via Moruzzi 1, I-56124, Italy
`silvano.chiaradonna@isti.cnr.it`
[3] University of Lisbon, Campo Grande 1749-016, Lisbon, Portugal
`pjv@di.fc.ul.pt`

Abstract. Critical infrastructures like the power grid are emerging as collection of existing separated systems of different nature which are interconnected together. Their criticality becomes more and more evident as the damage and the risks deriving from wrong behaviors (both accidental and intentionally caused) are increasing. It is becoming evident that existing (legacy) subsystem must be interconnected together following some disciplined and controlled way. This is one of the challenges taken by the European Project CRUTIAL, where an infrastructure architecture seen as a WAN of LANs is being proposed, where LANs confine existing sub-systems, protected by special interconnection and filtering devices (CIS - CRUTIAL Information Switches). Previous work led to the definition of the CIS internal and interconnection architecture, so that a set of CIS can collectively ensure that the computers controlling the physical process correctly exchange information despite accidents and malicious attacks. CIS resilience is achieved thanks to replication for intrusion tolerance and replica recovery for self-healing.

This chapter analyzes the redundant architecture of the CIS, with a set of objectives: identifying the relevant parameters of the architecture; evaluating how effective is the trade-off between proactive and reactive recoveries; and finding the best parameter setup. Two measures of interest were identified, a model of the recovery strategy was constructed and the quantitative behavior of the recovery strategy was analyzed. The impact of the detection coverage, of the intrusions and of the number of CIS replicas was analyzed and discussed. The directions for refining and improving the recovery strategy were proposed.

1 Introduction

Critical infrastructures (e.g., the power grid) are basically physical processes controlled by computers interconnected by networks [1]. Some years ago those systems were highly isolated and hence secure against most security threats. During the last years the Information and Communications Technology (ICT) part

R. de Lemos et al. (Eds.): Architecting Dependable Systems V, LNCS 5135, pp. 78–100, 2008.

of those critical infrastructures evolved in several aspects: i) hardware and software devices (station computers, networks, protocols,...) are no longer ad-hoc and proprietary, instead standard components (COTS[1]) are used; ii) most of the station computers are connected to corporate networks and to the Internet. Therefore these infrastructures are nowadays greatly exposed to cyber-attacks coming from the Internet [2,3], so they have a level of vulnerability similar to other systems connected to the Internet, but the socio-economic impact of their failure can be huge. This scenario, reinforced by several recent incidents, is generating a great concern about the security of these infrastructures, especially at government level [4].

A reference architecture [5] was recently proposed to protect the power grid in the context of the CRUTIAL[2] EU-IST project. Since the power grid is formed by facilities (power transformation substations, corporate offices, etc.) interconnected by a wider-area network (WAN), [5] proposes to represent facilities using protected LANs interconnected by a WAN, leading to the WAN-of-LANs architecture. Using such an architecture, the problem of protecting the power grid (and similar critical infrastructures) is reduced to the problem of protecting LANs from the WAN or other LANs.

In the CRUTIAL reference architecture each LAN is connected to the WAN through a special interconnection and filtering device, the CIS (CRUTIAL Information Switch), which ensures that both the incoming and outgoing traffic satisfies the security policy defined to protect the infrastructure (the so called CIS Protection Service). A CIS is hence a kind of improved firewall that works at the application layer and that is intrusion tolerant. CIS resilience is achieved thanks to replication for intrusion tolerance and replica recovery for self-healing [6,7]. Replication is used in order to guarantee system correct operation when some replicas are compromised. Rejuvenation is instead used to remove the effects of malicious attacks aiming to compromise some replicas and to break the system. The replica rejuvenation strategy, PRRW (Proactive-Reactive Recovery Wormhole), is based both on periodic (proactive) recoveries and on event triggered (reactive) recoveries, seeking perpetual unattended correct operation.

The proactive-reactive recovery strategy aims to both increase CIS dependability and guarantee CIS availability, despite of faults, intrusions and recoveries. In particular, recoveries have beneficial effects (e.g., reactive recoveries rejuvenate replicas detected as incorrect), but also negative effects (e.g., the proactive recovery of a correct replica makes the replica unavailable for the whole duration of the recovery). The key property of the PRRW strategy is that, as long as the fault exhibited by the replica is detectable, this replica will be recovered as soon as possible, ensuring that there is always an amount of replicas available to sustain correct operation [7].

This chapter analyzes the redundant architecture of the CIS, with a set of objectives: evaluating how effective is the trade-off between proactive and reactive recoveries, identifying the relevant parameters of the architecture and finding the

---

[1] Commercial Off-The-Shelf components.

[2] CRitical UTility InfrastructurAL resilience: `http://crutial.cesiricerca.it`

best parameter setup. Two dependability and availability measures of interest were identified. A model of the recovery strategy was constructed in order to analyze the quantitative behavior of the recovery strategy. The impact of the detection coverage, of the intrusions and of the number of CIS replicas on the measures of interest was analyzed and discussed. The directions for refining and improving the recovery strategy were proposed.

The rest of the chapter is organized as follows. Section 2 gives an overview of the reference architecture used in CRUTIAL; Section 3 gives an overview both of the CIS and the PRRW recovery strategy; Section 4 presents the models and the quantitative analysis of the PRRW strategy; Section 5 identifies the directions for improvements and refinements on the recovery strategy. Finally, concluding remarks are presented in Sect. 6.

2   CRUTIAL Reference Architecture Overview

The infrastructure architecture in CRUTIAL is modeled as a WAN-of-LANs [5]. All the Information and Communications Technology (ICT) parts necessary for the control of the whole power grid[3] are logically grouped in substations and finally in local area networks (LANs). LANs are interconnected by a global interconnection network, called WAN. The WAN is a logical entity owned and operated by the critical information infrastructure operator companies, which may or not use parts of public network as physical support. All traffic originates from and goes to a LAN, so packets are switched by the WAN through substation gateways called CRUTIAL Information Switches (CIS).

CIS collectively act as a set of servers providing distributed services aimed to control both the command and information flow among the ICT parts of the critical infrastructure, securing a set of necessary system-level properties. This set of servers must be intrusion-tolerant, prevent resource exhaustion providing perpetual operation, and be resilient against assumption coverage uncertainty, providing graceful degradation or survivability. An assumed number of CIS can be corrupted; in consequence, a logical CIS is implemented as a set of replicated physical units (CIS replicas) according to fault and intrusion tolerance needs. Likewise, CIS are interconnected with intrusion-tolerant protocols, in order to cooperate to implement the desired services.

3   CIS Overview

CIS is the substation gateway interfacing a protected LAN with the WAN, as shown in Fig. 1. In order to be intrusion-tolerant, the CIS is replicated (with diversity) in n machines and follows its specification as long as at most f of

---

[3] Some examples are the administrative clients and the servers LANs, the operational (SCADA) clients and servers LANs, the engineering clients and servers LANs, the Public Switched Telephone Network (PSTN) modem access LANs, the Internet and extranet access LANs, etc.

these machines are attacked and behave maliciously, both toward other replicas and toward the station computers in the protected LAN. Both the incoming and outgoing traffic is managed by "Traffic Replication Devices" that behave like Ethernet hubs: when they receive a packet from a port, they broadcast it to all the other ports. This way, the traffic received by the CIS from the WAN is spread to all the replicas, and the traffic generated by each replica is spread to all the other replicas and to the protected LAN.

The CIS is implemented using an hybrid architecture, so it is composed by two parts: the payload and the wormhole [8]. The payload is an asynchronous system where applications and protocols are executed; the wormhole is a secure and synchronous system providing services to the payload part through a well-defined interface. The wormhole part of each replica (local wormhole) is connected to the other local wormholes through a synchronous and secure control channel, isolated from other networks.

CIS intrusion tolerance is enhanced by rejuvenating CIS replicas through recoveries. In order to guarantee system availability despite the unavailability of recovering replicas, the number of replicas in the system is set to $n \geq 2f + 1 + k$, where k is the maximum number of replicas allowed to recover in parallel. This way, the system is able to tolerate at most f Byzantine replicas and recover k replicas simultaneously.

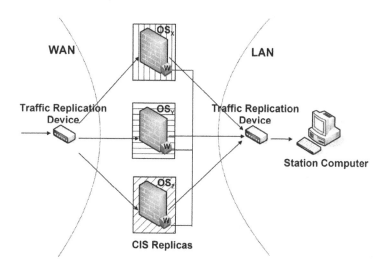

Fig. 1. CIS intrusion tolerant hybrid architecture

The CIS protection service, executed in each payload replica, verifies whether the incoming messages comply with the security policy (OrBAC[4] [9]), notifying their (positive) approval to its local wormhole. The wormhole collects message approvals coming from the local wormholes; an incoming message m is signed by

---
[4] OrBAC (Organization Based Access Control).

the wormhole if and only if the wormhole collects at least $f+1$ different approvals for m. Messages signed by the wormhole are considered valid messages and they are forwarded to their destination only by a distinguished payload replica, the leader (so there is no unnecessary traffic multiplication inside the LAN).

Each payload replica has to verify whether the leader forwards all the signed messages and has to check whether invalid messages are sent toward the LAN. The wormhole is in charge of both triggering the recoveries when necessary, ensuring that there is an amount of replicas to sustain system's correct operation, and managing the election of the new leader.

3.1   Fault Model and Assumptions

This Section describes [7] the fault model and the assumptions on which the fault model is based on. Station computers are assumed to only accept messages signed by the wormhole (a symmetric key K is shared between the station computer(s) and the CIS wormhole). The following faults are considered:

f1) The faults related to communication involve both the traffic replication devices and the communication channels among them and the replicas (except the control channel connecting local wormholes). Traffic replication devices can lose messages coming from a port or sometimes delay the traffic forwarding on some ports (for an unbounded time); traffic replication devices cannot generate spurious messages or alter messages. Communication channels can lose messages or unpredictably delay the traffic forwarding.

f2) A payload replica can be intruded, and hence can be affected by Byzantine faults.

f3) A local wormhole can only fail by crash; at most $f_c \leq f$ local wormholes are assumed to fail by crash. The crash of a local wormhole is detected by a perfect failure detector. When a local wormhole crashes, the corresponding payload is forced to crash together.

f4) Fault-independence is assumed for payload replicas, i.e., the probability of a replica being faulty is independent of the occurrence of faults in other replicas (this assumption can be substantiated in practice through the extensive use of several kinds of diversity [10]).

f5) The same attack on the same replica has always the same probability of success (this is a working assumption that could be relaxed in future work).

f6) Station computers cannot be compromised (it is the trusted network that we aim to protect, exactly in the sense of preventing it from being compromised).

f7) Replicas are correct after their recovery.

f8) The security policy verified by the CIS is assumed to be perfect; this means that a correct replica applies perfectly the policy verification and there are no policy inconsistencies between replicas (i.e. all correct replicas verify the same policy).

Given the set of faults just described, the corresponding failure modes for a payload replica are:

- Crash. The payload replica crashes because of the crash of the corresponding local wormhole (f3) or as the effect of an intrusion (f2).
- Omission. The payload replica is subjected to a transient omission because of communication problems (f1) or as the effect of an intrusion (f2). For example, a transient omission occurs when the leader payload is not forwarding a signed message because it never received it from the traffic replication device (f1).
- Invalid. The payload replica is failing by value as the effect of an intrusion (f2), e.g., it is sending illegal messages toward the LAN or it is flooding the WAN and the LAN aiming to delay the forwarding of legal messages.

For ease of modeling, we assume that a replica, as soon as it is successfully intruded, explicitly manifest failures (of any kind) and that a failure caused by an intrusion is permanent.

The system is unavailable if the number of correct working replicas is less than $f+1$ (so quorums cannot be reached) or if there are more than $f+1$ correct replicas, but the leader is omitting (so legal messages are not forwarded). The system fails if the number of invalid replicas is greater than f (the correctness of the system cannot be guaranteed) or if the necessary resources are unavailable for a fixed duration (CIS seeks perpetual operation).

3.2 The PRRW Strategy

We now explain the PRRW (Proactive-Reactive Recovery Wormhole) strategy that we are going to evaluate, laid down in [7]. The PRRW strategy manages the CIS replica recoveries using a mix of proactive and reactive recoveries, and it is characterized by the following parameters:

- The maximum time interval T_P (cycle or recovery period) between consecutive recoveries on the same replica (each replica is hence recovered at most after T_P).
- The worst case execution time T_D of a recovery.
- The maximum number k of replicas that may recover simultaneously.
- The maximum number f of simultaneously corrupted replicas that the system can tolerate.

The PRRW strategy is organized as shown in Fig. 2: time is divided in $\lceil n/k \rceil$ different time slots that are cyclically repeated. Each slot is divided in two tasks: task A and task R_i, with $i = 1, \ldots, \lceil n/k \rceil$.

Proactive (periodic) recoveries are executed during task R_i only; up to k replicas recover simultaneously in each task R_i, according to the replica index. Replica i, with $i = 1, \ldots, k$, are recovered in task R_1, replica i, with $i = k + 1, \ldots, 2k$, are recovered in task R_2 and so on. Task R_i lasts for (at most) T_D and it is executed again after a period T_P.

Two types of reactive (a-periodic) recoveries can be triggered on replica i:

1. "Immediate" reactive recovery, triggered if a quorum of $f+1$ accusations exists about i sending illegal messages; in this scenario replica i is "detected" of being compromised, because at least one correct replica detected that replica i is failed.

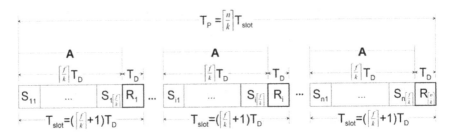

Fig. 2. The PRRW scheduling

2. "Delayed" reactive recovery, triggered if a quorum of at least $f+1$ accusations exists about the current leader i, some about i sending illegal messages, other about i not forwarding a signed message (the signed messages was not forwarded for more then O_t times). In this scenario the leader replica i is "suspected" of being compromised, because at least one correct replica raised an accusation about leader replica i, but the wormhole is not able to identify which accuser replica is correct, so it is not able to identify which kind of accusation is correct about leader replica i.

"Immediate" reactive recoveries are immediately triggered on replica i as soon as the replica is detected of being compromised.

"Delayed" reactive recoveries are only triggered on the leader replica, are executed during task A and are coordinated with proactive recoveries. If no "immediate" reactive recovery is already triggered for replica i, the PRRW strategy finds the closest recovery sub-slot where the recovery of replica i does not endanger the availability of the CIS. If the found sub-slot is located in the slot where replica i will be proactively recovered, the "delayed" reactive recovery is not performed. Task A is divided into $\lceil f/k \rceil$ recovery sub-slots identified as S_{ij}; up to k replicas can be recovered simultaneously in each sub-slot. Task A lasts for (at most) $\lceil f/k \rceil T_D$.

Each slot lasts hence for up to $(\lceil f/k \rceil + 1)T_D$ with period T_P. After each R_i task has been executed once, each replica has been proactively recovered once.

A new leader is elected by the wormhole if the current leader is recovering or if the local wormhole of the current leader is detected to be crashed. The new leader is chosen as the (currently not crashed) replica more recently recovered by a proactive recovery.

4   PRRW Quantitative Analysis

This Section presents a quantitative analysis of the PRRW strategy. The relevant measures of interest are identified and the relevant parameters are described. The model representing the PRRW strategy is described and finally the results of the performed simulations are presented and discussed.

The quantitative analysis of the PRRW strategy aims to evaluate how effective is the trade-off between proactive and reactive recoveries. Proactive recoveries rejuvenate the replicas in predefined instants of time, without being based on any fault detection. This means that proactive recoveries treat all the faults, including also the latent and hidden ones, which cannot be treated in other way, but they recover also correct replicas, weakening the availability of the system. On the other side, reactive recoveries are triggered only on replicas detected or suspected of being faulty; replicas not detected or suspected of being faulty are never recovered, even if they are actually faulty, weakening the dependability of the system.

Recoveries determine a discontinuity in the CIS configuration caused by the temporary unavailability of the replicas subjected to a recovery. Therefore it is possible to represent the entire operational life split into different periods of deterministic duration called "phases". This feature allows a reconfiguration strategy belonging to the Multiple Phased System (MPS) class for which a modeling and evaluation methodology exist [11], supported by the DEEM tool [12]. Using DEEM, the model is split into two logically distinct sub-nets: the Phase Net (PhN) representing the schedule of the various phases, each one of deterministic duration, and the System Net (SN) representing the behavior of the system. Each net is made dependent on the other by marking-dependent predicates that modify transition rates, enabling conditions, reward rates etc. Reward measures are defined as Boolean expressions, functions of the net marking. Both the analytic [11] and simulation solutions [13] can be used in order to exercise the models; the measures of interest defined in our quantitative analysis were evaluated by simulation.

Different studies were performed on the modeled system varying several parameters; the relevant parameters are the following:

1. Mission time t.
2. Probability p_I of intrusion within a replica manifesting as a permanent invalid behavior; intrusions can manifest themselves as permanent omissions with probability $1 - p_I$. Parameter p_I impacts on the PRRW strategy because invalid and omission failures are treated in different ways.
3. Detection coverage c_M of malicious behavior of a replica. Parameter c_M impacts on the PRRW strategy because only detectable faults can trigger reactive recoveries.
4. Number n of replicas in the system.

The quantitative analysis aims to evaluate how these parameters impact on the measures of interest.

4.1   Measures of Interest

We are interested in measuring both the system failure probability $P_F(t)$ and the system unavailability $P_U(0, t)$ at time t.

The system fails at time t if one of the following conditions holds:

1. the number of invalid replicas gets over f;
2. the system is unavailable for an interval of time greater then T_O.

Let $P_{\mathrm{FI}}(t)$ be the probability of the system being failed at time t because of condition 1, given that it was correctly functioning at time $t = 0$. Let $P_{\mathrm{FO}}(t)$ be the probability of the system being failed at time t because of condition 2, given that it was correctly functioning at time $t = 0$. $P_{\mathrm{F}}(t)$ is defined as the probability of the system being failed at time t, given that it was not failed at time $t = 0$, and it is obtained as

$$P_{\mathrm{F}}(t) = P_{\mathrm{FI}}(t) + P_{\mathrm{FO}}(t).$$

The system is unavailable at time t if one of the following conditions holds:

1. the number of correct replicas is less than $f+1$ (quorums cannot be reached);
2. there are more than $f + 1$ correct replicas, but the leader is omitting (legal messages are not forwarded).

Let $T_{\mathrm{U}}(0, t)$ be the total time the system is not failed but unavailable within $[0, t]$ because of one of the above conditions. Let $T_{\mathrm{A}}(0, t)$ be the total time the system is not failed within $[0, t]$. System unavailability, denoted by $P_{\mathrm{U}}(0, t)$, is defined as the probability of the system being unavailable within $T_{\mathrm{A}}(0, t)$, given that it was correctly working at time $t = 0$; system unavailability is obtained as

$$P_{\mathrm{U}}(0,\ t) = \frac{T_{\mathrm{U}}(0,\ t)}{T_{\mathrm{A}}(0,\ t)}.$$

4.2   The PRRW Model

The Phase Net (PhN). The phase net (Fig. 3) models the PRRW scheduling shown in Fig. 2. The deterministic transitions *TsubSlot* and *TRi* model the times to perform the tasks A and R$_i$, respectively. Place *Sij* contains a token during the task A (a-periodic recovery phase) and *Ri* contains a token during the task R$_i$ (periodic recovery phase). The marking of *CountSubSlot* counts the number of the current recovery sub-slot (S$_{ij}$) within the current recovery slot. The marking of *CountSlot* counts the number of the current recovery slot within the current cycle. The marking of *CountWin* counts the number of the current cycle. The immediate transition *tNextSlot* fires when a periodic recovery slot ends, resetting the marking of *CountSubSlot* to 1. The immediate transition *tNextWin* fires when a new cycle is started, resetting the marking of *CountSlot* to 1. The immediate transitions of the phase net have priority less than the priorities of the immediate transitions of the system net.

The System Net (SN). The system net of the PRRW model is composed by $n \leq 6$ similar subnets (one subnet for each replica), a subnet to keep track of system failures and a subnet to model the initialization (the description of this last subnet is omitted without affecting the comprehension of the model).

Figure 4 shows the subnet modeling replica 1. The left part of the subnet models the replica failures, while the right part of the subnet models the replica recovery and leader election. Places which name ends with digit "1" model replica 1, while the other places (*Leader* and *kRec*) are shared by all the replicas.

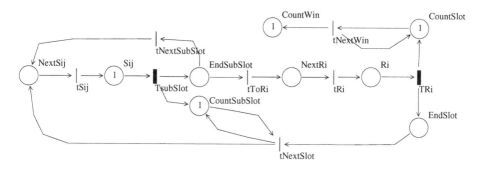

Fig. 3. The phase net of the PRRW model

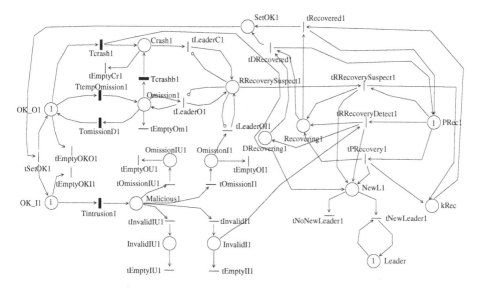

Fig. 4. The subnet of SN modeling replica 1

Replica failures are modeled as follows. As long as both OK_O1 and OK_I1 contain one token each, replica 1 is correctly working. One token in places $Crash1$ or $Omission1$ represents the crash of the replica or an omissive behavior as a consequence of a transient omission, respectively. The exponential transitions $Tcrash1$ and $Tcrashb1$ represent the time to the crash with rate λ_1^c; when the replica crashes, place OK_I1 is emptied (the replica cannot be no more intruded). $TtempOmission1$ represents the time to a transient omission exponentially distributed with rate λ_1^o. A transient omission disappears after a time modeled by the exponential transition $TomissionD1$ with rate λ^{eo}.

The exponential transition $Tintrusion1$ represents the time to intrusion with rate λ_1^a; the effect of the intrusion is modeled by the following immediate transitions (enabled in the same marking) and the associated places:

- *TomissionIU1* for an undetectable omission failure, with probability $(1 - c_M)(1 - p_I)$,
- *TomissionI1* for a detectable omission failure, with probability $c_M(1 - p_I)$,
- *TinvalidIU1* for an undetectable invalid failure, with probability $(1 - c_M)p_I$,
- *TinvalidI1* for a detectable invalid failure, with probability $c_M p_I$,

where p_I and c_M are the probability of an intrusion manifesting as a permanent invalid behavior and the detection coverage of malicious behavior, respectively.

The replica recovery is modeled as follows. Place *PRec1* contains a token as long as replica 1 is not recovering, while place *Recovering1* contains one token as long as the replica is recovering. Place *DRecovering1* contains a token during a reactive recovery triggered by detections. Place *kRec* is used to count the number of replicas currently recovering. Place *RRecoverySuspect1* contains a token if a crash, an omission or a malicious omission occurs.

Recoveries are triggered by one of the following immediate transitions (ordered by increasing priorities): *tRRecoverySuspect1* (reactive recovery triggered by suspects), *tRRecoveryDetect1* (reactive recovery triggered by detections) or *tPRecovery1* (proactive recovery). The immediate transition *tRRecoverySuspect1* fires if a new a-periodic recovery sub-slot is starting (*NextSij* contains a token) and less than k replicas are recovering (*kRec* contains less than k tokens) and the replica is not going to be proactively recovered in the next periodic slot (the index of the replica is not in the interval $[(Mark(CountSlot) - 1)k + 1, Mark(CountSlot)k]$). The immediate transition *tRRecoveryDetect1* fires if a new recovery sub-slot is starting (*NextSij* contains a token or NextRi contains a token). The immediate transition *tPRecovery1* fires if a periodic recovery slot is starting (*NextRi* contains a token) and less than k replicas are recovering (*kRec* contains less than k tokens) and the index of the replica is in the interval $[(Mark(CountSlot) - 1)k + 1, Mark(CountSlot)k]$.

After the starting of a recovery of the replica, all the immediate transitions which name starts with *tEmpty* fire, emptying the following places: *OK_O1*, *OK_I1*, *Crash1*, *Omission1*, *InvalidIU1*, *InvalidI1*, *OmissionIU1* and *OmissionI1*. Immediate transitions *tRecovered1* or *tDRecovered1* fire when the current recovery ends, resetting the replica subnet.

The election of the leader replica is managed as follows. The marking of place *Leader* corresponds to the index of the current leader; when replica 1 either is going to be recovered or is crashed, one token is added in place *NewL1*. *tNewLeader1* fires if replica 1 is the current leader, triggering the mechanism of election of a new leader, otherwise *tNoNewLeader* fires. The arc from place *Leader* to place *tNewLeader1* has multiplicity equal to *Mark(Leader)*, while the arc from place *tNewLeader1* to place *Leader* has multiplicity equal to the index of the replica that will be elected as the new leader. The new leader should be the last (not crashed) replica proactively recovered, that is replica with index $j = ((n + (Mark(CountSlot) - 2)k) mod n) + k$. If replica j is currently crashed, the next attempt is made on replica $j - 1$, until a not crashed replica is found.

The subnet shown in Fig. 5 models the system failure. Place *OKSysN* contains a token as long as the system is not failed and it is not omitting (there are

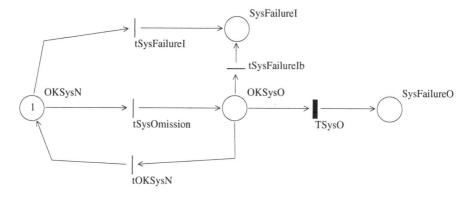

Fig. 5. The subnet of SN modeling the system failure

more than f correct replicas and the leader is not crashed or omitting). Place *OKSysO* contains a token when the system is not failed but it is omitting. Place *SysFailureI* contains a token when the system is failed because of invalid behavior (there are at least $f+1$ invalid replicas). Place *SysFailureO* contains a token when the system is failed because the resource unavailability lasted for an unacceptable period of time represented by the exponential transition *TSysO* with rate $1/T_O$.

Different priorities are associated to the immediate transitions of SN, when no probabilistic choices are required. For example, all the immediate transitions of a replica i have priorities lower than those of replica j, if $i < j$.

Reward Structures. The evaluation of the measures of interest $P_F(t)$ and $P_U(0, t)$ involves specifying a performance (reward) variable and determining a reward structure for the performance variable, i.e., a reward structure which associates reward rates with state occupancies and reward impulses with state transitions [14]. System failure probability $P_F(t)$ was evaluated in terms of an "instant of time" performance variable which is based on the following reward structure:

```
if (Mark(OKSysO)=0 and Mark(OKSysN)=0) then (1) else (0)
```

System unavailability $P_U(0, t)$ was evaluated as $P_U(0, t) = \dfrac{T_U(0, t)}{T_A(0, t)}$.

$T_U(0, t)$ was evaluated defining an "interval of time" performance variable which reward structure is the following:

```
if (Mark(OKSysO)=1) then (1) else (0)
```

$T_A(0, t)$ was evaluated defining an "interval of time" performance variable which reward structure is the following:

```
if (Mark(OKSysO)=1 or Mark(OKSysN)=1) then (1) else (0)
```

4.3   Model Evaluation and System Analysis

In this Section the results of the evaluation of the measures of interest are shown. The measures of interest were evaluated by simulation [13] with a confidence level of 95% and a half-length confidence interval of 1%.

All the model parameters and the default values used for the evaluations are shown in Table 1; the value for T_D was taken from [7]. The relevant parameters are:

1. Mission time t. This is the time during which the system is exercised since it starts to work. t varies in $[2628, 42048]$ sec.
2. Probability p_I of intrusion within a replica manifesting as a permanent invalid behavior. p_I varies in $[0, 1]$. If $p_I = 0$ then all intrusions manifest as a permanent omissive behavior; in this case, only "delayed" reactive recoveries (on the leader replica) can be triggered. If $p_I = 1$ then all intrusions manifest as a permanent invalid behavior; in this case, intrusions on each replica can only trigger "immediate" reactive recoveries.
3. Detection coverage c_M of malicious behavior of a replica. c_M is the probability of detecting an intruded replica, and hence the probability of reactively recovering an intruded replica. c_M varies in $[0, 1]$. If $c_M = 0$ then no intrusions are detected; in this case, all intrusions are treated by proactive recoveries and reactive recoveries are only triggered by crash or communication omissions. If $c_M = 1$ then all intrusions are detected and treated by reactive recoveries.
4. Number n of system replicas in the system, maximum number f of corrupted replicas tolerated by the system itself and maximum number k of system replicas recovering simultaneously, with $n = 2f + 1 + k$.

A first study was performed observing both system failure probability $P_F(t)$ and system unavailability $P_U(0, t)$ over mission time t for three different values of p_I.

Figure 6(a) shows how $P_{FI}(t)$ and $P_{FO}(t)$ change over mission time t, with $P_F(t) = P_{FI}(t) + P_{FO}(t)$. $P_F(t)$ increases exponentially over time for all the values of p_I. $P_F(t)$ behaves in fact like a geometric random variable for the following reasons. System failure probability during each recovery period (cycle) is not null; after each cycle the system is rejuvenated, so we can assume that the system failure probability during the next cycle is the same as the previous one. So system failure probability $P_F(t)$ cumulates over the recovery periods as a geometric random variable. The values of $P_F(t)$ are over 0.01 because of the values assigned to the system parameters. As p_I varies from 0 to 1, $P_F(t)$ increases of about 30% for low values of t and increases of about 17% for high values of t. For $p_I = 0$, $p_I = 0.5$ and $p_I = 1$ the value of $P_{FI}(t)$ is about 0%, 17% and 50% of the value of $P_F(t)$, respectively, independently on the values of t.

If $p_I = 0$ then $P_{FI}(t) = 0$, because there is no invalid behavior, and hence $P_F(t) = P_{FO}(t)$. As p_I varies from 0 to 1, $P_{FO}(t)$ changes from 100% of $P_F(t)$ to 50% of $P_F(t)$; the number of intrusions does not change, but the effect of intrusions changes. In fact, the value of $P_{FO}(t)$ depends on the time during

Table 1. Parameters and their default values

Name	Default Value	Meaning
t	2628	Mission time (sec)
n	4	Number of replicas in the system
k	1	Max number of replicas recovering simultaneously
f	1	Max number of corrupted replicas tolerated by the system
T_D	146	Time duration of a recovery operation (sec)
T_O	60	Duration of system omission before considering the system failed (sec)
λ_i^c	[1.9E-7, 3.8E-7]	Crash rate of replica i. Each replica has a diverse crash rate (from 1 per 60 days to 1 per 30 days)
λ_i^o	[1.9E-6, 3.8E-6]	Transient omission rate of replica i. Each replica has a diverse rate (from 1 per 6 days to 1 per 3 days)
λ^{eo}	3.3E-2	Omission duration rate of a replica. A transient omission lasts for 30 seconds (on average)
λ_i^a	[5.8E-5, 1.2E-5]	Successful attack (intrusion) rate of replica i. Each replica has a diverse rate (from 5 per day to 1 per day)
p_I	0.5	Probability of intrusion within a replica manifesting as a permanent invalid behavior (if $p_I = 0$ all intrusions manifest as permanent omissions)
c_M	0.7	Probability of detecting malicious behavior of a replica

which replicas are unavailable, which for $p_I = 0$ is given by the sum of the following durations:

- the time spent waiting for a "delayed" reactive recovery of the omissive leader;
- the time spent during the recovery on the omissive leader;
- the time spent waiting for proactive recoveries of (not leader) omissive replicas;
- the time spent for proactive recoveries (not varying for the different values of p_I).

If $p_I = 1$ then the time during which replicas are unavailable is given by the sum of the following durations:

- the time spent during "immediate" reactive recoveries on replicas detected as intruded; the number of these recoveries is about n times the number of "delayed" reactive recoveries performed for $p_I = 0$;
- the time spent for proactive recoveries.

Therefore, the value of $P_{FO}(t)$ for $p_I = 1$ mainly represents the impact of recoveries (both proactive and reactive) on $P_F(t)$ (crashes and transient omissions are still present, but have lower rates than intrusions). The value of $P_{FO}(t)$ for $p_I = 1$ shows that the impact of recoveries on $P_F(t)$ is high (about 50%).

Figure 6(b) shows how $P_U(0, t)$ changes over mission time t. $P_U(0, t)$ increases over time for all the values of p_I. For $p_I = 0.5$ and $p_I = 1$ the value of

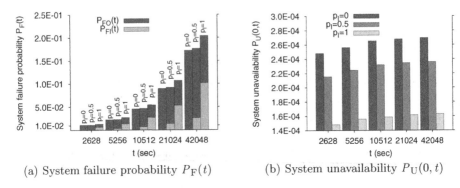

(a) System failure probability $P_F(t)$ (b) System unavailability $P_U(0, t)$

Fig. 6. System failure probability $P_F(t)$ and system unavailability $P_U(0, t)$ over mission time t for different values of p_I

$P_U(0, t)$ is about 87% and 60% of the value of $P_U(0, t)$ for $p_I = 0$, respectively, independently on the values of t.

The trend of $P_U(0, t)$ for varying p_I is similar to the trend of $P_{FO}(t)$ shown in Fig. 6(a); for $p_I = 1$ the value of $P_U(0, t)$ is mainly due to the recoveries, for $p_I = 1$ and $p_I = 0.5$ the value of $P_U(0, t)$ is influenced by the fact that the number of recoveries decreases but the number of omission increases.

Another study was devoted to evaluate both system failure probability $P_F(t)$ and system unavailability $P_U(0, t)$, varying both the detection coverage c_M and the probability p_I of intrusions manifesting as invalid behavior. This study shows how reactive recoveries improve the measures of interest with regard to treating intrusions with proactive recoveries only.

Figures 7(a) and 7(b) show how $P_{FI}(t)$ and $P_{FO}(t)$, respectively, change over detection coverage c_M for different values of p_I; in order to make easier their comparison, the same scale for the y-axis is used. $P_{FI}(t)$ decreases as c_M increases from 0 to 1 for all the values of p_I. $P_{FI}(t)$ takes the largest values for $p_I = 1$ and the lowest values for $p_I = 0$. If $p_I = 0$ then the values of $P_{FI}(t)$ for different values of c_M are 0 and are not shown in Fig. 7(a). $P_{FI}(t)$ takes the smallest values for $p_I = 0.2$ and is almost constant. The curve corresponding to $p_I = 1$ decreases quicker than the other curves (it decreases for about one order of magnitude) as c_M increases. $P_{FO}(t)$ shows an opposite behavior with respect to $P_{FI}(t)$: it increases as c_M increases from 0 to 1. $P_{FO}(t)$ takes the largest values for $p_I = 0$ and the lowest values for $p_I = 1$. The curve corresponding to $p_I = 1$ increases quicker than the other curves (it increases for about 2.5 times); the curve corresponding to $p_I = 0$ is almost constant. The largest variations in the values of $P_{FI}(t)$ and $P_{FO}(t)$ for varying c_M occur for $p_I = 1$.

The values of $P_{FI}(t)$ and $P_{FO}(t)$ for $c_M = 0$ correspond to the system configuration in which all the intrusions are treated only by proactive recoveries. The difference between the values of $P_{FI}(t)$ (and $P_{FO}(t)$) for $c_M = 0$ and $c_M = 1$ is due to the effect of treating all the intrusions by reactive recoveries. Increasing c_M there are two opposite effects with respect to $P_{FI}(t)$ and $P_{FO}(t)$: $P_{FI}(t)$

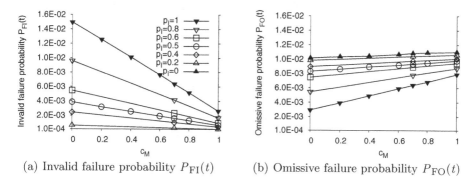

Fig. 7. Impact of detection coverage c_M on both $P_{FI}(t)$ and $P_{FO}(t)$ for different values of p_I

decreases, because invalid replicas reactively recovered are no longer weakening the system; $P_{FO}(t)$ increases, because replicas, while recovering, do not contribute to system operation. The overall effect, shown in Fig. 8(a), is that, when most of the intrusions behave as invalid ($p_I \geq 0.4$), system failure probability $P_F(t)$ decreases as detection coverage c_M increases. On the contrary, when most of the intrusions behave as omissions ($p_I < 0.4$), the impact of c_M on $P_F(t)$ is negligible. This stresses that, in order to improve the value of $P_F(t)$, it is useful to trigger reactive recoveries and hence to set the value for c_M as higher as possible.

Figure 8(b) shows how system unavailability $P_U(0, t)$ changes over detection coverage c_M for different values of p_I. The trend of $P_U(0, t)$ for varying c_M is similar to the trend of $P_{FO}(t)$ shown in Fig. 7(b). $P_U(0, t)$ increases as c_M increases from 0 to 1 for all values of p_I. $P_U(0,t)$ takes the largest values for $p_I = 0$ and the lowest values for $p_I = 1$. If $p_I = 0$, $P_U(0, t)$ is almost not

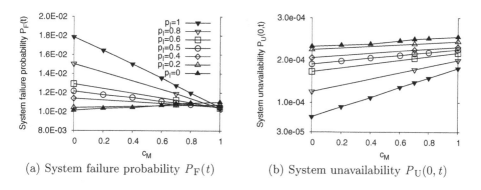

Fig. 8. Impact of detection coverage c_M on system failure probability $P_F(t)$ and system unavailability $P_U(0, t)$ for different values of p_I

influenced by changing the detection coverage, while increasing p_I the influence of c_M becomes more evident (almost an order of magnitude for $p_I = 1$).

It turns out that $P_U(0, t)$ is negatively affected by a larger value for c_M, because the larger is the detection coverage, the more reactive recoveries are triggered; the above trend is more evident as the probability p_I increases, because recoveries triggered by invalid behavior involve all replicas, not only the leader.

The results of this study show that increasing the detection coverage of intrusions has conflicting effects on system failure probability $P_F(t)$ and system unavailability $P_U(0, t)$: as c_M increases, $P_F(t)$ improves and $P_U(0, t)$ gets worsen; the impact of this effect depends on the behavior of the (invalid or omissive) intrusions, i.e. on the value of the parameter p_I. Since a low $P_F(t)$ and a low $P_U(0, t)$ are conflicting goals, the proper tuning of c_M entails defining their relative importance. Thus, if $P_F(t)$ has to be optimized, high values of c_M are required, while low values of c_M optimize $P_U(0, t)$. More generally, parameters for the CIS system can be tuned once the system designer has given constraints on the desired behavior of the system, e.g., $P_F(t)$ must be optimized while $P_U(0, t)$ must take values lower than a given threshold.

The last study performed aimed to evaluate the impact of the number of replicas on both system failure probability $P_F(t)$ and system unavailability $P_U(0, t)$. When dealing with the number of replicas in the system, three parameters are relevant: n, the overall number of replicas in the system, f, the maximum number of corrupted replicas tolerated by the system and k, the maximum number of replicas simultaneously recovering without endangering the availability of the system, with $n = 2f + 1 + k$. The following system configurations were evaluated:

1. $n = 4, f = 1, k = 1$
2. $n = 5, f = 1, k = 2$
3. $n = 6, f = 1, k = 3$
4. $n = 6, f = 2, k = 1$

Figures 9(a) and 9(b) show system failure probability $P_F(t)$ (decomposed in $P_{FI}(t)$ and $P_{FO}(t)$) and system unavailability $P_U(0, t)$ for the system configurations described above. $P_{FI}(t)$ decreases as n (and k) increases. The trend of $P_F(t)$ is mainly due to the trend of $P_{FO}(t)$. For the same value of $n = 6$, the higher is f and the lower is $P_F(t)$ (both $P_{FI}(t)$ and $P_{FO}(t)$), although k is lower. $P_{FI}(t)$ is lower because of the intrusion tolerance scheme is more robust ($f = 2$); $P_{FO}(t)$ is lower because the frequency of proactive recoveries is lower ($k = 1$). The trend of $P_U(0, t)$ is the same of $P_F(t)$.

We suppose that the increment of the value of $P_{FO}(t)$ varying from configuration 2 to 3 is due to the combined effect of a larger number of failures (n varies from 5 to 6, but $f = 1$) and a higher frequency for proactive recoveries (k varies from 2 to 3). It turns out that for the setting used (as shown in Table 1) the lower values for $P_F(t)$ and $P_U(0, t)$ are obtained for the system configuration 4, i.e., for higher values of f, independently of k.

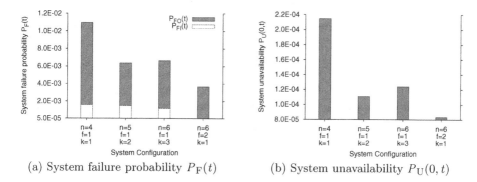

(a) System failure probability $P_F(t)$ (b) System unavailability $P_U(0, t)$

Fig. 9. System failure probability $P_F(t)$ and system unavailability $P_U(0, t)$ for different system configurations at mission time $t = 2628\,\mathrm{sec}$

4.4   Discussion about the PRRW Strategy

The CIS intrusion tolerance is currently obtained through a recovery strategy (PRRW) based on a combination of proactive and reactive recoveries. The use of both proactive and reactive recoveries shows to be effective since the two techniques possess complementary characteristics.

Proactive recoveries periodically rejuvenate all the replicas, without any need of fault detection mechanisms (also latent/hidden faults are treated). The period of the proactive recoveries defines a bounded temporal window (between two recoveries of the same replica) which represents a time limit for an attack attempt to be successful. In fact, this is the time an attacker has for conquering a majority of the replicas and thus for taking the control of the entire CIS. On the other side, being an "unconditional" recovery, the proactive recovery is applied also to correct replicas which become unavailable for the time necessary to perform the recovery. Moreover, if only proactive recovery is used in a system, a replica hit by a fault will be unavailable until the end of its next proactive recovery.

On the contrary, a reactive recovery is triggered only when a fault of a replica is detected, so its effectiveness depends on the assumed fault model and on the coverage of the detection mechanism used (latent/hidden faults are not treated). As shown in Fig. 8(a), reactive recoveries of the faulty replicas contribute to decrease system failure probability; they are in fact performed as soon as possible, however within the duration of $\lceil f/k \rceil T_D$, without waiting the next periodic recovery on the same replica. In this way, the recovery and the rejuvenation of a faulty replica is anticipated with respect to its next proactive recovery, so the (faulty) replica becomes active and correct earlier.

This behavior apparently suggests that the more reactive recoveries are performed, the worse is system availability, as it appears evidently in Fig. 8(b) for $p_I = 1$. In this case, all the intrusions manifest as invalid behavior and all the detected intrusions trigger a reactive recovery. In reality, what happens is that the system ability to survive gets increased, whereas for low values of the coverage (thus less reactive recoveries) the system fails as soon as replicas get affected by faults.

The PRRW strategy, as our analysis reveals, makes a significant difference in the way omission and invalid behaviors are treated. This is made evident by observing all the curves at varying values for p_{I}. Actually, invalid behaviors are detected with coverage c_{M} and trigger a reactive recovery, whereas omissive behaviors are essentially not detected: only the omission of the leader is detected and triggers some action, the omissions of the followers are removed only with the proactive recovery. Increasing the capability to detect (and quickly react) to omissive behaviors is a way to improve the overall fault tolerance strategy.

5   Direction for Improvements/Refinements

This Section identifies the directions for refining and improving the recovery strategy. An extended fault model is introduced and some modifications to the recovery schemes are presented.

5.1   New Extended Fault Model

The reactive recovery of the PRRW strategy is based on distinguishing and detecting a limited set of faults in replicas, amongst those possible to occur. Obviously, the remainder faults are treated, thanks to the strategy of proactive recoveries. We analyze this situation, under the light of the evaluation just performed, and enumerate a possible set of additional faults to be taken into account, in the sense of improving both system dependability and availability.

In the PRRW strategy, the correct replicas detect the following faults:

- Leader Benign Fault (LBF): The faulty leader omits to send a signed message to the LAN. A correct replica will suspect the leader to be "silent" after O_{t} consecutive leader omissions on the same signed message.
- Replica Malicious Fault (RMF): The faulty replica (being it either the leader or a follower) sends an unsigned message to the LAN; a correct replica will immediately detect the faulty replica to be a "malicious sender".

It comes out that the PRRW schema takes into account both omissive and malicious faults in the leader replica, but only malicious faults in the follower replicas. The idea is that if a follower is going to have an omissive behavior, the problem will be eventually treated either by the proactive recovery or by the election of the replica as a leader (the replica will be extensively monitored in this case). In both cases, the negative effects of the faults will be eventually eliminated.

An additional set of faults might be considered by the current reactive recovery mechanisms, since detecting such faults and treating them using reactive recoveries would improve both dependability and availability of the system. These faults are listed below:

- Malicious Approval (MA): A faulty replica approves an illegal message; the faulty replica is intruded, because all correct replicas verify the same security policy.
- Omitted Approval (OA): A faulty replica omits to approve a legal message; the omission could be caused by communication problems (the replica never received the legal message), but it could be also the effect of an intrusion.
- Malicious Suspect (MS): A faulty replica signals the wormhole an accusation about a correct replica; the faulty replica is intruded, because a correct replica does not show any incorrect behavior.
- Omitted Suspect (OS): A faulty replica does not signal the wormhole any accusation about a faulty replica; the omission could be caused by communication problems (the replica never received the legal message), but it could also be the effect of an intrusion.

In the MA and MS cases, the faulty replica is intruded, so it needs to be recovered as soon as possible; if the faulty replica is not detected as such, it is still considered correct. In the OA and OS cases, faults could be caused either by communication omissions (no recovery is useful to solve the problem) or as an effect of intrusions manifesting as omissive behavior (a recovery could solve the problem). Devising the adequate mechanisms for faithful detection is a subject of further study, but we underline possible avenues in the next section.

5.2 Architectural Modifications for the Detection of the Extended Set of Faults

This Section describes the architecture modifications necessary to detect the faults described in Sect. 5.1 and trigger the reactive recoveries. In order to perform the detection of the above faults it is necessary to allow each payload replica to be informed about all the approval results and manifested suspects taken by all the other payload replicas.

A shared virtual memory (SVM) mechanism [15,16] can be implemented as a reliable repository where each replica posts all its approval results and suspects; a majority of correct replicas is thus able to identify which replicas took the wrong approval decisions (if any) or manifested the wrong suspect (if any).

Approval results are stored for each incoming message as a data structure containing i) an identification for the incoming message m, ii) the approval decisions collected from all the replicas about m, iii) the final vote given by the wormhole about m. Suspects are stored as a data structure containing the suspecter(s), the suspected and the kind of suspect. Information is stored in the shared virtual memory, using it as a circular buffer in order to make room for newer information; therefore the SVM is used as a queue of dimension q. If the information to be broadcasted should be too heavy to be managed through the wormhole, some form of "compression" can be found.

Each message is identified using its MAC. Each approval decision is stored in an array of n elements, where the i-th element represents approval result of replica i about message m:

- "ACCEPT": replica i approves m;
- "REJECT": replica i does not approve m;
- "null": no approval information still received from replica i about m;
- "recovering": replica i is currently recovering.

The final vote can be one of the following: "LEGAL", "ILLEGAL" and "VOTING".

The follower payload behavior is monitored as follows. When message m comes from the WAN, each replica decides whether approving it or not, posting the final decision in the SVM. Not all the replicas will receive m in the same instant, and each replica will need some time in order to take the approval decision and post it in the repository, but a certain number of approval results about m will be available in the SVM at worst within T_{vote} time after the first post. Replicas that did not take any approval result till that moment and that were not recovering (those corresponding to the "null" array elements) will be suspected of omission (they could not have received m because of communication faults or they could have omit maliciously). Given the final vote about m, all the correct replicas (i.e. all the replicas which approval result is in agreement with the final vote) will be able to identify all the faulty ones (i.e. all the replicas which approval result is in disagreement with the final vote) and suspect them as malicious faulty replicas.

6   Concluding Remarks

This chapter analyzed the basic components of the CIS (CRUTIAL Information Switch) architecture proposed in the framework of the European Project CRUTIAL, where an infrastructure architecture seen as a WAN of LANs has been proposed. LANs confine existing sub-systems, protected by special interconnection and filtering devices (CIS); a set of CIS can collectively ensure that the computers controlling the physical process correctly exchange information despite accidents and malicious attacks.

We identified two dependability and availability measures of interest. We constructed a model of the the CIS recovery scheme, called PRRW, and we performed a preliminary analysis of the quantitative behavior of the PRRW. We analyzed and discussed the impact of some relevant parameters as the detection coverage, the intrusions and the number of CIS replicas, on the measures of interest, aiming to evaluate how effective is the trade-off between proactive and reactive recoveries. In particular, we have shown that increasing the detection coverage of intrusions has conflicting effects on both dependability and availability measures, and that these effects depend also on the behavior of invalid or omissive intrusions. The directions for refining and improving the recovery strategy were proposed.

Further studies are envisioned mainly in the following directions. We will deeply analyze the impact on the measures of interest of some PRRW parameters not yet investigated, like, for example, the false positive in intrusion detection, the threshold of duration of system omission before considering the system failed. We will deeply analyze the impact of the number of replicas (parameters n, f

and k) and the duration of the recovery period (i.e. the frequency of proactive recoveries). We will analyze alternative recovery policies, for example a recovery strategy where proactive recoveries are anticipated to the first available slot (slots where reactive recoveries are not requested).

Acknowledgments

This work has been partially supported by the European Community through the IST Projects CRUTIAL (Contract n. 027513).

References

1. Madani, V., Novosel, D.: Getting a grip on the grid. Spectrum, IEEE 42, 42–47 (2005)
2. Dawson, R., Boyd, C., Dawson, E., González Nieto, J.: SKMA: a key management architecture for SCADA systems. In: ACSW Frontiers 2006: Proceedings of the 2006 Australasian workshops on Grid computing and e-research, pp. 183–192. Australian Computer Society, Inc., Darlinghurst (2006)
3. Wilson, C.: Terrorist capabilities for cyber-attack. In: Dunn,, Mauer, V. (eds.) Int. CIIP Handbook, CSS, ETH Zurich, vol. II, pp. 69–88 (2006)
4. Gordon, L., Loeb, M., Lucyshyn, W., Richardson, R.: 2006 CSI/FBI computer crime and security survey (2006)
5. Veríssimo, P., Neves, N., Correia, M.: CRUTIAL: The blueprint of a reference critical information infrastructure architecture. In: 1st International Workshop on Critical Information Infrastructures @ ISC 2006 (2006)
6. Sousa, P., Neves, N., Lopes, A., Veríssimo, P.: On the resilience of intrusion-tolerant distributed systems. DI/FCUL TR 6–14, Department of Informatics, University of Lisbon (2006)
7. Sousa, P., Bessani, A., Correia, M., Neves, N., Veríssimo, P.: Resilient intrusion tolerance through proactive and reactive recovery. In: 13th IEEE Pacific Rim Dependable Computing conference (2007)
8. Veríssimo, P.: Travelling through wormholes: a new look at distributed systems models. SIGACT News 37, 66–81 (2006)
9. El Kalam, A.A., El Baida, R., Balbiani, P., Benferhat, S., Cuppens, F., Deswarte, Y., Miège, A., Saurel, C., Trouessin, G.: Organization based access control. In: 4th IEEE Int. Workshop on Policies for Distributed Systems and Networks (2003)
10. Obelheiro, R., Bessani, A., Lung, L., Correia, M.: How practical are intrusion-tolerant distributed systems? DI/FCUL TR 06–15, Department of Informatics, University of Lisbon (2006)
11. Mura, I., Bondavalli, A.: Markov regenerative stochastic Petri nets to model and evaluate the dependability of phased missions. IEEE Transactions on Computers 50, 1337–1351 (2001)
12. Bondavalli, A., Mura, I., Chiaradonna, S., Filippini, R., Poli, S., Sandrini, F.: DEEM: a tool for the dependability modeling and evaluation of multiple phased systems. In: DSN-2000 IEEE Int. Conference on Dependable Systems and Networks (FTCS-30 and DCCA-8), pp. 231–236 (2000)
13. Moretto, M.: Progettazione, realizzazione ed utilizzo di un generatore di simulatori per sistemi a fasi multiple. Master's thesis, Università degli Studi di Pisa (2004)

14. Sanders, W., Meyer, J.: A unified approach for specifying measures of performance, dependability and performability. In: Avizienis, A., Laprie, J. (eds.) Dependable Computing for Critical Applications. Dependable Computing and Fault-Tolerant Systems, vol. 4, pp. 215–237. Springer, Heidelberg (1991)
15. Nitzberg, B., Lo, V.: Distributed shared memory: a survey of issues and algorithms. Computer 24, 52–60 (1991)
16. Morin, C., Puaut, I.: A survey of recoverable distributed shared virtual memory systems. IEEE Transactions on Parallel and Distributed Systems 8, 959–969 (1997)

A Robust Semantic Overlay Network
for Microgrid Control Applications

Geert Deconinck, Koen Vanthournout, Hakem Beitollahi, Zhifeng Qui, Rui Duan,
Bart Nauwelaers, Emmanuel Van Lil, Johan Driesen, and Ronnie Belmans

K.U. Leuven – ESAT, Kasteelpark Arenberg 10, 3001 Leuven, Belgium
geert.deconinck@esat.kuleuven.be

Abstract. Control systems for electrical microgrids rely ever more on heterogeneous off-the-shelf technology for hardware, software and networking among the intelligent electronic devices that are associated with dispersed energy resources. For distributed microgrid applications in a dynamic environment, *overlay networks* provide an opportunity for a flexible and robust logical communication infrastructure among these intelligent electronic devices. Agora is a semantic overlay network that allows to efficiently route queries -related to microgrid control- in the overlay network, based on an XML description of the static and dynamic characteristics of the intelligent electronic devices. It is robust against changes in the microgrid and ICT infrastructure, and provides graceful degradation in case of unrecovered failures.

1 Motivating a Flexible, Dependable Information Infrastructure

More and more small-scale *dispersed energy resources* (DERs) (e.g. wind turbines, photovoltaic panels, coupled heat-power units) are being deployed in the electrical distribution grid. This puts extra stress on the power grid in an era where electricity is one of the most important commodities for economical, industrial and everyday activities. Main factors causing this shift from centralised electricity production to a decentralised power generation with DERs are the availability of small-scale units, which offer an increased flexibility in the liberalized energy market, and the growing trend towards sustainable development which favours energy efficient and low CO_2-emitting plants [1, 2]. Regarding power system reliability, integrating DER units can bring benefits, as well as deteriorated grid performance. Therefore new control strategies are being proposed to maintain the desired degree of dependability for the electricity supply [3-5]. As such, many of these distributed control algorithms rely on distributed computer and communication systems, running on several computing nodes with an off-the-shelf ICT infrastructure for communication. Many DERs and loads become intelligent electronic devices (IEDs) that are interconnected over this information infrastructure, as indicated in Fig. 1. This trend can also be found in many other critical infrastructures (gas, water, transport, telecommunication, etc.).

Over this information infrastructure, new services can be delivered by exploiting both the power and ICT infrastructure simultaneously. For instance, external information such as the instantaneous electricity price from real-time market places, can be

R. de Lemos et al. (Eds.): Architecting Dependable Systems V, LNCS 5135, pp. 101–123, 2008.
© Springer-Verlag Berlin Heidelberg 2008

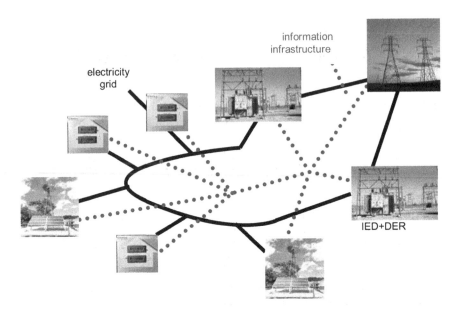

Fig. 1. Microgrids, consisting of DER interconnected via the electricity grid (thick lines) and corresponding IEDs interconnected via the information infrastructure (dotted lines)

incorporated into the control strategies in order to optimise economic benefits; intelligent loads can be switched on or off in order to implement demand side management and avoid costly electricity peak costs, etc. [1, 6].

Dispersed electricity generation is proliferating rapidly; this requires an equally proliferating -dependable- information infrastructure to support it. If sufficient generation (and storage) facilities are available in a part of the electrical grid, such part can become an energy island (or *microgrid*) which functions independently from the major grid (e.g. during a blackout or for economic reasons). In such islanding mode, the control algorithms are different from non-islanding mode, which requires several fundamental issues regarding system protection and control that need to be solved by power engineers [5]. Many of these proposed solutions require an appropriate communication and control infrastructure that continues to function in both modes (as an islanded microgrid or connected to the main grid) [7]. It is indispensable that this information infrastructure is dependable. Such information infrastructure is the scope of this paper.

Control algorithms in microgrids can be separated according to two axes: whether or not communication is involved (local vs. distributed) and whether or not real-time requirements need to be fulfilled. Table 1 provides examples of representative microgrid control applications algorithms. The distributed algorithms can be implemented in a *centralised* (hierarchical) or *decentralised* way.

However, the information infrastructure for microgrid control is not there yet. Generally speaking, communication and control systems that underpin electric power systems did not change significantly over the last 40 years; in spite of SCADA systems that became much more powerful and computation power that has increased

Table 1. Microgrid control applications

	Non real-time	*Real-time*
Local	Data aggregation, logging	Primary control (droop control)
Distributed	Smart metering, system monitoring, demand side management, peak shaving, secondary control, tertiary control, power quality analysis, market & trading	Load shedding (if generated power < demand), power quality mitigation, resynchronisation after islanding

significantly, control remains largely centralised and several control loops contain human interference communicating via telephone, fax and email [8, 9]. Even more, humans can only process a limited amount of information, as a result of which more than 99 % of the captured data is not used directly, but only in an aggregated way.

For cost reasons, this information infrastructure follows the trend of deploying heterogeneous off-the-shelf information and communication technology for hardware, software and networking [10]. This also allows new ICT paradigms to be integrated, such as peer-to-peer networking, resource discovery, distributed control, etc.

In general, off-the-shelf ICT components provide application flexibility, but imply vulnerabilities as the electrical energy infrastructure depends on the correct functioning of the information infrastructure in spite of accidental and malicious faults. Examples of accidental faults include the random physical faults that affect computation or communication components; typical examples of malicious faults to the ICT infrastructure of power systems include [11]:

- Denial-of-service (DoS) attacks on control systems via their communication backbone.
- Intrusions into communication flow among IEDs and subsequent execution of faked commands (spoofing, man-in-the-middle attacks).
- Exploiting vulnerabilities in standardised application layer protocols.
- Accidental or malicious infections by worms or viruses in the IED network caused by maintenance or not-allowed activities of control personnel.

Hence – in order to provide robust behaviour for energy applications – such information infrastructure needs to be fault-tolerant to both accidental and malicious faults, as well as be able to deal with a dynamic environment (such adapting to unforeseen changes in generation or load consumption, as well as coping with the addition or removal of DERs); middleware can provide the required graceful degradation in case of unrecovered failures, rather than resulting in a complete breakdown [12-15].

This paper shows a design of a dependable information infrastructure in the context of decentralised microgrid control applications where IEDs interact over a peer-to-peer overlay network, called Agora. Section 2 explains the approach to using overlay networks for microgrid control applications. Section 3 evaluates the resilience of overlay networks to accidental and malicious faults via simulation, while Section 4 provides experimental results of a microgrid control implementation.

2 Overlay Networks for Microgrid Control

Many distributed microgrid control applications can be considered as *unbounded* systems for which it is not possible to establish a global view at run-time. This is especially the case in a DER-context where not all energy producers (wind, photovoltaic panels) or loads are available all the time; neither is it known beforehand which electrical loads, storages and generators will work together in a particular microgrid control application. In this context, it is relevant that the information infrastructure autonomously determines the neighbours of an IED, and establishes communication links among them, i.e. it has to create an overlay network which is a set of logical set interconnections on top of the physical communication links. In such overlay network, *interacting* IEDs are located logically close to each other (e.g. DERs and loads that need to be balanced shall be connected over a short communication distance, even if they are physically located away from each other).

The microgrid control applications on top of the overlay network rely not only on a static configuration of IEDs, but this configuration will be modified during the application's execution. For instance, due to switching of generators and loads in a dispersed generation application, the IEDs that need to communicate vary over time, and hence, the logical communication topology (and overlay network) has to follow accordingly.

Besides, many IEDs in the microgrid control network change their parameters dynamically, which means that the overlay network has to be updated accordingly (e.g. the amount of power produced by a photovoltaic system or windmill).

Such overlay networks that interconnect dynamically changing IEDs are different from classical overlay networks that are used e.g. to download files (audio or video) which are static resources that can be replicated and do not change over time [16].

Because of these dynamic changes, resource discovery is important, as to be able to quickly find appropriate IEDs for the microgrid application at hand among the multitude of available IEDs.

Several architectural configurations are possible for this resource discovery, such as a centralized or hierarchical indexing system, or a decentralized system in the form of a peer-to-peer network. For a distributed microgrid control application, a peer-to-peer overlay approach is preferred, due to its inherent fault tolerance (no single-point-of-failure – see below), scalability, and automatic adaptation to changes.

Agora is such a peer-to-peer network, specifically designed for microgrid control applications [17, 18]. The dynamically varying (and static) characteristics of the IEDs are semantically represented in XML, so to enable to build the most suited overlay network for a particular microgrid control applications, i.e. a network that logically interconnects interacting IEDs. As such, Agora is a *semantic overlay network* that allows IEDs to query specific resources of other IEDs based on their (dynamically varying) attributes.

2.1 Semantic Distance

Key to the construction of semantic overlays is the ability to quantitatively describe semantic similarities between IEDs, which represents the way probability that they will interact for a giving microgrid control application. As such, a semantic distance metric yields a number proportional to the difference between the functionality of two IEDs.

The functionality of an IED, which will become a *node* of the overlay network, is defined by the combination of the node's resources, its mission targets and the external resources it requires to fulfil those targets. By describing this functionality via attributes, querying these attributes should be straightforward. The most widely used attribute-based language is the Extensible Mark-up Language (XML), which hence is a logical choice for constructing functionality descriptions, and to calculate semantic distances to build the overlay network.

```xml
<?xml version="1.0"?>
<entityDescription>
 <description>
  <IntelligentDevice>
   <static>
    <deviceOwner>ELECTA</deviceOwner>
    <deviceSegment>Arenberg-ESAT</deviceSegment>
    ...
    <intelligentDeviceType>
     <electricalDeviceType>
      <generator> <windTurbine/> </generator>
     </electricalDeviceType>
    </intelligentDeviceType>
   </static>
   <dynamic>
    <workingStatus>1</workingStatus>
    <IPAddress>10.33.135.149</IPAddress>
    <TCPport>20001</TCPport>
   </dynamic>
   <ElectricalDevice>
    <static>
     <maximumPowerInW>500</maximumPowerInW>
     <minimumPowerInW>0</minimumPowerInW>
    </static>
    <dynamic>
     <activePowerInW>164</activePowerInW>
     <reactivePowerInW>65</reactivePowerInW>
     <frequencyInHz>50</frequencyInHz>
     <lineVoltageInV>300</lineVoltageInV>
     <gossipingPeriodInms>3000</gossipingPeriodInms>
    </dynamic>
   </ElectricalDevice>
  </IntelligentDevice>
 </description>
 <interests/>
</entityDescription>
```

Fig. 2. XML fragment of the IED of a wind turbine, for use in a microgrid control application

A node functionality description is a XML file composed of two parts: the description of the node itself and a list of expressions of interest, which describes the resources and services needed by that IED during the operation of the microgrid control application. These expressions of interest are XML *queries* which syntactically take the same form as the description of the target device itself, expanded with search masks and tags. Furthermore, all data is marked as either static or dynamic, with the latter comprising all runtime parameters.

An example XML description file can be found in Fig. 2 for the IED of a wind turbine. The static parameters include location (segment) of the wind turbine and its power, frequency and voltage ratings; the dynamic parameters include its IP address as well as its actual power generation, voltage levels and actual frequency.

Having an XML description for each IED in the microgrid, it is possible to determine a suited overlay network in which interacting IEDs are logically close to each other – based on the semantic differences between two IEDs.

The generic form of the formula to calculate the semantic distance $\delta(u, v)$ between node u with description file XML_u and node v with description file XML_v, both conform the same XML schema, is: $1 - size(N_{common}) / [size(N_{common}) + size(N_{nc,xml_u}) + size(N_{nc,xml_v})]$ with N_{common} the set of common XML nodes, where an XML node is defined as common if and only if the node and all its ancestors exist in both files.

Text and values can only be contained by leaf nodes and count as a separate node for the purpose of the distance metric. Attributes are ignored. *, which yields an automatic match, is allowed for text fields in expressions of interest that are used to set up the overlay network for a particular microgrid control application. N_{nc,xml_i} is the set of non-matching nodes in XML file i.

This semantic distance metric is the novelty, but also the weakness of the proposed semantic overlay system. It allows the construction of a semantic overlay, but ill-constructed XML deteriorates that very construction. Well-designed schemas respect the rule that the depth of the data in the XML is inversely proportional to the importance of that data.

2.2 Node Links

To enter an Agora overlay network, a node only requires the address of one active node in that network. Using that entry point, this node will establish four types of node links.

1) *Companion links.* Every Agora node forms a pre-defined number of companion links, i.e., every node u, member of the Agora overlay network composed of the set of nodes V ($|V| = n$) has a set of companions C_u which is of fixed size $T_{|C|}$ (provided n is at least $T_{|C|} + 1$ and u has converged – see below). Companions are those nodes are semantically closest to u: $\forall u \in V, \forall v \in C_u, v \neq u, \forall w \in V \backslash C_u, w \neq u : \delta_c(u, v) \leq \delta_c(u,w)$, with δ_c the companion distance, i.e., the semantic distance calculated after all expression of interest fields are dropped, together with the dynamic data. The latter is to ensure a stable network structure, as taking into account dynamic data, i.e., run-time variable data, would result in continuous overlay structure changes. The formation of companion links ensures that *group*-locality emerges. In the microgrid control application, these companion links will cluster IEDs of similar DERs.

2) *Pupil links.* The second set of neighbours is the pupil set P, which composes of nodes semantically closest to the expressions of interest in the XML functionality description. $\forall u \in V, \forall v \in P_u, v \neq u, \forall w \in V \backslash P_u, w \neq u : \delta_p(u, v) \leq \delta_p(u, w)$ with $\delta_p(u, v)$ the pupil distance, i.e., the smallest distance obtained by applying the semantic distance formula on the sets of XML files acquired by taking the description field of node v and comparing it to the different expression of interest fields of node u. Additionally, as for δ_c, all dynamic data is excluded. The target size of P ($T_{|P|}$) is predefined separately for each node, as it relates strongly to the microgrid control application running on the node. Pupil links realise the support of time-locality, as they pre-link IEDs to the resources they require. In a particular microgrid control application, these pupil links will connect IEDs of generators to these of loads and storage elements in order to e.g. provide balancing between electricity generation and consumption.

3) *Far links.* If nodes only form companion and pupil links, the resulting clustering by functionality also brings along a high probability of network partitioning. To ensure a connected graph, far links are introduced (set F). All nodes within an Agora semantic overlay network have a probability P_{fl} of constructing a far link ($T_{|F|} = 0$ *or* 1) in addition to the above links: $\forall u \in V, \forall v \in F_u, v \neq u, \forall w \in V \backslash F_u, w \neq u : \delta_{fl}(u, v) \geq \delta_{fl}(u, w)$, with $\delta_{fl}(u, v)$ the far link distance, i.e., the average distance obtained by applying the semantic distance formula on the sets of XML files acquired by taking the description field of node v and comparing it to the description field and the different expression of interest fields of node u. As for δ_c and δ_p, dynamic data is excluded.

Far links are the equivalent of the rewired links in the small-world construction method [19], which takes a regular graph and transforms this to a small-world graph by randomly reconnecting a small percentage of links. These links provide *shortcuts* in the network which significantly reduce its diameter, with only a small distortion of the regular structure. Consequently, the combination of companion/pupil links (functional clustering) with far links (low diameter) result in a small-world topology. Experiments show that $P_{fl}=0.5$ is sufficient to prevent partitioning, while low enough to avoid strong distortion of the clustered topology. For the microgrid control applications, these far links result in efficient routing through the overlay network.

4) *Orphans & orphan links.* Orphan nodes are nodes with indegree zero, i.e., nodes which can reach other nodes, yet cannot be reached themselves, as they have no incoming links. These can emerge, e.g., if a node refers to functionally similar nodes, yet is too different of those companions for them to refer to the orphan and no far links, nor pupil links lead to it. Solution is to have each node refer to the $T_{|O|}$ last nodes that announced a link (see below) and to which no link is active: the orphan links (set O, which operates as a first-in-first-out buffer). Experiments show that, depending on the used XML schema, $T_{|O|}$ equal to one or two eliminates the orphan phenomenon. For the microgrid control applications, these orphan links results that IEDs are reachable for bidirectional communication.

2.3 Convergence

When a newly entered node has established a link to its initial entry point node, it starts to converge, i.e., the node progressively searches for the semantically closest nodes using δ_c, δ_p and δ_{fl}, by periodically transmitting a *request message* for each of these metrics. A request message is composed of the requesting node v's XML functionality description, a request threshold Θ, a hoplimit Λ, the node's current associated neighbour set C, P or F and a list of visited nodes V. After transmitting the request messages, the converging node waits for a fixed period of time (T_{cycle}) in which it listens for and evaluates replies with the addresses of potentially better neighbours. If that candidate neighbour is semantically closer than one of the current members of the associated set, a new link is established.

In case of a *companion request message* $\Theta = max(\forall i \in C_v : \delta_c(v,i))$, unless if $|C| < T_{|C|}$, then $\Theta = \delta_{max}$. For pupil requests $\Theta = max(\forall i \in P_v : \delta_p(v,i))$ ($\Theta = \delta_{max}$ if $|P| < T_{|P|}$) and for far link requests $\Theta = min(\forall i \in F_v : \delta_{fl}(v,i))$ ($\Theta = \delta_{fl,min}$ if $|F| < T_{|F|}$).

Reason for Θ not being 1 (for companion and pupil requests) or 0 (for far link requests) if the respective set target sizes are not yet reached, is to limit the initial burst of traffic that is the result of a converging node with (few) unfit neighbours making requests with high, respective low thresholds, which results in a high number of nodes qualifying for neighbourhood membership. Instead δ_{max} or $\delta_{fl,min}$ are employed, which are system parameters that have to be determined in function of the used XML description set and the microgrid control applications.

After expiration of the waiting interval T_{cycle}, the node checks if convergence is reached, i.e. if the neighbour sets are optimal, in which case it stops. Convergence is detected if no node replied to the latest request messages. If no convergence is detected, another convergence cycle is started and new request messages are sent into the overlay network. This procedure is visualised in Fig. 3, which shows a node entering an Agora overlay network and its subsequent hopping through the overlay to its optimal position. Periodically, all nodes re-converge (period T_{conv}), as to allow adaptation to changing network compositions. Fig. 4 and Fig. 5 contain, respectively, the convergence and reply processing algorithms.

Every request message is sent with a prefixed hoplimit Λ. Each time a node u receives a request $\mathfrak{M}$ and its hoplimit $\Lambda_{\mathfrak{M}}$ ($\Lambda_{\mathfrak{M}} \leq \Lambda$) is >0, then it will forward the message using the *request forward strategy* (see below), after decrementing $\Lambda_{\mathfrak{M}}$ and completing the visited node set. Additionally, upon receipt of a request, each node checks if any members of its neighbour set N are semantically closer to the requester than the attached request threshold, using the semantic distance metric associated with the request. If so, a reply is sent to that requester with the address of the candidate neighbour and the metric result.

All messages contain a unique id, which is composed of the requester's network address, combined with a message sequence number, which is calculated using the TCP packet sequence number mechanism. All nodes have a first-in-first-out buffer containing the last processed messages, which allows detection and blocking of duplicate messages, e.g., to limit the overhead caused if flooding is used as forward strategy. Fig. 6 provides the request processing algorithm.

Several *request forwarding algorithms* can be used, e.g., traditional blind search strategies such as flooding or random forwarding. However, it is better to use semantic distances to realise a heuristic search as it can be used to estimate the distance to

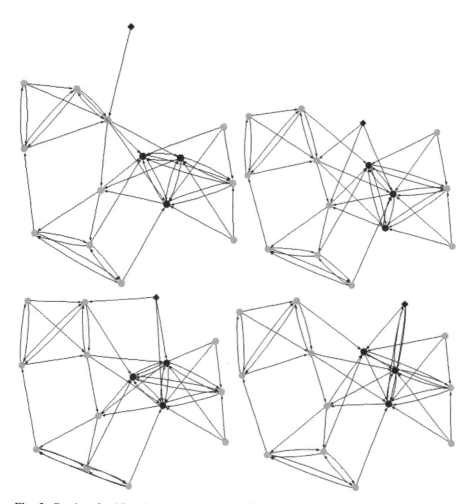

Fig. 3. Graphs of a 15-node Agora network while a new node *(diamond shaped)* enters the overlay network *(upper left)*. It forms a link to its entry point and starts converging. The three black nodes are the nodes semantically closest to the new node (and should eventually become companion nodes). The *upper right and lower left* figures show how the node progressively 'walks' through the network towards its companions, which are reached in the *lower right* figure, after which the new node detects convergence and stops sending request messages. Also the companions (and other nodes in the network) in turn adapt to the newcomer and, if suited, form links to it.

the resource that is searched for. More specifically, node u forwards requests to the neighbour i, unvisited by the request, semantically closest to the requester v (using the semantic distance metric associated with the request) and not yet member of N_v. Or: $i: i \in N_u \backslash V_{\mathfrak{M}} \backslash R_{\mathfrak{M}}, \ \forall j \in Nu \backslash V_{\mathfrak{M}} \backslash R_{\mathfrak{M}}, j \neq i: \delta(v,i) < \delta(v, j)$[1]. This results in heuristic depth-first search with cycle-checking and without backtracking [20].

---

[1] In case of a far link request, the expression $\delta_{fl}(v,i) > \delta_{fl}(v,j)$ is used.

---

converge(v)

do
    $R = \emptyset$
    $\mathfrak{m}_c \leftarrow composeCompanionRequest()$
    if $\mathcal{T}_{|P|} > 0$
      then $\mathfrak{m}_p \leftarrow composePupilRequest()$
    if $\mathcal{T}_{|F|} > 0$
      then $\mathfrak{m}_{fl} \leftarrow composeFarLinkRequest()$
    random nodes $r_1, r_2, r_3 : r_1, r_2, r_3 \in N_v$
    $send(\mathfrak{m}_c \rightarrow r_1)$
    if $\mathcal{T}_{|P|} > 0$
      then $send(\mathfrak{m}_p \rightarrow r_2)$
    if $\mathcal{T}_{|F|} > 0$
      then $send(\mathfrak{m}_{fl} \rightarrow r_3)$
    for $time(T_{cycle})$
      do $receive(\mathfrak{m}_{reply})$
        $R = R \cup \{\mathfrak{m}_{reply}\}$
    $\forall \mathfrak{m}_i \in R : processReply(v, \mathfrak{m}_i)$
while $R \neq \emptyset$

Fig. 4. Convergence algorithm for node v. $\mathfrak{M}$ symbolises a message and $N_v = C_v \cup P_v \cup F_v \cup O_v$ is the neighbour set of node v.

---

processReply($v, \mathfrak{m}$)

if $\delta_{\mathfrak{m}} = \delta_c$
  then $A = C_v$
if $\delta_{\mathfrak{m}} = \delta_p$
  then $A = P_v$
if $\delta_{\mathfrak{m}} = \delta_{fl}$ [5]
  then $A = F_v$
if $w \notin A$
  if $|A| < \mathcal{T}_{|A|}$
    then $A = A \cup \{w\}$
      $O = O \setminus \{w\}$
      announce($v \rightarrow w$)
    else node $y \in A, \forall i \in A, i \neq y : \delta_{\mathfrak{m}}(v, y) \geq \delta_{\mathfrak{m}}(v, i)$
      if $\delta_{\mathfrak{m}}(v, w) < \delta_{\mathfrak{m}}(v, y)$
        then $A = A \cup \{w\} \setminus \{y\}$
        $O = O \setminus \{w\}$
        announce($v \rightarrow w$)

Fig. 5. Algorithm used to process reply message $\mathfrak{M}$, containing candidate node w. $\delta_{\mathfrak{M}}$ is the semantic distance metric associated with $\mathfrak{M}$.

---

processRequest(v, $\mathfrak{m}_u$)

if $\mathfrak{m}_u \notin M_v$
  then *oldest* id $x, x \in M_v : M_v = M_v \setminus \{x\}$
      $M_v = M_v \cup \{id(\mathfrak{m}_u)\}$
      for $\forall$ nodes $i : i \in N_u \setminus (V_{\mathfrak{m}_u} \cup R_{\mathfrak{m}_u})$
        if $metr_{\mathfrak{m}_u} = \delta_c \wedge \delta_c(u, i) < \Theta_{\mathfrak{m}_u}$
          then $\mathfrak{m}_{reply,i} \leftarrow composeRequestReply(i)$
            $send(\mathfrak{m}_{reply,i} \rightarrow u)$
        if $metr_{\mathfrak{m}_u} = \delta_p \wedge \delta_p(u, i) < \Theta_{\mathfrak{m}_u}$
          then $\mathfrak{m}_{reply,i} \leftarrow composeRequestReply(i)$
            $send(\mathfrak{m}_{reply,i} \rightarrow u)$
        if $metr_{\mathfrak{m}_u} = \delta_{fl} \wedge \delta_{fl}(u, i) > \Theta_{\mathfrak{m}_u}$
          then $\mathfrak{m}_{reply,i} \leftarrow composeRequestReply(i)$
            $send(\mathfrak{m}_{reply,i} \rightarrow u)$
      if $\mathcal{L} > 0$
        then $\mathcal{L} = \mathcal{L} - 1$
          $V_{\mathfrak{m}_u} = V_{\mathfrak{m}_u} \cup \{v\}$
          forward(v, $\mathfrak{m}_u$)

Fig. 6. The algorithm to process a request from node u by node v

The successive convergences of all nodes result in a *self-organising* system, in which nodes continuously adapt to changes and, as a result of those local interactions, the network as a whole converges to a state in which nodes are clustered by functionality via the companion links and linked to the clusters of their interest via the pupil links, while the far links ensure small world properties. A converging self-organising system always evolves towards an attractor. However, such an attractor can be a local minimum. For a system to jump out of such a local minimum, enough energy or noise must be added. In Agora, this energy is added by having requesters perform the first hop randomly (see Fig. 4), which prevents requests of a converged node from constantly following the same path. A second method is to increase the hoplimit, which speeds convergence and allows nodes to sense beyond the borders of a local attractor, at the cost of more network traffic.

2.4   Link Announcements and Dynamism

The formation of a link consists of the node locally storing a copy of its new neighbour's description (XML) file and announcing the new link to the new neighbour. When a node receives such a link announcement, it evaluates if the originator qualifies for neighbourhood membership. Reason for this is twofold: First, it speeds up adaptation of the overlay network to a changed situation (see, e.g., Fig. 3), since otherwise a node will only adapt to a new situation during the convergence cycles. Second, without announcements a new node becomes an orphan permanently as it has no incoming links; indeed, a new node establishes only outgoing links and an indegree of at least one is required for requests to be able to reach a node. If no requests reach the node, no incoming links will be established. To limit the size of an announcement message from node u to node v, $\delta_c(v,u)$, $\delta_p(v,u)$ and $\delta_{fl}(v,u)$, calculated using the locally stored XML description file of v at u, are attached, rather than the entire XML description file of u. These metrics can also be buffered at u to reduce the processing requirements.

Link announcements are periodically repeated (period T_{ann}), as they also implement the orphan prevention mechanisms and deal with dynamism. Attached to a link announcement is the checksum of the currently stored copy of the neighbour's XML description file. Upon receiving an announcement, nodes match this checksum to their (up-to-date) XML file. If this match fails, the latest version is replied to the announcing node. Note that this is a *pull* system and that hence a delay may grow between description changes and description updates. However, the alternative to a pull system, a *push* system, would require all nodes to know all nodes of which they are a neighbour, ergo, a bidirectional graph, which is difficult and costly to maintain.

The periodic announcement algorithm can be found in Fig. 7, the algorithm executed when a node receives a link announcement in Fig. 8.

---

periodicAnnouncement(u)

repeat with period T_{ann}
    for $\forall$ nodes $i : i \in N_u$
        do $send(\mathfrak{m}_{ann,i} \rightarrow i)$
            $receive(\mathfrak{m}_{reply,i})$
            if $\exists \mathcal{XML}_i \in \mathfrak{m}_{reply,i}$
                then $\mathcal{XML}_{i,local} = \mathcal{XML}_i$

Fig. 7. The link announcement algorithm executed by every node $u \in V$

---

handleAnnouncement(u, $\mathfrak{m}_{ann,v}$)

do evaluatePeer(v)
    if $v \notin N$
        then if $|O| = T_{|O|}$
            then *oldest* member $w, w \in O : O = O \setminus \{w\}$
            $O = O \cup \{v\}$
            announce($u \rightarrow v$)
    if $(hash(\mathcal{XML})_{\mathfrak{m}_{ann,v}} = \emptyset)$
        $\vee (hash(\mathcal{XML})_{\mathfrak{m}_{ann,v}} \neq hash(\mathcal{XML}))$
        then $send(\mathfrak{m}_{upd} \rightarrow v)$
        else $send(\mathfrak{m}_{ack} \rightarrow v)$

Fig. 8. The algorithm a node u executes upon the receipt of an announcement message from node v. The evaluatePeer(v) algorithm checks if the announcing node qualifies for companion, pupil and/or far link membership.

2.5 Semantic Routing Support

A converging node searching for semantically close nodes is a process highly similar to *semantic routing* of queries for IEDs with which a microgrid control application has to be jointly executed. Analogously to the convergence mechanisms, the group- and time-locality based structure of a semantic overlay network allows the use of the semantic distance as a heuristic to realise semantic routing more efficiently than with e.g. flooding or random walkers. Fig. 9 illustrates the gain of using heuristic search in Agora networks to realise semantic routing, compared to random forwarding. Note that also random walkers gain from time-locality based structures, as the change for early hits increases when routing to announced nodes.

2.6 Agora Summary

The overlay network Agora allows applications to query specific resources based on attributes defining the resources; hence a *semantic overlay network*. The topology of these semantic networks is based on XML descriptions of resources, where neighbours of a single node are chosen based on a distance metric between its own XML description and the other node's XML description. This topology allows to route attribute-queries based on these XML distances. As such, the logical topology of the semantic overlay network clusters IEDs with similar functionality (electricity meters, manageable loads, storage elements and generators, etc.), ensuring group locality via companion links. It interconnects IEDs to cooperate in a control application via the pupil links via the interest descriptions in the XML file. Although this topology provides no deterministic query results, the overall efficiency is higher than *unstructured* overlay networks. Its query efficiency is lower than for *deterministic* overlay networks; but its added value is the broader range of supported applications, thanks to the functionality based organization and the resulting support of attribute-based semantic routing.

Such peer-to-peer network needs to periodically check for modifications: entities or links may appear, disappear or re-appear due to functional behaviour (no wind), due to electrical faults (short-circuits), or due to physical faults in the information infrastructure (controller or network breakdown). Indeed as parameters and functionality of entities change dynamically, so does the XML description describing these entities; hence, the overlay network needs to be adapted accordingly over time, to both retain its logical topology and to recover from errors. This ensures the *time* locality.

These semantic overlay networks fill the gap among existing decentralized resource discovery algorithms typically used in peer-to-peer systems, that is, the lack to search resources based on (a certain range of) values of several attributes [16].

Simulations show that a semantic overlay network such as Agora has a *small-world* property, meaning the average number of hops to reach any node from any other node is small (e.g. 4 to 5 hops), in spite of the size of the networks (some hundreds of nodes) [18].

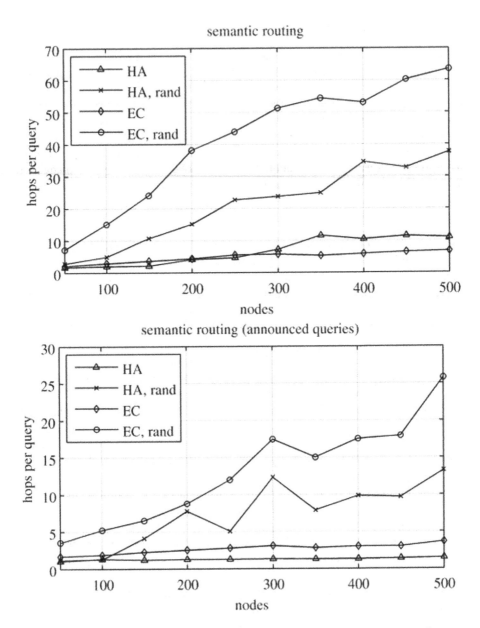

Fig. 9. (*top*) The average number of hops required for semantic routing messages to locate a matching node for Agora networks of increasing sizes, comparing random forwarding ("*rand*") to heuristic search (*no label*). Two XML description file sets are used: HA indicates use of a set of XML description files for a microgrid control application based on home automation devices, while EC displays the results for a set based on a combination of IEDs and regular file sharing resources. Data points are averages for messages issued from and composed for each node and consist for 50% of messages to devices in which an interest was announced. (*bottom*) Average number of hops in identical circumstances, but for messages to announced nodes only.

3 Microgrid Control on Top of Agora

The main functionality the Agora overlay network offers is automatic resource discovery and the related semantic routing service with attribute-based addressing. As such, a structure is created for data and information aggregation, and for distributed cooperation and control among the IEDs. Many of the microgrid control applications of Table 1 are based on some basic distributed control primitives, such as gossiping.

3.1 Gossiping for Overlay Communication

Gossiping is a scalable distributed primitive for data dissemination and aggregation, based on the periodic exchange of status data by all devices with a randomly selected neighbour in the peer-to-peer network [21]. A low characteristic path length of the overlay network is required for efficient gossiping; this is obtained in Agora thanks to the small-world property.

Within Agora, every IED exchanges information at fixed time intervals with one of its neighbours (chosen randomly). If that neighbour exchanges this new information with one of its neighbours (and so forth), the news spreads in the network.

Using this basic communication paradigm, some control functions can be implemented in overlay networks. One of the basic functions using gossiping based communication is distributed averaging: every node has a certain value (any real number) and using only gossiping, an overlay-network-wide average can be calculated. Such distributed averaging algorithm can be used in microgrid applications for secondary control (to maintain voltage and frequency within normal range). During gossiping the following steps happens:

IED C1	_IED C2_
send current average Average1→C2 receive average Average2	send current average Average2 → C1 receive average Average1
calculate new average Ave.1→(Ave.1+Ave.2)/2	calculate new average Ave.2→(Ave.2+Ave.1)/2

Eventually, all IEDs will have the same value, equal to the average of all values.

3.2 Agora Resilience against Accidental Faults

Small-world overlay networks are known to be quite resilient to crash failures [22]. They can tolerate a large number (10+%) of failures affecting arbitrary nodes without significant influence on the overlay's regularity and small diameter or before breaking down into several partitions. Additionally, small-world systems have proven to be capable of automatic and swift adaptation to errors. This is due to the fact that in a decentralised architecture no single node is crucial for overlay network construction and maintenance; hence, no single-point-of-failure exists. Secondly, overlay networks are built to deal with dynamic environments: new and/or leaving nodes, changing functionality or resource availability, etc. In fact, also accidental faults represent a change to which the network must adapt. Since overlay networks incorporate the former, usually by means of self-organisation, they are well capable of the latter.

Within Agora, this self-organisation can be tracked down to two algorithms; one providing error detection, the other providing error handling, which together result in graceful degradation in the advent of errors [18].

- An announcement mechanism (Fig. 7) ensures that each node attempts to contact all its neighbours periodically, as to update its internal data structures to runtime description changes. Since every communication serves a secondary function as error detection mechanism, this puts an upper-bound on the error detection latency.
- Every node periodically also reconsiders its links in the overlay and reconverges as to adapt to topological changes elsewhere in the overlay (Fig. 4). This same mechanism allows recovery from failed or unreachable nodes, posterior to their detection. The result is that Agora overlay networks establish smaller, yet internally optimised networks in the advent of errors.

A dedicated environment (implemented in the C language on a monoprocessor workstation) has been set up that is able to simulate the Agora algorithms with a varying number of nodes (10-1000) in the overlay network. It allows to represent the topology of the overlay networks, and to see the effects of the Agora algorithms on different performance indices (network diameter, convergence speed, etc.).

Fig. 10 shows this effect of self-organisation. The simulations start from a converged overlay network with all nodes operational and tests the resilience of Agora networks to node failures: a percentage of the nodes is selected, which is then forced to fail simultaneously. At this point the failed nodes become ghost nodes, which must be removed as quickly as possible from the overlay (no more links lead to the failed node). At time $1.5 \times T_{ann}$ the failed nodes recover, yet with loss of all internal memory; they become drifting nodes (worst case situation), which are consecutively absorbed by the overlay. Two different tests are performed: one in which the failing nodes are selected randomly, a second with a dedicated attack to the nodes with the highest indegree (number of incoming links). The simulation results show that when nodes fail, the overlay network is updated within a single period T_{ann}, and the recovery is completed within a few periods.

This graceful degradation may however result in the permanent splitting of the overlay into separate partitions. If all links from one partition to another are lost, it renders this partitioning irreversible, even after repair of the errors that caused it. This is a problem all overlay networks suffer and, without extra measures, can only be solved by means of manually inserted cross-partition links. However, this process can also be made automatic, by ensuring that pointers from one partition to the other endure. As such, every Agora node maintains a small FIFO buffer of fixed size which contains the n addresses of the n last nodes that were detected as having failed (*deceased* list). The result is that cross-partition pointers emerge, but also that pointers to failed nodes endure. In order to detect the recovery of previously failed nodes, each Agora node periodically attempts to contact the members of this deceased list again. If this succeeds, a connection attempt is made to that recovered node, which consists of the transmission of a link request and a link announcement to the recovered node. Together, this constitutes the network merge detection algorithm. How often this algorithm must be invoked is a trade-off between reaction speed and network load. For Agora, a network merge detection is performed at the beginning of each periodic convergence cycle, as this is the

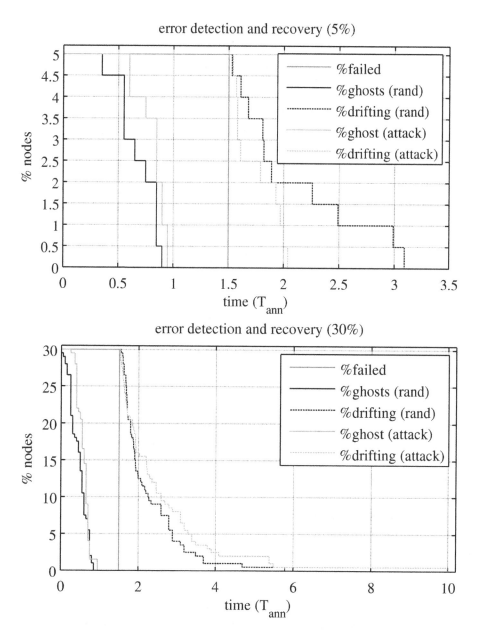

Fig. 10. Effect of a failure of 5% (*top*) or 30 % (*bottom*) of the overlay nodes (random and dedicated attack), i.e., *ghost* nodes removal time and time required to reinsert recovered *drifting* nodes

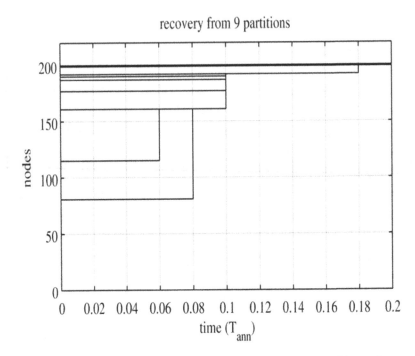

Fig. 11. Partition sizes of a split overlay network with 200 nodes in 9 partitions, after recovery of the communication network. The last remaining partition -composed of a single node- is only merged with the remainder of the overlay after time $2.24 \times T_{ann}$ (not shown).

point where the node already attempts to adapt to any changed network compositions with network merge detection being merely a different aspect of this. This periodic cycle is identical for all Agora nodes. Simulations with several hundreds of nodes confirmed the validity of this partition recovery (Fig. 11) [18].

4 Experimental Evaluation

In order to evaluate performance and dependability characteristics, a test bed has been developed which integrates the electric power system and the information infrastructure. It consists of several power electronic converters [23]. These converters are *electrically* interconnected via a microgrid and their IEDs are *logically* interconnected a communication network, as was depicted in Fig. 1. (This information infrastructure can be deployed on top of off-the-shelf communication protocols, such as TCP/IP, or on more secure implementations, such as SSL/TLS, VPN or IPsec. For the experiments, a TCP/IP based intranet was used, because the objective of the experiment was functionality and not security aspects). Each converter can be used to emulate generators or loads in a dispersed electricity generation environment. This platform allows different control algorithms (see Table 1) to be developed in a high level programming tool such as Matlab, after which they can be prototyped on a 4-quadrant power electronic converter (allowing to emulate electricity consumer as well as generators), whereby the control algorithms are downloaded on high performance hardware which manages the power electronics. As these converters are connected to PCs, they can be interconnected via TCP/IP modules in order to extend the control scope from local towards hierarchical and decentralized control algorithms. To improve information security of TCP/IP, it can be complemented by SSL/TLS mechanisms or by implementing secure channels via VPN or IPSEC; this is however outside the scope of this paper that aims at showing that accidental faults and targeted attacks to the overlay network can be coped with, due to the dynamic adaptation properties of Agora.

As a case study, decentralised secondary and tertiary control in a microgrid has been evaluated. Besides the electrical connection between all DERs -generators, load and storage units- in a grid segment, the associated IEDs are connected via the self-organizing semantic peer-to-peer network Agora. At start-up, all entities broadcast some identification information (type, static and dynamic information) which results in the setup of a peer-to-peer network. On top of this communication overlay network control applications are run. Primary control is realized by means of an enhanced droop control [5, 24], which requires no communication, thus guaranteeing a stable system, even when all communication fails. Secondary and tertiary control is performed by exploiting the peer-to-peer network. Secondary control consists of a gossiping-based distributed PI-controller (proportional-integral controller), which keeps voltage and frequency into the correct range. The economic optimization or tertiary control is based on a variation of the averaging gossiping algorithm, using local generation cost-curves at each generator to re-dispatch the generated power, such that all operate at the same marginal cost.

The experimental results for these microgrid control applications with four IEDs (a photovoltaic (PV) unit, a coupled heat power (CHP) unit, a battery and an intelligent load) interconnected by an Agora overlay network, subject to a mix of load and supply variations, are shown in Fig. 12, assuming specific cost functions for each of the four IEDs.

From t = 0 to 100 s, demand is very low, while the battery is nearly full and the PV unit provides few electricity, because it is cloudy. The intelligent load is fully activated, and the small excess power is absorbed by the battery. The marginal cost is about 40 €/MWh, determined by the most expensive activated unit, being the battery.

At t = 100 s, the load increases to 1.3 kW. Due to the primary control algorithm, both battery and CHP unit generate power, the former at full, the latter at partial output. Tertiary control equalises marginal costs which increase to 100 €/MWh.

Between t = 200 and 300 s, the load increases further to 2.3 kW. The battery gets emptied, changing its marginal cost. While the battery lowers its generation somewhat, the CHP unit compensates by increasing output and the intelligent load reduces demand, as to compensate both the load increase and the battery generation output decrease. The marginal cost increases to approximately 165 €/MWh.

At t = 300 s, the battery is empty, and its cost increase furthers, halting its generation. The power is taken over partly by the CHP increasing its power output somewhat, and especially by the intelligent load further decreasing its power demand. The marginal cost increases further to about 167 €/MWh.

At t = 500 s, concurrently the load decreases back to 1.3 kW and the sun breaks through, allowing to increase the power output of the PV unit to potentially 3 kW

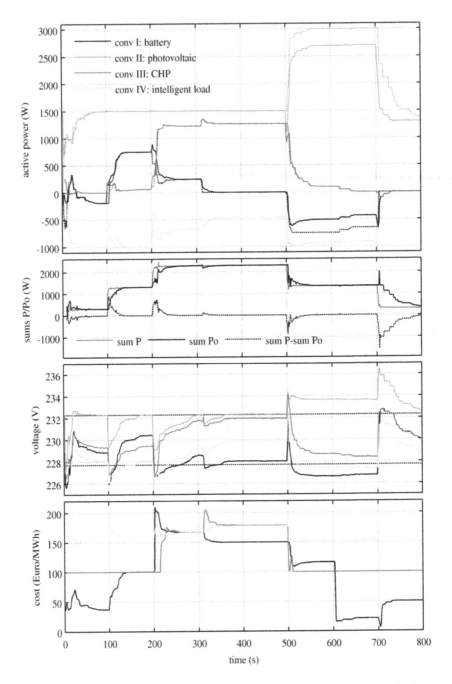

Fig. 12. Experimental validation with microgrid control applications in four IEDs interconnected by an Agora overlay network, subject to a mix of load and supply variations

(lowering its marginal costs), more than sufficient to cover the entire demand. As a result, the CHP stops generating, the battery starts recharging and the intelligent load again consumes at full power. However, the high output of the PV unit disturbs the voltage profile and it is no longer possible to keep the voltage between the 230 V ± 1 % tight margins and the secondary control comes in to correct the situation by curtailing both the power production of the PV unit (from 3 to 2.7 kW), the charging rate of the battery (from -0.7 to -0.5 kW) and the consumption of the intelligent load (from -1 to -0.9 kW). Disregarding the secondary control actions, the marginal cost would be determined by the CHP unit producing at partial load at 100 €/MWh. However, due to the local voltage quality constraints, the battery operates at a marginal cost of 115 €/MWh and the intelligent load reduces demand at a marginal cost of even 155 €/MWh, whereas the PV unit on the other hand, having a zero marginal cost, needs to curtail its power output.

At t = 600 s, the battery is sufficiently recharged, allowing it to lower its marginal cost, reflecting its willingness of further charge only at much lower marginal cost. As a result the CHP unit becomes uneconomic to operate, causing the marginal cost to fall dramatically to about 10 €/MWh, resulting in the battery still recharging almost as much as before. However, again the voltage quality constraints disturb the picture, causing secondary control to come in and the battery to recharge more slowly at slightly higher marginal cost and the PV unit still being curtailed, be it marginally less than before. Of course, the tight voltage constraints result in uneconomic operation as supply from the PV unit at zero marginal cost is replaced by other units increasing supply or curtailing demand at much higher marginal costs. The difference reflects the cost of maintaining the voltage quality. The situation here is aggravated by the very tight voltage quality constraints combined with a power line with a rather large resistance value. In practical setups, if such situations would often occur, alternative solutions like increasing the line cross sections or relocating the generators closer to the demand should be considered to prevent the costs associated with the uneconomic operation of the DER units due to voltage constraints.

Finally, at t = 700 s, the load decreases to 0.3 kW, while the battery is now fully charged (lowest costs). The capacity of the PV unit is larger than remaining demand of the intelligent load. As a result, the marginal cost falls to zero and the power generation of the PV unit is further curtailed, initially due to the primary control action, gradually replaced by the secondary.

Other experimental results (not shown here) confirm that the temporary or permanent unavailability of the communication links does not affect the control applications, as they are handled at middleware level by an adaptation of the overlay network, only resulting in a negligible delay for the secondary and tertiary control algorithms that are not time-critical [15]. Malicious faults however, are more dangerous as they can lead to overvoltages which trigger the protection mechanisms in the platforms. Future work will hence focus on integrating intrusion prevention and intrusion tolerance mechanisms in the overlay network [25].

Acknowledgements. This work was supported by the K.U.Leuven Research Council (GOA2007/09) and the European Union (IST 4-27513 CRUTIAL).

References

1. Kueck, J.D., Kirby, B.J.: The Distribution Grid of the Future. The Electricity Journal (Elsevier Science), 78–87 (June 2003)
2. Pepermans, G., Driesen, J., Haeseldonckx, D., Belmans, R., D'Haeseleer, W.: Distributed generation: definition, benefits and issues. Energy Policy 33, 787–798 (2005)
3. Chandorkar, M.C., Divan, D.M., Adapa., R.: Control of parallel connected converters in standalone ac supply systems. IEEE Trans. on Industry Applications 29, 136–143 (1993)
4. Marwali, M.N., Jung, J.-W., Keyhani, A.: Control of Distributed Generation Systems — Part II: Load Sharing Control. IEEE Trans. on Power Electronics 19, 1551–1561 (2004)
5. De Brabandere, K., Bolsens, B., Van den Keybus, J., Woyte, A., Driesen, J., Belmans, R.: A Voltage and Frequency Droop Control Method for Parallel Inverters. IEEE Trans. on Power Electronics, 1107–1115 (2007)
6. Rigole, T., Vanthournout, K., Brabandere, K.D., Deconinck, G.: Agents Controlling the Electric Power Infrastructure. Int. Journal of Critical Infrastructures IJCIS (Inderscience) 4, 96–109 (2008)
7. Mak, S., Radford, D.: Communication system requirements for implementation of a large scale demand side management and distribution automation. IEEE Trans. on Power Delivery 11, 683–689 (1996)
8. Hauser, C.H., Bakken, D.E., Bose, A.: A Failure to Communicate. IEEE Power & Energy Magazine 3, 47–55 (2005)
9. Stefanini, A., Servida, A.: The future of ICT for power systems: emerging security challenges. Joint DG INFSO, DG RTD and JRC workshop on R&D challenge. European Commission, Brussels, Belgium (2005)
10. Adamiak, M., Premerlani, W.: Data communications in a deregulated environment. IEEE Computer Applications in Power 12, 36–39 (1999)
11. Dondossola, G., Szanto, J., Masera, M., Fovino, I.N.: Evaluation of the effects of intentional threats to power substation control systems. In: Proc. Int. Workshop on Complex Network and Infrastructure Protection (CNIP 2006), Rome, Italy, pp. 309–320 (2006)
12. Amin, M.: Towards self-healing energy infrastructure systems. IEEE Computer Applications in Power 14, 20–28 (2001)
13. Deconinck, G., De Florio, V., Botti, O.: Software-implemented fault-tolerance and separate recovery strategies enhance maintainability. IEEE Trans. on Reliability 51, 158–165 (2002)
14. Deconinck, G., Rigole, T., Beitollahi, H., Duan, R., Nauwelaers, B., Van Lil, E., Driesen, J., Belmans, R., Dondossola, G.: Robust Overlay Networks for Microgrid Control Systems. In: Proc. Workshop on Architecting Dependable Systems (WADS 2007), co-located with 37th Ann. IEEE/IFIP Int. Conf. on Dependable Systems and Networks (DSN 2007), Edinburgh, Scotland (UK), pp. 148–153 (2007)
15. Rigole, T., Vanthournout, K., Deconinck, G.: Resilience of Distributed Microgrid Control Systems to ICT Faults. In: 19th Int. Conf. and Exhibition on Electricity Distribution (CIRED-2007), Vienna, Austria, p. 4 (2007)
16. Vanthournout, K., Deconinck, G., Belmans, R.: A Taxonomy for Resource Discovery. Personal and Ubiquitous Computing Journal (Springer) 9, 81–89 (2005)
17. Vanthournout, K., De Brabandere, K., Haesen, E., Van Den Keybus, J., Deconinck, G., Belmans, R.: Agora: Distributed tertiary control of distributed resources. In: Proc. 15th Power Systems Computation Conf (PSCC-15), Liège, Belgium, p. 7 (2005)
18. Vanthournout, K.: A semantic overlay network based robust data-infrastructure, applied to the electric power grid. Vol. PhD. K.U.Leuven, ESAT-ELECTA, p. 263 (2006)

19. Watts, D.J., Strogatz, S.H.: Collective dynamics of small-world networks. Nature 393, 409–410 (1998)
20. Poole, D.L., Mackworth, A.K., Goebel, R.: Computational Intelligence: A Logical Approach. Oxford University Press, Oxford (1998)
21. Jelasity, M., Montresor, A., Babaoglu, O.: Gossip-based aggregation in large dynamic networks. ACM Transactions on Computer Systems 23, 219–252 (2005)
22. Albert, R., Jeong, H., Barabasi, A.: Error and attack tolerance of complex networks. Nature 406, 378–382 (2000)
23. Van den Keybus, J., Bolsens, B., De Brabandere, K., Driesen, J.: Using a fully digital rapid prototype platform in grid-coupled power electronics applications. In: Proc. 9th IEEE Conf. on Computers and Power Electronics (COMPEL), Urbana-Champaign, USA, p. 10 (2004)
24. De Brabandere, K., Vanthournout, K., Driesen, J., Deconinck, G., Belmans, R.: Control of Microgrids. In: Proc. IEEE Power Engineering Society General Meeting, Tampa, Florida USA, p. 7 (2007)
25. Dondossola, G., Deconinck, G., Giandomenico, F.D., Donatelli, S., Kaaniche, M., Verissimo, P.: Critical Utility InfrastructurAL Resilience. In: Proc. Int. Workshop on Complex Network and Infrastructure Protection (CNIP 2006), Rome, Italy, p. 4 (2006)

Architecting Dependable and Secure Systems Using Virtualization

Bernhard Jansen[1], HariGovind V. Ramasamy[2],
Matthias Schunter[1], and Axel Tanner[1]

[1] IBM Zurich Research Laboratory, Rüschlikon, Switzerland
{bja,mts,axs}@zurich.ibm.com
[2] IBM T.J. Watson Research Center, Hawthorne, New York, USA
hvramasa@us.ibm.com

Abstract. We outline ways of leveraging virtualization for enhancing system dependability and security, and describe the practical realization of some of these enhancements using the Xen open-source virtual machine monitor (VMM). Using combinatorial modeling, we perform reliability analysis of multiple design choices when a single physical server is used to host multiple virtual servers. The analysis shows that unless certain conditions (e.g., regarding the number of virtual servers) are met, virtualization could decrease the reliability of a single physical server. The analysis also shows that improving the reliability of the VMM is crucial to improving the reliability of a virtualized physical node. Motivated by this observation, we show how the enhancements we have implemented can be combined to produce a more reliable Xen VMM architecture, called *R-Xen*. The Xen VMM consists of a hypervisor core and a privileged virtual machine (VM) called Dom0. Dom0, being much bulkier than the hypervisor core, is the weak link for Xen reliability. Consequently, R-Xen focuses on improving the reliability of Dom0 through replication in which Dom0 replicas mutually monitor each other for intrusion and faults. R-Xen converts more severe Dom0 replica faults into fail-stop behavior, and rejuvenates a failed replica. The approach is transparent and does not require any modifications to regular Xen VMs (user domains).

1 Introduction

Introduced in the 1960s, virtualization has lately enjoyed a great surge of attention. Virtualization allows one to abstract away the real hardware configuration of a system. One method of virtualizing the hardware resources of a computer involves using a layer of software called the Virtual Machine Monitor (VMM) to provide the illusion of real hardware for multiple virtual machines (VMs). Inside each VM, the operating system (often called the *guest* OS) and applications run on the VM's own virtual resources, such as virtual CPU, virtual network card, virtual RAM, and virtual disks. A VMM can be hosted directly on the computer hardware (e.g., Xen [1]) or in a host operating system (e.g., VMware Workstation).

In this paper, we explore opportunities for dependability and security made available by virtualization, and provide detailed information on how virtualization affects system reliability. We make four contributions: (1) a survey of dependability and security enhancements enabled by virtualization, (2) a prototype demonstrating the effectiveness

R. de Lemos et al. (Eds.): Architecting Dependable Systems V, LNCS 5135, pp. 124–149, 2008.

of hypervisor-based intrusion detection, (3) reliability models and analysis of the effects of virtualization, and (4) an architecture for a reliability-enhanced Xen VMM that leverages a subset of the enhancements.

We describe ways of leveraging virtualization for dependability and security enhancements, such as response to load-induced failures, administration of patches in an availability-preserving manner, enforcement of fail-safe behavior, proactive software rejuvenation, and intrusion detection and protection. We describe in detail a Xen-based implementation of a subset of these enhancements, particularly, intrusion detection and protection. The intrusion detector, called X-Spy, uses a privileged Xen VM to monitor and analyze the complete state of other VMs co-located on the same physical platform. X-Spy is close enough to the target monitored to have a high degree of visibility into the innards of the target (like host-based intrusion detection schemes). At the same time, thanks to the isolation provided by the VMM, X-Spy is far enough from the target to be unaffected even if the target becomes compromised (like network-based intrusion detection schemes). A key challenge in implementing X-Spy was the *semantic gap*, i.e., the proper interpretation of process information gathered from the VMs monitored in a completely different VM.

We provide detailed information on how virtualization affects an important dependability attribute, namely reliability. The VMM is increasingly seen as a convenient layer for implementing many services such as networking and security [2] that were traditionally provided by the operating system. We show why such designs should be viewed with more caution. We use combinatorial modeling to analyze multiple design choices when a single physical server is used to host multiple virtual servers and to quantify the reliability impact of virtualization. In light of the prevailing trend to shift services out of the guest OS into the virtualization layer, we show that this shift, if not done carefully, could adversely affect system reliability.

We describe a reliability-enhanced Xen VMM architecture, called *R-Xen*, that combines replication, intrusion detection, and rejuvenation. Normally, the Xen VMM consists of a relatively small hypervisor core and a full-fledged privileged VM called *Dom0* that runs a guest OS (Linux). Regular VMs running on the Xen VMM are called *user domains* or *DomUs*. Because of its size and complexity, Dom0 is the weak point in the reliability of the Xen VMM. R-Xen focuses on improving Dom0 reliability (and thereby improving the Xen VMM reliability) through three-fold replication. The three Dom0 replicas each contain X-Spy implementations to mutually monitor each other and thus detect the presence of faults and/or intrusions in the other two. If two replicas report to the hypervisor that the third is corrupted, the hypervisor terminates and rejuvenates the corrupt replica. If the replica terminated happens to be the *primary* replica that provides device virtualization for user domains, then one of the two backups becomes the new primary.

The remainder of the paper is organized as follows. Section 2 describes related work in the area of virtualization-based dependability and virtualization-based intrusion detection. In Section 3, we describe at a high-level several dependability and security enhancements (including intrusion detection and protection) that are made possible by virtualization. Section 4 describes X-Spy, our Xen-based prototype implementation of intrusion detection and protection. Section 5 analysis the reliability impact

of virtualization and highlights the importance of VMM reliability to the overall reliability of a virtualized physical node. Motivated by the conclusions of our reliability
analysis and leveraging our X-Spy implementation, Section 6 describes an architecture
for a more reliable Xen VMM. Finally, in Section 7, we present our conclusions.

2   Related Work

We now provide a sampling of related work in the area of using VMs for improving dependability. We also compare our X-Spy intrusion detection framework with previous
hypervisor-based intrusion detection systems. Many of these works, including ours, implicitly trust the virtualization layer to function properly, to isolate the VMs from each
other, and to control the privileged access of certain VMs to other VMs. Such a trust can
be justified by the observation that a typical hypervisor consists of some tens of thousands lines-of-code (LOC), whereas a typical operating system today is on the order of
millions LOC [3]. This allows a much higher assurance for the code of a hypervisor.

Bressoud and Schneider [4] implemented a primary-backup replication protocol tolerant to benign faults at the VMM level. The protocol resolves non-determinism by
logging the results of all non-deterministic actions taken by the primary and then applying the same results at the backups to maintain state consistency.

Double-Take [5] uses hardware-based real-time synchronous replication to replicate
application data from multiple VMs to a single physical machine so that the application
can automatically fail over to a spare machine by importing the replicated data in case
of an outage. As the replication is done at the file system level below the VM, the
technique is guest-OS-agnostic. Such a design could provide the basis for a business
model in which multiple client companies outsource their disaster recovery capability
to a disaster recovery hot-site that houses multiple physical backup machines, one for
each client.

Douceur and Howell [6] describe how VMMs can be used to ensure that VMs satisfy determinism and thereby enable state machine replication at the VM level rather
than the application level. Specifically, they describe how a VM's virtual disk and clock
can be made deterministic with respect to the VM's execution. The design relieves
the application programmer of the burden of structuring the application as a deterministic state machine. Their work is similar to Bressoud and Schneider's approach [4]
of using a VMM to resolve non-determinism. However, the difference lies in the fact
that whereas Bressoud and Schneider's approach resolves non-determinism using the
results of the primary machine's computation, Douceur and Howell's design resolves
non-determinism *a priori* by constraining the behavior of the computation.

Dunlap *et al.* describe ReVirt [7] for VM logging and replay. ReVirt encapsulates the
OS as a VM, logs non-deterministic events that affect the VM's execution, and uses the
logged data to replay the VM's execution later. Such a capability is useful to recreate the
effects of non-deterministic attacks, as they show later in [8]. Their replay technique is
to start from a checkpoint state and then roll forward using the log to reach the desired
state.

Joshi *et al.* [8] combine VM introspection with VM replay to analyze whether a
vulnerability was activated in a VM before a patch was applied. The analysis is based

on vulnerability-specific predicates provided by the patch writer. After the patch has been applied, the same predicates can be used during the VM's normal execution to detect and respond to attacks.

Backtracker [9] can be used to identify which application running inside a VM was exploited on a given host. Backtracker consists of an online component that records OS objects (such as processes and files) and events (such as read, write, and fork), and an offline component that generates graphs depicting the possible chain of events between the point at which the exploit occurred and the point at which the exploit was detected.

An extension of Backtracker [10] has been used to track attacks from a single host at which an infection has been detected to the originator of the attack and to other hosts that were compromised from that host. The extension is based on identifying causal relationships, and has also been used for correlating alerts from multiple intrusion detection systems.

King *et al.* [11] describe the concept of time-traveling virtual machines (TTVMs), in which VM replay is used for low-overhead reverse debugging of operating systems and for providing debugging operations such as reverse break point, reverse watch point, and reverse single step. Combining efficient checkpointing techniques with ReVirt, TTVMs can be used by programmers to go to a particular point in the execution history of a given run of the OS. To recreate all relevant state for that point, TTVMs log all sources of non-determinism.

Garfinkel and Rosenblum [3] introduced the idea of hypervisor-based intrusion detection, and pointed out the advantages of this approach and its applicability not only for detection, but also for protection. Their Livewire system uses a modified VMware workstation as hypervisor and implements various polling-based and event-driven sensors. Compared with Livewire, our X-Spy system employs more extensive detection techniques (e.g., by checking not only processes, but also kernel modules and file systems) and protection techniques (such as pre-checking and white-listing of binaries, and kernel sealing) with an explicit focus on rootkit detection. In addition, X-Spy enables easy forensic analysis.

Zhang *et al.* [12] and Petroni *et al.* [13] use a secure coprocessor as the basis for checking the integrity of the OS kernel running on the main processor. However, as the coprocessor can only read the memory of the machine monitored, only polling-based intrusion detection is possible. In contrast, X-Spy can perform both polling-based and event-driven intrusion detection. Specifically, it can intercept and deny certain requested actions (such as suspicious system calls), and therefore has the capability to not only detect but also protect.

Laureano *et al.* [14] employ behavior-based detection of anomalous system call sequences after a learning phase in which "normal" system calls are identified. Processes with anomalous system call sequences are labeled suspicious. For these processes, certain dangerous system calls will in turn be blocked. The authors describe a prototype based on a type-II hypervisor, namely, User-Mode Linux (UML) [15].

The ISIS system of Litty [16] is also based on UML. ISIS runs as a process in the host operating system and detects intrusions in the guest operating system by using the `ptrace` system call for instrumenting the guest UML kernel. Unlike X-Spy, ISIS focuses mostly on intrusion detection and not protection.

Jiang *et al.* [17] describe the *VMwatcher* system, in which host-based anti-malware software is used to monitor a VM from within a different VM. X-Spy and VMwatcher are similar in that both use the hypervisor as a bridge for cross-VM inspection, and both tackle the semantic gap problem. While their work focuses on bridging the semantic gap on a multitude of platforms (hypervisors and operating systems), our work focuses on employing more extensive detection mechanisms (such as checking not only processes, but also kernel modules, network connections, and file systems) on a single hypervisor. In contrast to X-Spy, VMwatcher does not include event-driven detection methods or protection techniques.

The Strider GhostBuster system by Beck *et al.* [18] is similar to X-Spy in that both use a differential view of system resources. Strider GhostBuster compares high-level information (such as information obtained by an OS command) with low-level information (e.g., kernel information) to detect malicious software trying to hide system resources from the user and administrator. However, such a comparison has limited effectiveness as detection takes place in the same (potentially compromised) OS environment. Beck *et al.* also compare the file system view obtained from a potentially compromised OS with the view obtained from an OS booted from a clean media. The disadvantage of such an approach is that it requires multiple reboots and is limited to checking only persistent data (such as file system) and not run-time data.

3   Using Virtualization for Dependability and Security

Commodity operating systems provide a level of dependability and security that is much lower than what is desired. This situation has not changed much in the past decade. Hence, the focus has shifted to designing dependable and secure systems around the OS problems. Thanks to the flexible manner in which VM state can be manipulated, virtualization can enable such designs. In particular, VM state, much like files, can be read, copied, modified, saved, migrated, and restored [2]. In this section, we give several examples of dependability and security enhancements made possible by virtualization.

Coping with Load-Induced Failures: Deploying services on VMs instead of physical machines enables a higher and more flexible resilience to load-induced failures without requiring additional hardware. Under load conditions, the VMs can be seamlessly migrated (using live migration [19]) to a lightly loaded or a more powerful physical machine. VM creation is simple and cheap, much like copying a file. In response to high-load conditions, it is much easier to dynamically provision additional VMs on under-utilized physical machines than to provision additional physical machines. This flexibility usually compensates for the additional resources (mainly memory) needed by the hypervisor.

Patch Application for High-Availability Services: Typically, patch application involves a system restart, and thus negatively affects service availability. Consider a service running inside a VM. Virtualization provides a way of removing faults and vulnerabilities at run-time without affecting system availability. For this purpose, a copy of the VM is instantiated, and the patch (be it OS-level or service-level) is applied on the copy rather than on the original VM. Then, the copy is restarted for the patch to take effect, after which the original VM is gracefully shut down and future service requests are directed to the copy VM. To ensure that there are no undesirable side effects due to the patch application, the copy VM may be placed under special watch for a sufficiently long time while its post-patch behavior is being observed before the original VM is shut down. If the service running inside the VM is stateful, then additional techniques based on a combination of VM checkpointing (e.g., [20]) and VM live migration [19] may be used to retain network connections of the original VM and to bring the copy up-to-date with the last correct checkpoint.

Enforcing Fail-Safe Behavior and Virtual Patches: The average time between the point in time when a vulnerability is made public and a patch is available is still measured in months. In 2005, Microsoft took an average time of 134.5 days for issuing critical patches for Windows security problems reported to the company [21]. Developing patches for a software component is a time-consuming process because of the need to ensure that the patch does not introduce new flaws or affect the dependencies between the component involved and other components in the system. In many cases, a service administrator simply does not have the luxury of suspending a service immediately after a critical flaw (in the OS running the service or the service itself) becomes publicized until the patch becomes available.

Virtualization can be used to prolong the availability of the service as much as possible while at the same time ensuring that the service is fail-safe. We leverage the observation that publicizing a flaw is usually accompanied by details of possible attacks exploiting the flaw and/or symptoms of an exploited flaw. Developing an external monitor to identify attack signatures or symptoms of an exploited flaw may be done independently of patch development. The monitor may also be developed much faster than the patch itself, because the monitor may not be subject to the same stringent testing and validation requirements.

Consider a service running inside a VM rather than directly on a physical machine. Then, a VM-external monitor, running in parallel to the VM, can be used to watch for these attack signatures or detect the symptoms of exploitation of the flaw. If attack signatures are known, the VM-external monitor can be used to block the attack, e.g. by filtering the incoming network stream, to terminate interaction with the attack source, or to protect targeted structures inside the VM, e.g. the system call table. If only symptoms of exploitation are known, detection of a compromise can be used to immediately halt the VM. The monitor could be implemented at the VMM level or in a privileged VM (such as Dom0 in Xen [1]). If it is important to revert the service to its last correct state when a patch becomes available, then the above technique can be augmented with a checkpointing mechanism that periodically checkpoints the state of the service with respect to the VM (e.g., [20]).

Proactive Software Rejuvenation: Rebooting a machine is an easy way of rejuvenating software. The downside of machine reboot is that the service is unavailable during the reboot process. The VMM is a convenient layer for introducing hooks to proactively rejuvenate the guest OS and services running inside a VM in a performance- and availability-preserving way [22]. Periodically, the VMM can be made to instantiate a *reincarnation VM* from a clean VM image. The booting of the reincarnation VM is done while the original VM continues regular operation, thereby maintaining service availability. One can view this technique as a generalization of the proactive recovery technique for fault-tolerant replication proposed by Reiser and Kapitza [22].

As mentioned above in the context of patch application, techniques based on VM checkpointing and live migration may be used to seamlessly transfer network connections and the service state of the original VM to the reincarnation VM. It is possible to adjust the performance impact of the rejuvenation procedure on the original VM's performance. To lower the impact, the VMM can restrict the amount of resources devoted to the booting of a reincarnation VM and compensate for the restriction in resources by allowing more time for the reboot to complete.

One can view the above type of rejuvenation as a *memory-scrubbing* technique for reclaiming leaked memory and recovering from memory errors of the original VM. More importantly, such a periodic rejuvenation offers a way to proactively recover from errors without requiring failure detection mechanisms (which are often unreliable) to trigger the recovery.

Intrusion Detection and Response: Based on the location of the intrusion detection sensors, intrusion detection system (IDS) implementations are broadly classified into host-based IDS (HIDS) and network-based IDS (NIDS) [23]. A NIDS monitors network traffic from and to the target, and analyzes the individual packets for signs of intrusion. Because of its isolation from the target monitored, a NIDS decreases its susceptibility to attacks and is largely unaffected by a compromised target. However, as network traffic becomes increasingly encrypted and as the NIDS has no direct knowledge of the effects or properties of the attack targets, the usefulness of NIDS is decreased. The fact that not all intrusions may manifest their effects in the form of malicious traffic also lowers the utility of NIDS. The sensors of a HIDS are placed on the target machine itself, giving them a high degree of visibility into the internals of the target, enabling closer monitoring and analysis of the target than NIDS does. However, the location of HIDS on the same "trust compartment" as the target is also a disadvantage: after an intrusion into the target, the HIDS may no longer be trusted.

Virtualization provides a way of removing the disadvantages of HIDS and NIDS, while retaining their advantages. In our approach, the sensors are placed in a special privileged VM (called the *secure service VM* or SSVM) used for monitoring other VMs hosting regular production services (called *production VMs* or PVMs). The placement of the sensors on the same physical machine but in a different VM allows monitoring and analysis of the complete state of other VMs via the VMM, and at the same time, keeps the sensor out of reach of a potentially compromised VM and in a secure vantage position.

The twin characteristics of proximity to the target and isolation from the target also make the SSVM a convenient location for implementing intrusion response mechanisms. The secure vantage point of the SSVM allows one to implement otherwise difficult responses, e.g., even a simple response like 'shutdown a compromised system' may not be effectively triggered from inside the compromised system. On the other hand, it is easy and effective to suspend the operations of a compromised PVM from the SSVM. In addition, the SSVM can instruct the VMM to provision a healthy replacement PVM or block suspicious system calls that may potentially tamper with the integrity of the kernel.

For effective rejuvenation of a compromised PVM by re-provisioning a new PVM, it is not sufficient to merely boot the new PVM from a clean state. The new PVM might still possess all the vulnerabilities of the compromised one. Hence, it is important to perform a forensic analysis of the compromised PVM's state to remove as many vulnerabilities as possible. Such an analysis is facilitated by the virtualized environment hosting the SSVM. The SSVM can obtain not only modified files of a suspended PVM, but also its complete run-time state from the memory dump created at the time of suspension. The memory dump can be examined using the same techniques as the one used to observe the state of a running PVM from the SSVM for the purpose of intrusion detection.

4 Xen-Based Implementation of Intrusion Detection and Protection

In this section, we describe the prototype implementation of a subset of the security enhancements mentioned above, namely, intrusion detection and protection for VMs. Later, in Section 6, we leverage the implementation for enforcing fail-safe behavior and for triggering software rejuvenation in our construction of R-Xen.

4.1 Intrusion Detection and Protection for Xen Virtual Machines

We have implemented an intrusion detection and protection framework called *X-Spy*. The core idea is to use a secure service VM (SSVM) that monitors one or more production VMs (PVM). The SSVM performs the following functions:

Lie Detection. The SSVM accesses the memory of the PVM and compares actual critical system data (processes, mounts, etc.) against data obtained by executing normal Unix commands inside the PVM. If the comparison yields discrepancies, then that is indicative of a compromised PVM. In contrast to earlier hypervisor-based intrusion detection work, X-Spy's detection mechanisms are more comprehensive and include lie detection at the level of processes, network connections, modules, and file system mounts.

Protection. We have added a system call inspector to Xen that allows the monitoring of the system calls within the PVM for the purpose of protecting relevant forensic information (like log files) and the integrity of the kernel (kernel structures, modules, and memory).

X-Spy uses the Xen [1] VMM developed by Cambridge University and guest VMs running the Linux 2.6 operating system. Nevertheless, the concepts such as system call analysis and lie detection can be applied to other operating systems such as Microsoft Windows. All X-Spy components are implemented either in the Xen hypervisor or in the SSVM. While their implementation logic depends on the guest OS, X-Spy does not require any modification to the guest OS of the PVM.

Limitations. To overcome the semantic gap, we assume some knowledge of the kernel structures of the guest operating system (specifically, Linux kernel 2.6) so that X-Spy components can be appropriately coded. If the guest operating system is upgraded to a newer version in which kernel structures are different, then the X-Spy components need to be re-coded appropriately. That fact may be an impediment to commercializing X-Spy, as it implies an ongoing commitment to develop and patch X-Spy components to keep pace with upgrades to the guest operating system.

For detecting hidden processes, X-Spy requires that the scheduler of the PVM's guest OS keep a list of processes that need to be scheduled in a standard place within a known memory structure. If an attacker is able to replace the scheduler with her own one having a different list of processes, the detection approach would be subverted. That is why it is important to protect the integrity of the kernel code (for example, using mechanisms that we describe in Section 4.4).

The SSVM needs read access to the memory of the PVMs for the purpose of monitoring them. In addition, it must be possible to do an SSH login to the PVM from the SSVM and execute normal Unix commands. These requirements are contrary to the isolation guarantees of the hypervisor. The SSVM itself could become a high-value attack target, and accordingly, needs stronger protection. Several measures can be taken to strongly reduce the potential of the SSVM getting compromised. For example, as the SSVM is a special-purpose VM (in contrast to PVMs), it can be hardened, its functionality reduced solely to that of monitoring the PVMs, and its access restricted through a specific administrative interface.

4.2   Architecture of X-Spy

The architecture of the X-Spy intrusion detection framework is shown in Figure 1 and that of the X-Spy intrusion protection framework is shown in Figure 2. Our architecture consists of a PVM and a SSVM running on top of the same hardware and Xen hypervisor. In our implementation, both the SSVM and the PVM run Linux kernel 2.6. The SSVM obtains the run-time state of the PVM through the Xen hypervisor, which is at a lower level of abstraction than both the SSVM and the PVM. The SSVM has access to the raw devices of the PVMs (memory, disk, network); however, the difficulty lies in the SSVM properly interpreting the data because of a semantic gap [24]. For example, the physical memory of the host system will be made available in chunks as *pseudo-physical* memory to the VMs. In addition, the (possibly different) operating systems of the VMs use a virtual address space on top of the physical memory, leading to the problem of properly interpreting raw memory locations in a different context.

4.3   Intrusion Detection by Means of a Lie-Detector

The basic idea of the Lie-Detector is to compare the insider and outsider views of the system to identify objects (processes, files etc.) that try to hide themselves from the operating system [18]. Such behavior is typical of *rootkits*, which are then used to hide other (typically malicious) software, but is also sometimes characteristic of DRM functionality (e.g. the XCP content protection technology by Sony BMG in 2005). The Lie-Detector (Figure 1) consists of three major functionalities:

1. PVM Information Collection: The Lie-Detector collects information about the PVM by two different means: the *native* interface and the *frontDoor* interface.

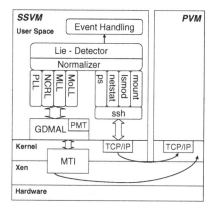

Fig. 1. Architecture of the X-Spy Lie-Detector components

2. PVM Information Normalization: The PVM information collected via the native interface is normalized to a format equivalent to that of commands executed through the frontDoor interface.

3. Analyze-and-Compare: The normalized information from the native and *frontDoor* interfaces is then compared to identify differences that are indicative of maliciously hidden system resources and to minimize false positives. Any findings will be reported through the *Event Handling* component.

We describe the above functionalities in detail below.

Memory Translation Interface (MTI) One of the main components of X-Spy is a Memory Translation Interface (MTI) that allows the SSVM full access to a PVM's pseudo-physical and virtual memory in a convenient fashion. The MTI has two parts:

1. An extension to the Xen hypervisor, which performs address translation and traversal of the page tables.

2. A Linux kernel device driver that runs in the SSVM kernel and provides two interfaces, namely, /dev/mem_domX and /dev/kmem_domX. These interfaces are functionally equivalent to the /dev/mem and the /dev/kmem device files, respectively, and allow the root user in the SSVM kernel access to the PVM's physical memory and kernel memory contents, respectively.

One challenge to overcome when implementing the MTI was that the SSVM cannot access a PVM's foreign memory as it corresponds to a different context. Therefore, the MTI has to emulate the memory management unit by translating the address to the right format and re-mapping it from the PVM memory space onto the memory space of the Lie-Detector process running in the SSVM. For this purpose, we have developed two user-space libraries that the MTI uses: the *Guest Domain Memory Access Library* or GDMAL and the *Process Memory Translator* or PMT. The GDMAL provides read-write access to the PVM's memory. Within the PVM's memory, the PMT allows access to the virtual address space of PVM processes. In addition, the PMT provides some helper functions to facilitate the use of the /dev/mem_domX and /dev/kmem_domX interfaces. The PMT performs the process address translation by extracting the memory management information for the process from the OS-specific task (process) description data structure. When the guest OS is Linux, as in our case, the PMT extracts the `mm_struct` data structure from the `task_struct` data structure.

The *native interface* is used to collect PVM information "from the outside" through the raw access made available by the Xen hypervisor, e.g. by accessing the PVM's memory via the MTI, and to collect host-specific data via special user-space libraries that we have developed, namely the process list library (PLL), the network connection and routing library (NCRL), and the module list library (MLL).

The second interface, called the *frontDoor interface*, is used to obtain PVM information by doing an SSH login to the PVM and executing normal Unix commands. The Lie-Detector normalizes the information collected from both interfaces, and then compares them. If the comparison yields discrepancies in the information collected from those two sources, this is strongly indicative of an intrusion. Obviously, it is not possible to obtain information through the frontDoor interface and the native interface at exactly the same time. This timing difference may lead to false positives, and we explain below how to overcome this problem. We implement comparison methods for processes, network connections, kernel modules, file system mounts and files.

The MTI provides access to the PVM's raw kernel virtual memory but lacks any semantic context. To fix this shortcoming, we manually created a *memory offset file* for each library[1]. Based on these files, the libraries such as PLL, NCRL, and MLL, implement the logic to extract all data values of interest from the raw kernel virtual memory. Each offset file stores the offset values of the start of each data item of interest from the beginning of the containing structure.

Process List. The PLL acts on information provided by the MTI to generate output similar to that of the `ps` command. This is done by accessing and then traversing the doubly-linked circular task list via the MTI.

Our comparison is based on the multitude of information extractable from this `task_struct` data structure, such as PID, state, parent, open files, registers, priorities, locks, and memory management information. However, not all fields in the data structure are used. For example, the running time of a process as seen by the native interface query and the frontDoor interface query are bound to slightly differ, owing to the difference in the time of query.

This comparison will detect processes in the PVM that actively try to hide their presence or change their appearance (e.g. the owner) from queries made from within the PVM. This will identify rootkit-like behavior, as non-hiding processes can be identified by more conventional (non-hypervisor-based) malware detection tools.

Note that simply comparing the process information from the native and frontDoor interfaces results in false positives because of frequent changes to the process table. We fix this by executing a native access (outsider view) before and after the frontDoor query (insider view). If a given process disappeared in the second query but is again visible in the third, we consider it to be an intrusion. If it does not reappear, we assume that the process merely terminated.

---

[1] With some effort, it is possible to generate the offset files automatically at kernel compilation time.

Network Connections and Routing. We obtain information about IPv4 connections, Unix socket connections, and IPv4 routing through the native and frontDoor interfaces. For the native interface queries, we have developed the NCRL library, which uses the MTI to collect information equivalent to that obtained from three commands: 'netstat -an -inet' for IPv4 connections, 'netstat -an -unix' for Unix Socket connections, and 'netstat -rn' for IPv4 routing. This information can then be used to discover hidden network connections.

Similar to the timing problem in the Lie-Detector comparison of process information, we face a timing problem in the comparison of network connection information because of network connections that were terminated or started in the time interval between the native interface query and the frontDoor interface query. The solution here is again to reduce false positives by using three queries[2].

Module List. To obtain information about the PVM's kernel modules we have developed another user-space library called the MLL for collecting information from the native interface query. The frontDoor interface query uses the lsmod command, which outputs the contents of /proc/modules displaying the kernel modules currently loaded. In addition to the native interface and frontDoor interface queries, the MLL also queries a third Xen interface for detecting hidden Linux loadable kernel modules (LKMs). LKMs are a way to link object code without interruption to the Linux kernel while it is running. Such LKMs are automatically registered at loading time, but it is possible for an LKM to un-register itself after loading. In such a case, the LKM can hide even from a native interface query (as the adore-ng rootkit indeed does; see Section 4.5). To address this issue, we established a *shadow module list* in the hypervisor. The hypervisor traps the init_module system call and analyzes the ELF header section of the object file to get the module name and stores the name in the shadow module list. The hypervisor also traps the delete_module system call to remove entries from the shadow module list. As the hypervisor address space cannot be accessed by the PVM, the shadow module list cannot be altered by an intruder. The Xen interface query shows the contents of the shadow module list and is taken as reference for comparison with the results of the native interface and frontDoor interface queries. If the results from the native interface and/or the frontDoor interface queries do not list an entry from the shadow module list, we conclude that the module in question is hidden.

Mounts. The frontDoor interface uses the cat /proc/mounts command, which provides a list of all mounted file systems in the PVM. An obvious alternative would have been to use the output of the mount command; however that alternative is less useful and secure because the command merely outputs the contents of the /etc/mtab file, and it is easy to mount a file system without an entry showing up in the /etc/mtab file by using the mount -n command.

The mount list library (MoLL[3]) operates on the PVM information about mounted file systems collected via the native interface query. The starting symbol for obtaining the information is the task_struct structure of the idle task (however, the entry for any

---

[2] Note that the frontDoor query is made through an SSH connection, which will show up only in the frontDoor query but in neither of the interface queries.

[3] The MoLL should not be confused with MLL, the module list library.

task would be adequate), from where the MoLL gains access to the `vfsmnt` circular list. The list provides complete information about all file systems currently mounted.

The mount information gathered from the native interface query is used as the reference against which the information from the frontDoor interface is compared. If there are mounted file systems that appear in the former but not in the latter, we take this as an indication of a hidden malicious process because mount information is relatively static, and hence false positives are not a big concern.

File System. In the case of the file system, bridging the semantic gap in general implies the use of raw access to the physical disk and the related traffic to rebuild the file system structures of the guest operating system of the PVM in the context of the SSVM. Accessing file systems mounted by another operating system is feasible even for disparate operating systems, e.g. Microsoft Windows and Linux, as for example shown in [17]. Xen can use a Linux file system existing on the Xen/Dom0 level to boot and launch guest domains. This same file system can then be mounted read-only by the SSVM. We then retrieve the file information via the frontDoor and compare it with the information of the file system mounted by the SSVM.

For efficiency and simplified forensic recording, we use a basic read-only file system and add the CoWNFS *copy-on-write* file system [25, 26]. This allows us to store the changes for multiple runs for later forensic analysis and protects the original state of the system from any (potentially malicious) changes. This combined file system was then used as an NFS mountable file system for booting the PVM.

4.4   Protection of System Integrity and Forensic Information by Means of System Call Inspection

We now outline how X-Spy's System Call Inspection component (Figure 2) is used to protect the system against intrusions.

Protection of Forensic Information. In case of a successful intrusion it is highly desirable to protect as much forensic information as possible. A smart intruder would want

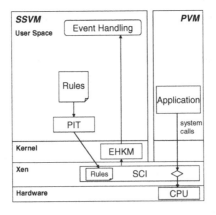

Fig. 2. Architecture of the X-Spy event-driven protection components

to hide all traces of the intrusion, e.g., by altering log-files[4] such as the wtmp/utmp and the /var/log/messages files. While these files cannot be modified by normal users, intruders with root access can. One way to address this issue would be to use a hardened system (e.g., SELinux). However, this protects only if the superuser is not allowed to change the SELinux rules in a running System.

In a virtualized environment as considered here, we have the possibility to protect important files by intercepting the system call sequence in the PVM through the Xen hypervisor (see Figure 2). For this purpose, we added a module to the Xen hypervisor, the *System Call Inspector* (SCI), which can inspect all[5] system calls occurring in the PVM and either block or accept calls depending on a set of *rules*. These rules are stored and edited in the SSVM (and therefore out of reach of any activity in the PVM), and can be loaded into the SCI (in binary form) via the Policy Installation Tool (PIT).

X-Spy implements a functionality for checking and fine-tuning system calls by instrumenting the system call handling chain. An int 0x80 instruction is intercepted by an interrupt handler located in the Xen context where checks against the previously introduced rule set are done. Only after passing the checks is the call redirected to the PVM Kernel, where the normal system call handler is invoked; otherwise, the call returns without any action being taken. In certain cases, the system call is allowed after some fine-tuning, e.g., a modification of the parameters so that the call conforms to the rule set specified. The amount of performance overhead depends on the type of checks and fine-tuning being done for a particular system call.

As the interception of the system call happens in the Xen context, the problem of semantic gap has to be overcome to determine which system calls actually merit additional checks. For our aim of protecting forensic information, system calls performing file operations are essential. We protect forensic information by preventing calls that rename, link, unlink, or delete log files. Furthermore, we limit access to log files by permitting only the append operation on them. To ensure that a malicious process cannot bypass the checking, we normalized the paths.

If the SCI finds that an application in the PVM tries to initiate a system call that is not allowed according to the rule set, it will block or modify it and send a corresponding event through an *event handling kernel module* (EHKM) in the SSVM to the high-level event handling component with information about the violated rule and the corresponding process in the PVM.

Protection of Binaries Against User-Space Rootkits. The mechanism used for protecting forensic information can also be used to protect binaries from being altered by an intruder. Many user-space rootkits try to alter ps or netstat to hide their presence or to install a back door by modifying the openssh binary. While earlier tools, such as Tripwire, can *detect* the alteration of a binary or a library, our event-driven approach to check system calls and their arguments can actually *prevent* their alteration.

---

[4] Note that the above protection scheme for log files can easily be extended to protect other important files, such as Xen VM configuration files, through additional rules in the rule set.

[5] Note that Xen implements a "fast trap" mechanism to enhance performance. If Xen calls are to be monitored as well, then this mechanism need to be disabled.

In addition, it is possible to restrict read/write access to an executable, but still allow its execution. Based on the corresponding rule set, the module we have implemented in the Xen hypervisor checks whether a system call is trying to change, delete, link, or rename a binary, and if so, the call is denied. As execution of a binary normally happens through the `execve` system call without actually opening the binary file, it is even possible to add a rule that forbids the opening of certain binaries completely without disallowing their execution.

Kernel Sealing. X-Spy also implements *kernel sealing*, a well-known method to protect a system or prevent intrusions. The kernel memory can be accessed directly by reading or, more dangerously, by writing to the `/dev/mem` or `/dev/kmem` device files. The rule set of the X-Spy event-driven module in the Xen hypervisor was updated to restrict access to those files, so that only read requests are allowed and write requests return an error result without performing the write operation.

Accessing the kernel memory by loading a kernel module or writing directly to /dev/(k)mem is potentially dangerous because it allows an intruder to establish its own interface to the kernel; thereafter, the intruder can easily place malicious code in the kernel and have full access to the file system and other kernel internals. X-Spy uses a technique called *white-listing* by which all kernel modules allowed to be loaded are explicitly specified along with their respective SHA-1 hash values. If the module to be loaded at run-time is not specified in the white-list or if it has an incorrect hash value, X-Spy prevents the module from being loaded by preventing the system call from reaching the PVM kernel space. Note that our X-Spy implementation does not offer protection against buffer overflows on systems calls.

Pre-Checking of Binaries. An effective way of protecting a PVM from user-space rootkits or other malicious software is to check the hash of every binary, prior to its execution, against a white-list of pre-calculated hashes and to allow its execution only if there is a match. Computing the hash of the binary has to be done out of the reach of a potential intruder in the PVM and should also not require modification of the PVM's OS. To meet these conditions, X-Spy computes the hash of the binary in the SSVM. To enable such a computation, it is necessary that the SSVM has all partitions of the PVM mounted; furthermore, the binary should not be on a RAM disk, on network file system, or on an encrypted file system that the SSVM cannot access. An alternative would be to do the computation in the hypervisor, which would require overcoming the semantic gap problem.

For computing the hash of the binary in the SSVM, we use a technique called *memory scanning*, which involves loading the complete `.text` and `.data` sections of an ELF binary into memory by setting the program counter to the next page, asking the PVM kernel to load the page, and then hashing it while handling the page fault.

If the hash cannot be verified the hypervisor invalidates all of the memory and returns the control back to the guest domain. Because of the invalid `.text` section to which the PC points, the process will crash. Note that relying on support from the PVM's guest OS does not necessarily constitute a security gap, because a non-cooperative PVM kernel would lead to a wrong hash value and in this case, as seen above, the process will be forced to quit.

4.5 Evaluation

While the conceptual limitations have been discussed in Section 4.1, we will now evaluate the effectiveness and efficiency of our implementation.

Functional Evaluation. The goal of the Lie-Detector is to expose malicious code. Once all information is visible, we no longer focus on whether a particular LKM or process is hostile.

We first evaluated our implementation using a set of functional tests that implement typical rootkit functionality, such as hiding processes, kernel modules, mounts, or network connections. Our Lie-Detector correctly exposed all attempts to hide such critical information.

We then tested the system using the adore-ng rootkit [27]. Adore-ng is an LKM-based rootkit for Linux kernels which allows one to hide files and directories, processes, and network connections. The basic rootkit consists of the kernel module and a user-space control program. While currently this is the only widely available rootkit for the Linux kernel 2.6, other similar rootkits exist for earlier kernel versions and may be ported to the 2.6 kernel.

In a fully protected X-Spy system, the rootkit cannot even be installed as the insertion of modules is restricted through the SCI interception of the respective system calls and the white-listing of allowed modules. After explicitly allowing the rootkit to insert itself into the kernel, we used its control program to hide processes, files, and network connections. The X-Spy Lie-Detector component reported these hidden resources faithfully by comparing the responses from the native and frontDoor interfaces as described in Section 4.3. Although the adore-ng kernel module will remove itself from the list of modules visible with `lsmod`, detection of the module by the Lie-Detector is possible with the help of the shadow module list (see discussion in Section 4.4).

The rule set used in X-Spy's event-driven protection mechanism contained about 110 rules, e.g. to protect forensically relevant files (e.g. `/var/log/messages` and `/var/log/wtmp`) and to prevent access to raw memory (`/dev/(k)mem`), security relevant configuration files (`/etc/ssh.config`), and operating system tools (`/bin/ls`). In addition, we specified an explicit list of allowed kernel modules (module white-listing). Once the rule set was active, it either generated security events with information about the offending processes in the PVM or successfully prevented the deletion or truncation of log-files and the modification of configuration and utility files.

Performance Impact. To measure the performance impact of the Lie-Detector and the event-driven approach, we used a single machine implementing a web server scenario. The PVM hosted an Apache web server, and multiple clients were simulated using the *ab* performance benchmarking tool (see `http://httpd.apache.org/docs/2.0/programs/ab.html`). The networks were virtual and internal to this machine.

Figure 3(a) shows that the performance impact of the Lie-Detector depends on how often it is run. The overhead is roughly 31% when it is running continuously, 20% when it is run every 10 sec, and 4% when it is run every 30 sec. Most practical applications will run infrequent scans. In this case, the performance impact of X-Spy is negligible, particularly when compared with the performance reduction of moving Linux into a VM.

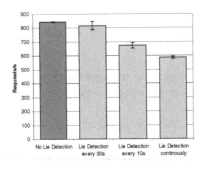
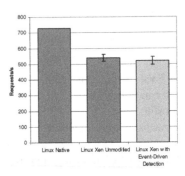

(a) Impact of Lie-Detector   (b) Impact of protective measures

Fig. 3. Performance impact of X-Spy components: number of fulfilled requests per second in the HTTP benchmark

In a real-world setting, the frequency of "Lie Detection" should be chosen based on the expected time until an intrusion occurs and the expected time until such an intrusion is detected. The latter is an important factor because it denotes the critical time window between the intrusion and its detection when the PVM is at the mercy of the intruder, who can take arbitrary actions (such as installing a fake website or copying private information onto a different system). If the PVM runs a critical service in which the critical time window should be minimized, then the Lie-Detector should be run continuously.

As seen in Figure 3(b), the event-driven method results in a performance loss of about 4%. Compared with the 34% overhead incurred by changing from a service running on a non-virtualized platform to that running on a Xen-based PVM, the loss incurred by the event-driven approach is minor.

5   Quantifying the Impact of Virtualization on Node Reliability

In this section, we use combinatorial modeling to perform a reliability analysis of redundant fault-tolerant designs involving virtualization on a single physical node and compare them with the non-virtualized case. The results of the analysis highlight the importance of improving the reliability of the hypervisor.

We consider a model in which multiple VMs run concurrently on the same node and offer identical service. We derive lower bounds on the VMM reliability and the number of VMs required for the virtualized node in order to have better reliability than in the non-virtualized case. We also analyze the reliability impact of moving a functionality common to all VMs out of the VMs and into the VMM. In addition, we analyze the reliability of a redundant execution scheme that can tolerate the corruption of one out of three VMs running on the same physical host, and compare it with the non-virtualized case. Our results point to the need for careful modeling and analysis before a design based on virtualization is used.

Combinatorial modeling and Markov modeling are the two main methods used for reliability assessment of fault-tolerant designs [28]. We chose combinatorial modeling because its simplicity enables easy elimination of "hopeless" choices in the early stage of the design process. In combinatorial modeling, a system consists of series and parallel combinations of modules. The assumption is that module failures are independent. In a real-world setting, where module failures may not be independent, the reliability value obtained using combinatorial modeling should be taken as an upper bound on the system reliability.

Non-Virtualized (NV) Node: For our reliability assessment, we consider a non-virtualized single physical node as the base case. We model the node using two modules: hardware (H) and the software machine (M) consisting of the operating system, middleware, and applications (Figure 4(a)) . Thus, the node is a simple serial system consisting of H and M, whose reliability is given by $R_{sys}^{NV} = R_H R_M$, where R_X denotes the reliability of module X (Figure 4(b)).

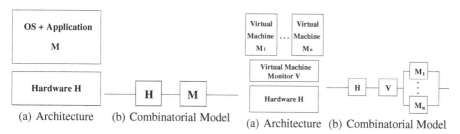

(a) Architecture   (b) Combinatorial Model

Fig. 4. Non-virtualized node

(a) Architecture (b) Combinatorial Model

Fig. 5. Node with n VMs

Virtualized Node with n Independent, Identical VMs: Figure 5(a) shows a physical node consisting of H, a type-1 VMM (V) that runs directly on the hardware (such a VMM is referred to as a *hypervisor*), and one or more VMs ($\{M_i\}, i \geq 1$). The VMs provide identical service concurrently and independently (i.e., without the need for strong synchronization). For example, each VM could be a virtual server answering client requests for static web content. Thus, the node is a series-parallel system (Figure 5(b)) whose overall reliability is given by $R_{sys}^n = R_H R_V [1 - \prod_{i=0}^n (1 - R_{M_i})]$. Here, we consider the reliability of the hardware to be the same as that in the non-virtualized case because the underlying hardware is the same in both cases. An obvious concern is whether the hardware in the virtualized node will register a significant drop in reliability due to load/stress compared with the non-virtualized node. However, this concern does not apply to our context of application servers in a data center, in which typical hardware utilization in a non-virtualized node is abysmally low (less than 5%) and n is typically in the low tens of VMs.

The condition for the n-replicated service to be more reliable than the non-virtualized service is given by $R_{sys}^n > R_{sys}^{NV}$. i.e., $R_H R_V [1 - \prod_{i=0}^n (1 - R_{M_i})] > R_H R_M$. For simplicity, let $R_{M_i} = R_M$ for all $1 \leq i \leq n$. This is a reasonable assumption, as each VM has the same functionality as the software machine M in the non-virtualized case. Then, the above condition becomes

$$R_V [1 - (1 - R_M)^n] > R_M. \tag{1}$$

Inequality (1) immediately yields two conclusions. First, if $n = 1$, then again the above condition does not hold ($R_V < 1$). What this means is that it is necessary to have some additional coordination mechanism or protocol built into the system to compensate for the reliability lost by the introduction of the hypervisor. In the absence of such a mechanism/protocol, simply adding a hypervisor layer to a node will only decrease node reliability. Second, if $R_V = R_M$, then it is obvious that above condition does not hold.

It is clear that the *hypervisor has to be more reliable than the individual VMs*. The interesting question is how much more reliable. Figure 6 shows that for a fixed R_M value, the hypervisor has to be more reliable when deploying fewer VMs. The graph also shows that, for fixed values of R_M and R_V, there exists a lower bound on n below which the virtualized node reliability will definitely be lower than that of a non-virtualized node. For example, when $R_M = 0.1$ and $R_V = 0.3$, deploying fewer than 4 VMs would only lower the node reliability. This is a useful result, as in many practical settings, R_M and R_V values may be fixed, e.g., when the hypervisor, guest OS, and application are commercial off-the-shelf (COTS) components with no source-code access.

The equation for R_{sys}^n also suggests that by increasing the number of VMs, the node reliability can be made as close to the hypervisor reliability as desired. Suppose we desire the node reliability to be R, where $R < R_V$. Then, $R = R_H R_V [1 - (1 - R_M)^n]$. Assume that the hardware is highly reliable, i.e., $R_H \simeq 1$. Then, the above equation becomes the inequality,

$R < R_V [1 - (1 - R_M)^n]$

$\implies (1 - R_M)^n < 1 - \frac{R}{R_V}$

$\implies n. \log(1 - R_M) < \log(1 - \frac{R}{R_V})$

Dividing by $\log(1 - R_M)$, a negative number, we obtain,

$$n > \frac{\log(1 - \frac{R}{R_V})}{\log(1 - R_M)}. \tag{2}$$

Inequality (2) gives a lower bound on the number of VMs required for a virtualized physical node to meet a given reliability requirement. In practice, the number of VMs that can be hosted on a physical node is ultimately limited by the resources available on that node. Comparing the lower bound with the number of VMs that can possibly be co-hosted provides an easy way of eliminating certain choices early in the design process.

Figure 7 shows the lower bound for n for two different R values (0.98 and 0.998) as the VM reliability (R_M) is increased from roughly 0.1 to 1.0, with the hypervisor reliability fixed at 0.999. The figure shows that for fixed R_V and R_M values, a higher system reliability (up to R_V) can be obtained by increasing the number of VMs hosted. However, when n is large, one is faced with the practical difficulty of obtaining sufficient diversity to ensure that VM failures are independent.

Moving Functionality out of the VMs into the Hypervisor: We now analyze the reliability impact of moving a functionality out of the VMs and into the hypervisor. As before, our system model is one in which a physical node has $n \geq 1$ independent and concurrently operating VMs providing identical service. Consider a functionality f

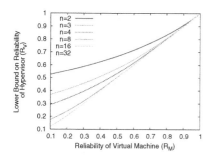

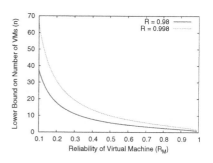

Fig. 6. Lower bound on the hypervisor reliability for a physical node with n independent and concurrently operating VMs providing identical service

Fig. 7. Lower bound on the number of VMs to achieve desired reliability R for a physical node with n independent and concurrently operating VMs providing identical service when $R_V = 0.999$

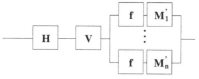

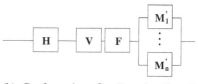

(a) Configuration C_1: Functionality f implemented within each VM

(b) Configuration C_2: Functionality F implemented as part of Hypervisor

Fig. 8. Moving functionality out of the VMs into the hypervisor

implemented inside each VM. Then, each VM M_i can be divided into two components, f and M_i', the latter representing the rest of M_i. Figure 8(a) shows the reliability model for a node containing n such VMs. Let us call this node configuration C_1. Further, suppose that the functionality f is moved out of the VMs and substituted by component F implemented as part of the hypervisor. Now, the new hypervisor consists of two components F and the old hypervisor V. Figure 8(b) shows the reliability model for a node with the modified hypervisor. Let us call this node configuration C_2.

We now derive the condition for C_2 to be at least as reliable as C_1. For simplicity, let us assume that $R_{M_i'} = R_{M'}$ for all $1 \le i \le n$. Then, the desired condition is
$$R_{sys}^{C_2} \ge R_{sys}^{C_1}$$

$$\implies R_H R_V R_F [1 - (1 - R_{M'})^n] \ge R_H R_V [1 - (1 - R_f R_{M'})^n]$$

$$\implies R_F \ge \frac{[1 - (1 - R_f R_{M'})^n]}{[1 - (1 - R_{M'})^n]}. \tag{3}$$

It is easy to see from Figure 8 that if there is only one VM, it does not matter whether the functionality is implemented in the hypervisor or in the VM. We can also confirm this observation by substituting $n = 1$ in inequality (3).

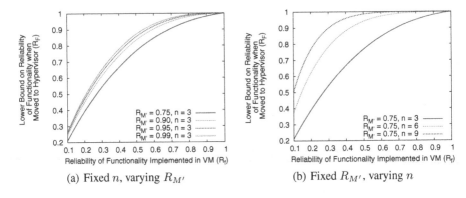

(a) Fixed n, varying $R_{M'}$

(b) Fixed $R_{M'}$, varying n

Fig. 9. Plot of $R_F \geq \dfrac{[1 - (1 - R_f R_{M'})^n]}{[1 - (1 - R_{M'})^n]}$

Figures 9(a) and (b) illustrate how R_F varies as R_f is increased from 0.1 to 1. The graphs show that for configuration C_2 to be more reliable than C_1, F has to be more reliable than f. Figure 9(a) shows that as $R_{M'}$ increases, the degree by which F should be more reliable than f also increases. Figure 9(b) shows that the degree is also considerably higher when more VMs are co-hosted on the same physical host. For example, even with modest $R_{M'}$ and R_f values of 0.75, F has to be ultra-reliable: R_F has to be more than 0.9932 and 0.9994 if $n = 6$ and $n = 9$, respectively. Thus, when more than a handful of VMs are co-hosted on the same physical node, a better system reliability is more likely to be obtained by retaining a poorly reliable functionality in the VM rather than by moving the functionality into the hypervisor.

Virtualized Node with VMM-level Voting: Consider a fault-tolerant 2-out-of-3 replication scheme in which three VMs providing identical service are co-hosted on a single physical node. The VMM layer receives client requests and forwards them to all three VMs in the same order. Assume that the service is a deterministic state machine; thus, the VM replicas yield the same result for the same request. The VMM receives the results from the VM replicas. Once the VMM has obtained replies from two replicas with identical result values for a given client request, it forwards the result value to the corresponding client. Such a scheme can tolerate the arbitrary failure of one VM replica, and is similar to the one suggested in the RESH architecture for fault-tolerant replication using virtualization [29]. Assuming that the VMs fail independently, the system reliability is given by

$$R_{sys}^{2-\text{of}-3} = R_H R_V [R_M^3 + \binom{3}{2} R_M^2 (1 - R_M)].$$

Then, $R_{sys}^{2-\text{of}-3} > R_{sys}^{NV}$ gives the condition for the 2-out-of-3 replication scheme to be more reliable than the non-virtualized service. Thus, we obtain

$$R_H R_V [R_M^3 + \binom{3}{2} R_M^2 (1 - R_M)] > R_H R_M$$

$$\implies R_V > \frac{1}{3R_M - 2R_M^2}. \tag{4}$$

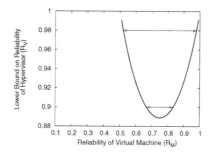

Fig. 10. Plot of $(3R_M - 2R_M^2)^{-1} < R_V < 1$

Inequality (4) gives a lower bound on the hypervisor reliability for the 2-out-of-3 replication scheme to have better reliability than the non-virtualized case. Figure 10 shows a plot of $\frac{1}{3R_M - 2R_M^2} < R_V < 1$. It is clear from the graph that there exists no R_V value that satisfies inequality (4) and is less than 1 when $R_M \leq 0.5$. In other words, if the VM reliability (i.e., the operating system and service reliability) is poor to begin with, then the 2-out-of-3 replication scheme will only make the node reliability worse even if the hypervisor is ultra-reliable. This result concurs with the well-known fact that any form of redundancy with majority voting is not helpful for improving overall system reliability when the overall system is composed of modules with individual reliabilities of less than 0.5 [28]. The graph also shows that the higher the hypervisor reliability, the larger the range of VM reliability values for which the 2-out-of-3 replication scheme has better reliability than the non-virtualized case. For example, when $R_V = 0.98$, the range of VM reliability values that can be accommodated is greater than the range when $R_V = 0.9$.

6 An Architecture for a More Reliable Xen VMM

As shown by the model-based analysis in Section 5, it is highly desirable to make the VMM as reliable as possible to improve the overall reliability of a virtualized node. In this section, we leverage our X-Spy implementation to propose a reliability-enhanced design of the popular Xen open-source VMM [1].

The Xen VMM (Figure 11(a)) consists of a hypervisor core and a privileged domain (or VM) called Dom0 or domain zero. The hypervisor core is small in size and concerned with virtualizing the memory and CPU. Dom0 is a full-fledged VM running a guest OS (Linux) and virtualizes other hardware devices (such as disks and network interfaces). Dom0 is the first domain that is created, and controls all other domains, called user domains or DomUs. For any given physical device in Xen, the native device driver is part of at most one VM. If the device is to be shared with other VMs, then the VM with the native device driver makes the device available through a *back-end driver*. Any VM that wants to share the device exports a virtual device driver called the *front-end driver* to the back-end driver. Every front-end virtual device has to be connected to a corresponding back-end virtual device; only then does the front-end device

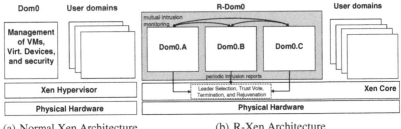

(a) Normal Xen Architecture   (b) R-Xen Architecture

Fig. 11. Enhancing the Reliability of the Xen VMM

become active. The mapping is one-to-one, i.e., each front-end virtual device from each user domain is mapped to a corresponding back-end virtual device. The communication between the back-end and front-end drivers takes places through shared memory and event channels. The event channel is used for sending simple lightweight notifications and the shared memory is used for sending requests and data.

As Dom0 is relatively large, we expect its reliability to be lower than that of the hypervisor core. Thus, improving the reliability of Dom0 is crucial to improving the reliability of the Xen VMM as a whole. We combine some of the technologies described in Section 3, namely, intrusion detection, enforcing fail-stop behavior, and intrusion response in form of software rejuvenation, to architect a more reliable Xen VMM, which we call *R-Xen*.

In R-Xen, we enhance the reliability of Dom0 by replication (Figure 11(b)). Dom0 is a single logical entity that actually consists of three privileged domains, *Dom0.A*, *Dom0.B*, and *Dom0.C*, with identical privilege levels. The three replicas mutually monitor each other using the techniques we described above in our X-Spy implementation. Specifically, each Dom0 replica is simultaneously the PVM and the SSVM for the other two Dom0s. Periodically, the Dom0 replicas submit a fault detection vote to the hypervisor core that indicates whether one of its two peers is thought to be compromised. If any given Dom0 replica is labeled as being faulty by its two peer SSVMs, then the replica will be terminated and rejuvenated by the hypervisor. In this way, we enforce fail-stop behavior of the replica despite the presence of a more severe kind of fault in the replica. The hypervisor core then starts a new Dom0 replica as a replacement of the terminated one.

One of the Dom0 replicas is designated as *active* by the hypervisor core, and it is this active replica that provides the back-end drivers for the devices of the user domains. The other two replicas are designated as *passive*, and do not provide any back-end devices. As mentioned above, each of the three Dom0 replicas monitors and is being monitored by the other two. If the hypervisor gets reports from two independent replicas labeling the third replica as faulty, then the hypervisor terminates that replica and replaces it with a new Dom0 replica. If the terminated replica is a primary, then the hypervisor designates one of the backups as the new primary replica by re-connecting the front-end devices of the user domain(s) to the replica's back-end devices. The disconnection and reconnection of the user domain(s) to a different Dom0 has already been implemented in Xen and is used for live migration of domains. Therefore, the code can be reused. The hypervisor itself has to actively give permissions for doing the reconnection and re-routing the data from the old Dom0 to the new one. It also has to shutdown the old Dom0 after the reconnection process has been completed. Using a previously started backup as the new primary results in less interruption to the user domain than using the replacement replica (which has to be booted from scratch) as the new primary. It also enables the booting of the replacement replica to occur concurrently to the reconnection of the front-end devices. Like other fault-detection-based techniques, there is the drawback of *detection latency*, i.e., a time delay between the actual occurrence of the fault and its detection. I/O requests sent by the user domain(s) during this latency period may have to be re-issued. On the positive side, our technique can be implemented in a manner that is completely transparent to the user domain(s). In other words, a DomU running on normal Xen should be able to run without modification on this type of R-Xen as well.

7   Conclusion

Virtualization offers enormous opportunities for flexible and cost-efficient management and deployment of systems. It is clear that the scope of virtualization will expand in the future. Hence, it is important to gain a better understanding of the impact of virtualization on non-functional system properties such as dependability and the opportunities it creates for improving them.

We have described methods of leveraging virtualization for improving system dependability and security, and described a Xen-based implementation of a subset of them. We used combinatorial modeling to analyze the reliability impact of introducing virtualization. Our results provide useful information on the type of conditions that need to be satisfied to uphold overall system reliability in the presence of virtualization. In light of the general trend to move services out of the guest OS into the virtualization layer, our results indicate the need for a more cautious approach. Future work includes more rigorous modeling and analysis of dependability attributes in the context of virtualization, particularly in dynamic situations such as VM migration.

Our analysis also highlighted the importance of the VMM's reliability in a virtualized system for overall system reliability. That motivated our work on R-Xen, a variant of the Xen open-source VMM designed for improved reliability. R-Xen employs threefold replication of the privileged Dom0, transparent and mutual monitoring of the Dom0 replicas based on our X-Spy intrusion detection and protection framework, enforcement of fail-safe behavior in a replica believed to be faulty, and rejuvenation of that replica.

References

1. Barham, P.T., Dragovic, B., Fraser, K., Hand, S., Harris, T.L., Ho, A., Neugebauer, R., Pratt, I., Warfield, A.: Xen and the Art of Virtualization. In: Proc. 19th ACM Symposium on Operating Systems Principles (SOSP 2003), October 2003, pp. 164–177 (2003)
2. Garfinkel, T., Rosenblum, M.: When Virtual is Harder than Real: Security Challenges in Virtual Machine Based Computing Environments. In: Proc. 10th Workshop on Hot Topics in Operating Systems (HotOS-X) (May 2005)

3. Garfinkel, T., Rosenblum, M.: A Virtual Machine Introspection Based Architecture for Intrusion Detection. In: Proc. Network and Distributed Systems Security Symposium (NDSS 2003) (February 2003)
4. Bressoud, T.C., Schneider, F.B.: Hypervisor-Based Fault Tolerance. ACM Trans. Comput. Syst. 14(1), 80–107 (1996)
5. VMware: VMware Double-Take, http://www.vmware.com/pdf/vmware_doubletake.pdf
6. Douceur, J.R., Howell, J.: Replicated Virtual Machines. Technical Report MSR TR-2005-119, Microsoft Research (September 2005)
7. Dunlap, G.W., King, S.T., Cinar, S., Basrai, M.A., Chen, P.M.: ReVirt: Enabling Intrusion Analysis through Virtual-Machine Logging and Replay. SIGOPS Operating System Review 36(SI), 211–224 (2002)
8. Joshi, A., King, S.T., Dunlap, G.W., Chen, P.M.: Detecting Past and Present Intrusions through Vulnerability-Specific Predicates. In: Proc. 20th ACM Symposium on Operating Systems Principles (SOSP 2005), pp. 91–104 (2005)
9. King, S.T., Chen, P.M.: Backtracking Intrusions. In: Proc. 19th ACM Symposium on Operating Systems Principles (SOSP 2003), October 2003, pp. 223–236 (2003)
10. King, S.T., Mao, Z.M., Lucchetti, D.G., Chen, P.M.: Enriching Intrusion Alerts through Multi-Host Causality. In: Proc. Network and Distributed System Security Symposium (NDSS 2005) (2005)
11. King, S.T., Dunlap, G.W., Chen, P.M.: Debugging Operating Systems with Time-Traveling Virtual Machines. In: Proc. 2005 Annual USENIX Technical Conference, April 2005, pp. 1–15 (2005)
12. Zhang, X., van Doorn, L., Jaeger, T., Perez, R., Sailer, R.: Secure coprocessor-based intrusion detection. In: Proc. 10th ACM SIGOPS European workshop, pp. 239–242 (2002)
13. Nick, L., Petroni, J., Fraser, T., Molina, J., Arbaugh, W.A.: Copilot - A Coprocessor-based Kernel Runtime Integrity Monitor. In: Proc. 13th USENIX Security Symposium, p. 13 (2004)
14. Laureano, M., Maziero, C., Jamhour, E.: Intrusion Detection in Virtual Machine Environments. In: Proc. 30th EUROMICRO Conference (EUROMICRO 2004), pp. 520–525 (2004)
15. Dike, J.: A User-Mode Port of the Linux Kernel. In: Proc. 4th Annual Linux Showcase & Conference, p. 7 (2000)
16. Litty, L.: Hypervisor-Based Intrusion Detection. Master's thesis, University of Toronto (2005)
17. Jiang, X., X.W., Xu, D.: Stealthy Malware Detection through VMM-based Out-of-the-Box Semantic View Reconstruction. In: Proc. 14th ACM conference on Computer and Communications Security (CCS 2007), pp. 128–138 (2007)
18. Beck, D., Vo, B., Verbowski, C.: Detecting Stealth Software with Strider GhostBuster. In: Proc. International Conference on Dependable Systems and Networks (DSN 2005), pp. 368–377 (2005)
19. Clark, C., Fraser, K., Hand, S., Hansen, J.G., Jul, E., Limpach, C., Pratt, I., Warfield, A.: Live Migration of Virtual Machines. In: Proc. 2nd Symposium on Networked Systems Design and Implementation (NSDI 2005), May 2005, pp. 273–286 (2005)
20. Agbaria, A., Friedman, R.: Virtual Machine Based Heterogeneous Checkpointing. Software: Practice and Experience 32(1), 1–19 (2002)
21. Washington Post: A Time to Patch (2006), http://blog.washingtonpost.com/securityfix/2006/01/a_time_to_patch.html
22. Reiser, H.P., Kapitza, R.: Hypervisor-Based Efficient Proactive Recovery. In: Proc. 26th IEEE International Symposium on Reliable Distributed Systems (SRDS 2007), pp. 83–92 (2007)
23. Debar, H., Davei, M., Wespi, A.: A Revised Taxonomy of Intrusion-Detection Systems. Annales des Telecommunications 55(7-8), 83–100 (2000)

24. Chen, P.M., Noble, B.D.: When Virtual is Better than Real. In: Proc. 8th Workshop on Hot Topics in Operating Systems (HotOS-VIII), May 2001, pp. 133–138 (2001)
25. Kotsovinos, E., Moreton, T., Pratt, I., Ross, R., Fraser, K., Hand, S., Harris, T.: Global-scale Service Deployment in the XenoServer Platform. In: Proc. 1st USENIX Workshop on Real, Large Distributed Systems (WORLDS 2004) (December 2004)
26. Ross, R.: CoWNFS, http://www.russross.com/CoWNFS.html
27. stealth: Adore-ng v0.42, http://packetstormsecurity.org/
28. Johnson, B.W.: Design and Analysis of Fault-Tolerant Digital Systems. Addison-Wesley, Reading (1989)
29. Reiser, H.P., Hauck, F.J., Kapitza, R., Schröder-Preikschat, W.: Hypervisor-Based Redundant Execution on a Single Physical Host. In: Proc. 6th European Dependable Computing Conference (EDCC 2006), p. S.2 (2006)

Model-Based Approaches for Dependability in Ad-Hoc Mobile Networks and Services*

Gergely Pintér, Zoltán Micskei, András Kövi, Zoltán Égel,
Imre Kocsis, Gábor Huszerl, and András Pataricza

Budapest University of Technology and Economics
Department of Measurement and Information Systems
{pinterg,micskeiz,kovi,zegel,ikocsis,huszerl,pataric}@mit.bme.hu

Abstract. This paper presents our results in the field of Model Driven Design (MDD) gained in dependable, distributed application development communicating over ad-hoc mobile networks. The context of the discussion is the Highly Dependable IP-based Networks and Services (Hidenets) research project. Our efforts involve (i) construction of the *platform's UML model*, (ii) construction of a *metamodel* illustrating the intended organization of applications running on the platform, (iii) defining a *UML profile* on the basis of the metamodel facilitating the integration of the basic services provided by the Hidenets platform to support high availability of the application and (iv) providing a set of dependability enforcing *design patterns* to support the implementation of applications built for the Hidenets platform using our profile. The paper highlights the benefits of applying model-based approaches in the context of complex dependability frameworks.

1 Introduction

The aim of Hidenets is to develop and analyze end-to-end resilience solutions for distributed applications and mobility-aware services in ubiquitous communication scenarios. Technical solutions will be developed for applications with *high dependability requirements* in the context of *ad-hoc communication* with infrastructure support. These solutions are essential for the deployment of future mission-critical applications as the use of *off-the-shelf components* (COTS) and *wireless communication* links will dramatically decrease the costs of market entry, making such ubiquitous scenarios both technically and commercially feasible. However, COTS components and wireless links in an ad-hoc network in which neither the participation nor any QoS of members is guaranteed leads necessarily to an *inherently unreliable* system, and therefore *end-to-end system-level resilience solutions* addressing both accidental and malicious faults are to be developed. Hidenets solutions are expected to contribute to users' perception of trustworthiness of future wireless services strongly impacted by availability and resilience aspects. Our efforts in the framework of the Hidenets project can be grouped into two main categories:

* This work was partially supported by IST-FP6-STREP-26979 (HIDENETS).

R. de Lemos et al. (Eds.): Architecting Dependable Systems V, LNCS 5135, pp. 150–174, 2008.

Modeling the platform including:
- Construction of the *use-case model* of key HA services, which organizes use-cases into a straightforward *package hierarchy* indicating explicitly the *dependency relations* between services. This model answers the question: *"What are the key services provided by the platform and what are the interdependency relations amongst them?"*.
- Definition of a *component model* of services, which specifies their *interfaces* and reflects the interdependency relations of *required and provided interfaces*. This model answers the question: *"What are the interfaces of services exposed by the platform to application developers and how are these interfaces used within the platform for interconnecting services?"*.

Application modeling support involving:
- Construction of a *metamodel* illustrating the intended organization of applications running on the platform. This metamodel identifies the *key concepts* from an application developer's point of view with respect to various services, introduces the corresponding *metaclasses* and connects these newly introduced metaclasses to core UML concepts. This step answers the question: *"What is the intended organization of applications running on the platform and how do the platform-related parts correspond to fundamental UML concepts?"*.
- Defining a *UML profile* for the metamodel; *stereotypes* and *tagged values* enable the annotation of models with dependability and platform-related information. This step answers the question: *"How to add platform-related information to ordinary UML models of dependable applications that are intended to take advantage of the platform?"*.
- Providing a set of *design patterns* to support the implementation of applications built for the platform using our profile. These patterns can be seen as detailed examples for implementing various dependability-related parts of applications. This step answers the question: *"What are the best practices for organization and implementation of various dependability-related parts of application intended to be executed on the platform?"*.

Conformance to the existing standards was a main objective thus emphasis was put on building the metamodel on such widely known and industrially accepted conceptual frameworks such as OMG's *UML Profile for Schedulability, Performance and Time* (SPT) [1] for modeling application–platform interaction or SA Forum's Application Interface Specification [2] integrating the most important means for HA assurance into a unifying framework.

The key part of the paper is organized according to the structure outlined above: Sec. 2 discusses the UML model of the platform involving the use-case model and the definition of components and their interfaces, Sec. 3 outlines our efforts concerning application development support involving the metamodel construction, profile definition and the set of design patterns. Sec. 4 introduces a case study illustrating the application of the profile and the design patterns. Finally, Sec. 5 presents methods for the verification of the developed application using testing and fault modeling.

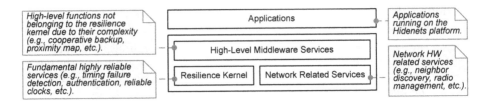

Fig. 1. The Hidenets Platform

2 Platform Model

This section provides an overview on the first group of modeling efforts: *construction of the platform's UML model*. The model consists of two key parts: (i) the *use-case model* indicating the services as use cases and outlining their interdependency relations and (ii) the *component model* specifying the interfaces of these services. Sec. 2.1 introduces the use-case model and Sec. 2.2 outlines interfaces and the organization of services into components.

2.1 Use-Case Model of Services

This subsection outlines the process of constructing a *use-case view* of services required by dependable mobile applications. The goal of this step was similar to the usual use case-modeling at the beginning of model-based software development process: (i) identification of the *system boundaries* i.e., a clear distinction of which are the services to be developed and which are the ones expected from the underlying HW/SW platform, (ii) discover the *dependency relations* amongst various services and (iii) ensuring that all the dependencies will be *resolved* i.e., all feature required by a service will be implemented or explicitly indicated as a requirement against the underlying platform.

In use-case modeling the modeler would like to get answers to the following questions: "Who/what *will use* the system to be developed and who/what *will be used* by the system?" (i.e., identification of *actors*), "*How* is an actor using the system or used by the system?" (i.e., identification of *use-cases*) and "From the entire structure of the problem, which are those *parts that are to be developed?*" (i.e., identification of *system boundaries*). By definition [3] an *actor* is an entity outside of the system; an actor can be a person, a hardware device or another system. A *use-case* is a set of activities to be performed by the system that is of value for one or more actors (systems are obviously developed to provide such valuable services). The indication of *system boundaries* enables us to clearly highlight which are those use cases that are to be developed by us.

The UML notation for actors is a *stick man icon*, use-cases are graphically represented by *ellipses*, while system boundaries are shown as a *rectangle* containing the use cases to be implemented; actors are connected to use-cases by solid lines. Various dependency relations (including, extension, etc.) can be indicated amongst use-cases by connecting the use cases by *dashed arrows*.

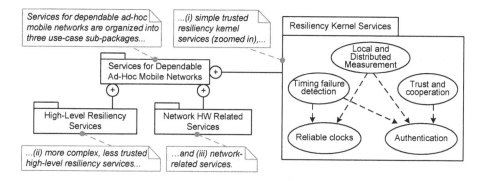

Fig. 2. Organization of Use-Case Packages

In case of a usual software development process it is relatively easy to identify actors since they are typically the *users* of the system; in case of a middleware the notion of *actor* usually represents those *applications* that rely on services of the platform thus explicit emphasis was not put on detailed modeling of actors: the single actor in the use-case model of the Hidenets platform represents those applications that use platform-specific services and this single actor was not indicated in the diagrams.

The Hidenets platform organizes resiliency-related services into three groups (Fig. 1): (i) fundamental, highly reliable core services, called *Resilience Kernel*, (ii) complex thus less trusted *middleware services* and (iii) *closely network hardware-related components.*

Use-cases obviously correspond to groups of services provided by the platform. In case of Hidenets over 30 services were identified thus their detailed discussion is out of the dimensions of this paper; after a brief summary the rest of the paper will be focused on two easy to understand services (authentication and timing failure detection) as examples. Use-cases are organized into *packages* in correspondence to the classification above (Fig. 2):

Resiliency Kernel Services are those relatively simple core services that are considered to be highly reliable parts of the platform: (i) *authentication* aims at identification of peers and securing their communication by providing various encryption, key negotiation, digital signature etc. functions; (ii) *local and distributed measurement* provides support for distributed measuring of some duration in time; (iii) *reliable clocks* are used for obtaining the actual local time on a node also taking into consideration the possible deviation from the global time estimation; (iv) *timing failure detection* checks whether a timed action appears (finishes, etc.) in time and (v) *trust and cooperation service* is able to evaluate locally the level of trust of neighboring entities and to manage cooperative operations.

High-Level Resiliency Services are those complex functionalities that do not belong the resiliency kernel due to their inherent complex nature: (i) *cooperative backup* aims at the discovery of storage resources in the vicinity of a node and negotiating a contract for using these resources for data backup purposes; (ii) *diagnostic management* judges whether various parts of the system are working properly or not; (iii) *network context repository* is a database for network and communication related information; (iv) *proximity map* maintains a local view in a node about its vicinity; (v) *QoS coverage management* evaluates whether the QoS requirements of an application are satisfied, or re-negotiation is needed; (vi) *reconfiguration management* recognizes if a reconfiguration is needed in the system and decides which policy has to be applied and (vii) *replication management* takes care of state sharing between replicated stateful services.

Network Hardware-Related Services involve (i) *multi-channel, multi-radio management* (coordinating multiple radio devices attached to a single node), (ii) *multi-channel, multi-radio routing* (advanced routing algorithms using the redundant radio devices), (iii) *neighbor discovery* (detecting the presence of other nodes in the vicinity), (iv) *ad-hoc topology control* (exchanging routing-related topology information amongst nodes), (v) *IP routing* (adapted to specialties of the ad-hoc domain), (vi) *IP forwarding and route resilience* (policing, marking and remarking of packets according to QoS classification and traffic contracts), (vii) *broadcast, multicast and geocast* (reducing the amount of traffic at the sender side and in the network due to multiple deliveries of the same content), (viii) *gateway agent* (connectivity between ad-hoc and infrastructure networks), (ix) *link failure detection* (detection of broken links), (x) *in-stack* and (xi) *performance monitoring* (various monitoring activities within the protocol stack), (xii) *communication adaptation* (improving the system level communication performance and user experience), (xiii) *QoS differentiation* (end-to-end QoS management), (xiv) *gateway network selection* (selection of network technologies or base stations), and (xv) *profile management* (describing the capabilities of nodes).

Obviously there are various *use dependency relations* amongst services, e.g., the *local and distributed measurement service* (see above) uses *reliable clocks* for performing local measurements and the *authentication* service for secure communication. These dependency relations were *discovered* by carefully investigating the initial verbal functional specification of services [4] to be developed and explicitly asking the corresponding project partners to collect what are those services that are used by the service developed by them. Since at the initial phase of the project exact interfaces of services were not available, the discovery of these dependencies aimed only at ensuring that there are no such services that are expected by a part of the platform but are actually not provided by anyone.

As shown in Fig. 2 use-cases are organized into four packages corresponding to the classification above; contents of the resiliency kernel package are explicitly shown: note that dependencies amongst services that were textually outlined above appear as UML *dependency relations* amongst use-cases.

In this step the services provided by the platform were identified, discovered the dependencies amongst services and organized this information into a UML use-case model. The benefits of this activity are not specific to the Hidenets

Table 1. Functionalities of the Authentication and Timing Failure Detection Services

	Function	**Arguments**	**Return value**
Authentication	Establish connection	peer identifier	session identifier
	Decrypt data	encryption key, data block	data block
	Decrypt message	session identifier, message	message
	Encrypt data	encryption key, data block	data block
	Encrypt message	session identifier, message	message
	Sign data	encryption key, data block	digital signature
	Sign message	session identifier, message	digital signature
	Verify data	data block, signature	Boolean (y/n)
	Verify message	message, signature	Boolean (y/n)
Timing failure detection	Initiate detection	deadline, call-back	detection identifier
	Shutdown detection	detection identifier	

project by any means: for any non-trivial system it is highly recommended to clearly identify the services to be implemented at the beginning of the project and by the clear indication of service dependencies to prevent the introduction of dependencies that can not be met.

2.2 Component Model and Interface Definitions

This subsection outlines the process of defining the *interfaces* of the various services. The key goal of this step was similar to the identification of *top-level components* of a complex software system, with the clear indication of *required* and *provided interfaces* – this clear separation of concerns enables *concurrent* team development of the individual components, without having to worry about integration difficulties at the end of the project. This section can be seen as an answer to the question: "*What are the interfaces of services exposed by the platform to application developers and how are these interfaces used within the platform for interconnecting services withing the framework?*".

In order to facilitate re-use of previously published field expertise, emphasis was put on the integration of our work to corresponding standards e.g., *timing related data types* (deadlines, intervals, etc.) were derived from the corresponding concepts of the SPT Profile [1], while *QoS related data types* (e.g., service level agreements of the QoS coverage management and QoS differentiation services) were derived from the corresponding concepts of the QoS and FT Profile [5].

This step consisted of walking through all the services to be provided by the platform (i.e., use-cases identified above) and *defining the interface* of the services i.e., for each functionality of each service the following information was collected (i) the *name*, (ii) the *argument list*, (iii) the *return type* and (iv) the terse textual *description* of the function. This step is illustrated with two examples: the authentication and the timing failure detection services.

The *authentication service* provides the following key functionalities (Tab. 1): (i) *establishing* a secure communication session with another peer, (ii) encrypting arbitrary data using a symmetric key, (iii) encrypting a message within the context of a session, (iv) decrypting arbitrary data using a symmetric key, (v) decrypting a message within the context of a session, (vi) digitally signing arbitrary data using a private key, (vii) digitally signing a message using a private key, (viii) verifying if given signature on arbitrary data is valid and (ix) verifying if a given message signature is valid.

The *timing failure detection service* is similar to a watchdog processor: in case of a distributed real-time application a client component that would like to use a real-time functionality sets up a *detection activity* to ensure that the called real-time function returns in time or a timing failure notification is received from the timing failure detection service. When initiating the detection activity the client specifies the deadline within the operation called should be finished and a call-back function: this call-back function of the client will be invoked by the timing failure detection service if the detection activity is not shut down before the expiration of the deadline – obviously upon receiving the answer from the real-time service within the deadline, the client explicitly shuts down the detection activity. Having outlined the operation, it is easy to see that the timing failure detection service provides two functions: (i) *initiating* and (ii) *shutting down* a detection activity (Tab. 1). With respect to the application of previous standards, it is easy to see that SPT's *time interval* concepts seamlessly fits to the *deadline* attribute to be specified at the initiation of a detection activity.

The functionalities provided by the services were organized into coherent *interfaces*, where individual functions appear as *operations* of the corresponding interface; e.g., for the authentication service (Fig. 3, left side) we introduced the *IAuthentication* interface (following the convention of prefixing the names of interfaces by the *I* letter) and added operations corresponding to the functionalities outlined above (writing function names according to the usual Java and UML style). For the unambiguous definition of operations on interfaces some *data types* had to defined, e.g., in case of the *IAuthentication::establishConnection* operation, the identifier of the peer is represented by the *PeerID* data type, while the session identifier is represented by the *SessionID* data type. UML's usual notation for interfaces is a rectangle with the keyword ≪*interface*≫, the name of the interface and indication of operations in the compartment below.

For each service a UML *component* was introduced and indicated the interfaces *provided* by the corresponding service; UML's notation for components is a rectangle with two smaller rectangles in its upper left part, the keyword ≪*component*≫ and the name of the component; provided interfaces are indicated by small circles attached to the component and indicating the name of the provided interface. Based on the *dependency information* stored in the use-case model the interfaces *required* by services was also indicated using UML's notation: a socket attached to the component with the name of the required interface; required and provided interfaces are attached to one-another by solid lines. In case of the timing failure detection service it is easy to see (Fig. 3, right side) that the *TimingFailureDetectionService* component *provides* the *ITimingFailureDetection* interface according to the naming convention above and requires the

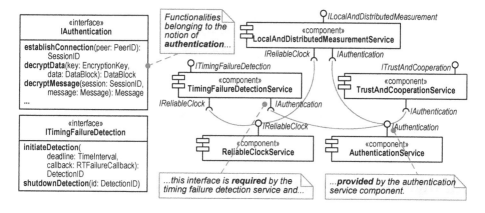

Fig. 3. Components with Required and Provided Interfaces

IReliableClock and *IAuthentication* interfaces, these interfaces are *provided* by components *ReliableClockService* and *AuthenticationService* respectively.

As mentioned in the introduction, emphasis was put on the integration of our model to previously published *standards*. General dependability concepts of the models are derived from relevant OMG specifications, e.g., this clearly appears in the definition of time-related data types: the notions of *time instances, intervals* etc. were derived from the corresponding concepts of the SPT Profile e.g., in case of the timing failure detection service the *deadline* for finishing a real-time operation was derived from the *time interval* concept of SPT. It may be beneficial to mention that the SPT profile is currently being replaced by OMG's novel proposal, MARTE (UML Profile for Modeling and Analysis of Real-Time and Embedded Systems) [6]; as fundamental time-related concepts are similar in SPT and MARTE, our data types can be easily fitted to the new profile once MARTE will be officially released. Second, the middleware service interfaces offered to the applications are aligned wherever possible with SA Forum's Application Interface Specification [2]. For example, the replication manager uses replicas similarly as the components are used in the Availability Management Framework. Re-using these concepts in our work offers the following benefits: (i) reduction of time needed for building the model, (ii) reduction of possibilities for introducing conceptual errors in the model and (iii) using the well-known fundamental concepts, the model is also easier to understand.

To put together: this step (i) clearly defined interfaces, (ii) introduced components for services, (iii) indicated provided and required interfaces of these components and (iv) introduced data types on the basis of previously published standards. The benefits and lessons learned in this step are not Hidenets-specific: the clear identification of interfaces enables project partners to work independently without having to worry about future interface incompatibilities while the integration to well-known standards enables the knowledge re-use.

2.3   Summary

This section has outlined the UML model of the Hidenets platform: (i) we presented a use-case model enumerating the services, organizing them into packages and indicating the dependency relations amongst them and (ii) we outlined the component model with the unambiguous definition of service interfaces. Obviously full models could not be presented here: rather two easy to understand services were selected to be used as examples throughout the entire paper; the detailed documentation of the platform model was published in the corresponding deliverable of the project [7] and research papers [8,9,10,11,12].

3   Modeling Applications

This section provides an overview on the second group of the modeling efforts: *providing practical support for the development of applications for the Hidenets platform*. Key parts of our corresponding work are as follows: (i) introducing a *metamodel* for some dependability-related features provided by the platform, (ii) definition of a *UML profile* on the basis of the metamodel and (iii) the specification of a set of *design patterns* providing support for application development. The main objective of these models, notations and supporting tools is the support of the best-practice exploitation of the high availability related services offered by the Hidenets platform.

Below Sec. 3.1 presents an introduction to fundamental concepts of the Model Driven Architecture, meta-modeling and UML profiles, then Sec. 3.2 introduces the metamodel, Sec. 3.3 defines the profile, finally Sec. 3.4 outlines some parts of the design pattern library.

3.1   An Overview on Model Driven Development

Our approach is organized according to OMG's Model Driven Architecture initiative (MDA) [13]. This subsection provides a short overview on MDA concepts.

MDA consists of three key steps: (i) platform independent modeling (PIM), (ii) platform specific modeling (PSM) and (iii) implementation. The *platform independent model* of the application is prepared focusing barely on the services to be delivered, organization of the internal structure etc. without taking into consideration the features or weaknesses of the target platform, e.g., in case of graphical user interfaces, a PIM model uses abstract concepts like window, button etc. without bounding itself to implementations of these concepts in Java Swing, Microsoft Windows, UNIX X-Window environment etc. The typical outcomes of PIM step are UML models, i.e., ordinary class, activity, etc. diagrams without using target-specific features. In the *platform specific modeling* step the PIM model is modified such way that features and weaknesses of the target platform are taken into consideration; according to our previous example, abstract GUI elements are mapped to concepts of the target windowing environment, e.g., the button class will be derived from Java Swing's JButton, etc. Clear separation of platform independent modeling and mapping the structure to specialties of the target environment results in *straightforward re-usability* of models since PIM models are not bound to the target platform. Thus porting the application to a new platform only requires the modification of the mapping between PIM and platform specific concepts. In the final *implementation step* the platform specific model is implemented in the target language e.g., Java in our example.

The abstract syntax of models built in subsequent steps is defined by so called *metamodels*. The metamodel of a modeling language defines *key concepts of the modeling language* (e.g., in case of UML class diagrams, classes, interfaces, attributes, associations, inheritance, etc.) as *metaclasses* and various relations of these metaclasses – this way one can imagine the metamodel of UML as a class model of UML itself. According to this observation, a UML model (containing the modeler-defined classes, packages, behavior etc.) can be seen as an *instance* of the UML metamodel. Metamodeling is a fundamental concept in MDA: the mapping between PIM and PSM actually means the introduction of such new metaclasses in the basic toolkit of UML that enable the developer to keep using the well-known syntax of UML while exploiting platform-specific features that may not have been known at all by designers of UML. For example in case of development of a software requiring dependable communication facilities, one can (i) initially design the application using plain UML class and interaction diagrams focusing only on the services to be delivered by the application (PIM) then (ii) decide which platform to use as the underlying dependable communication middleware, (iii) introduce platform specific metaclasses e.g., derive a *dependable communication link* metaclass from the UML built-in communication link metaclass and finally (iv) indicate in her/his model that the link between two endpoints must be highly dependable.

An important question however is *how to introduce new metaclasses into UML* since theoretically this would require the modification of the internal model representation format of the modeling environment. In order to overcome this difficulty, OMG has introduced the concept of *UML profiles*. A UML profile is a light-weight incremental modification of the metamodel: a profile does not aim at defining an *entire metamodel* just the *difference* between the original and the desired one. New metaclasses are to be derived from already existing ones and these new metaclasses will appear as *stereotypes* attached to their built-in ancestors, e.g., according to the example above, the newly introduced *DependableLink* metaclass is derived from the *Link* metaclass, thus the profile declares the ≪DependableLink≫ stereotype; if this stereotype is applied to a link in the model, that link is considered to be a *DependableLink* instance.

3.2   A Metamodel for Dependable Ad-Hoc Mobile Services

This subsection presents a more in-depth investigation of some services provided by the Hidenets platform to answer the question: *"What is the intended organization of applications running on the platform and how do the platform-related parts correspond to fundamental UML concepts?"*. This investigation is necessitated by the easy to see fact that a set of interfaces barely carries enough information for properly using any nontrivial services. This subsection will

(i) identify those parts of applications that are relevant for some Hidenets services, (ii) describe these application-level concepts at the abstraction level of the UML metamodel and (iii) provide design patterns that illustrate how to use Hidenets services from well-organized applications. It will focus again on authentication and timing failure detection services also discussed above.

First the textual description of how to use services from an application developer's point of view is presented:

Authenticated communication is a communication of two *peers* in a distributed application. In a software model these peers appear as *classes* of the application, the fact that they are in some communicating relation is indicated by the *association* between them. From an application developer's point of view it would be beneficial to *explicitly indicate* those *classes* that have to be authenticated and those *associations* through which authenticated communication is performed. Once having marked peers and channels of authenticated communication, the actual authenticated communication should be implemented using the authentication service; this involves (i) *initialization* of the authenticated channel by calling the *IAuthentication::establishConnection* function of the authentication service components on both nodes, (ii) sending messages by first letting them *signed* (encrypted, etc.) by calling *IAuthentication::signMessage* and (iii) upon the reception of a message *verifying* the digital signature on the message by calling *IAuthentication::verifyMessage* – detailed description of this scenario would be beneficial for developers actually learning the usage of the platform.

Timing failure detection aims at detecting that a *real-time operation* has violated the deadline of service delivery; this communication involves two entities: the *provider* of the service and the *client* of the service. Upon the violation of a deadline, the timing failure detection service calls a *call-back operation* of the client. The deadline of the operation is indicated in a *real-time service agreement* between the two entities. From an application developer's point of view, real-time service providers and clients are *classes* or components; the communication of entities is indicated by the *association* between them; as the real-time service agreement does not directly belong to any of entities, this information is best stored in an *association class* attached to the association between them; finally a straightforward model of real-time services and call-back function is to add them as *operations* to the corresponding classes. The usage of timing failure detection feature of the platform is as follows: (i) the client first *initiates* a detection activity by calling *ITimingFailureDetection::initiateDetection* (specifying the deadline and the call-back function to be called upon deadline violation), (ii) *calls* the real-time service operation and starts waiting for the answer, if the answer is delivered within the deadline (iii-a) the client *shuts down* the timing failure detection activity by calling *ITimingFailureDetection::shutdownDetection*, otherwise upon violation of the real-time contract (iii-b) the timing failure detection service *notifies* the client by invoking its call-back function.

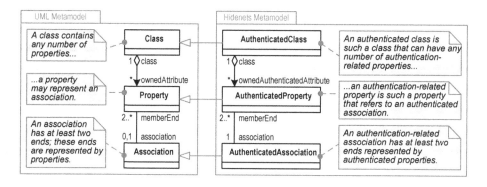

Fig. 4. Metaclasses Corresponding to the Authentication Service

The definitions above carry information about both the intended *organization* of the application (classes, associations, operations, etc.) and the intended *usage pattern* of services. This information will be formally defined by providing a *metamodel* of applications running on the Hidenets platform and presenting *design patterns* as guidelines for application developers.

In correspondence to the definition of metamodels and profiles above, those relevant concepts of ad-hoc mobile applications will be captured that are non-standard UML features. In case of the authentication service three metaclasses are introduced (Fig. 4): (i) *AuthenticatedClass* (corresponding to peers of an authenticated communication, derived from the core UML *Class* concept), (ii) *AuthenticatedAssociation* (corresponding to the association through which the authenticated communication is performed, derived from UML's *Association* metaclass) and (iii) as association are connected to classes through *properties* the *AuthenticatedProperty* was derived from the *Property* UML concept.

In case of the timing failure detection service the following metaclasses were introduced (Fig. 5): (i) *RTServiceProvider* and (ii) *RTServiceClient* (corresponding to providers and clients of real-time services respectively, both derived from the core UML *Class* concept), (iii) *RTService* (representing a real-time operation of the provider, derived from UML's *Operation* metaclass), (iv) *RTFailureCallback* (representing call-back functions to be called by the timing failure detection service upon detecting the violation of a real-time service agreement, obviously derived from *Operation*), (v) *RTServiceProvision* and *RTServiceAccess* properties (see above remark about properties above), finally *RTServiceAgreement* (representing real-time service contracts between the provider and the client, derived from UML's *AssociationClass* metaclass).

In order to avoid confusion, the relations between metaclasses introduced above are shown in the separate diagram of Fig. 6; the organization reflects UML's relations between the corresponding ancestor metaclasses (Fig. 5, top part): the real-time service provider class contains real-time services, while the client class contains the call-back operation. The two classes are connected through the corresponding properties by the real-time service agreement

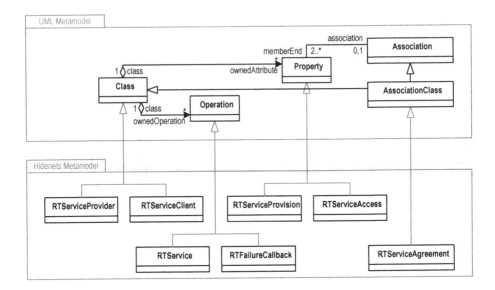

Fig. 5. Metaclasses Corresponding to the Timing Failure Detection Service

association class; note that a time interval attribute to this metaclass was added representing the deadline of operation.

3.3   UML Profile for Hidenets Applications

This subsection defines a UML profile in correspondence to the metamodel discussed above. The profile answers the question: *"How to add platform-related information to ordinary UML models of dependable applications that are intended to take advantage of the platform?"* Note that since Hidenets hides most of mobility-related issues, these concepts do not appear in the profile either, rather the profile focuses on general dependability concepts.

Translation of a metamodel whose elements were directly derived from UML concepts as shown above is relatively straightforward: *stereotypes* have to be introduced to be attached to built-in concepts and *tagged values* have to be created in correspondence to attributes of newly introduced metaclasses. For example if a new metaclass *DerivedMC* is derived from the core UML metaclass *CoreMC* a stereotype has to introduced to be attached to those instances of *CoreMC* that are actually instances of *DerivedMC*; let this stereotype be called *derived*; this way *CoreMC* model elements can be tagged with the stereotype ≪*derived*≫ to indicate that they are actually instances of *DerivedMC*. If *Derived* has an attribute *attr*, it has to be indicated that for classes with stereotype ≪*derived*≫ the value of attribute *attr* can be specified in the model.

In case of the metamodel outlined above for all the metaclasses stereotypes were introduced by prefixing the name of the represented metaclass with *hi*; Tab. 2 shows the stereotypes corresponding to metaclasses defined

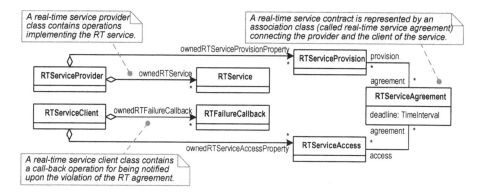

Fig. 6. Relation of Metaclasses Corresponding to the Timing Failure Detection Service

Table 2. Stereotypes, Represented Metaclasses and Tagged Values

Stereotype	Represented metaclass	Attached to...	Tags
hiAuthenticatedClass	AuthenticatedClass	Class	–
hiAuthenticatedProperty	AuthenticatedProperty	Property	–
hiAuthenticatedAssociation	AuthenticatedAssociation	Association	–
hiRTServiceProvider	RTServiceProvider	Class	–
hiRTServiceClient	RTServiceClient	Class	–
hiRTService	RTService	Operation	–
hiRTFailureCallback	RTFailureCallback	Operation	–
hiRTServiceProvision	RTServiceProvision	Property	–
hiRTServiceAccess	RTServiceAccess	Property	–
hiRTServiceAgreement	RTServiceAgreement	AssociationClass	deadline

in the context of authentication and timing failure detection services, e.g., the ≪*hiRTServiceAgreement*≫ stereotype can be attached to association classes indicating that the model element is actually a real-time service agreement (i.e., instance of *RTServiceAgreement*); classes marked with this stereotype may specify the value of the *deadline* attribute.

An example for the usage of the profile is shown in Fig. 7: the designer introduced a class *SomeRTServiceProvider* to provide some real-time service by its single member function called *someOperation* and stereotyped these entities according to the profile, another class using this service was called *SomeRTServiceClient* with the call-back function *someCallback*; the real-time agreement between the two classes is represented by the association class *SomeRTServiceAgreement* marked with the proper stereotype; the deadline is indicated by specifying the value of the *deadline* tagged value within braces.

3.4   A Design Pattern Library for Hidenets Applications

This subsection presents some *design patterns* that provide straightforward examples for the implementation of dependability-related application parts built on

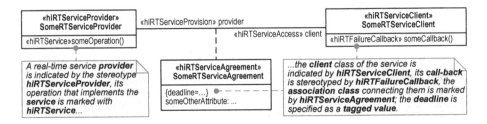

Fig. 7. Example for the Application of the Profile

the platform. The discussion can be seen as an answer to the question: *"What are the best practices for organization and implementation of various dependability-related parts of application intended to be executed on the platform?"*. Note that we did not aim at proposing novel dependability solutions, but indicating the way of application of well-known patterns [14] in the context of Hidenets by explicitly connecting the concepts of our profile to design pattern elements.

The design pattern for *authenticated communication* (Fig. 8) illustrates the model organization and implementation in case of two communicating classes (*PeerA* and *PeerB* respectively). The top part of the figure presents the static organization: the communicating peers are stereotyped classes, the association between them (called *channel* in the figure) is also stereotyped according to the profile introduced above. Both classes are associated to authentication service components (in case of a distributed application the two classes may be running on different nodes thus the platform service components used by them may also be running on different nodes; for simplicity reasons both service components were called *AuthenticationService* in the example). The lower part of the figure presents the interaction model for setting up a secure communication channel and sending a digitally signed message whose signature is verified upon reception.

The design pattern for *detecting violations of real-time service agreements* (Fig. 9) illustrates the model organization and the implementation in case of a class providing a real-time service and its client (called *Provider* and *Client* respectively. The top part of the figure presents the static organization: both the provider and client are stereotyped classes, there is an association class between them representing the real-time service agreement stereotyped again according to the profile introduced above. The client class is associated to a timing failure service component. The lower part of the figure presents the interaction model for initiating a detection, calling the service and depending on whether the provider provides the response within the deadline shutting down the detection activity by the client or notifying the client by the timing failure detection service.

3.5   Observations on the Support of Standard Profiles

During the development of the Hidenets metamodel several standardized UML profiles were used, like the SPT or the QoS profiles. With the help of these specifications basic concepts did not have to be redefined, e.g., time or quality

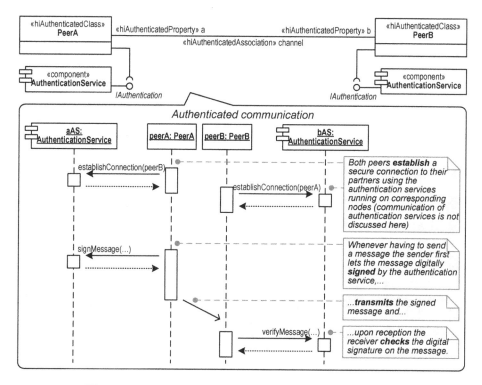

Fig. 8. Design Pattern for Authenticated Communication

of service, which saved a huge amount of effort and allowed us to focus on domain-specific issues. However, the following issues were found during the implementation of the profile, which may hinder the everyday use of UML profiles.

Although most of the UML CASE tools offer a way to create and share profiles, no downloadable versions even for these popular profiles were found for any UML versions. Creating a profile from OMG's document is usually a straightforward task, but probably more people would use them if the profiles could simply be imported to a UML tool. The other key problem faced was that there are few examples for the standard profiles. The SPT profile is referenced in several academic paper, however for the UML 2.0 testing profiles [15] there are only two examples available so far. The specifications mostly just list the concepts of the profiles, without examples showing how to use them making them hard to apply.

In order to overcome these practical weaknesses, our profile will be released not only in textual format of project reports but also in downloadable modules that are easy to import into such popular modeling environments as the IBM Rational Software Architect, etc.

3.6 Summary

This section has outlined our modeling efforts in the context of application development support: (i) introduced a metamodel for some dependability-related

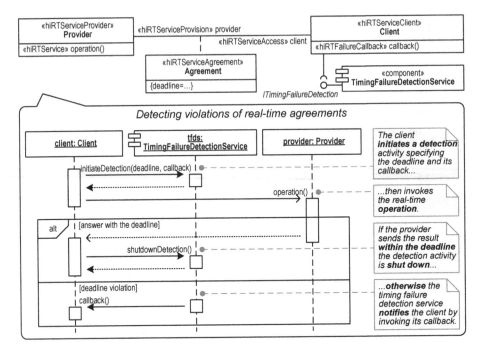

Fig. 9. Design Pattern for Detecting Violations of Real-Time Agreements

features provided by the Hidenets platform, (ii) defined the corresponding UML profile and (iii) specified a set of design patterns as straightforward examples for implementing dependability-related parts of applications intended to run on the Hidnets platform. Obviously full discussions could not be presented here: the focus was again rather on the same services used as examples in the previous key part of the paper; the detailed documentation of the metamodel and the profile was published in the corresponding deliverable of the project [7].

4   A Case Study for the Application of the Profile

This section presents an example for using our profile in the context of the demonstrator application developed by us in the sixth work package of the Hi-denets project. The software developed is a simplified version of an intelligent cruise control application (mentioned in the context of the "platooning use-case" in [4]); it will be refered as the Platoon Driver Support Software (PDSS). Below the key concepts of PDSS are briefly defined and the functional and non-functional requirements enumerated.

The *platoon* consists of *vehicles*, which are driven by human drivers. The first vehicle in the platoon is called the *head vehicle*, other vehicles are called *slave vehicles*. Slave vehicles should adjust their speed according to the head vehicle – this speed adjustment is supported by the PDSS software. The functional requirements against the PDSS application can be summarized as below:

- The software periodically *collects* various parameters of vehicles (speed, acceleration, etc.) and using the head vehicle as reference *calculates* the actuations to be applied to slave vehicles.
- The software presents the *map of the current area* to the driver of the head vehicle similarly to a usual GPS device with additional annotations indicating various traffic circumstances; the database of traffic conditions is stored on the infrastructure and managed by (human) operators of the company.
- The software periodically reports the *actual position* of the platoon to the infrastructure. On the infrastructure side the operators can follow the movement of platoons on a display.

The non-functional requirements against PDSS are as follows:

- Controlling slave vehicles requires *up-to-date information* about the actual state of vehicles and the actuations calculated by the software should be applied to the slaves within short deadlines.
- The data channel between vehicles should be temper proof i.e., communication should be *encrypted*, and peers should be *authenticated*.
- The decisions of platoon drivers are taken according to up-to-date traffic conditions thus the information provided by the infrastructure should be trusted thus peers of this communication should be *authenticated*.

This section focuses on the application of the UML profile introduced above; it will show how to model the *real-time requirements* for collecting sensor information from slave vehicles and the *authentication* requirement for the communication between vehicles. The context of the introduction is the control loop between vehicles, i.e., the activity in which the software collects reference sensor values from the head vehicle, obtains sensor information from slaves, calculates the actuation to be applied to slaves and transmits this information. The key control logic is running on the head vehicle, slaves only provide information upon request and apply the actuation data sent to them. (Note that some design decisions were drawn in order to be able to *demonstrate some platform-specific features* instead of directly focusing on the most straightforward implementation of the application itself.)

The high-level organization of the software is shown in the deployment diagram of Fig. 10: (i) there are two computer node types, one for the head vehicle (*HVComputer*) and another for slaves (*SVComputer*); obviously this organization does not require actually different hardware, the distinction was made purely for modeling purposes; (ii) the two key software artifacts deployed to the computers are the Hidenets platform (*HidenetsPlatform*, deployed to both computers) and head and slave parts of the control loop (*HVSoftwareImage* and *SVSoftwareImage* deployed to the head and slave vehicle computers respectively); (iii) the software image deployed to the head vehicle contains (according to UML's terminology *manifests*) the code for sensors of the head vehicle (component *HVSensors*) and the head part of the control loop (component *HVControl*); (iv) the software image deployed to slave vehicles contains the code for sensors of slave vehicles (component *SVSensors*) and the slave part of the control loop (component *SVControl*). Sensor components (*HVSensors* and *SVSensors*) provide the

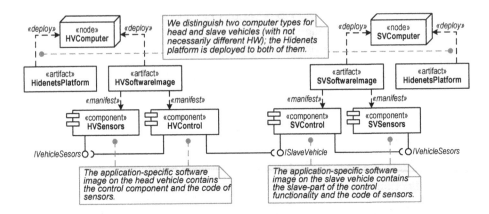

Fig. 10. Deployment Model of the Platoon Driver Support Software

IVehicleSensors interface, this interface is required by the corresponding control components; the component implementing the slave part of the control loops provides the *ISlaveVehicle* interface to the head part of the control loop (these interfaces are specified in Fig. 11).

The internal structure of the component implementing the head part of the control loop (*HVControl*) is shown in Fig. 11: (i) the interfaces required by the component are accessed through two ports: (a) the local sensor port (*LocalSensorPort*) uses the *IVehicleSensors* interface of the head vehicle while (b) the slave vehicle port (*SlaveVehiclePort*) uses the *ISlaveVehicle* interface of the slave parts' control component; (ii) the core intelligence is implemented in the *runControlCycle* member operation of the control algorithm class (*ControlAlgorithm*); (iii) the control cycle is periodically invoked by a timer class (*Timer*).

It is easy to see that (i) according to the real-time requirements above there is a *real-time service agreement* between the control algorithm class and the port providing the necessary sensor data (subtleties of the inter-vehicle communication is hidden within the port class thus it is more straightforward to model the real-time service relation between the algorithm and the port than modeling the real-time requirements between the algorithm and the slave part of the control loop); furthermore (ii) due to the authentication requirements the port communicating with slave vehicles should be *authenticated*:

– The real-time service relation is indicated by labeling *ControlAlgorithm* with the stereotype ≪*hiRTServiceClient*≫ (being the client of a real-time service) and labeling *SlaveVehiclePort* with the stereotype ≪*hiRTServiceProvider*≫ (being the provider of a real-time service). The association class attached to the association between them (*SensorFreshnessAgreement*) is labeled with the stereotype ≪*hiRTServiceAgreement*≫. Note that the deadline to deliver sensor data is indicated as a tagged value in *SensorFreshnessAgreement*.

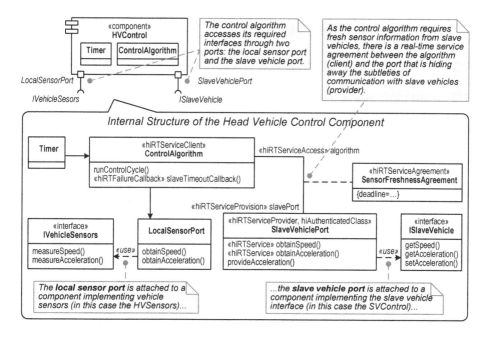

Fig. 11. Internal Structure of the Head Vehicle Control Component

- The authentication requirement is indicated by attaching the
  ≪*hiAuthenticatedClass*≫ stereotype to *SlaveVehiclePort*; although not
  indicated in the figure, the slave counterpart of the communication should
  also be marked by this stereotype.

A control cycle is shown in the interaction diagram of Fig. 12. Heads of life lines
indicate cooperating entities: (i) the timer that invokes the control loop, (ii) the
control algorithm, (iii) the authentication service deployed to the head vehicle,
(iv) the local sensor port of the head vehicle, (v) the slave vehicle port, (vi) the
timing failure detection service deployed to the head vehicle and (vii) interface
of the component implementing the slave part of the control loop. The key steps
in the interaction are highlighted by the comments of the diagram.

The example has demonstrated two key benefits of having applied a model-
driven approach in the project: (i) application of our *UML profile* enabled the developers to clearly and declaratively indicate requirements that naturally emerge
in applications running on mobile ad-hoc platforms and (ii) the implementation
was greatly simplified by organizing the behavior of the application according
to the *design patterns* outlined above. The joint application of a fully elaborated
profile and a detailed set of design patterns can also build the foundations of
code generation approaches that are capable of automatically transforming the
UML model of the application into source code. For more detailed discussion of
the demonstrator application see [16].

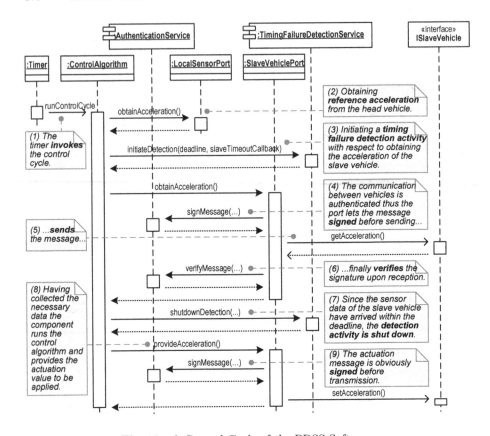

Fig. 12. A Control Cycle of the PDSS Software

5   Testing and Fault Modeling

Following a rigorous application development method and relying on a well-defined metamodel greatly enhances the dependability of the developed system, however cannot guarantee that it will satisfy all requirements. Being aware of this issue, in Hidenets (i) a *testing framework* is developed, fitted to specialties of the ad-hoc mobile domain and (ii) an *error propagation* and *static analysis* solution is elaborated; this section presents a brief overview on these areas.

5.1   Testing Ad-Hoc Mobile Applications

Testing is one of the most popular V&V activities. Testing of distributed systems offers several challenges, e.g., the behavior of the system is highly asynchronous or the final verdict has to be assigned using the partial verdicts returned by the different testing components. However, ad-hoc mobile networks (MANET) introduce further issues to test development and execution. Ad-hoc networks are by nature very dynamic, which implies that (i) test cases have to be created which cover scenarios where nodes are appearing or disappearing, (ii) test platforms should be able to simulate the specialties of mobile networks (e.g., frequent disconnects or high latencies).

To better understand the new testing related challenges a case study [17] was performed, the analysis of a mobile Group Membership Protocol was carried out. The insights gained from this case study can be summarized as follows. Standard UML was appropriate to model the structure and behavior of one node (by static structure diagrams, statecharts, activity diagrams etc.), but it was inconvenient for modeling a complex scenario which included several nodes, due to the lack of formal semantics assigned to sequence diagrams, lack of an unambiguous notation for broadcast messages etc. Moreover, services and applications in mobile settings rely heavily not just on user input but also on context information, like current location data. A test execution engine should be able to feed the System Under Test (SUT) not only with the messages coming outside from the SUT but also these contextual data.

Taking into account these experiences a testing framework is elaborated based on scenario languages. Work is focused on (i) defining a testing language for test requirements and test purposes, (ii) identifying the extensions needed for the mobile setting, and (iii) creating a test platform. The current and recommended semantics for UML Sequence Diagrams is not precise enough to describe test cases, thus, after investigating the semantics issues, a subset of the elements was selected, which can be used to specify testing artifacts. The stereotypes in the profile presented in the previous Section mark the dependability requirements of an application, these are the exact behaviors that should be the starting points for test planning. Finally, it will be investigated how existing network simulators and context controllers developed for MANETs could be integrated into test platforms to execute test cases.

5.2 Error Propagation Modeling and Static Analysis

Even carefully designed and tested components may fail to deliver their services, thus if an application has strict dependability requirements, it is important to analyze what *combination* of these failures could lead to a violation of the requirements. Treating the platform's services and parts of the application as separate components with defined fault modes and using the information about the relations between the services contained in the platform model, error propagation modeling could answer the above question.

In the classic taxonomy of dependability [18], components of a system may fail to show the behavior expected from them, a phenomenon called component service *failure*. As components have internal states as well as observable ones (input and output, essentially), deviation in state from the reference behavior is called *error*, what may lead to component service failure. Specifically, erroneous input and output states are called *data errors*. By definition, the adjudged or hypothesized cause of an error is called a *fault*, that can be *internal* or *external* by origin. The phenomenon of erroneous states propagating in a system along data and resource dependencies is called *error propagation*.

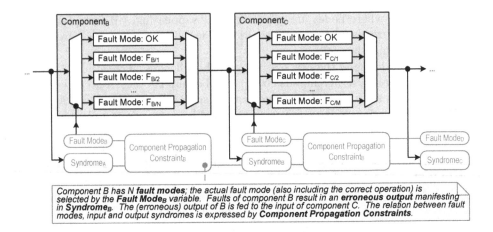

Fig. 13. Error Propagation Modeling

Analyzing error propagation in a system of numerous components thus relies on (i) capturing the behavior of components (under faults as well as during normal operation) and (ii) capturing the dependencies between the components. Although the taxonomy implies a state-based, dynamic modeling approach, its general applicability is questionable. Formal analysis approaches dealing with state space representations (as for example model checking) are usually constrained by the maximal number of states, which can be quite early exhausted due to state space explosion by composing components into a system. Also, state space based analysis is inapplicable for on-line diagnosis or impact analysis due to run time reasons.

These problems can be managed in our approach [19] by using *qualitative modeling* and *abstraction*, leading to a stateless error propagation description. First, partitioning the deviations on input and output into a qualitative set of data error classes (a spatial abstraction) transforms input and output data sequences into input and output error sequences. Second, establishing a total ordering on each resulting input and output error language (in the simplest form, an 'error seriousness' ordering) allows for characterizing any error run on an input or output with one single error, what is effectively a qualitative partitioning of the error runs (temporal abstraction). The characteristic error of a run is called *syndrome*. Note that resource dependencies and failures can also be modeled via errors and syndromes. Additionally, the internal fault mode of a component has to be represented, as error propagation characteristics drastically differ under different internal faults (or in case there is no fault). Internal faults are also partitioned into a qualitative set of *component fault modes*.

This way, error propagation of components can be characterized by input-output syndrome tuples plus a fault mode value, resulting in a relation in the mathematical sense over inputs, outputs and component fault mode. The modeling granularity depends on the available expert knowledge, empirical data and the analysis needs and as such needs human effort to set up; however, this can be done on a per *component type* basis.

This model naturally translates to *finite domain constraint satisfaction problems* (CSP) [20], with propagation relations and connectivity as *constraints* and syndromes and fault modes as *variables*. Diagnosis and impact analysis in this setting are search for consistent variable binding with an initially partially bound variable set (fault activation assumption/knowledge and syndrome value assumption/knowledge).

With pure CSP supported problem solving, the analysis pattern is an iterated model – execute – evaluate loop. Constraint logic programming (CLP) [21] over finite domains is an amalgamation of logic programming and finite domain CSP: the state of a program is the current goal and a so-called constraint store, that stores the currently possible domains of select variables. Special predicates allow for posting new constraints to the store and searching for store-consistent variable bindings; CSP failure (inconsistent store) and backtracking are reflected back to the logic program via the CSP predicates. Accordingly, a CLP search tree is the logic programming search tree with current goals as nodes, the nodes also attributed with the current constraint store of that node.

Finally we have to highlight some aspects regarding *performance issues* and *implementation possibilities*. Finite domain CSP solving, the heart of the approach, is in general an NP-complete problem – however in our case this issue does not apply due to the (relatively) *high level of modeling abstraction*. The application of state of the art logic programming environments featuring support for dynamic predicates and meta calls even enables the *on-line operation* of propagation analysis.

6   Conclusions

This paper presented a model-based approach to develop resilient solutions. Although the work was focused on the setting of ad-hoc mobile networks, the methods used and the experience gained can be used to architect any dependable system. The following steps contributed to the dependability of the overall solution (i) creating the *platform's UML model* helped to identify the boundaries of the system and design the architecture of the services, (ii) elaborating a *UML profile* and *design pattern library* supports the application development by offering the key concepts and structures of the target domain as built-in modeling elements, (iii) presenting a *case study* showed how the above profile and design patterns could be applied to a complex application, and finally (iv) developing *testing* and *error propagation modeling* methods contributed to the verification of the system's dependability requirements.

References

1. Object Management Group: UML Profile for Schedulability, Performance and Time (January 2005)
2. Service Availability Forum: Application Interface Specification (2007), http://www.saforum.org
3. Object Management Group: Unified Modeling Language: Superstructure (2007)

4. Radimirsch, M., Matthiesen, E.V., Huszerl, G., Reitenspiess, M., Kaâniche, M., Svinnset, I.E., Casimiro, A., Falai, L.: Use Case Scenarios and Preliminary Reference Model (Deliverable of the Hidenets Project – D-1.1) (2006)
5. Object Management Group: UML Profile for Modeling Quality of Service and Fault Tolerance Characteristics (2006)
6. Object Management Group: UML Profile for Modeling and Analysis of Real-Time and Embedded Systems (MARTE) (2007)
7. Kövi, A., Pataricza, A., Rákosi, B., Pintér, G., Micskei, Z.: UML Profile and Design Patterns Library (Deliverable of the Hidenets Project – D-5.1)
8. Moniz, H., Neves, N.F., Correia, M., Casimiro, A., Verissimo, P.: Intrusion Tolerance in Wireless Environments: An Experimental Evaluation. In: PRDC 2007: 13th IEEE Pacific Rim International Symposium on Dependable Computing, Melbourne, Australia (2007)
9. Courtes, L., Killijian, M.O., Powell, D.: Security Rationale for a Cooperative Backup Service for Mobile Devices. In: 3rd Latin-American Symposium on Dependable Computing (LADC), Morelia, Mexico (2007)
10. Matthiesen, E.V., Schwefel, H.P., Renier, T.J.: A Selection Metric for Backup Group Creation in Inter-Vehicular Networks. In: IST Mobile and Wireless Communications Summit, Budapest, Hungary (2007)
11. Bondavalli, A., Ceccarelli, A., Falai, L.: A Self-Aware Clock for Pervasive Computing Systems. In: 15th Euromicro International Conference on Parallel, Distributed and Network-Based Processing (PDP 2007) (2007)
12. Hansen, A.F., Lysne, O., Cicic, T., Gjessing, S.: Fast Proactive Recovery from Concurrent Failures. In: IEEE International Conference on Communications (ICC 2007) (2007)
13. Object Management Group: MDA Guide. OMG (June 2003)
14. Douglass, B.P.: Real-Time Design Patterns: Robust Scalable Architecture for Real-Time Systems. Addison-Wesley, Boston (2002)
15. Object Management Group: UML Testing Profile (2005)
16. de Bruin, I.: Specification of the HIDENETS Laboratory Set-up Scenario and Components (Deliverable of the Hidenets Project – D-6.1)
17. Waeselynck, H., Micskei, Z., Nguyen, M.D., Riviere, N.: Mobile Systems from a Validation Perspective: a Case Study. In: ISPDC 2007: Proc. of the Sixth Int. Symp. on Parallel and Distributed Computing, Hagenberg, Austria, July 5–8, 2007, IEEE, Los Alamitos (2007)
18. Avizienis, A., Laprie, J., Randell, B., Landwehr, C.: Basic Concepts and Taxonomy of Dependable and Secure Computing. IEEE Transactions on Dependable and Secure Computing 1(1), 11–33 (2004)
19. Pataricza, A.: Model Based Design of Dependability. Dissertation for the Degree of Doctor of Sciences from the Hungarian Academy of Sciences (2006)
20. Tsang, E.: Foundations of Constraint Satisfaction. Academic Press, San Diego (1993)
21. Jaffar, J., Maher, M.J.: Constraint Logic Programming: A Survey. Journal of Logic Programming 19/20, 503–581 (1994)

Design, Implementation and Deployment of State Machines Using a Generative Approach

Graham N.C. Kirby, Alan Dearle, and Stuart J. Norcross

School of Computer Science, University of St Andrews,
North Haugh, St Andrews, Fife KY16 9SX, Scotland
{graham,al,stuart}@cs.st-andrews.ac.uk

Abstract. We describe an approach to designing and implementing a distributed system as a family of related finite state machines, generated from a single abstract model. Various artefacts are generated from each state machine, including diagrams, source-level protocol implementations and documentation. The state machine family formalises the interactions between the components of the distributed system, allowing increased confidence in correctness. Our methodology facilitates the application of state machines to problems for which they would not otherwise be suitable.

We illustrate the technique with the example of a Byzantine-fault-tolerant commit protocol used in a distributed storage system, showing how an abstract model can be defined in terms of an abstract state space and various categories of state transitions. We describe how such an abstract model can be deployed in a concrete system, and propose a general methodology for developing systems in this style.

1 Introduction

The finite state machine (FSM) is a widely used abstraction for describing and reasoning about distributed algorithms [1]. Here we address the problem of developing a FSM formulation for an algorithm whose generality precludes its expression as a single FSM. Instead, the algorithm may be characterised as a family of related FSMs, each corresponding to a particular value of some parameter to the general algorithm. Although family members differ in their individual states and transitions, they share a common structure dictated by the general algorithm.

Our approach is to develop an abstract model that captures the common architecture of the family of FSMs. This can be executed with chosen parameter values to generate any particular member of the FSM family. The output of the abstract model is a FSM representation, from which various concrete artefacts may be generated. These include textual FSM descriptions, FSM diagrams and source-level algorithm implementations.

This approach can also be applied to the generation of a single extended finite state machine [2,3] from the abstract model.

We describe the approach via the motivating example of a Byzantine-fault-tolerant (BFT) commit algorithm. We think that the technique could also be applied to development of other fault-tolerant protocols, making it directly relevant to the area of architecting critical infrastructures.

R. de Lemos et al. (Eds.): Architecting Dependable Systems V, LNCS 5135, pp. 175–198, 2008.
© Springer-Verlag Berlin Heidelberg 2008

2 Background

The motivation for this work arose during development of a particular algorithm within a distributed storage system [4]. The aim of the ASA project is to develop a resilient, logically ubiquitous storage infrastructure with the following attributes:

- ease of use
- operation on non-trusted platforms
- flexibility allowing users to trade-off resilience of data, performance and capacity
- scalability
- provision of an historical record of data

Several aspects of our approach follow directly from these goals. From the scalability requirement, we avoid a physically centralised architecture. From the requirement for operation on non-trusted infrastructure (i.e. Byzantine fault-tolerance), we avoid reliance on any single node behaving correctly. Thus all operations invoked by a user must be either intrinsically verifiable, or involve the agreement of multiple independent nodes.

The high-level ASA architecture is shown in Fig. 1. File system adapters connect individual user operating systems to a single distributed abstract file system, which is in turn built on a generic distributed storage layer. This storage layer is itself implemented on a peer-to-peer (P2P) key-based routing infrastructure [5], which dynamically maps a given key to a unique live node, even though nodes may join and leave the network at arbitrary times.

We have developed a P2P application framework, the purpose of which is to provide functionality useful in implementing various P2P style applications, and to abstract over the details of particular P2P protocols. This allows the P2P layer to be varied without affecting the layers above. Currently we use a Java implementation of

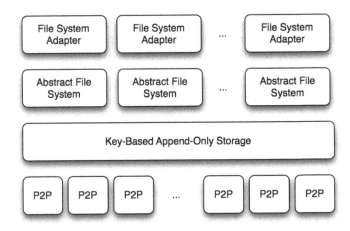

Fig. 1. Architecture of motivating distributed storage infrastructure

the Chord protocol [6]. In Chord, all participating nodes are organised into a logical circle, and messages routed around the circle. The protocol takes its name from the chords across the circle, which are additional 'short-cut' links maintained by each node, yielding routing performance that scales logarithmically with the size of the network.

The generic key-based storage layer provides resilience by replicating data and meta-data on multiple P2P nodes, and actively maintaining those replicas as nodes fail, misbehave or leave the P2P overlay.

The API presented to users by the generic storage layer does not include any destructive update operation; data can only be appended. Internal processes manage 'cleaning' of the historical record, guided by user policies controlling the trade-off between completeness of the record and consumption of resources.

The generic storage layer provides a ubiquitous resilient mutable storage facility for unstructured data, with an historical record. To support the historical record, updates are appended rather than being destructive. The main entities supported are data blocks, PIDs, and GUIDs:

- A data block contains unstructured data. Blocks have arbitrary size and are immutable.
- A PID (Persistent Identifier) is used to denote a particular data block. This might correspond to a particular version of a file, a fragment of a file, or some other object.
- A GUID (Globally Unique Identifier) is used to denote something with identity, such as a file or object.

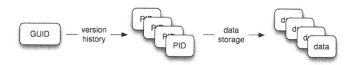

Fig. 2. Logical entities in the generic storage layer

The main algorithms operating in the generic storage layer maintain two distributed services: the data storage service (mapping a PID to an immutable data block) and the version history service (mapping a GUID to a sequence of PIDs). In each case, the service is structured as a service endpoint communicating with a set of collaborating servers. Both services are required to be Byzantine-fault-tolerant [7].

2.1 Data Storage

To store a new data block, the service endpoint calculates a unique PID for the data using a secure hashing algorithm (SHA1 [8]). It then determines which participating nodes should store replicas of the data, by applying a globally known function that deterministically generates a set of keys from a single PID. The service endpoint then uses the P2P routing layer to locate the nodes managing those keys. In the current prototype, the key generation function returns a set of keys that are evenly distributed in key space. The number of keys is determined by the data replication factor. Having located the replication nodes, referred to as the *peer set* for the data key, the service endpoint sends a copy of the data to each of the hosts. To achieve Byzantine fault tolerance, the storage operation completes once $(r-f)$ nodes have replied indicating that they have successfully stored the data, where r is the replication factor and f is the maximum number of faulty nodes that can be tolerated. In common with all Byzantine fault tolerance schemes, r must be greater than $3f$. This ensures that even if the $(r-f)$ replies include f misleading ones from faulty nodes, at least $(f+1)$ correctly functioning nodes have stored replicas of the data.

To retrieve a data block for a given PID, the replica nodes are located as above. It is then sufficient to pick a single replica node (at random, or guided by some 'closeness' metric) and request the data block from it. The secure hash function can then be used to verify that the block received does indeed correspond to the requested PID. If this check fails, another node can be tried.

2.2 Version History

The motivating example for this paper is provided by the *commit* protocol used to record a new GUID-PID mapping in the version history. The algorithm is executed by all members of the current peer set for the specified GUID; these are the nodes on which that GUID's version history is replicated.

Peer set members are located in a similar manner to that already described for the data storage service. Since the addition of a new version to the version history is an update operation, it is necessary to operate a serialisation algorithm to ensure that a globally consistent view emerges in the face of concurrent updates. Otherwise, it would be possible for different members of the peer set for a given GUID to record different orderings in the version history. This means that it is necessary for the members of each peer set to maintain contact with one another, and to adjust their views of the set membership as the topology of the P2P network changes. When a request to store a new version is received by the members of a peer set they execute a *commit* protocol amongst themselves, only completing once all have agreed which is the next version to be recorded in the global history. Again, this protocol is tolerant of Byzantine nodes in the peer set.

On retrieval of a particular version, it is not possible for the service endpoint to verify the integrity of the result from any individual member of the peer set, since there are no constraints on what PID may be mapped to by a given GUID. It is thus necessary to compare the results as they arrive from the peer set members, and to select the (only possible) one that is returned consistently by at least $f+1$ nodes.

We now sketch the operation of the *commit* protocol[1]. To simplify peer set maintenance, all members of a peer set have equal status, so that there is no need for a leader election process when membership changes. The protocol is essentially a majority voting consensus algorithm, in which peer set members vote among potentially competing update requests for the GUID. The result is an agreed ordering of the requests among all peer set members. This agreed ordering is achieved as follows:

The protocol proceeds in two phases, involving the counting of *vote* and *commit* messages among peer set members respectively. When a client issues an update for a

---

[1] Further details are available at *http://asa.cs.st-andrews.ac.uk/abstractmodel/*.

particular GUID, a request is sent to all members of the peer set for that GUID. Each peer set member votes for particular updates in the order in which it receives the requests. Voting involves sending a *vote* message to all of the other members. Once a particular candidate update receives $2f+1$ votes, all members agree that the update should be the next to be appended to the global history. This agreement is established by the exchange of *commit* messages. Consistent ordering arises since each committed update has been approved by a majority of the non-faulty members (of which there are between $2f+1$ and $3f+1$), and by allowing an update voted for by a sufficiently high number of other peer set members to proceed ahead of a previous locally selected update. Since there is no guarantee that any one of a set of concurrent updates will gain enough votes to reach this threshold, the algorithm may deadlock. It is thus necessary for the service endpoint to operate a timeout/retry scheme. Various schemes such as random or exponential back-off, or fixed or random server ordering, could be used to attempt to reduce the probability of repeated deadlocks.

The protocol is tolerant to Byzantine-faulty behaviour by members of the peer set, to the extent that at least $3f+1$ members are needed to give tolerance to f failures. Hence for a replication factor r, yielding r replicas of each version history, the protocol tolerates at most $floor((r-1)/3)$ faulty participants. Some examples of practical values for r and f are given in section 4.4.

Background processes regenerate missing replicas and replace faulty nodes, thus here the limit of f tolerable failures applies to the duration of a particular execution of the *commit* protocol, rather than to the lifetime of the system. Additional replicas need to be generated whenever the set of nodes storing replicas of a given data item is temporarily reduced. This may occur due to fail-stop faults, which are straightforwardly detected through timeouts, or due to the detection of malicious nodes. Such nodes are eventually detected, with high probability, using periodic cross-checks between replica nodes.

3 General Approach to State Machine Generation

3.1 Mapping Algorithm to State Machine

Initially, we designed a single generic algorithm that appeared to meet the requirements outlined in the previous section, parameterised by the replication factor. In an effort to gain greater insight into its operation, we then developed a FSM model for a selected replication factor—four, being the simplest scheme to yield a BFT algorithm. Although neither the algorithm (about 500 lines of pseudo-code) nor the FSM (33 states with 3-4 transitions from each) is especially complex, they are non-trivial.

The original algorithm maintains the following variables for every ongoing *commit* operation:

- *update_received*: a flag recording whether an update request for the given update has been received
- *votes_received*: a count of *vote* messages received
- *vote_sent*: a flag recording whether a *vote* message has been sent
- *commits_received*: a count of *commit* messages received
- *commit_sent*: a flag recording whether a *commit* message has been sent

- *could_choose*: a flag recording whether a future update could be voted for: this is *false* if another update is currently in progress
- *has_chosen*: a flag recording whether the update currently in progress was voted for locally.

The upper bound on both *votes_received* and *commits_received* is one less than the number of participants, which itself is given by the replication factor. Thus in total there are five boolean variables and two integer variables that range from 0 to $r-1$ for replication factor r.

In the FSM model, each peer set member maintains a separate FSM instance for every ongoing update. Each instance encodes the possible values of the variables listed above in its states. For a replication factor of 4, there are 512 possible states, comprising all combinations of 5 boolean variables and 2 integer variables ranging from 0 to 3. Of these 512 states, only 33 are actually reachable in practice. Fig. 3 shows three states and some state transitions from our original state diagram[2]. The names of the states encode the number of *votes* received, *votes* sent, *commits* received and *commits* sent. In the diagram, a transition from state *1/0/1/0* to *2/1/1/1* is triggered by the receipt of a vote message (labeled *<-vote*), since the threshold for committing has been reached (in this case 2 *votes* and 1 *commit* received); the node sends a *commit* message and moves into the state *2/1/1/1*.

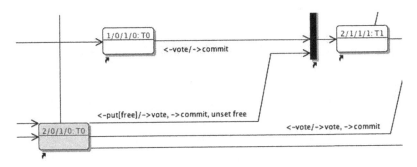

Fig. 3. Excerpt from FSM for replication factor 4

Even though we are satisfied (informally) that the FSM is correct, there is no strong correlation between the code and the FSM—thus its creation achieves little in terms of building confidence in the algorithm.

The main reason for the disparity between the FSM and the algorithm is that the former is specific to a fixed replication factor, while the algorithm is generic. The individual states in the FSM correspond to the counts of messages that have been sent and received at particular points during the algorithm's execution. The maximum values of these counts are dependent on the replication factor, thus the number of states in the FSM is also dependent on the replication factor. This implies that it is not possible to construct a single FSM that is equivalent to the generic algorithm.

---

[2] The diagram was constructed at an early stage in the design process, at which point it appeared that only four variables were necessary.

3.2 A Spectrum of Possible State Machines

In this approach, the process of transforming an algorithm to a FSM involves identifying particular ranges of values for the algorithm's internal variables, and mapping them to states. A given range corresponds to an equivalence class, in the sense that the algorithm must behave identically for all values within that range, since it maps to a single state in the FSM.

In the *commit* algorithm described, each state in the FSM corresponds to a single value for each of the discrete (boolean and integer) variables. Thus the FSM encodes in its states all possible variable values. The original algorithm and the resulting FSM may be viewed as extremes on a spectrum trading off number of states against number of variables. The original algorithm has, effectively, one state and many variables, while the FSM has many states and no variables.

Intermediate points on this spectrum are also possible. For example, extended finite state machines (EFSMs) allow transitions and actions to depend on internal variables as well as states [2,3]. In an EFSM formulation of an algorithm, the original variable values that map to a given state are not restricted to an equivalence class, since the transitions and actions from that state may depend on the internal variables. This means that an EFSM typically has fewer states than a corresponding FSM.

For a given algorithm, a FSM is likely to be simpler in structure than an EFSM, but is more likely to suffer from state space explosion. The other significant difference is that a single EFSM may be used in place of a family of related FSMs. In the main part of this paper we focus on the use of FSMs; section 5.3 compares this with the use of EFSMs, and argues that the generative approach is also beneficial for EFSMs.

3.3 Generation Process

To unify the FSM model and the generic algorithm, the FSM must be generalised in some way. The key insight is to identify how both the state space and the state transitions are determined by the replication factor. The state space is defined straightforwardly by the various combinations of the possible message counts, themselves bounded by the replication factor. For transitions, the important point is that some denote simple increments in message counts, whereas others denote actions to be performed—such as the sending of messages to other participants in the distributed algorithm. We term the latter category of transitions *phase transitions*. By identifying where in the state diagram phase transitions occur, and relating these to the replication factor, it is possible to produce a generic description defining a family of related FSMs.

For our commit algorithm, we proceeded as follows:

- We developed an abstract model that captured the common structure among the members of the FSM family.
- We executed the abstract model with a replication factor of 4 to generate an abstract representation of a specific FSM, which we then checked for consistency with the original FSM.
- Once satisfied with the correctness of the abstract model, we developed tools to generate various FSM artefacts, including diagrams and source-level implementations.

The overall generation process is illustrated in Fig. 4.

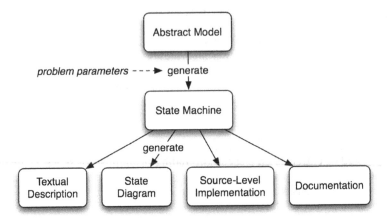

Fig. 4. State machine generation scheme

The abstract model describes the components of the states, the rules for state update on message receipt, and the actions to be carried out when particular state transitions occur. The abstract model is implemented in Java by a class *AbstractModel*. The method *generateStateMachine()* takes the replication factor as a parameter, and generates a representation of the corresponding FSM in the form of an instance of class *StateMachine*. The FSM contains a collection of states linked by transitions. Both states and transitions may be annotated for documentation purposes. Transitions also refer to associated actions to be performed by the FSM. These classes are outlined in Fig. 5.

```
class AbstractModel {
    StateMachine generateStateMachine(int replication_factor);
}
class StateMachine {
    String[] messages;
    State[] states;
    State start_state;
    State finish_state;
}
class State {
    String state_name;
    Transition[] transitions;
    String[] annotations;
}
class Transition {
    State resultant_state;
    String[] actions;
    String[] annotations;
}
```

Fig. 5. Corresponding Java classes

Fig. 6 shows an example of the use of these classes; the code fragment generates a particular FSM with replication factor 4, and uses another class, *TextRenderer*, to render it in a textual format.

```
AbstractModel abstract_model = new AbstractModel();
StateMachine machine_4 = abstract_model.generateStateMachine(4);

println(new TextRenderer().render(machine_4));
```

Fig. 6. Generating a FSM

3.4 Defining the Abstract Model

The abstract model is a model of the structure common to all members of the FSM family. The steps involved in the generation of a particular member of the family—an instance of *StateMachine*—are as follows:

1. generate a data structure containing representations of all possible states
2. for each state, generate the transitions resulting from all possible messages, and record in the data structure
3. prune any unreachable states
4. combine any sets of equivalent states

The final data structure forms the resulting *StateMachine* instance. Of these steps, *1, 3* and *4* can be performed fairly mechanically, whereas step *2* embodies the core logic of the algorithm.

Generating possible states. To generate all possible states, the state space must be defined in terms of the problem parameters—in our case, the replication factor. The state comprises the union of the 5 boolean and 2 integer variables listed in section 3.1. Hence the space of possible states, containing all combinations of values, has the size $2^5 r^2$. This gives 512 states for the smallest sensible value of $r=4$. The *generateStateMachine()* operation iterates through all of these combinations, generating a list of *State* objects. A simplified example of the data structure at this stage is shown in Fig. 7.

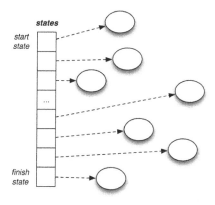

Fig. 7. Data structure after step 1

Generating transitions. The core of the abstract model defines the transitions between states. For any given state, it determines the effects of each of the possible messages, in terms of actions performed and the resulting state. Given that a state transition represents a change in the variables tracking the messages sent and received, a transition can be categorised as either a simple state transition or a phase transition.

On a simple state transition, the sole effect is to increment one of the received message counts; no action is performed. A phase transition occurs when the receipt of a message causes some threshold to be reached, triggering an action. For example, in the commit algorithm, when the total number of votes sent and received reaches the number of non-faulty nodes, a *commit* message is sent to all the nodes. Fig. 8 illustrates this distinction for an abstract state space: thin arrows show simple transitions, whereas thick arrows show phase transitions.

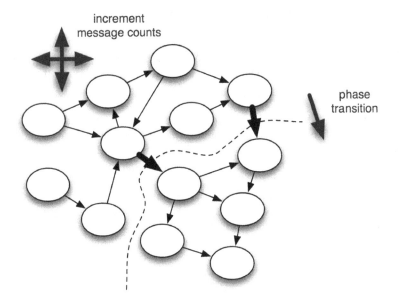

Fig. 8. Simple transitions and phase transitions

The second step in the generation of a FSM is to iterate over each of the state representations in the data structure generated during the first step. For each state, the abstract model determines which transitions would result from each of the possible messages, if received by the running FSM in that state. Each transition, along with any corresponding actions, is recorded in the FSM data structure.

Fig. 9 shows an abstract representation of the entire abstract model, which defines how the FSM should react on receipt of each of the possible messages, depending on its current state. In each case the reaction is defined in terms of reads and writes to the state variables, and outgoing messages to be sent.

```
update message
    set update_received
    if could_choose and !has_chosen and vote_sent:
        send vote message, set vote_sent, unset could_choose
        if total votes sent and received reaches threshold:
            if commit_sent:
                send commit message, set commit_sent
        set has_chosen
        send not free message

vote message
    increment corresponding count
    if total votes sent and received reaches threshold:
        if !vote_sent:
            if could_choose:
                set has_chosen, send not free message
            send vote message, set vote_sent, unset could_choose
        if commit_sent:
            send commit message, increment count

commit message
    increment corresponding count
    if total commits received reaches threshold:
        if !vote_sent:
            send vote message, set vote_sent, unset could_choose
        if commit_sent:
            send commit message, set commit_sent
        if has_chosen:
            send free
        finished

free message
    if !vote_sent and !has_chosen:
        set could_choose
        if update_received:
            send vote message, set vote_sent, unset could_choose
            if total votes sent and received reaches threshold:
                if !commit_sent:
                    send commit message, set commit_sent
            set has_chosen
            send not free message

not free message
    if !vote_sent and !has_chosen:
        unset could_choose
```

Fig. 9. Abstract model pseudo-code

The abstract model pseudo-code is now used as a guide to implementation. Fig. 10 shows the implementation of the operation *generateTransitionOnVote()*, defined within the abstract model, determining the transitions from a given state on receipt of a *vote* message[3]. The control decisions that would be taken dynamically in a generic algorithm are here being taken at generation time.

The list *actions* is used to accumulate representations of any outgoing messages to be sent as the full consequences of receiving the vote message are elaborated. Utility methods such as *targetOnVoteReceived()* and *targetOnVoteSent()* simply calculate the state reached as a result of the corresponding state variable change. A series of

---

[3] Similar logic in the abstract model generates documentation describing the states and the rationale for each transition.

```
void generateTransitionOnVote(State s) {
    List<String> actions = new ArrayList<String>();
    try {
        State s1 = targetOnVoteReceived(s, actions);
        if (reachedNonFaultyThreshold(s1.getTotalVotes())) {
            // Phase transition: vote threshold exceeded.
            if (!s1.getVoteSent()) {
                if (s1.getCouldChoose()) {
                    s1 = targetOnHasChosenSet(s1, actions);
                    s1 = targetOnNotFreeSent(s1, actions);
                }
                s1 = targetOnVoteSent(s1, actions);
            }
            if (!s1.getCommitSent()) {
                s1 = targetOnCommitSent(s1, actions);
            }
        }
        s.recordTransition(Message.VOTE, actions, s1);
    }
    catch (InvalidStateException e) {
        // Ignore - message not applicable in this state.
    }
}
```

Fig. 10. Implementation of part of abstract model

updates to the state variable *s1* generate all the required state variable changes following receipt of the *vote* message. Finally, the resulting state transition is recorded in the FSM representation of the current state, together with any necessary actions.

Fig. 11 shows the data structure after representations of the state transitions have been generated.

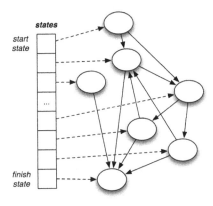

Fig. 11. Data structure after step 2

Pruning unreachable states. Once the complete transition graph has been generated, a reachability analysis is performed. Depending on the application, there may exist states that could never be reached via transitions from the start state. For example, the *commit* algorithm completes as soon as $f+1$ *commit* messages have been received, thus there are no reachable states where the *commit* count exceeds f. For simplicity, such states are removed from the generated model. With a replication factor of 4, this step reduces the state space from its initial size of 512 to 48. Fig. 12 illustrates the result of pruning.

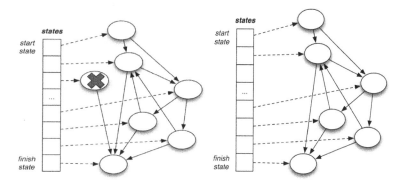

Fig. 12. Data structures before and after step 3

Combining equivalent states. The generated FSM may be further simplified by identifying and combining sets of states that are equivalent, in the sense that the outgoing transitions from each perform the same actions and lead to the same destination state. With a replication factor of 4, this process results in 33 states. Fig. 13 illustrates the result of this step.

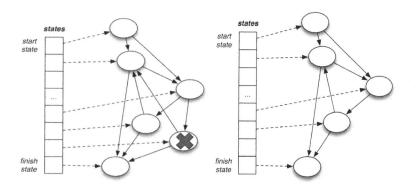

Fig. 13. Data structure before and after step 4

3.5 FSM Artefacts

The abstract representation of a FSM generated by the abstract model can be rendered to yield various concrete artefacts, including:

- a simple textual representation
- a state transition diagram
- source code for an implementation of the corresponding protocol

```
state: T/2/F/0/F/F/F
--------------------
Description:

Have received initial update from client.
Have not voted since another update has already been voted for.
Have received 2 votes and no commits.
Have not sent a commit since neither the vote threshold (3) nor the external
commit threshold (2) has been reached.
May not choose since another ongoing update has been voted for.
Have not chosen this update since another ongoing update has been chosen.
Waiting for 1 further vote (including local vote if any) before sending commit.
Waiting for 2 further external commits to finish.


Transitions:

    message: VOTE
        action: ->vote
        action: ->commit
        transition to: T/3/T/0/T/F/F


    message: COMMIT
        transition to: T/2/F/1/F/F/F


    message: FREE
        action: ->vote
        action: ->commit
        action: ->not free
        transition to: T/2/T/0/T/T/T
```

Fig. 14. Example generated state description

Fig. 14 shows the textual representation of an example state and its outgoing transitions. The name of the state encodes the variable values (*update_received*, *votes_sent* etc) in that state. The commentary describing the state in terms of the generic algorithm is entirely automatically generated, derived from annotations specified within the abstract model implementation. These annotations were omitted from Fig. 10 for brevity; in the full code, each successive assignment to the state variable $s1$ is accompanied by a call to a method that records a textual annotation describing the reason for the change. A FSM may be rendered as a state diagram by generating an XML diagram representation that can be imported into a diagramming tool (in this case, Together [9]). Fig. 15 shows an example, with a small part of the diagram magnified.

A FSM can also be rendered, automatically, as a source code implementation. Fig. 16 shows a fragment of generated code, comprising part of the handler method for incoming *vote* messages. Whenever a *vote* message for a particular GUID/PID update is received by a peer set member, the *receiveVote()* method of the corresponding FSM instance is invoked.

The body of the handler message consists of a large case switch on the current machine state, with a branch for each possible state. Each state is represented by a generated variable of the form *F-0-F-0-F-F-F*, encoding the corresponding values of the state variables. Although the structure embodied in the generated code is equivalent to

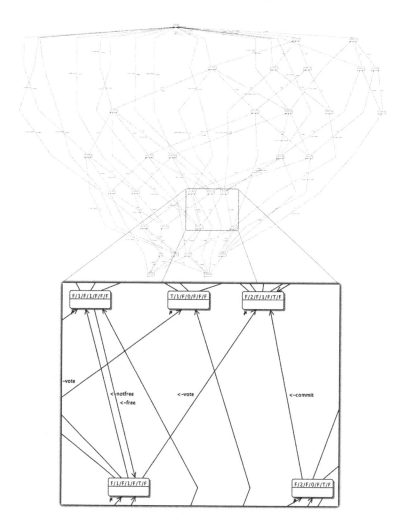

Fig. 15. Automatically rendered diagram of generated FSM

that shown in Fig. 14, its organisation differs in that all possible states are grouped under each message, rather than vice-versa.

As illustrated in all of the branches shown, the result of executing a particular branch is to move the FSM into the appropriate new state. In some branches, as illustrated in the third branch, a number of external actions are also performed—in this case, the sending of a *commit* message to the other members of the peer set. This corresponds to a phase transition.

Commentary on states and transitions, as illustrated in Fig. 14, is also included in the generated code.

```
void receiveVote() {

    switch (getState()) {

        case (F-0-F-0-F-F-F) : {
            setState(F-1-F-0-F-F-F);
            break;
        }
        case (F-0-F-0-F-F-T) : {
            setState(F-1-F-0-F-F-F);
            break;
        }
        ...
        case (T-1-T-1-F-T-T) : {
            sendCommit();
            setState(T-2-T-1-T-T-T);
            break;
        }
        ...
    }
}
```

Fig. 16. Example generated source code

4   Use in Practice

Having outlined our general approach to designing and implementing a distributed algorithm as a family of FSMs, we now discuss several practical issues:

- how to write a source code generator to produce an implementation from a FSM representation
- when to perform source code generation
- how to incorporate generated code into an application
- the execution cost of generation.

4.1   Writing Generative Code

Generative code, which produces a representation of new source code when executed, is often difficult to write and to understand. Typically, generative code involves either much hard-to-read string manipulation, or operations on an abstract syntax tree. In either case, discerning the intended structure of the generated code from the generator can be challenging.

Fig. 17 illustrates the most straightforward approach, using a string buffer to accumulate the code being generated. The code fragment shown here contains most of the logic involved in rendering a FSM as a source code implementation. It iterates through each of the message types defined for the FSM, and generates a handler method for each one. Within each handler, a case switch over all states is generated—Fig. 16 illustrates one such handler.

Such generative code is undoubtedly unwieldy. We have previously experimented with the development of GUI tools to assist with the construction of generative code [10]. Here we take a simpler approach, restricting ourselves to string manipulation,

```
for (String m : machine.getMessages()) {

    buffer.append("void receive" + m + "() {\n");
    buffer.append("    switch (getState()) {\n");

    for (State state : machine.getStates()) {

        Transition t = state.getTransition(m);

        buffer.append("        case (" +
            state.getStateName() + ") : {\n");
        buffer.append("            setState(" +
            t.getResultantState().getStateName() + ");\n");
        buffer.append("            break;\n");
        buffer.append("        }\n");
    }

    buffer.append("    }\n");
    buffer.append("}\n");
}
```

Fig. 17. Generative code for state machine implementation

```
// Adds the specified items to the output buffer.
void add(StringBuffer buffer, String... items);

// Adds the specified items to the output buffer, with newline.
void addLn(StringBuffer buffer, String... items);

// Opens a new block and increases indent level.
void enterBlock(StringBuffer buffer);

// Exits current block and decreases indent level.
void exitBlock(StringBuffer buffer);

// Increases the indent level.
void increaseIndent();

// Decreases the indent level.
void decreaseIndent();

// Resets indentation.
void resetIndent();
```

Fig. 18. Generation utility methods

with a small set of utility methods to assist with legibility of both generative and generated code, as outlined in Fig. 18.

While apparently trivial, the use of such methods makes a significant difference to
legibility, by reducing the amount of explicit string concatenation code, and by avoiding the need to control indentation of the generated code via white space defined
explicitly in the generative code. Without such simple abstractions, there is a direct
trade-off between readability of generative and generated code. Fig. 19 illustrates the
same generative code as Fig. 17, using these abstractions.

It would also be possible for generative code to manipulate an abstract syntax representation. In practice, we have found that this yields less intelligible generative
code.

```
for (String m : machine.getMessages()) {

    addLn(buffer, "void receive" + m + "()");
    enterBlock(buffer);
    addLn(buffer, "switch (getState())");
    enterBlock(buffer);

    for (State state : machine.getStates()) {

        Transition t = state.getTransition(m);

        addLn(buffer, "case (" + state.getStateName() + ") :");
        enterBlock(buffer);
        addLn(buffer, "setState(" +
            t.getResultantState().getStateName() + ");");
        addLn(buffer, "break;");
        exitBlock(buffer);
    }

    exitBlock(buffer);
    exitBlock(buffer);
}
```

Fig. 19. Generative code using simple abstractions

4.2   When to Perform Generation

Given the ability to generate on demand an implementation of a FSM solution to a distributed algorithm, for a given parameter value, there are several options as to when such generation could be performed:

- once, during the initial development of the overall application of which the solution forms part
- every time the algorithm needs to be executed
- whenever a new value of the parameter is encountered

Clearly, the appropriate point on this spectrum depends largely on the degree to which the required parameter value varies. We have incorporated a generated FSM solution for the distributed *commit* algorithm into the ASA infrastructure. Since the replication factor is expected to change only rarely, we executed the abstract model with the default replication factor, generated source code from the resulting FSM, and copied that into the code-base.

Should we wish in future to support dynamic change to the replication factor, this may be achieved by dynamically generating implementations on the fly. Since such changes are not expected to be frequent in the distributed storage application, the amortised cost of such regeneration should not be significant.

Other variants on generation policy include generating an implementation each time the application is initialised, and caching generated implementations to avoid the need for regeneration of versions that have been encountered previously [11].

4.3   Incorporation of Generated Code

For one-off generation followed by copying and pasting into an existing code base, there is no real issue regarding incorporation of generated code into the surrounding application. Once added, the generated code is treated in exactly the same way as previously existing code during the build process.

For code generated on the fly, however, it is necessary to compile, load and bind to the resulting executable code dynamically. Various approaches have been used [11-13]; more recently, Java 6 has provided explicit run-time access to the compiler [14].

4.4   Execution Cost

As indicated above, given the expected styles of use, the execution cost of generation is unlikely to be particularly important. Nonetheless, we performed a short series of measurements, for FSMs supporting various replication factors in our distributed storage application. The results are shown in Table 1, which lists the characteristics of FSMs of various complexities. The columns f and r show the degree of Byzantine-fault-tolerance and replication factor respectively. The next two columns show the numbers of states before and after pruning. The final column shows the approximate wall-clock times taken to generate the FSMs on an Apple MacBook Pro (3GB, 2.33GHz Intel Core 2 Duo).

Table 1. Times to generate state machines of various complexities

f	r	initial states	final states	generation time (s)
1	4	512	33	0.10
2	7	1568	85	0.12
4	13	5408	261	0.38
8	25	20000	901	2.2
15	46	67712	2945	19.1

The size of the initial state space, before pruning, is proportional to the square of r, the replication factor, since the state space encodes two independent variables with r legal values. The size of the final pruned state space appears to grow slightly slower than r^2. The relationship between state space size and generation time cannot be asserted with any confidence from this small sample. The pragmatic conclusion, however, is that generation time does not appear likely to be a limiting factor in the application of this technique.

We have not yet compared the execution efficiency of a running FSM implementation with that of a non-FSM solution. However, we do not expect any significant difference, given that very little computation is required to respond to an incoming message in an algorithm of the style suitable for the FSM treatment.

5   Methodology

We conclude our discussion of this approach by summarising the key features, identifying a general methodology that could be applied to problems other than the original motivating distributed storage system, and speculating on the scope of such applicability.

5.1 A General Methodology

To recap, the main steps involved in the approach, which we have illustrated in the context of the *commit* algorithm, are:

- identify the core variables used in the algorithm, which in combination define the state space
- identify the messages that can be received by a FSM
- identify the phases intrinsic to the algorithm, and the actions that should result from phase transitions
- define an abstract model that captures the state transition logic
- encode the above in the form of an abstract model implementation that can be used to generate FSMs for various parameter values
- define renderers to produce various concrete artefacts from an FSM representation, the most important of which is a source code renderer that can generate specific FSM implementations

The resulting abstract model can then be used to produce implementations as required.

Since completing the abstract modelling process for the ASA distributed *commit* algorithm, as illustrated throughout the paper, we have refined the infrastructure to make it more generic, and thus applicable to other problems. Since much of the manipulation of FSM representations is independent of the details of the algorithm being modelled, the implementation of these steps was extracted into an abstract superclass. Problem-specific abstract models can be derived from this.

Rather than containing hard-wired definitions of the state components and messages, these are now represented by a data structure with which the generic abstract model is initialised. Fig. 20 shows how the abstract model for the *commit* algorithm is now configured. Each instance of *IntComponent* defines the maximum value of the corresponding state component.

The source code renderer is now completely generic with respect to the algorithm being modelled, so it is possible to apply the methodology to new algorithms without writing any new generative code. The rendering code is parameterised with a class defining appropriate action methods, such as *sendCommit()* in Fig. 16. The generated class inherits from this specified class, allowing it to access the action methods.

```
StateComponent[] state_components = {
  new IntComponent("votes_received",
    replication_factor - 1),
  new IntComponent("commits_received",
    replication_factor - 1),
  new BooleanComponent("update_received"),
  new BooleanComponent("vote_sent"),
  new BooleanComponent("commit_sent"),
  new BooleanComponent("could_choose"),
  new BooleanComponent("has_chosen")};

String[] messages = {"update", "vote",
  "commit", "free", "not_free"};

initAbstractModel(state_components, messages);
```

Fig. 20. Initialising generic abstract model

5.2 Applicability of the Methodology

We believe that the technique of generating FSM families is applicable to a range of distributed applications that can be broadly characterised as *message counting algorithms*. There are a number of different algorithms that may be characterised in this manner including consensus algorithms, distributed termination algorithms, distributed garbage collection algorithms, and threshold signature algorithms.

The algorithm with which we demonstrated the technique in this paper is essentially a consensus algorithm. Perhaps the best known consensus algorithm is that proposed by Chandra and Toueg [15]. In that algorithm, each of n processes counts rounds with a rotating coordinator. In each round, the participants and the coordinator exchange beliefs upon which they are trying to agree. Each process maintains three pieces of state: the actual *decision*, a *counter* storing the round number, a *belief* containing an estimate of the decision and the round number in which the decision was made. Like the algorithm described in this paper, the state held at each node and the messages themselves are relatively simple and amenable to being processed by a FSM.

A distributed computation may be defined as being terminated when each process in it has locally terminated and no messages are in transit. Alternately this may be defined as when the number of messages sent is equal to the number of messages received [16]. Consequently, most distributed termination algorithms are based upon message counting. Furthermore, the state carried in both the messages and held by the processes is relatively simple. We therefore believe that the techniques described in this paper may be applied to such algorithms.

Tel and Mattern [17] have shown that at least one distributed termination algorithm can be automatically derived from a distributed garbage collection algorithm. In [18], Blackburn *et al* demonstrate the reverse mapping, that is the combination of any known distributed termination algorithm with a centralised garbage collector to produce a distributed garbage collector. It is therefore unsurprising that we believe that the technique described here can also be applied to distributed garbage collection. However, the problems of doing so may outweigh the benefits. In [18] an algorithm called *task balancing* is described, in which each site counts (a) the number of tasks of each job sent by each site to each other site, and (b) the number of tasks received by and completed at each site. The encoding of such data structures in a FSM, even one that has been mechanically derived, may prove overly complex due to an explosion in the state space. In such cases, EFSMs may be useful, as discussed in the next section.

5.3 Generating Extended Finite State Machines

As mentioned briefly earlier, the process of mapping an algorithm to a state machine formulation can be thought of as involving a spectrum of target state machines. At one end of the spectrum lies the original algorithm, viewed as a state machine with a single state and multiple internal variables. At the other end lies the FSM or family of FSMs, with multiple states and no internal variables. At intermediate points lie various EFSMs, with a number of internal variables and fewer states than the FSMs. The designer selects an appropriate point on this spectrum through decisions on which variables in the original algorithm should be mapped to variables in the state machine, and which should be encoded in the state space.

The *commit* protocol can be implemented as an EFSM in which the message counting variables are mapped to EFSM variables. The effect is to coalesce the states within each state phase of the original FSM, so that all state transitions in the EFSM correspond to phase transitions in the FSM. For example, all of the FSM states that differ only in the number of *vote* messages below the threshold become a single EFSM state. The resulting EFSM contains 9 states.

Besides the reduction in state space size, the other benefit of the EFSM formulation in this example is that the EFSM is generic with respect to the replication factor. Its states do not encode the values of the message counts, the possible values of which depend on the replication factor, but simply whether or not they have reached their respective thresholds. The state space of the EFSM is thus not dependent on the replication factor.

Nonetheless, it is not straightforward to construct the EFSM in this example. It appears that it may still be beneficial to use a similar approach to that outlined for FSMs, defining an abstract model and then generating an EFSM from it.

6 Related Work

This work is obviously strongly related to the extensive literature on FSMs, for example [1,19]. Traditional FSMs are used to model computations with fixed numbers of states. EFSMs [2] permit greater flexibility, by allowing transitions to depend on internal variables.

[3] describes the generation of FSMs from abstract state machines, in which the states of an abstract state machine are grouped into hyperstates, corresponding to FSM states. The algorithm is approximate in that some links or states may be missing; since the method is targeted at very large state spaces this is an acceptable trade-off for tractability.

Architectural style languages [20,21] allow families of related systems to be characterised in terms of their shared high level system structure, and specialised to produce particular instances. The work described here is less general since it focuses explicitly on the FSM paradigm; the generic abstract model could be thought of as one particular architectural style.

We have previously used generative techniques to build generic object browsers [11] and to support highly generic strongly typed code [12].

An alternative strategy is to apply formal specification and verification techniques to fault-tolerant algorithms. For example, in [22] a protocol is specified as logical assertions and verified using an interactive proof checker. In [23] an extended actor algebra is used to specify fault-tolerant software architectures. These approaches offer the possibility of formal proofs, whereas here we intend to provide a less formal aid to understanding, at significantly lower cost.

7 Conclusions

We have outlined an approach to generating an EFSM, or a family of related FSMs, and corresponding protocol implementations from a unifying abstract model. In the ASA project this has allowed us to produce a FSM style description of our original BFT distributed commit algorithm. This has increased our confidence in the correctness of the algorithm; indeed several errors in the original version were identified during the process.

We have applied this approach to a specific BFT distributed algorithm, and believe the approach to be applicable to other critical infrastructure problems involving message-counting protocols where the number of states is dependent on a set of parameters.

Acknowledgments

This work was supported by EPSRC grant GR/S44501/01 and by a Royal Society of Edinburgh / Scottish Executive Support Research Fellowship. Markus Tauber and Rob MacInnis contributed to the development of the distributed commit algorithm.

References

1. Minsky, L.M.: Computation: Finite and Infinite Machines. Prentice Hall, Englewood Cliffs (1967)
2. Cheng, K.T., Krishnakumar, A.S.: Automatic Functional Test Generation using the Extended Finite State Machine Model. In: 30th Design Automation Conference, Dallas, Texas, pp. 86–91. ACM, New York (1993)
3. Grieskamp, W., Gurevich, Y., Schulte, W., Veanes, M.: Generating Finite State Machines from Abstract State Machines. ACM SIGSOFT Software Engineering Notes 27(4), 112–122 (2002)
4. Kirby, G.N.C., Dearle, A., Norcross, S.J., Tauber, M., Morrison, R.: Secure Location-Independent Storage Architectures (ASA) (2004),
   http://asa.cs.standrews.ac.uk/
5. Dabek, F., Zhao, B.Y., Druschel, P., Kubiatowicz, J., Stoica, I.: Towards a Common API for Structured Peer-to-Peer Overlays. In: Kaashoek, M.F., Stoica, I. (eds.) IPTPS 2003. LNCS, vol. 2735. Springer, Heidelberg (2003)
6. Stoica, I., Morris, R., Karger, D., Kaashoek, F., Balakrishnan, H.: Chord: A Scalable Peer-to-Peer Lookup Service for Internet Applications. In: ACM SIGCOMM 2001, San Diego, CA, USA, pp. 149–160 (2001)
7. Lamport, L., Shostak, R., Pease, M.: The Byzantine Generals Problem. ACM Transactions on Programming Languages and Systems 4(3), 382–401 (1982)
8. Eastlake, D., Jones, P.: RFC 3174 - US Secure Hash Algorithm 1 (SHA1) (2001),
   http://www.faqs.org/rfcs/rfc3174.html
9. Borland: Borland Together (2007),
   http://www.borland.com/us/products/together/

10. Kirby, G.N.C., Connor, R.C.H., Morrison, R.: START: A Linguistic Reflection Tool using Hyper-Program Technology. In: Persistent Object Systems: 6th International Workshop on Persistent Object Systems (POS6), Tarascon, France. Workshops in Computing, pp. 355–373. Springer, Heidelberg (1994)

11. Dearle, A., Brown, A.L.: Safe Browsing in a Strongly Typed Persistent Environment. Computer Journal 31(6), 540–544 (1988)

12. Kirby, G.N.C., Morrison, R., Stemple, D.W.: Linguistic Reflection in Java. Software - Practice & Experience 28(10), 1045–1077 (1998)

13. Kirby, G.N.C.: Dynamic Java Compiler (2005),
    `http://www-systems.cs.st-andrews.ac.uk/wiki/`
    `Dynamic_Java_Compiler`

14. Sun Microsystems: JavaCompiler Interface (2007),
    `http://java.sun.com/javase/6/docs/api/javax/tools/`
    `JavaCompiler.html`

15. Chandra, T., Toueg, S.: Unreliable Failure Detectors for Reliable Distributed Systems. Journal of the ACM 43(1), 225–267 (1996)

16. Mattern, F.: Algorithms for Distributed Termination Detection. Distributed Computing 2(3), 161–175 (1987)

17. Tel, G., Mattern, F.: The Derivation of Distributed Termination Detection Algorithms from Garbage Collection Schemes. ACM Transactions on Programming Languages and Systems 15(1), 1–35 (1993)

18. Blackburn, S.M., Hudson, R.L., Morrison, R., Moss, J.E.B., Munro, D.S., Zigman, J.N.: Starting with Termination: A Methodology for Building Distributed Garbage Collection Algorithms. In: 24th Australasian Computer Science Conference (ACSC 2001), Gold Coast, Queensland, pp. 20–28 (2001)

19. Brand, D., Zafiropulo, P.: On Communicating Finite-State Machines. Journal of the ACM 30(2), 323–342 (1983)

20. Garlan, D., Allen, R.J., Ockerbloom, J.: Exploiting Style in Architectural Design Environments. In: 2nd ACM SIGSOFT Symposium on Foundations of Software Engineering, New Orleans, Louisiana, USA, pp. 175–188 (1994)

21. Medvidovic, N., Taylor, R.N.: A Classification and Comparison Framework for Software Architecture Description Languages. IEEE Transactions on Software Engineering 26(1), 70–93 (2000)

22. Hooman, J.: Verification of Distributed Real-Time and Fault-Tolerant Protocols. In: Johnson, M. (ed.) AMAST 1997. LNCS, vol. 1349. Springer, Heidelberg (1997)

23. Dragoni, N., Gaspari, M.: An Object Based Algebra for Specifying a Fault Tolerant Software Architecture. Journal of Logic and Algebraic Programming 63, 271–297 (2005)

Handling Emergent Nondeterminism in Replicated Services

Joseph Slember and Priya Narasimhan

Carnegie Mellon University, Pittsburgh PA 15213, USA
`jslember@ece.cmu.edu, priya@cs.cmu.edu`

Abstract. When distributed applications are replicated for fault tolerance, the presence of even a single nondeterministic service can lead to emergent system-wide nondeterminism that compromises replica consistency. Our approach, Midas identifies and addresses multiple sources of nondeterminism (including system calls, multithreading, etc.) in a multi-service replicated distributed architecture. Midas involves a synergistic combination of compile-time dependency, concurrency and nondeterminism analyses, followed by the performance-sensitive compensation of nondeterminism at runtime. This approach upholds existing application semantics and allows services to continue to be nondeterministic, while yet maintaining their replicas consistent. We demonstrate Midas' scalability through a microbenchmark that shows the underlying trade-offs under different kinds of dependencies between clients, services and invocations in a distributed system. We also validate our claims by modeling a representative multi-service application using Java Pathfinder.

1 Introduction

Distributed applications are moving from the realm of simple, client-server applications to larger, more complex, multi-service applications. Most enterprise applications are of this multi-service nature, often composed of a series of interconnected services (e.g., web servers, file servers, name servers, storage servers, auction services, database servers) that together process a client's request. Even in peer-to-peer applications, a request can traverse multiple distributed entities, each of which can be regarded as a service, before a response is returned to the requestor.

Each constituent service is typically developed independently, but is combined with other services to form larger, more complex, and often more useful, distributed applications. When invoked, a service can, in turn, dispatch a request to another service, which can invoke yet another service, and so on, leading to a variety of inter-service dependencies and communication patterns. Additional emergent interactions and configurations of the distributed application can arise when multiple (seemingly independent) clients (entities in their own right, but that never proffer any services within the system) are thrown into the mix.

A common way to provide fault-tolerance for these kinds of applications is to replicate the critical components, i.e., the services, in the system. When replication is superimposed on a multi-service, distributed application, the complexity

R. de Lemos et al. (Eds.): Architecting Dependable Systems V, LNCS 5135, pp. 199–224, 2008.

of the system increases further. One of the major challenges in dealing with replication is ensuring that the replicas of each service remain consistent in state and behavior during that service's execution.

1.1 Nondeterminism: The Bane of Consistent Replication

A service can be considered to be deterministic (from a replication-centric viewpoint) if different replicas of the service, when starting from the same initial state and fed the same set of input messages, reach the same final state and produce the same output. Clearly, determinism is essential to consistent replication, and lack of determinism (or *nondeterminism*) can lead to replica divergence, thereby compromising fault-tolerance. Common nondeterministic features include multithreading, local timers, system calls, etc.

Most practical systems deal with the requirement of determinism through one of three possible strategies: (i) eliminating all nondeterminism within each service prior to replication, thereby altering the original intent of the application programmer by producing a new version of each service with altered semantics, (ii) using special replication styles, like primary-backup replication [9], effectively eliminating state-machine replication [16] as a choice for nondeterministic services; we argue why even a primary-backup replication strategy is not proof against nondeterministic side-effects in a multi-service setting, or (iii) transparently forcing synchronization between replicas on every system call, requiring them to coordinate effects on their respective states and their outputs; while this is effective, it can be overkill, if potential sources of nondeterminism do not actually manifest into replica divergence.

1.2 Midas in a Nutshell

Our approach, Midas, focuses on handling nondeterminism of all forms (multithreading, system calls, etc.) for multi-service distributed applications that employ replication for fault tolerance. These applications can cause emergent nondeterminism due to the possibility of just a single service's nondeterminism percolating to other (perhaps otherwise deterministic) services, simply due to the dependencies and communication among the services.

If a service employs state-machine replication, each replica actively processes the same ordered set of incoming requests and updates its local state identically, without needing to consult with its fellow replicas. This continuous, automatic maintenance of consistency across replicas is advantageous because it provides for rapid failover and also masks single-replica failures from clients. However, state-machine replication obviously requires the service to be deterministic so that its replicas are all identical in behavior and state and can, therefore, collectively provide a fault-tolerant version of the service. Thus, state-machine replication and nondeterminism are often considered to be mutually exclusive design choices.

We postulate that consistent replication can be achieved for distributed applications consisting of multiple, interconnected, nondeterministic services, where each service can employ state-machine replication for fault tolerance. Midas' inter-disciplinary approach exploits program analysis to address the problems of distributed fault tolerance. We leverage the compile-time static analysis of multi-service applications to reveal insights that enable the subsequent runtime compensation of any nondeterminism within the application. The inherent value of Midas lies not only in its ability to identify, and prepare for, any nondeterminism ahead of deployment, but also in its ability to handle nondeterminism, without compromising fault tolerance, regardless of the number of services or clients within the application.

1.3   Contributions

Cross-service dependency analysis: Our analysis extracts the dependencies that can arise between services, clients and requests. While this analysis helps to handle nondeterminism, a side-benefit is that it produces a concurrency model of the application's architecture that can be useful in other situations (e.g., orchestrating application upgrades). This model allows us to understand how dependencies affect concurrency (and, therefore, multithreading-induced nondeterminism) at different levels of the system.

Forward and backward nondeterminism: We address the "contamination", or propagation, of nondeterminism across services, distinguishing between forward and backward nondeterminism. In a service, forward nondeterminism can occur prior to the service issuing a request (thereby potentially contaminating the request), and backward nondeterminism can occur prior to the service returning a reply (thereby potentially contaminating the reply). Identifying the two types of nondeterminism, as well as their co-dependencies, allows us to minimize the amount of work that needs to be performed to handle the ensuing nondeterminism.

Formal model: We formally model our approach for a relatively simple multi-service application using Java Pathfinder. We demonstrate that our compile-time modifications do not alter the programmer's semantics and that our runtime compensation does indeed address nondeterminism without compromising fault tolerance.

Experimental evaluation: We design and implement a variety of performance-sensitive techniques for the runtime compensation of nondeterminism: these range from the transfer of the entire checkpoint of a service's replica to its fellow replicas at strategic points in execution, to the selective re-execution of code at the fellow replicas. Through a multi-service microbenchmark, we evaluate the overheads, the scalability, and underlying trade-offs of compensation in the face of different amounts/types of nondeterminism, and dependencies among clients and services.

2   Problem Description

Figure 1 illustrates the progressive complexity that can arise when multiple services, clients and replication are added to a distributed application. Consider

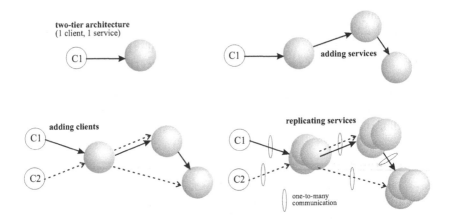

Fig. 1. Increasing application-level complexity with services, clients and replication added

a single client in a multi-service, non-replicated application. Suppose that the client invokes the first service, which then invokes a second service, and so on, until all of the services in the system are utilized in some fashion. Thus, the client's original request is fulfilled by the entire collection of services, with each service performing some amount of processing before issuing its own request to the next needed service.

We can view this as an *end-to-end operation* originating at the client and spanning all of the services, and that can be decomposed into individual requests between pairs of services. We call this the forward, or downstream, request-path (client → service 1 → service 2 → ...). The operation unfolds in the reverse direction: the final service to receive a request sends a reply to its invoking service, which then replies, in turn, to its invoking service, and so on, until the client ultimately receives a reply to its original request. There is, thus, a corresponding backward, or upstream reply-path (client ← service 1 ← service 2 ← ...).

Neither the client nor any of the services is required to be synchronous, i.e., blocked while waiting for a response. Also, there can be any number of distinct requests between a pair of services due to the overall end-to-end operation. For instance, a service receiving an incoming request can make several requests of, and receive/process the corresponding replies from, another service before responding, in its turn, to its invoking service.

Contamination can occur if a service's nondeterminism somehow propagates, through service-level or request-level interactions, potentially rendering some other service nondeterministic. Multiple clients serve to aggravate this situation because each client likely issues its end-to-end operations concurrently with and independent of other clients; however, the mixture of requests and replies from different clients in progress at a service can lead to increased multi-threading, and an increase in the number of possible scenarios to consider for handling nondeterminism. Effectively, the *emergent leakage of a service's nondeterminism into other services, requests and replies* can make it difficult to handle nondeterminism in a scalable way. A secondary effect of contamination is that, even if with only one nondeterministic service in the system, we cannot completely rule out the possibility of other (otherwise deterministic) services becoming nondeterministic, without sufficient analysis of the application.

Superimposing service replication on this picture, as shown in Figure 1, only serves to render it all the more complex. With the state-machine replication of a service X, more communication ensues because every replica processes, responds and issues every request. If X has 3 replicas (say, X_1, X_2, X_3), then, each time that X issues a request, there will be 3 distinct copies of the same request, one from each replica. Add to this the fact that each replica's request can be nondeterministic and differ from those of its fellow replicas, i.e., the content of the same request from the 3 replicas can be different because each replica's respective nondeterminism might impact the outgoing request. Any other service, Y, that now communicates with replicated service X will typically select and process the first-received request from X's replicas, and discard the corresponding requests from the other replicas of X. Thus, Y's nondeterminism past this point can be influenced by that replica of X whose request was selected by Y. The same replica might not be selected the next time around that Y hears again from X; the selected replica is always the one whose request makes it to Y ahead of all of its fellow replicas' corresponding requests. Now, if Y is also replicated, it is easy to see how a third service, Z, that communicates with Y might be influenced by X's nondeterminism.

Primary-backup replication [9] is often considered to alleviate the difficulties posed by nondeterminism in the case of state-machine replication. With primary-backup replication, a designated primary replica processes all of the requests and replies, and synchronizes itself with its backup replicas by periodically transferring checkpoints of its state to them. One advantage is only a single replica of a service is processing all requests/replies and we do not need to worry about inconsistencies across replicas in the fault-free case. However, given the possible propagation of nondeterminism through service-level dependencies, to ensure consistency, great care must be exercised in checkpointing. For instance, checkpoints cannot necessarily be taken independently at the primary replica of any service without sufficient consideration of the remaining services in the system. Another concern arises when faults occur that require the election of a new primary replica of a service – in these cases, nondeterminism can leak to communicating services.

In this paper, we focus specifically on the consistent state-machine replication of services where emergent nondeterministic behavior arises when services interact. The challenges of consistent primary-backup replication and Midas' support for consistent coordinated checkpoints without system-wide blocking, even under failures, is outside the scope of this paper. That work is likely the subject of a future submission.

2.1 Objectives

We expect our approach to exhibit certain properties. The **required properties** of our solution include:

- *Dependency tracking:* Because of the nature of the dependencies across services and requests in the kinds of applications that we target, we require our solution to extract dependency and concurrency information from the application.
- *Independence of replication style:* We require our solution to be equally applicable to both state-machine and primary-backup replication, although we refrain from a detailed discussion of the latter due to lack of space.
- *Unmodified application semantics:* We require our solution to retain the application's intended semantics, i.e., the handling of nondeterminism should not affect the expected semantic behavior of the application. Nondeterminism should be allowed to continue to exist within the application. We note that our approach might affect the timing, but not the logical, behavior of the application.
- *Generic:* We require our solution to handle all known forms of nondeterminism, including multithreading and system calls.

The **desired properties** of our solution include:

- *Scalability:* Increasing the number of services and clients increases the amount of nondeterminism and the dependencies that need to be considered. We desire our solution to be scalable with respect to the number of services and clients, i.e., our solution should ideally display a linear behavior in compensation performance with increasing number of clients or services.
- *Sustain concurrency:* Although concurrency can lead to nondeterminism, we desire our solution to permit as much concurrency as the application programmer wishes.

2.2 Assumptions and Limitations

We assume that we have access to all of the source code of the distributed application. This is required for us to determine all of the cross-service and cross-request dependencies, as well as the nondeterminism and state at the application level. We assume that all of these dependencies and state can be identified through static analysis. This implies that dynamic functionality (such as dynamic memory allocation, pointers to functions, pointer aliasing, etc.) that might affect nondeterministic state or dependencies cannot be handled in our current implementation of Midas. We have, however, begun to incorporate some support for dynamic functionality into our framework and can currently perform basic pointer aliasing analysis as well as dynamic memory allocation. These restrictions or limitations typically do not affect Java applications as much as C++ applications. It is important to note that Midas is inherently pessimistic. It marks all state and execution as nondeterministic and works to ascertain that which is deterministic. Reflection is one of the one features of a Java application that causes Midas problems with efficiency. However, the use of reflection is typically rare. Additionally, we require the ability to modify the application's source code to track and compensate for the nondeterminism.

While we target application/service-level nondeterminism in this paper, we can just as well extend our compile-time analyses to include other architectural layers as well (as in our recent work on identifying middleware-level nondeterminism [17]). We note that our approach currently covers all of the operating-system libraries loaded by the application at compile-time. Additionally, since we do consider nondeterminism due to thread scheduling, our approach also compensates for this source of nondeterminism due to the operating system.

We assume that all of the services within the application are replicated. Our fault hypothesis is restricted to process- and node-crashes, and message-loss faults. We assume that replicas and nodes fail independently. Malicious, or arbitrary, faults are outside our current scope.

3   Application-Level Insights for Scalability

We define two new abstractions, slivers and compensation service-pairs, that allow us to handle nondeterminism between immediately communicating services, rather than across the entire set of services in the system. This allows our approach to scale and also ensures that nondeterminism does not spread rampant throughout the system, but rather, is contained between communicating services.

3.1   Slivers

As described in Section 2, a service's nondeterminism can leak due to its emergent interactions with other services. To regain some level of leakage containment in order to handle nondeterminism scalably, we propose splitting up the work done at any service into sequential blocks of execution that we call *slivers*. A service will typically execute the following sequence multiple different times: (1) receiving an incoming request from an upstream service, (2) some post-request processing that might lead to execution and local state changes, (3) dispatching an outgoing (nested) request to some downstream service, (4) receiving incoming replies for requests sent in the previous step, (5) some post-reply processing that might lead to additional execution and local state changes, and (6) dispatching an outgoing reply to the upstream service that issued the request in step 1.

Steps 3, 4 and 5 might repeat several times before step 6 is finally executed. For simplicity, assume that only one downstream request is made (i.e., steps 3, 4 and 5 occur only once, followed by step 6). We propose decomposing these execution blocks and state into multiple sequences that make intuitive sense from the viewpoint of handling nondeterminism. The sequence {1, 2, 3} represents forward state/execution or a forward sliver, while the sequence {4, 5, 6} represents backward/execution or a backward sliver. The associated nondeterminism due to the forward and backward sliver is labeled, respectively, as forward or backward nondeterminism.

Now, assume that steps 3, 4 and 5 execute twice back-to-back because of two nested requests from the service to yet another service. We denote the two corresponding sub-sequences as {3a, 4a, 5a} and {3b, 4b, 5b}, giving us an overall sequence of {1, 2, 3a, 4a, 5a, 3b, 4b, 5b, 6} at the service. Thus, there will exist two forward slivers in this case, {1, 2, 3a} and {4a, 5a, 3b}, and one backward sliver, {4b, 5b, 6}.

The sliver abstraction affords us advantages that will be made apparent in Section 4.5. The sliver can be regarded as a basic unit of encapsulation of nondeterminism – leveraging this abstraction, we can compensate for nondeterminism on a local, sliver-wise basis rather than on a global scale.

3.2   Compensation Service-Pairs

For the purpose of compensation, we also propose to group a service with its communicating services. The idea is to have the basic unit of compensation span a pair of communicating services so that the nondeterminism compensation becomes tractable. This proves far less complex then allowing nondeterminism to leak, unchecked, from one service to the next, and then trying to unravel the dependencies and inconsistencies on a global scale.

Assume that we have a four-service application, $C \rightleftarrows S1 \rightleftarrows S2 \rightleftarrows S3 \rightleftarrows S4$, where the client C1 first invokes service S1; the end-to-end operation travels downstream through S2, S3 and finally to S4. The corresponding replies make their way back to the client, from one service to the next, in the reverse/upstream direction. In this case, the compensation service-pairs are (S1, S2), (S2, S3), and (S3, S4). S2 is a member of two different compensation service-pairs because it dispatches downstream requests and upstream replies. If S2 also made a direct downstream request to S4, there would be an additional compensation service-pair, (S2, S4). We distinguish between forward-compensation service-pairs and backward-compensation service-pairs depending on whether the compensation action is due to the execution of a forward or a backward sliver, respectively. Thus, for downstream requests, we consider forward-compensation service-pairs, while for upstream replies, we consider backward-compensation service-pairs.

Thus, for an end-to-end operation in a distributed multi-service setting, if n individual requests are made between services to fulfill the overall end-to-end operation, there will exist n compensation service-pairs. Note that this definition is indifferent to the number of actual distinct requests between the services that form a pair.

4   Midas' Implementation

The handling of nondeterminism occurs in two phases. The first phase involves identifying the various sources of nondeterminism and the slivers at each service. This is done through Midas' compile-time analysis framework described in Section 4.1. The subsequent phase involves using Midas' runtime technique to compensate for any state divergence across a service's replicas. Section 4.5 describes how our performance-sensitive compensation techniques accomplish this phase.

4.1 Compile-Time Analysis Framework

Midas supports consistent fault-tolerance for any C++ or Java distributed application; our only additional piece of infrastructure, described in Section 4.3, is an underlying reliable, totally ordered group communication protocol to convey the application's messages. Our initial work involved converting C++ applications to C-based equivalents to render them amenable to static analysis; the limitations of converting from C++ to C, and then reannotating the information lost in the conversion was time-consuming, extensive and possibly incomplete, depending on the complexity of the C++ application.

Recognizing these drawbacks, we have redesigned our current Midas framework so that it no longer needs to convert applications from C++ to C in order to perform its analysis. The entire analytical framework centers around a custom handwritten C++ compiler front-end that converts C++ source code into a variation of an abstract syntax tree (AST). More specifically, we perform parsing on the source code. Our lexical analysis breaks the source code up into tokens that are then fed into our syntax analysis to ensure that the token stream forms a correct sequence according to our grammar. We do not generate code from the extracted AST. The output of the syntax analysis is a parse tree.

More specifically, we built an LALR(1) parser with little shift/reduce or reduce/reduce error. The grammar that we used is an updated version of the ANSI C++-compliant grammar ([10]) that was proposed as a standard and we did not encounter any issues with the applications that we ran through our parser. We could use a more complex GNU C++ front-end for this process. The parse-tree generation is fairly straight forward and the details are omitted here for lack of space.

The parse-tree is stripped of all non-semantic information for ease of use, effectively rendering it an AST. We now perform semantic analysis and annotate the tree heavily with this information. Several passes are made over the tree in order to gain information for identifying/handling nondeterminism (see Section 4.2) and for dependency/concurrency analysis (see Section 4.6).

4.2 Identifying Nondeterminism

We regard pure nondeterminism as any execution or state that is the direct, or root, source of nondeterminism, e.g., system calls like `gettimeofday` and shared state among threads. Contaminated nondeterminism covers any execution or state that is "touched" by pure nondeterminism or other contaminated nondeterminism. We need to identify the various sources of nondeterminism, as well as the extent to which nondeterminism has pervaded the application. Given our extracted parse-tree, we perform control-flow analysis over the entire tree to determine all of the possible control paths. We perform data-flow analysis to determine which variables are dependent on each other. The data- and control-flow analyses are combined to form dependency annotations that are control-flow dependent.

The first analysis pass over each end-to-end invocation is special. It actually splits up the application source-code into different segments that directly correspond to the forward and backward slivers described in Section 3.1. For each service, all of the external invocations are first identified, followed by the identification of forward and backward slivers. Recall that, in response to an incoming downstream request I, a service can issue one or more outgoing (nested) requests O_1, O_2, ... to other services, and receive replies R_1, R_2, ..., respectively, from them. Forward slivers at a service can encapsulate the following: (i) the execution and state between $\{I, ..., O_1\}$, i.e., between the incoming downstream request I and the first ensuing nested request O_1, or (ii) execution and state between $\{R_1, ..., O_2\}$, $\{R_2, ..., O_3\}$, etc., i.e., between the reply from a service and the next nested request that immediately follows. The concept of forward slivers does not distinguish whether a service makes requests O_1, O_2, etc. to a downstream or an upstream service.

This analysis pass, in essence, builds a call-path for the distributed application, mapping out all of the potential paths involved in an end-to-end operation. Note that there does not exist a one-to-one mapping between slivers and requests. It is possible for a single sliver to lead to multiple requests, e.g., through the repeated execution of a loop. At the same time, because our analysis examines all of the possible control paths that are possible at a service, we might identify multiple possible slivers for a downstream request. Ultimately, only one of these slivers will ever execute at runtime based on the control path chosen then. However, to account for all of the possibilities, our analysis will identify all of the possible resulting slivers.

The next pass over the parse tree discovers all of the sources of pure nondeterminism within each sliver. These include system calls involving local timers, hostname or anything that is node-specific, and all of the shared state between threads at a service. We treat inter-thread shared state in a special way – each access to a shared state-variable by a thread is considered to be a separate source of nondeterminism. For example, consider a single shared variable between two threads; if each thread accesses this variable four times, then, there exist eight separate instances of pure nondeterministic state. It is immaterial that these eight instances happen to revolve around the same variable. This view of inter-thread shared state frees us from having to worry about thread interleaving or when the thread actually executes. This would apply also to system calls that might be used repeatedly in a loop.

Once all of the pure nondeterminism within each sliver has been identified, we perform several recursive passes to find all of the state "touched" by the pure nondeterministic sources, and consider these to be contaminated nondeterminism. Any state that is then touched by that contaminated state is also marked as contaminated. Once all of the contaminated and pure nondeterminism have been identified and marked, dynamic data structures are built to store just the pure nondeterminism or both the pure+contaminated nondeterminism, depending on the specific compensation technique (of those described in Section 4.5) that we elect to use. We instrument the source code to track this nondeterministic state and execution, and copy it to the data structures at runtime. We employ dynamic data structures because different control-flow paths can be taken depending on the request.

We also add code to enable the runtime decision of whether or not a service requires either the compensation of nondeterminism or the application of a supplied checkpoint. The trickiest part of handling nondeterminism is the creation of the code-snippets that recreate nondeterministic state at run-time. This is discussed in later chapters.

4.3   Runtime Replication Infrastructure

Our approach handles the issues of nondeterminism for consistent replication in fault-tolerant applications. However, there are other requirements for consistent replication – reliable, totally ordered delivery of messages to replicas, duplicate detection and suppression, etc.

Total order guarantees that all of the replicas of a service will see the same set of messages in the same order. Reliable delivery guarantees that messages sent by a service will not be lost. We leverage the open-source Spread group communication protocol [3] to obtain the total ordering and reliable delivery guarantees. The additional overhead of Spread can be quite significant and is typically dependent on the number of replicas in a Spread group. Spread has a very simple interface and wrappers can be used to make it transparent to the application above. It is quite common to demand totally ordered, reliable delivery of messages. In any fault-tolerant distributed system, that is not using a cold-passive technique, it is required.

Because we focus on state-machine replication, a replicated service will lead to multiple duplicate requests and replies, one from each of its replicas. For example, when a three-way replicated service X invokes a two-way replicated service Y, each of Y's replicas will receive three requests, one from each of X's replicas; on the return path, each of X's replicas will receive two replies, one from each of Y's replicas. Clearly, we cannot allow X's/Y's replicas to process the duplicate messages, or their states will be wrong (unless the operations are idempotent).

At every receiving replica, we dispatch the first-received unique message (request or reply) to the replica, and drop any duplicates of the dispatched message using identification information that we embed in the messages. This identification takes the form of four pieces of information, {service-id, request-id, callback-id, client-id}. If these four numbers are identical for any two received messages, they are duplicates of each other in a semantic sense.

The duplicate detection-suppression process introduces other considerations for nondeterminism. Given that every replica can differ from its fellow replicas (due to the nondeterminism that we allow to exist at the application), every replica's outgoing request/reply will differ from that of its fellow replicas' counterparts. In the example above, X's replicas (X_1, X_2 and X_3) might each send a different request to Y; similarly, Y's replicas (Y_1 and Y_2) might each send a different reply to X. This is how nondeterminism can propagate between

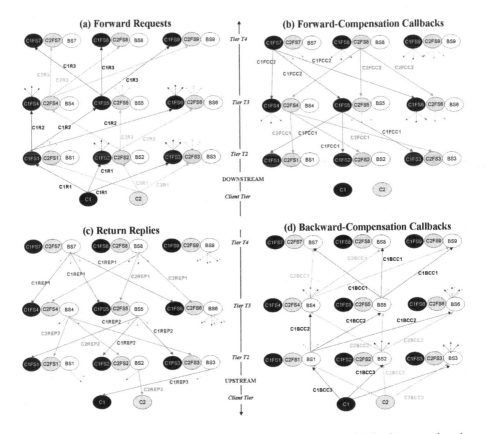

Fig. 2. Normal interactions and compensation actions across multiple clients and multiple replicated services

communicating services, based on which sending replica's message was selected at the receiving service. Because of total order, all of Y's replicas will make the identical decision about which X-replica's request was selected; if X_1's request is chosen by Y_1, the same decision will occur at Y_2 as well.

4.4   Multiple Clients, Multiple Replicated Services

We demonstrate the superimposition of the various interaction patterns due to multiple clients and multiple, replicated services in Figure 2. Here, we have a four-service, two-client architecture with three replicas each of services S2 through S4. To show how we can handle any propagation/combination of nondeterminism, we assume that nondeterminism exists in both the forward and backward direction at each of the services. Additionally, the backward nondeterministic state is dependent on its forward counterpart at every service. Figure 2(a) represents the flow of forward/downstream requests, Figure 2(c) represents the flow of the corresponding backward/upstream replies.

The terms forward-compensation and backward-compensation callbacks represent the additional communication that we use to compensate for the nondeterminism across the replicas of every service. For the purpose of this section, we assume that the forward and backward callbacks effect the required compensation actions and render the replicas consistent in their forward and backward states, respectively, after they are processed. We describe the actual, behind-the-scenes processing actions of these callbacks in Section 4.5.

Before introducing the interactions of the second client, C2, we explain what would happen if there was only one client, C1, in Figure 2(a). C1 issues a request, C1R1, to service S2. The arrival of C1R1 at each replica of S2 leads to the local creation of forward state at that replica, respectively denoted by C1FS1, C1FS2 and C1FS3 at the three distinct replicas. Note that the forward state is client-associated (therefore, the prefix C1), while there is only one piece of backward state across all clients; however, as with forward state, the backward state can also vary across replicas, i.e., BS1, BS2 and BS3 for the three replicas of S2. The S2 replicas invoke service S3, leading to the downstream request, C1R2. In the figure, the three-pronged arrows arising from each replica denote the reliable ordered multicast of the associated message, one prong for each replica of the receiving service. All of the communication in this figure is assumed to occur over totally ordered reliable multicast. The transmission of C1R2 creates the C1-associated forward states C1FS(4,5,6) across the three respective replicas of service S3. C1R3, the ensuing downstream request, similarly results in the creation of C1-associated forward states C1FS(7,8,9) at the three respective replicas of service T4.

Assume, now, that client C2 is also present in Figure 2, and concurrently invokes service S2 along with C1. If C1 arrives at service S2 earlier, C1R1 leads to the creation of forward states C1FS(1,2,3) before C1R2 is dispatched. Service S2's replicas will await the forward-compensation callback, C1FCC1, from service S3 in order to compensate for any nondeterminism across the forward states of S2's replicas. Once S2's replicas have their forward states compensated, they can be considered consistent once more, and can be ready to process a new client's request. Service S2 does not need to wait for a reply to its pending request, C1R2, if it can process a new incoming request without violating application semantics/dependencies. This concurrent processing of both C1's and C2's requests at a service is possible only if the C1-associated forward state, C1FSx, at each of the service's replicas is not dependent on the local backward state, BSx (as we assume in this figure); otherwise, there is no clean separation between the service's local forward and backward state, and the backward state would "touch" the forward state in the reply phase. If the forward state is dependent on the backward state, end-to-end locking semantics must be locally enforced at the service for consistency reasons, and concurrent processing of multiple clients by that service (and at its other communicating services, as a consequence) is effectively forbidden.

When C2's request comes into the picture at service S2, we might need to make a local copy of the forward state at S2's replicas for the purpose of C2.

This creation of a forward-state copy only needs to occur if the backward state BSx is dependent on the forward state C1FSx at the service (as we assume in this figure). In this case, we make a local copy of C1FSx and denote it as C2FSx; note that C2FSx starts out being identical to C1FSx, but changes as C2's requests get processed by the service. This process is repeated for every incoming request at a service.

Figure 2(b) represents all of the forward-compensation communication required to compensate for the nondeterminism across a service's replicas due to the execution of a forward sliver. For every downstream outgoing request from service Si to service Sj, there is a corresponding forward-compensation callback, Sj → Si, between the associated forward-compensation service-pair (Si, Sj) if nondeterminism is present at the service, Si, issuing the downstream request. In the figure, an example is service S2 issuing request C1R2 to service S3, forming the forward-compensation service-pair (S2, S3). Service S3 immediately responds with a forward-compensation callback, C1FCC1, to service S2.

Figure 2(c) and Figure 2(d) are the same as Figure 2(a) and Figure 2(b), respectively, except that they represent the upstream replies and backward-compensation callbacks. We consider communicating services to form backward-compensation service-pairs in this case. For every outgoing reply from service Sj to service Si, there immediately follows a matching backward-compensation callback, Si → Tj, if the backward state at service Si that was used to process the reply was nondeterministic.

Without the application-level knowledge extracted through Midas' analytical framework, we could not derive these key insights about forward state, backward state and the need for compensation callbacks. We could also not support concurrent clients without significant concerns about compromising consistent replication and fault tolerance. More details of the concurrency and dependency analyses are in Section 4.6.

4.5   Runtime Compensation

This section describes what the callbacks actually accomplish, for four performance-sensitive compensation techniques that we have developed. In this section, we assume that compensation is required across the replicas of service Si and that service Sj issues the callback to effect this. Thus, (Si, Sj) constitute a compensation service-pair. After processing the callback, each Si replica is consistent and is ready to process a new request. We discuss the techniques for a typical backward-compensation callback, i.e., the compensation occurs as a consequence of service Si sending a reply to service Sj. A similar discussion applies to forward-compensation callbacks.

Full-Checkpoint Transfer (transfer-ckpt): During our compile-time analysis, we instrument the code of every service to allow for the extraction and assignment of its entire state (checkpoint). At runtime, every replica of Si retrieves and multicasts its checkpoint, along with its reply, to service Sj. The replicas of Sj accept the first response, store the identifier of the corresponding (selected) Si replica and that replica's state. Because all of the requests and replies are totally ordered, all of service Sj's replicas will always select the same Si replica. Service Sj's replicas immediately multicast a callback to service Si containing this saved information (including the checkpoint of the selected Si replica). Each receiving Si replica examines this information to see if it was the selected replica, at the Sj side, for the reply. The selected Si replica does not need to do any compensation work, but the remaining Si replicas apply the callback's contents (basically, the checkpoint).

Differential-Checkpoint Transfer (`transfer-diff-ckpt`): During our compile-time analysis, we instrument the code of every service to allow for the extraction and assignment of state at all of the places where the processing of a reply might modify state. At runtime, only the actually executed change-points in Si's replicas are captured and the associated state (called a differential check-point) is multicast to service Sj as a callback. The remainder of the technique is the same as `transfer-ckpt`.

Transfer Contaminated-Nondeterminism (`transfer-contam`): Each Si replica piggybacks its actual nondeterministic state (both pure and contaminated) to its reply to Sj. During our compile-time analysis, we create within Si's code a `struct` that encapsulates the pure and contaminated nondeterminism within each Si replica. At runtime, all of the nondeterministic changes to the data are stored in this `struct` and dispatched in a callback from Si to Sj. The remainder of the algorithm is the same as the `transfer-ckpt` technique.

Reexecute Contaminated-Nondeterminism (`reexec-contam`): Each Si replica tracks only its pure nondeterministic state and piggybacks this state to its reply to Sj. During our compile-time analysis, we insert prepared portions of code that Si can execute at runtime to regenerate the contaminated nondeterminism if given the pure nondeterministic state as input. In `reexec-contam`, every receiving Sj replica extracts the piggybacked nondeterministic `struct`, as in `transfer-contam`. This nondeterministic `struct` is then multicast from Sj to Si in the compensation callback. Each Si replica that needs to compensate first assigns the pure nondeterministic part of its state to the received nondeterministic `struct`, and then executes the compile-time-inserted code to regenerate the corresponding contaminated nondeterminism.

4.6   Dependency and Concurrency Analyses

An alternative way to handle the nondeterminism in Figure 2 would have been to track all of the nondeterministic information at each service on the forward request-path of the call chain all the way up to service S4. On the backward reply-path, we would then compensate one service at a time, all the way back to the client. After a service is compensated and its replicas rendered consistent, the service can start processing its next incoming request. The point of the immediate callbacks is the gain in concurrency, and the savings in time by issuing a callback and attaining compensation/consistency while the end-to-end operation is still in progress elsewhere in the system.

214 J. Slember and P. Narasimhan

Concurrency analysis plays a big role in implementing the callback-based compensation. There are two kinds of dependencies to determine during our analysis of the abstract syntax tree. The first kind is whether the forward state is dependent on the backward state, i.e., if the forward state at a service is modified based on the backward reply received from a downstream service. This scenario does not allow for concurrency, and would necessitate blocking at all services until the end-to-end operation completes.

Our analysis also determines a second kind of dependency, namely, whether the backward state depends on the forward state. In this case, the backward state at a service is affected by the service's forward state on the return reply-path. This form of dependency permits concurrency across multiple client requests at the service, through our forward-state copy mechanism. This concurrency also implies that a service can have multiple outstanding requests that it has dispatched to different downstream services.

The caveat here is that the incoming replies on the return path must be processed by a receiving service in the order in which that service previously dispatched the corresponding downstream requests. However, this is the case only when the service's backward slivers are co-dependent, i.e., there exists some overlap in the state accessed by backward slivers at the service. If the backward slivers at a service are independent, then, incoming replies can be processed out of order. The number of clients is irrelevant to this analysis.

The four-service example in Figure 2 assumes that nondeterminism existed in all of the forward and backward slivers at all of the services. Clearly, this might not be the case in some applications. If no forward nondeterminism exists, no forward-compensation callbacks would be needed; a similar argument applies to backward nondeterminism. Our analysis can determine just to what extent nondeterminism exists in the forward and backward paths so that we compensate only for nondeterminism that actually manifests.

Apart from the concurrency benefits of the callback-based compensation strategy, the other advantage is that the compensation does not need to be conducted on a global scale, but can be performed at the scale of compensation service-pairs. This also allows us the flexibility of selecting the appropriate strategy (of the four listed in Section 4.5) for various pairs of services. For instance, one compensation service-pair might elect to use `transfer-ckpt` because the service to be compensated has a small amount of state; another service-pair might employ `reexec-contam` because the service to be compensated has a large amount of state but small processing time.

4.7 Inadvertently Introduced Nondeterminism?

Since Midas' approach instruments the application to capture and compensate for the nondeterminism, we need to consider the possibility that our instrumentation inadvertently introduces further nondeterminism. We argue that this is not the case by examining our two kinds of instrumentation.

The first kind simply collects a service's nondeterministic information into a data structure and dispatches this structure between replicas. This kind of instrumentation is read-only and does not introduce any nondeterminism of its own. The second kind of instrumentation is the compensation code that we insert. Given that the replication infrastructure in the system is based on a reliable multicast transport layer, we know that all of a service's replicas will act on the same nondeterministic information for the purposes of compensation. Thus, the compensation will be applied identically across all of a service's replicas. There should be no inadvertent nondeterminism introduced through Midas' instrumentation.

5 Substantiating Midas' Claims

In our approach, we make two claims that we substantiate through formal modeling. The first claim is that Midas itself does not violate application semantics by modifying the source-code or changing the application's state at runtime. The second claim is that Midas maintains consistency in the face of nondeterminism in a multi-service architecture.

For our modeling, we chose to use Java PathFinder [24], a runtime analysis tool that verifies executable Java bytecode. It can be used as a software model-checker to examine all of the possible execution paths of a program in order to look for violations of specific properties. Java PathFinder provides particular support for examining multi-threaded programs.

We created a simple, but sufficiently representative, multi-service distributed application that could actually be modeled by Java PathFinder (JPF). This application is composed of two communicating services, as shown in Figure 3. Each service has two replicas. The intermediate service is state-machine replicated and contains nondeterminism in the form of multithreading. We vary the number of threads from two to eight, with the threads sharing some state (an array of 100 integers). Half of the threads add numbers to the shared array, while the other half of the threads multiply numbers with the shared state. We intentionally do not use any locking mechanisms to protect the shared state.

The interleaving of the threads will determine the state of the intermediate service. The client sends a request to the intermediate service, which invokes an interleaved-thread operation that sums up the numbers in the array and sends the result to the end service. The end service, also state-machine replicated, adds a random integer to the received value and returns the result to the intermediate service. The intermediate service resumes thread interleaving using the value in the reply from the end service; after some processing, the intermediate service sends its reply to the client. While there might be no useful semantic meaning to the application's functionality, there exist dependencies between the intermediate and end services in terms of both forward and backward state. We note that, given the initial state of the intermediate service's shared array, there are only a finite number of possible outcomes depending on the size of the shared array. This observation is important because it helps in the determination of correctness and consistency. JPF is able to traverse the space completely given the limited number of outcomes. However, with all model-checkers, this would not scale well.

JPF supports three ways of enforcing properties in a model on an executing application. The first is through assertions that are checked at specific points in time. This is the most straightforward way of checking whether or not something is true at a given point in time. However, assertions are not necessarily the easiest to use in the face of multithreading. The second JPF mechanism is to write a search property function. This function will be executed after every state transition in the bytecode. The search function allows for more complex and long running analysis compared to using assertions. A third way is to employ search listeners and virtual-machine (VM) listeners that can be used to gain more detailed information about VM-level state transitions. This is more complex than we need for the purposes of checking our model. Unfortunately, JPF is not built for distributed systems, but for single processes running in a VM environment. Therefore, we model our multi-service distributed application in Figure 3 as a single process, with each node modeled as a thread. We use five threads: one for the client, one for each intermediate-service replica, and one for each end-service replica. We select one of our compensation techniques, namely, reexec-contam, to substantiate our claims.

We inserted several different assertions and checks using JPF. When the client sends a request to service S1, both S1 replicas receive the request and process it. Their state will change but will be divergent due to nondeterminism in the intermediate service, as demonstrated in Figure 3. At this point an assertion is made that the output state of both replicas is valid. This is checked by determining all of the possible resultant states. After each S1 replica finishes processing the forward request, they each invoke service S2. S1's replicas each piggyback their nondeterminism to this request. Just prior to this downstream request, another assertion/check is made. Within this assertion, each replica's nondeterministic state (prior to the issue of the downstream request) is copied over to some temporary state. We then invoke the reexecution snippet that has already been generated.

The assertion then checks that the resultant temporary state is equivalent to the replica's state just prior to the downstream call. This validates the captured state, as well as the reexecution snippet. Next, S2's replicas choose one of the incoming S1 requests and drop the other. They strip off the piggybacked nondeterministic information from the request. They then attach this state to a forward callback which is immediately returned to S1. Both S1 replicas receive this callback, but only one of them needs to process it because it was not chosen by S2. At this point, another assertion/check is performed by JPF.

At every stage that a replica's state might change, an assertion is made to verify the validity of the state. At the end of the callback's execution, consistent replication should be exhibited by S1. Similarly, on the S2 end, assertions serve to track the updates to S2's state, as well as the effect of any compensation callbacks or piggybacked nondeterminism. The various assertion checks are shown in Figure 3.

We ran this simple JPF-supported application repeatedly while varying the workload on the machines, in order to force the threads to interleave in different ways. It is important to note that we were not running this for performance.

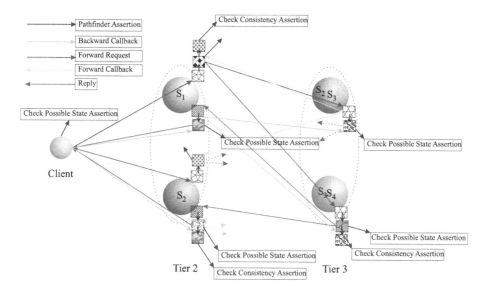

Fig. 3. Java Pathfinder-based model-checking architecture with assertions

We continuously ran the experiments until the majority of interleavings were exhibited. Depending on the thread scheduling, we observed emergent nondeterminism occur. However, the assertion checks continued to demonstrate that we do not inadvertently introduce nondeterminism with our approach, and that our compensation does indeed result in consistent replication.

6 Empirical Evaluation

6.1 Microbenchmark Application

We evaluated our implementation and compensation techniques using variations of a basic multi-service, multi-client, micro-benchmark application on Emulab [21]. Each service performs the same amount of processing, and each client has identical functionality. Every server replica and every client is located on a different Pentium III, 850MHz machine with 256MB RAM running TimeSys Linux 2.4 over a 100 Mbps LAN. The application is multithreaded with shared state across threads. Additionally, nondeterministic system calls (e.g. random()) are used by the application. Our goal in using this microbenchmark is to show the scalability of our approach with respect to the number of clients, the number of services, and the number of replicas/service. Additionally, we vary the amount of forward and backward nondeterminism. We varied our experimental configurations to change (i) the number of clients to 2 and 4, (ii) the number of services to 2 and 4, (iii) the number of replicas/service to 2 and 4, (iv) the forward nondeterminism to 0%, 5% and 60% of the total state within the service, (v) the backward nondeterminism to 0%, 5% and 60% of the total state within the

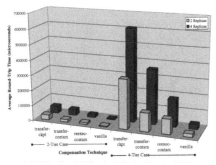 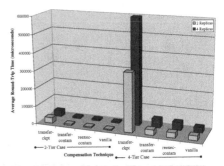

(a) 60% forward & backward nondeter-   (b) 5% forward & backward nondeterminism   minism

Fig. 4. Overhead for compensation techniques for varying number of services and service replicas

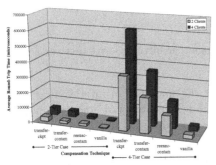 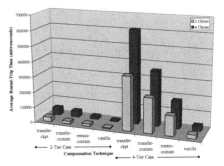

(a) 60% forward & backward nondeter-   (b) 5% forward & backward nondeterminism   minism

Fig. 5. Overhead for compensation techniques for varying number of clients

service, and (vi) the compensation techniques, ranging from `transfer-ckpt`, `reexec-contam`, `transfer-contam`. The `vanilla` case simply serves as a baseline for performance comparison, and allows replicas to remain nondeterministic and does not involve any compensation. The vanilla case does also include the underlying reliability layer. This is important because we are comparing the relative overheads of the techniques, regardless of the underlying layer. If vanilla did not include the reliability layer, then the comparison of techniques would be dependent on the overheads introduced by Spread, which would not be a fair comparison since any group communication protocol could be used. The metric that we use for evaluation is round-trip time as measured at a client. For each configuration, we compute the average round-trip time across all the clients for 300 end-to-end invocations/client.

The "total state" of a service is represented by two arrays (one forward and one backward) of 10,000 `longs` each. In our microbenchmark, each time a forward

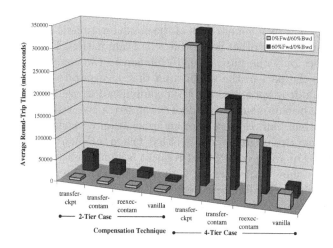

Fig. 6. Overheads of having all forward vs. all backward nondeterminism. There are 4 clients and 4 replicas/service with either 60 % forward or 60 % backward nondeterminism.

sliver is executed, all of the forward array is touched; similarly, all of the backward array is touched when a backward sliver executes. Therefore, $x\%$ forward nondeterminism and $y\%$ backward nondeterminism mean that $x\%$ of the forward array is nondeterministic on the forward request-path and $y\%$ of the backward array is nondeterministic on the backward reply-path. The backward state depends on the forward state if the latter is accessed by the incoming/backward reply.

We have two major sources of nondeterminism: multithreading with shared state and nondeterministic system calls. By changing the amount of overlapping state across threads, the amount of pure nondeterminism can be varied. Changing the amount of state modified by a purely nondeterministic system call can vary the amount of contaminated nondeterminism. These two sources of nondeterminism are split equally for the purposes of introducing varying amounts of nondeterminism in our micro-benchmark's experimental configurations. Therefore, if 60% of the total state is nondeterministic, 30% of state is shared across the threads, and 30% of state is due to contaminated nondeterminism.

6.2   Observations from Results

Scalability w.r.t. degree of replication. Figure 4(a) keeps the amount of forward and backward nondeterminism constant at 60% each and the number of clients at four. It is apparent that `transfer-ckpt` has the highest overhead, with round-trip time almost 30 times that of `vanilla`. This technique transfers all of the checkpoint of each service across each request, reply, and callback, thereby adding significant overhead. `transfer-contam` performs better than `transfer-ckpt` because only 60% of the state has to be transferred between and within services. `reexec-contam` performs the best of the three techniques because in our micro-benchmark, half of the nondeterministic state is due to pure nondeterminism and the other half is due to contamination. The `reexec-contam` technique passes only the pure nondeterminism in the compensation callback, and reexecutes the part of the application that incorporates the contaminated nondeterminism. It is apparent that the communication overhead dominates the processing time because removing half of the state transfer reduces the round-trip by a little less than half. However, for an application with significant processing time, `reexec-contam` might be costlier that `transfer-contam`.

The overhead of going from 2 to 4 replicas is significant, with the round-trip time almost doubling in most cases; with each additional replica, the communication overhead and the duplicate-detection costs increase linearly. This is more noticeable in the 4-service case than in the 2-service case. The 2-service case does not show as dramatic an increase because the client makes a backward-compensation callback to its neighboring service, and is effectively done and can proceed with its work. Thus, the actual compensation callback's overhead does not affect the round-trip time significantly. However, the 4-service case shows more significant increase in round-trip time due to the added compensation-related communication and the associated callbacks.

Figure 4(a) also serves to demonstrate that our techniques can handle a rather extreme amount of nondeterminism (even 60% forward nondeterminism and 60% backward nondeterminism), albeit with significant overhead. The graph also shows that `transfer-ckpt` is not ideal in this case because it represents the highest possible overhead that could occur.

Figure 4(b) is the same as Figure 4(a), except that the amount of forward and backward nondeterminism is only 5% each. The overheads of `transfer-contam` and `reexec-contam` are more reasonable, even in the 4-service, 4-replica case. Note that `transfer-ckpt` is more or less identical across Figure 4(a) and Figure 4(b) because this technique transfers the entire state, and the amount of state does not change across the two graphs. Basically, the amount of nondeterminism does not impact `transfer-ckpt`. At such lower amounts of nondeterminism, the overheads of `reexec-contam` and `transfer-contam` with varying number of replicas and the number of services are low; thus, these techniques scale well in this case. Unlike Figure 4(a), `reexec-contam` does not incur half the latency of `transfer-contam`. The amount of state being transferred is small, and the number of compensation messages is the dominant factor, and not the amount of state. In the 2-service case, there is little difference across `vanilla`, `reexec-contam`, and `reexec-contam` because only a single compensation callback is required.

Scalability w.r.t. number of clients. Figures 5(a) and 5(b) are similar to 4(a) and 4(b), respectively, but with a fixed 4 replicas/service and a varying number of clients. The workload across the services doubles when the number of clients doubles. This is demonstrated by the linear increase in round-trip times for the 4-service case in Figure 5(a). However, the 2-service case in Figure 5(a), as well as the 2-service and 4-service cases in Figure 5(b), show that `reexec-contam` scales well.

Varying forward and backward nondeterminism. Figure 6 compares the cases where the amounts of forward and backward nondeterminism differ widely, for a fixed number of clients and services. The 4-service case is the most interesting as the amount of forward and backward nondeterminism affects each of our techniques differently. The `transfer-contam` technique actually fares better with more backward nondeterminism while the `reexec-contam` incurs significantly lower overheads with more forward nondeterminism. This comparison is significant from an application developer's viewpoint. When an application is being developed, if nondeterministic execution can be relocated between a server's forward and backward slivers, this can influence the compensation technique chosen. This can also me done by using compiler techniques that understand dependencies and are able to perform code-motion. If most of the nondeterminism can be placed in the backward sliver, `transfer-contam` would be preferable, but if the nondeterminism could be entirely relocated to the forward sliver, `reexec-contam` might be better. Note that `reexec-contam`'s latencies will increase with server-side processing time. Therefore, these scalability of each technique in its own right is more relevant for a given application than its comparison to the other techniques. The 2-service 0% forward-nondeterminism results are fairly constant because there is nothing to compensate for.

7   Related Work

Considerable research efforts have been expended to handling nondeterminism in distributed fault-tolerant systems.

Gaifman [12] targets nondeterminism that arises in concurrent programs due to environmental interaction. This technique involves backup replicas lagging behind the primary to ensure consistency. The Multithreaded Deterministic Scheduling Algorithm [13] aims to handle multithreading transparently by providing for internal and external queues that together enforce consistency. The external queue contains a sequence of ordered messages received via multicast, while each internal queue focuses on thread dispatching, with an internal queue for each process that spawns threads. Basile [5] addresses multithreading using a preemptive deterministic scheduler for active replication. The approach uses mutexes between threads and the execution is split into several rounds. Because the mutexes are known at each round, a deterministic schedule can be created.

The fault-tolerant real-time MARS system requires deterministic behavior [15] in highly responsive automotive applications that are nondeterministic due to time-triggered event activation and preemptive scheduling. Determinism is enforced using a combination of timed messages and a communication protocol for agreement on external events. Delta-4 XPA's semi-active replication [4] addresses nondeterminism through a hybrid replication style that employs primary-backup replication for all nondeterministic operations and active replication for all other operations. In SCEPTRE 2 [6], nondeterminism arises from preemptive scheduling. Semi-active replication is used, with deterministic behavior enforced through the transmission of messages from a coordination entity to backup replicas for every nondeterministic decision of the primary's. Similarly, Wolf's piecewise deterministic approach [22] handle nondeterminism by having a primary replica that actually executes all nondeterministic events, with the results being propagated to the backups at an observable, deterministic event.

X-Ability [11] is based predominantly on the execution history resulting from previous invocation. The approach is not necessarily transparent to the programmer because the proposed correctness criterion must be followed for consistency. The advantage is that it is independent of the replication style. Slye et al. [19] track and record the nondeterminism due to asynchronous events and multithreading. While nondeterminism is not eliminated, the nondeterministic executions are recorded so that they can be replayed to restore replica consistency in the event of rollback.

The Transparent Fault Tolerance (TFT) system [7] enforces deterministic computation on replicas at the level of the operating system interface. The object code of the application binaries is edited to insert code that redirects all nondeterministic system calls to a software layer that returns identical results at all replicas. Hypervisor-based fault tolerance [8] involves a virtual machine that ensures that all nondeterministic data is consistent across replicas. This is accomplished by using a simulator to execute all environmental instructions, and then requiring system-wide lock-step synchronization on this execution.

Zagorodnov et al. [23] target nondeterminism that is inherent to service protocols used by network servers. The solution involves the interception of I/O streams of replicas, and the appropriate handling of input and output streams.

Taiani et al. [20] propose adding fault-tolerance to complex architectures. Their technique handles nondeterminism transparently by introducing a meta-level object protocol. The technique is demonstrated by handling multithreading-induced nondeterminism at the middleware layer; however, the approach might be expanded to handle application-level nondeterminism. This approach does permit some semantic analysis to determine what possible sources of nondeterminism need to be controlled.

Napper and Alvisi set out to make a JVM fault-tolerant in [1]. Thread synchronization, clock-driven scheduling and timers were some of the sources of nondeterminism that they had to handle inside the JVM. They targeted nondeterminism due to multithreading in the JVM and were able to achieve success with under 100 percent overhead for the majority of the applications tested.

Alvisi et al. [2] performed a survey of different rollback-recovery techniques, both checkpoint and log-based. The techniques they discussed target only those that did not rely on special language features. Asynchronous signals and system calls are the two sources of nondeterminism that they discuss with respect to these techniques.

8   Conclusion

We presented a non-transparent approach that allows nondeterminism to exist in multi-service, multi-client distributed fault-tolerant systems. The approach involves a synergistic combination of compile-time dependency, concurrency and nondeterminism analyses, followed by the performance-sensitive compensation of nondeterminism at runtime. Due to the possibility of nondeterminism propagating in multi-service, multi-client architectures, we introduce the concepts of forward/backward slivers as well as forward/backward nondeterminism. These abstractions allow for finer granularity and scalability in the handling of nondeterminism. Through a formal model, we also demonstrate that our approach itself does not inadvertently introduce nondeterminism of its own. We believe it is sufficient to show that Midas does not violate application semantics or introduce nondeterminism in a simple example since the vast majority of modeling tools do not scale to allow for true testing on a large application.

We evaluate our approach with a microbenchmark that compares our compensation techniques for varying number of clients, number of replicas/service, and number of services. Our approach appears to scale well with reasonable levels of nondeterminism, and can also handle increased amounts of nondeterminism, albeit with significant overheads.

References

1. Alvisi, L., Napper, J.: Transparent Fault Tolerant Java Virtual Machine. In: DSN, San Francisco, CA, pp. 425–434 (June 2003)
2. Alvisi, L., Elnozahy, E., Wang, Y.M., Johnson, D.B.: A Survey of Rollback-Recovery Protocols in Message-Passing Systems. ACM Computing Surveys 34(3), 375–408 (2002)
3. Amir, Y., et al.: A low latency, loss tolerant architecture and protocol for wide area group communication. In: DSN, New York, pp. 327–336 (June 2000)
4. Barrett, P., et al.: The Delta-4 extra performance architecture (XPA). In: FTCS, pp. 481–488 (1990)
5. Basile, C., et al.: A preemptive deterministic scheduling algorithm for multi-threaded replicas. In: DSN, San Francisco, CA, pp. 149–158 (June 2003)
6. Bestaoui, S.: One solution for the nondeterminism problem in the SCEPTRE 2 fault tolerance technique. In: Euromicro Workshop on Real-Time Systems, Odense, Denmark, pp. 352–358 (June 1995)
7. Bressoud, T.C.: TFT: A software system for application-transparent fault tolerance. In: FTCS, Munich, Germany, pp. 128–137 (June 1998)
8. Bressoud, T.C., et al.: Hypervisor-based fault-tolerance. ACM Transactions on Computer Systems 14(1), 90–107 (1996)
9. Budhiraja, N., Marzullo, K., Schneider, F., Toueg, S.: Distributed Systems. In: The Primary-Backup Approach, ch.8, 2nd edn., pp. 199–216 (1993)
10. http://www.csci.csusb.edu/dick/c++std/cd2/gram.html
11. Frolund, S., et al.: X-ability: A theory of replication. In: PODC, Portland, OR, pp. 229–237 (2000)
12. Gaifman, H., et al.: Replay, recovery, replication, and snapshots of nondeterministic concurrent programs. In: PODC, Montreal, Canada, pp. 241–255 (August 1991)
13. Jimenez-Peris, R., et al.: Deterministic scheduling for transactional multithreaded replicas. In: SRDS, pp. 164–173 (2000)
14. Orgiyan, M., et al.: Tapping TCP streams. In: IEEE International Symposium on Network Computing and Applications, Cambridge, MA, pp. 278–289 (October 2001)

15. Poledna, S.: Replica Determinism in Fault-Tolerant Real-Time Systems. PhD thesis, Technical University of Vienna, Vienna, Austria (April 1994)
16. Schneider, F.B.: Implementing fault-tolerant services using the state machine approach: A tutorial. ACM Computing Surveys 22(4), 299–319 (1990)
17. Slember, J.G., et al.: Nondeterminism in ORBs: The perception and the reality. In: Workshop on High Availability in Distributed Systems, Krakow, Poland (September 2006)
18. Slember, J.G., et al.: Living with nondeterminism in replicated middleware systems. In: Middleware, Melbourne, Australia, pp. 81–100 (November 2006)
19. Slye, J.H., et al.: Supporting nondeterministic execution in fault-tolerant systems. In: FTCS, Sendai, Japan, pp. 250–259 (June 1996)
20. Taiani, F., et al.: A multi-level meta-object protocol for fault-tolerance in complex architectures. In: DSN, Yokohama, Japan, pp. 270–279 (June 2005)
21. White, B., et al.: An integrated experimental environment for distributed systems and networks. In: OSDI, Boston, MA, pp. 255–270 (December 2002)
22. Wolf, T.: Replication of Non-Deterministic Objects. PhD thesis, Ecole Polytechnique Federale de Lausanne, Switzerland (November 1988)
23. Zagorodnov, D., et al.: Managing self-inflicted nondeterminism. In: HotDep, Yokohama, Japan (June 2005)
24. Visser, W., et al.: Model Checking Programs. Automated Software Engineering Journal 10(2) (2003)

Toward Architecture Evaluation through Ontology-Based Requirements-Level Scenarios

Mamadou H. Diallo, Leila Naslavsky,
Thomas A. Alspaugh, Hadar Ziv, and Debra J. Richardson

Department of Informatics
Donald Bren School of Information and Computer Sciences
University of California, Irvine
{mamadoud,lnaslavs,alspaugh,ziv,djr}@ics.uci.edu

Abstract. We describe an approach for evaluating whether a candidate architecture dependably satisfies stakeholder requirements expressed in requirements-level scenarios. We map scenarios to architectural elements through an ontology of requirements-level event classes and domain entities. The scenarios express both functional requirements and quality attributes of the system; for quality attributes, the scenarios either operationalize the quality or show how the quality can be verified. Our approach provides a connection between requirements a stakeholder can understand directly, and architectures developed to satisfy those requirements. The requirements-level ontology simplifies the mapping, acts as the focus for maintaining the mapping as both scenarios and architecture evolve, and provides a foundation for evaluating scenarios and architecture individually and jointly. In this paper, we focus on the mapping through event classes and demonstrate our approach with two examples.

1 Introduction

Designing architectures that are consistent with their requirements is crucial in the development of large software systems. Software architecture evaluation methods have been proposed as a way of determining the fitness of an architecture with respect to its functional requirements as well as its quality attributes such as availability, reliability, performance, maintainability, and security [4,7,15,18,23,31]. These quality attributes are in general expressed by stakeholders in natural language sentences, which are difficult to use in the evaluation methods. Scenarios have been used as an alternative (and sometimes complementary) way to express requirements and system behavior throughout the phases of software development. Scenarios have been used by the evaluation methods to relate requirements and architectures [3]. However, in most methods this relationship is not conserved for later use. For evaluation methods to be more useful and effective, the relationship between requirements and architectures needs to be maintained to support the evolving nature of these two processes.

Scenarios are used with different representations and semantics across software phases. They can describe a system at different levels of abstraction [1], can be

R. de Lemos et al. (Eds.): Architecting Dependable Systems V, LNCS 5135, pp. 225–247, 2008.
© Springer-Verlag Berlin Heidelberg 2008

linked to software architecture, and be used for testing [9,14]. At the requirements level, scenarios can be expressed in many forms, including prose. We use the ScenarioML language [1,2]. It provides a scenario syntax with a well-defined structure for events, and user-defined ontologies defining domain concepts.

This paper describes a four-step approach to architecture evaluation that aids software architecture designers. First, user requirements are specified using a structured scenario language; second, the architecture is described using an architectural description language; third, requirements scenarios are mapped into architectures using elements from the structured scenario and components in the architecture; and fourth, the resulting architectures are evaluated against original requirements scenarios.

An architectural description comprises structural and behavioral specifications. Our proposed approach is not dependent on a particular Architectural Description Language (ADL). It does require, however, that each component in the architecture description have precisely defined responsibilities and services, which are provided through their interfaces. In this paper, we use structural descriptions written in xADL [12], an XML-based ADL. In addition, we adopt an extension of xADL for behavioral description that uses statecharts, proposed in [25].

We propose an approach that maps domain events, classes, and individuals used in requirements scenarios (described using ScenarioML) to architectural components (described using xADL). This approach supports evaluation of consistency between architecture and requirements. Our approach's main contribution is leveraging ScenarioML to establish the relation from requirements to architecture more effectively and evolvably. This is possible because ScenarioML supports an ontology of domain events and entities, which enables a straightforward and compact mapping from events in the requirements to the components responsible for those events in the architecture.

We use a domain ontology as the basis for the mapping between requirements and architectures because it facilitates the mapping. In this work, an *ontology* is a collection of domain class, individual, and event type definitions that are typically interrelated. ScenarioML supports and encourages reuse of event types as templates for specific events in scenarios, and unambiguous links to domain classes and individuals wherever these are referred to. The ontology not only improves the clarity of the scenarios [2], but also effectively reduces the complexity of links between the requirements and architecture elements. Without the ontology, each appearance of a scenario element is linked individually to all relevant architecture elements; with the ontology, the appearances are linked to its definition in the ontology, and only that definition is linked to the architecture elements. The more extensive the reuse of the ontology definitions in the scenarios, the greater is the reduction in complexity. ScenarioML supports reuse of event types that appear as equivalent events in the same or several scenarios; specialization and generalization of events through their event types; explicit relationships among a parameterized event type's instances with different arguments; and domain classes and individuals referred to in events. In the initial work presented here, we focus on reuse of equivalent events.

To illustrate how our approach supports evaluation of software architectures against requirements-level scenarios, we apply it to two examples. The first example shows how our approach identifies inconsistencies between functional requirements and architecture. The second example shows that our approach can be applied to distributed systems and can also evaluate the architecture against non-functional requirements (e.g. availability, and reliability).

The remainder of the paper is organized as follows. Section 2 briefly discusses the portion of ScenarioML used by our approach. We present our approach to architecture evaluation in Section 3, and illustrate its application to two example systems in Section 4. Section 5 discusses some of our findings. We place the research in the context of related work in Section 6, and summarize in Section 7. Section 8 outlines our future work.

2 ScenarioML

ScenarioML is a language for expressing scenarios that provides structures to represent the aspects of textual scenarios that people treat and interpret consistently [1,2]. It makes use of the division of scenarios into events; natural language *simple events* whose meaning is understood by humans; *compound events* consisting of subevents in a temporal pattern; *event schemas* for alternation, iteration, and the like; *episodes* that reuse an entire scenario as a single event of another; *ontologies* defining domain concepts; and a number of other features. It is designed to support being read and written by all stakeholders (using software tools), and to accommodate machine processing. Here we discuss only the parts of ScenarioML most significant for our approach.

A ScenarioML *ontology* consists of a collection of domain class, individual, and event type definitions. The definitions typically refer to each other and are interrelated. A domain class (an *instanceType*) defines a class of entities in the domain that are in some sense equivalent. A domain individual (an *instance*) in the ontology defines a specific entity of a class whose existence is assumed or guaranteed; ScenarioML also provides structures for referring to individuals that are newly created or identified during the course of a scenario. An event type (*eventType* in ScenarioML) acts as a template for reusing the same event in several scenarios or several times in the same scenario. A domain class may be specified to be subsumed by another in a subclass/superclass relationship, as can an event type. Both domain classes and event types may be parameterized, in which case their instances are as well and must be given an argument for each parameter.

3 Approach

In this section, we describe our approach for evaluating a software architecture against requirements-level scenarios. The requirements-level scenarios need to describe not only functional requirements, but also non-functional requirements as discussed below. With these scenarios one can evaluate whether the architecture meets the functional requirements. They also enable one to assess how well a selected architecture style can support the dependability qualities of the system such as availability, reliability, maintainability, and safety. The software architecture needs to be expressed in an ADL, with precisely defined responsibilities and services for each component.

The requirements-level scenarios are modeled with ScenarioML. The ScenarioML ontology models the actions performed by different actors in the scenarios using *eventType* and associated elements such as *super* and *parameter*. The scenarios are expressed by instantiating the *eventType*. Indeed, ScenarioML is the foundation of our approach.

We use xADL for describing the architecture in the examples presented in Section 4. However, any other ADL with similar features could be used. xADL is an XML-based architectural description language that is highly extensible. It supports structural [12] description of architectures and also behavioral [25] description of architectures using statecharts. Additionally, it has tool support for runtime and design time modeling, architecture configuration management, and model-based system instantiation.

3.1   Overview of Approach

Our approach takes requirements-level scenarios described in ScenarioML and evaluates them against the architecture of the system described with components and connectors. The scenarios describe the functional and non-functional requirements that are important to the stakeholders. The approach is based on explicit mappings between *eventTypes* in the ontology and components in the architecture. The mapping is created by examining in conjunction the meaning of the event in the scenarios and the roles played by different components in the architecture.

The approach comprises four main steps: (1) description of the important scenarios of the system in ScenarioML, (2) description of the architecture using an architectural description language, (3) mapping the ontology event types to the architectural components, and (4) walkthroughs of the scenarios in the architecture. Figure 1 shows an overview of the approach.

3.2   Scenarios Description in ScenarioML

Description of scenarios with ScenarioML can be accomplished through the following three steps:

1. Identify actors of the scenarios and actions they perform. Then, generalize the actions where possible to reduce the eventual number of event types. The fewer the event types, the simpler it is in the approach's later steps.
2. Define the event types based on the identified actions in the first step using the *eventType*. This includes sub-typing and parameterizing events where appropriate. For example, a group of related events can be grouped under a

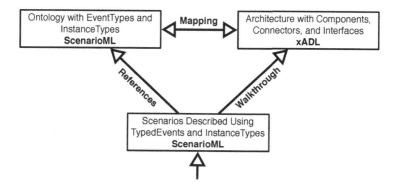

Fig. 1. Overview of the approach

super-event, or a general event can include parameters to allow specialization to particular contexts.

3. Write scenarios using the previously defined event types. The element used for this purpose is the *typedEvent* element, which references and reuses a defined *eventType*.

The requirements scenarios for a system are often quite numerous. Our approach does not propose a method for ranking scenarios by importance, so that limited evaluation time can be focused on the most important ones. In general, we expect that the importance of a scenario is determined by the system's designers.

3.3 Architecture Description

We assume the architecture is described with an ADL that supports both structural and behavioral descriptions. The structural description provides the infrastructure for mapping, while the behavioral description allows dynamic checking of the architecture against scenarios. The architecture description should include components, connections, and constraints on the communication between the components. The role of each component must be specified unambiguously to facilitate the mapping of event types and components. If the architecture decomposes the components into subcomponents, the responsibilities of each subcomponent should be identified precisely. It this case, the mapping can be done at the subcomponent-level, which can give more detailed information about the fitness of the architecture in regard to requirements.

3.4 Mapping Ontology Elements to Architectural Components

The mapping is performed between event types in the ontology and components in the architecture's structural description. It is based on the meaning of the events of the scenarios and the responsibilities of the components. For example, in the PIMS (Personal Investment Management System) system [21] described later in Section 4, the event "The user enters the portfolio's name" is matched to the component "Master Controller", which manages the user interface; the event "The system authenticates the user" is matched to the component "Authentication", which is responsible for the authentication task. A table can be used to capture the mapping, with row headings representing the events and column headings the components (such as Table 1).

The mapping is many-to-many. One event type from the requirements-level scenario describes a high level action that can be decomposed into several of a component's low level actions. Therefore, to execute an event type from the requirements-level scenario, multiple low level actions may be executed. In addition, each component supports many low level actions, where each action can result from the decomposition of different event types from the requirements-level scenario.

3.5   Architecture Evaluation against Scenarios

The task of evaluating an architecture against a set of scenarios consists of going through the sequence of the events in the scenarios, using the established mapping to match events to components, while simulating the behavior of the matched components. The resulting architecture behavior is then evaluated for inconsistencies with the scenario.

The architecture can be inconsistent with the requirements in a number of ways. The inconsistency can take the form of a missing link between two components that is required by the scenarios. If two successive events match two components, where the first event in the sequence matches the first component and the second event matches the second component, then the two components may need to be able to communicate. In this case, the structural description of the architecture should allow such communication, else the architecture may be inconsistent with the requirements. The architecture satisfies the requirements-level scenario if the second component provides an interface to the first component to allow it to request the necessary services, for example.

Another possible inconsistency occurs when the structural description of the architecture violates constraints imposed by the requirements. For instance, a requirement for a distributed system could be "Clients need to communicate through a central server." This constraint can be violated if the architecture allows two clients to communicate directly, bypassing the central server.

Some quality attributes can be more effectively described using *negative scenarios*. A negative scenario describes an undesirable behavior of a system. In this case, the inconsistency is identified by a successful execution of the negative scenarios. For instance, for security reasons a requirement for a distributed system could be "Users need to be authorized to access the network." A scenario could describe a user with inadequate authentication information accessing the system. The successful execution of such a scenario implies the system is not secure.

4   Two Applications

In this section, we illustrate our approach by applying it to two example applications. The first example is a single-process textbook system, which we used to show how our approach detects inconsistencies between functional requirements of a system and its architecture. The second example is a realistic distributed and decentralized system, which we used to demonstrate how our approach can be used to analyze the fitness of an architecture with regard to non-functional requirements (quality attributes). Both the functional and non-functional requirements of this system are described using scenarios.

We chose these applications rather than real-world industrial systems because they have relatively complete requirements and architectures. Our earlier study found that few if any publicly available industrial systems have both [13].

For this study, we selected xADL to describe the architecture of the systems. We used Archipelago, a user-friendly graphical editor for xADL included in Arch-Studio 4 to describe the PIMS's architecture [12]. ArchStudio 4 is an open-source software and systems architecture development environment. It is an environment of integrated tools for modeling, visualizing, analyzing and implementing software and systems architectures, based on the Eclipse open development platform.

4.1   PIMS

The first example we selected for this study is PIMS (Personal Investment Management System), included in Jalote's book [21] and presented in detail on the book's website as an extended case study. PIMS is used by customers to keep track of their invested money in institutions such as banks and in the stock market. It includes all the development artifacts from the requirements documents to the Java source code.

The PIMS functional requirements are presented in the form of use cases. In total the system's requirements comprise 22 uses cases. Each use case contains a main scenario and some alternative scenarios. The system contains only few non-functional requirements, which pertain to performance, security, and fault tolerance. For the purpose of demonstrating our approach, we focus on two functional scenarios, "Create portfolio" and "Get the current prices of shares." The scenario "Create portfolio" describes the steps required to create a new portfolio and "Get the current prices of shares" lists the steps to be performed to get the current prices of shares from the Internet (Figure 2).

The PIMS use cases in this example are:

"Create portfolio" main scenario: (1) User initiates the "create portfolio" functionality. (2) System asks the user for the portfolio name. (3) User enters the portfolio name. (4) An empty portfolio is created.

"Create portfolio" alternate scenario: (4.a) Portfolio with the same name exists. (4.a.1) System asks the user for a different name. (4.a.2) User enters a different name. (4.a.3) Empty portfolio gets created.

"Get the current prices of shares" main scenario: (1) User initiates the "download current share prices" functionality. (2) The system downloads the current share prices from a particular website. (3) The system display the current share prices. (4) The system save the current share prices.

"Get the current prices of shares" alternate scenario: (2.a.1) The system is not able to download (due to network failure, site down, ...). (2.a.2) The system gets current value saved from before. (2.a.3) The system display current value saved from before; ask the user to change it.

The PIMS architecture (Figure 3) is designed using the Layered Architectural Style. The architecture not only includes the main architecture diagram, but also the different modules and their interfaces comprising in each component. It comprises a data access layer separating the business logic and data repository. Data retrieval and modification is done via this data access layer, while all the processing of data or implementation of the business logic done in the business logic layer. The fourth layer is the presentation layer ("Master controller") which is responsible for interacting with the user and invoking modules of the business logic layer.

PIMS ScenarioML Scenarios. This first step of the approach comprises using the ScenarioML language to develop an ontology for PIMS, and describing the selected PIMS scenarios using the ontology elements. The two principal actors of the system are "User" and "System". Based on the various scenarios, the actions performed by each actor were identified and described using the ScenarioML ontology. This description included generalizing and parameterizing the actions for simplicity and clarity, and identifying equivalent events that can be defined once and shared. Figure 2 shows some actions performed by the actor "User" expressed using the ontology element *eventType*. In addition to defining the events for each actor, the general concepts of the system are also captured using the elements *term* and *instanceType* of the ontology and included in the PIMS ontology.

Based on the *eventTypes* defined in the ontology, the selected scenarios are described. Figure 2 shows the description of the scenarios "Create portfolio" and "Get the current prices of shares" respectively. The important events in these scenarios are defined using *typedEvents*, which refer to the *eventTypes* in the ontology.

PIMS Architectural Description in xADL. In this second step, we described the PIMS architecture using xADL. Figure 3 shows the structure description of the PIMS architecture. We used the Archipelago editor in the ArchStudio 4 environment to draw the diagram and define all the elements of the architecture.

Mapping PIMS Ontology Elements to PIMS Components. In this third step, we created a mapping between PIMS ontology elements and the PIMS architecture components. The description of the PIMS architecture is presented in Figure 3. The architecture comprises the components with their interfaces and connectors, that can be visualized graphically. Each component in this architecture has a well defined role, which facilitated the mapping from event types to

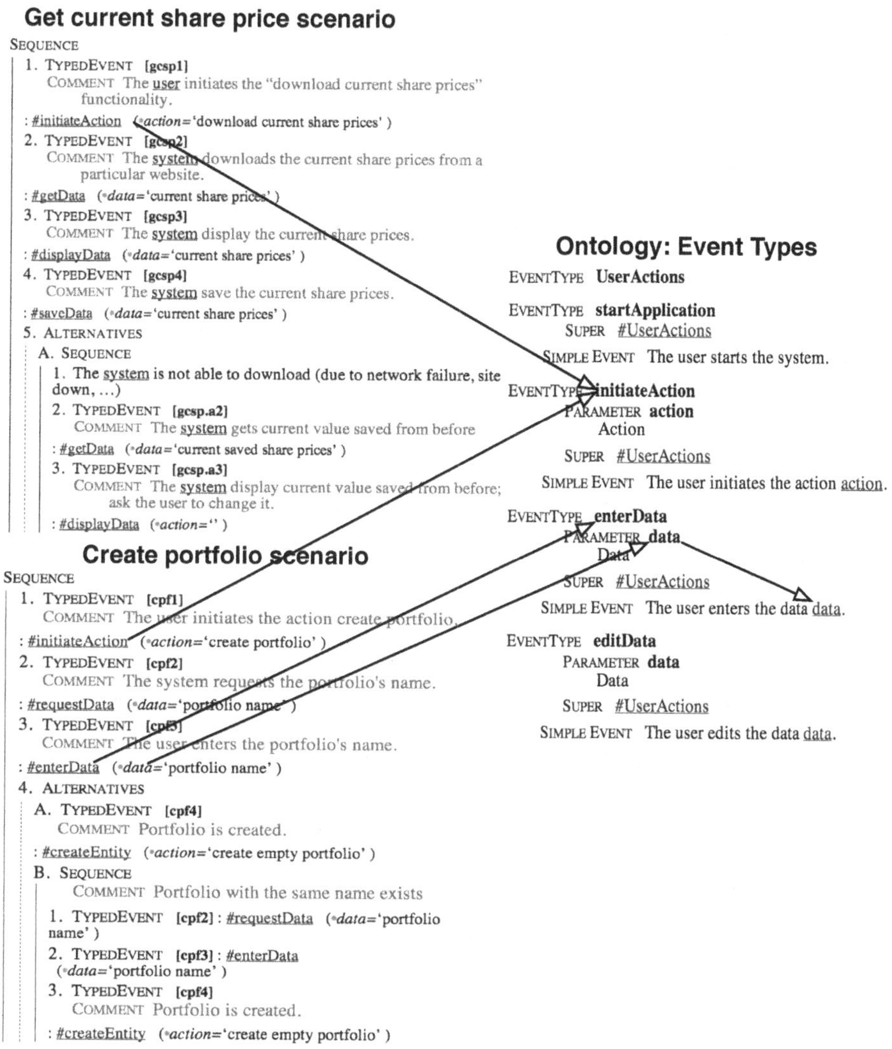

Get current share price scenario

SEQUENCE
1. TYPEDEVENT [gcsp1]
   COMMENT The user initiates the "download current share prices" functionality.
   : #initiateAction (*action*='download current share prices')
2. TYPEDEVENT [gcsp2]
   COMMENT The system downloads the current share prices from a particular website.
   : #getData (*data*='current share prices')
3. TYPEDEVENT [gcsp3]
   COMMENT The system display the current share prices.
   : #displayData (*data*='current share prices')
4. TYPEDEVENT [gcsp4]
   COMMENT The system save the current share prices.
   : #saveData (*data*='current share prices')
5. ALTERNATIVES
   A. SEQUENCE
      1. The system is not able to download (due to network failure, site down, ...)
      2. TYPEDEVENT [gcsp.a2]
         COMMENT The system gets current value saved from before
         : #getData (*data*='current saved share prices')
      3. TYPEDEVENT [gcsp.a3]
         COMMENT The system display current value saved from before; ask the user to change it.
         : #displayData (*action*='')

Create portfolio scenario

SEQUENCE
1. TYPEDEVENT [cpf1]
   COMMENT The user initiates the action create portfolio.
   : #initiateAction (*action*='create portfolio')
2. TYPEDEVENT [cpf2]
   COMMENT The system requests the portfolio's name.
   : #requestData (*data*='portfolio name')
3. TYPEDEVENT [cpf3]
   COMMENT The user enters the portfolio's name.
   : #enterData (*data*='portfolio name')
4. ALTERNATIVES
   A. TYPEDEVENT [cpf4]
      COMMENT Portfolio is created.
      : #createEntity (*action*='create empty portfolio')
   B. SEQUENCE
      COMMENT Portfolio with the same name exists
      1. TYPEDEVENT [cpf2] : #requestData (*data*='portfolio name')
      2. TYPEDEVENT [cpf3] : #enterData (*data*='portfolio name')
      3. TYPEDEVENT [cpf4]
         COMMENT Portfolio is created.
      : #createEntity (*action*='create empty portfolio')

Ontology: Event Types

EVENTTYPE **UserActions**

EVENTTYPE **startApplication**
SUPER #UserActions
SIMPLE EVENT The user starts the system.

EVENTTYPE **initiateAction**
PARAMETER **action**
Action
SUPER #UserActions
SIMPLE EVENT The user initiates the action action.

EVENTTYPE **enterData**
PARAMETER **data**
Data
SUPER #UserActions
SIMPLE EVENT The user enters the data data.

EVENTTYPE **editData**
PARAMETER **data**
Data
SUPER #UserActions
SIMPLE EVENT The user edits the data data.

Fig. 2. PIMS scenarios and part of mapping to PIMS ontology

components. Table 1 shows the mapping between some elements of the ontology and some components of the architecture. Each ontology event type is mapped at least to one component and each component is mapped to by at least by one ontology event type.

PIMS Scenarios Walkthrough. In this final step, we performed a walk-through of the scenarios in the architecture. Since the PIMS architecture was carefully designed to be part of a book, we were not surprised to find it is consistent with all the scenarios describing the system functional requirements.

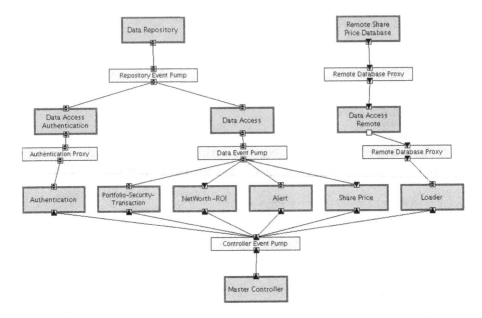

Fig. 3. The architecture of PIMS described in xADL

In order to illustrate how our approach discovers inconsistencies between requirements and architecture, we artificially introduced an error in the PIMS architecture by excising the link between the "Data Access" and "Loader" components. In introducing this error, our expectation was that the walkthrough of the "Create portfolio" scenario would succeed while the "Get the current prices of shares" scenario would fail.

We performed the walkthroughs of the two scenarios manually. The "Create portfolio" main scenario contains four simple events in a chain and matches four components in the architecture. As expected, the walkthrough was successful because the sequence of the events in the scenario matches an appropriate sequence of the components.

The "Get the current prices of shares" main scenario is also composed of four simple events in a chain and matches four components in the architecture.

Table 1. Mapping between ontology event types and architecture components

eventTypes	Components
startApplication	Master Controller
initiateAction	Master Controller
enterData	Master Controller
requestData	Master Controller
executeAction	Authentication, Data Access Authentication, Data Repository
reportError	Master Controller

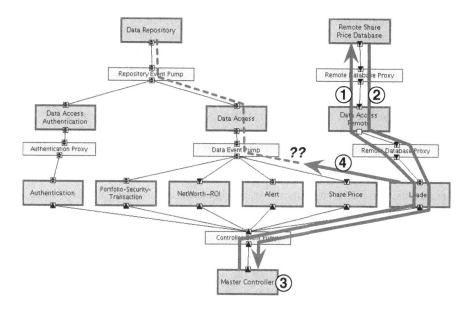

Fig. 4. Failed walkthrough of "Get the current prices of shares" scenario

However, the sequence of the events in the scenario does not succeed in the modified architecture due to the excised link between the "Data Access" and "Loader" components. Figure 4 illustrates the walkthrough of this scenario. The first event sends a request from the "Master Controller" component through intervening connectors and components to the "Remote Share Price Database". The second event transfers data back to the "Master Controller", and the third event displays it there. The fourth event would transfer specific data from the "Loader" through "Data Access" to the "Data Repository" to be saved. Since the necessary first link along this path between the "Loader" and "Data Access" was excised, and other paths do not support transfer of this data, the current prices of shares cannot be sent to the "Data Repository" to be saved. Therefore, the modified architecture does not cover this scenario.

4.2 CRASH System

The second system we chose to illustrate our approach is CRASH (Crisis Response and Situation Handling), a decentralized and distributed system developed in our department for case studies [27]. CRASH models a collection of governmental and non-governmental organizations cooperating in response to emerging situations in order to make decisions. The system contains the following decision-making organizations: Police Department, Fire Department, Search and Rescue, Red Cross, St. Elsewhere Hospital, a Charitable Organization, and the Department of Public Works. Each CRASH peer is divided into three sub-system classes: Display, Information Gathering Sources, and Command and Control. The Display sub-system is responsible for visualizing the information currently known to the organization such as deployment of resources and other vital information. Information Gathering Source sub-systems provide feedback and information to the entity's Command and Control sub-system, for example by relaying reports from the public. These sub-systems are connected to the entity's Command and Control through internal ad hoc networks. Additionally, each entity's Command and Control center is also connected to the Command and Control centers of other organizations, perhaps, again, through ad hoc networks. An entity's Command and Control center is then responsible for aggregating data received from its information sources as well as information from other organizations. Ultimately, the Command and Control system is responsible for making decisions on behalf of the entity and conveying information and instructions to its affiliated resources. A high-level architecture of the system is illustrated with two peers in Figure 5.

For the CRASH system to be dependable, it needs to be available, reliable and secure. Since the system is intended to be used to manage crisis in critical times, its availability is crucial. The continuity of correct service of the system is necessary to successfully coordinating the activities of the different organizations during the execution of the operations. Secondly, the CRASH system needs to be reliable so that all the services it delivers during the operations are correct. Finally, the system also needs to be secure to ensure that malicious entities cannot join the network and perform malicious behavior.

In this section, we focus on two scenarios that illustrate several dependability issues of CRASH.

The first scenario in concerned about the availability of the system. In the CRASH system, it is important to know what are the available entities at any given time. The availability of a system can be compromised by hardware and software failures. In this example scenario, we focus on the software failure. The following scenario operationalizes the availability requirement by showing how the system handles the failure of a component.

Entity Availability scenario: (1) The Police Department shuts down its Command and Control entity. (2) The Fire Department's Command and Control sends a request message to the Police Department's Command and Control. (3) The Network sends a failure message to the Fire Department. (4) The Fire Department receives the failure message.

The second scenario focusses on the reliability of the system. In order for the CRASH system to deliver reliable services, the communication between the entities in the system need to be effective. One aspect of this is the sequence in which messages are received; messages received out of order can create a mistaken understanding of what has occurred. The following scenario shows how the reliability requirement can be verified by testing whether the messages sent by a peer are received by other peers in the same sequence they are sent.

Message Sequence scenario: (1) Fire Department's Command and Control sends a request message to the Police Department's Command and Control. (2) Fire Department's Command and Control sends a second request message to the Police Department's Command and Control after 5 seconds. (3) The Police

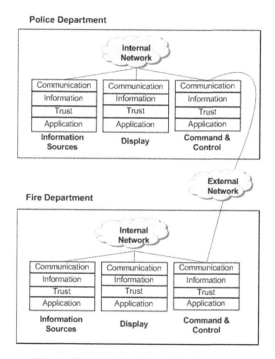

Fig. 5. CRASH High-Level Architecture

Department's Command and Control receives the first message. (4) The Police Department's Command and Control receives the second message.

The architecture style used to design the CRASH system is C2 [28]. A C2 architecture is composed of components and connectors that are organized into layers. Components in a layer are only aware of components in the layers above and have no knowledge about components in layers below. Components communicate with each other using two types of asynchronous event-based messages, requests and notifications. Request messages travel up the architecture while notification messages move down the architecture.

CRASH ScenarioML Scenarios. In this step, an ontology and scenarios for the non-functional requirements were developed for the CRASH system. The principle actors of the system are "User", "System", "Entity", and "Network". Based on the non-functional requirements scenarios, the actions performed by each actor were identified and described using the ScenarioML ontology. This description included generalizing and parameterizing the actions for simplicity and clarity and for a minimal set of event types. The description in ScenarioML of the ""Entity Availability" scenario is presented in Figure 6, and that of the ""Message Sequence" is presented as part of Figure 8.

CRASH Architectural Description in xADL. In this step, we again used Archipelago to define the CRASH architecture. The full architecture is too large

SEQUENCE

1. TYPEDEVENT **[ac1]**
   COMMENT The Police Department shuts down its Command and Control entity.
   : #shutdownEntity (•*entity*='Police Department' , •*component*='Command and Control')

2. TYPEDEVENT **[ac2]**
   COMMENT The Fire Department's Command and Control (from the UI component)
   sends a request message to the Police Department's Command and Control.
   : #sendMessage (•*sender*='Fire Department' , •*message*='Request Message'
   , •*receiver*='Police Department')

3. TYPEDEVENT **[ac3]**
   COMMENT The Network (Multicast Manager component) sends a failure message
   to the Fire Department (UI Component).
   : #sendMessage (•*sender*='Network (Multicast Manager)' , •*message*='Failure Message'
   , •*receiver*='Fire Department (UI)')

4. TYPEDEVENT **[ac4]**
   COMMENT The Fire Department (UI Component) receives the failure message.
   : #receiveMessage (•*sender*='Network (Multicast Manager)' , •*message*='Failure Message'
   , •*receiver*='Fire Department (UI)')

Fig. 6. "Entity Availability" scenario

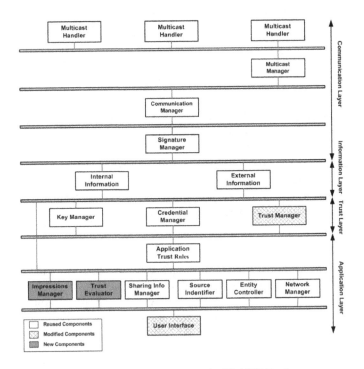

Fig. 7. Architecture of each CRASH Entity

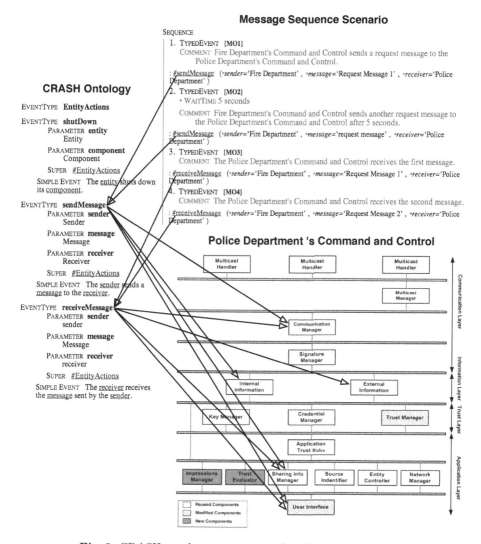

Fig. 8. CRASH ontology, scenario, and architecture mapping

to show here; as an illustration, we show the internal architecture of the Police Department's Command and Control center in Figure 7.

Mapping CRASH Ontology Elements to CRASH Architecture Components. Figure 8 gives a general overview of the relationships between ontology, scenarios, and architecture in our approach. It illustrates the mapping between the event types in the CRASH ontology and the components in the CRASH architecture. For example, the event type "sendMessage" is mapped to three components: "User Interface", "Sharing Info Manager", and "Communication Manager". It also shows how event types in the ontology are instantiated as typed events in the scenarios.

CRASH Scenarios Walkthrough. The two selected scenarios, "Entity Availability" and "Message Sequence", are concerned with availability and reliability respectively. In general, static walkthroughs have limited effectiveness for evaluating satisfaction of quality attributes by an architecture. These two quality attributes can be determined effectively only at run-time. Since we have not implemented our tool for supporting the execution of the architecture with scenarios, we demonstrate the concept by describing what could have happened when the execution of the scenarios on the architecture is simulated.

The "Entity Availability" main scenario contains four simple events in a chain that match a number of components in the architecture. The result of the walkthrough of this scenario is as follow. If the architecture provides a mechanism for detecting the availability of the entities, than the User Interface component of the Fire Department's Command and Control, which initiated the first event in the scenario, will receive an error message alerting the unavailability of the Police Department's Command and Control. Otherwise, Fire Department's Command and Control will not receive any alert about the unavailability of Police Department. This scenario is effective in determining if the an entity is available at any given time.

The "Message Sequence" main scenario is also composed of four simple events in a chain that match a number of components in the architecture. The main concern in this scenario is the preservation of the messages order in the architecture. The result of the walkthrough is as follow. If first message sent by the Fire Department's Command and Control arrives first in the Police Department's Command and Control, then the order is preserved; otherwise the order not preserved.

5   Discussion

A challenge of using scenarios to evaluate architecture is finding the necessary behavioral information in the architecture in order to exercise the architecture convincingly with a requirements scenario. This difficulty is highlighted when one tries to match events in scenarios to appropriate components and services in architectures. One aspect of the challenge is that requirements events are typically described at a finer granularity than architectural components, with several successive events often mapping to a single component. A requirements-level ontology can support generalization and specialization of the actions performed by actors in the scenario events, giving more flexibility in the conceptual level of the events. For instance, in the CRASH system, the message for saving, updating, and deleting information, can be generalized under one more-abstract message action, especially if the architecture handles all three similarly. Then the more-abstract *eventType* for that action can be mapped more straightforwardly and dependably to the architecture. The method by which it is specialized for the three cases (by parameters, or by event subtypes, or a combination) then provides a specific direction from which to evaluate how the architecture supports each of the cases.

Another challenge for scenario-based architecture evaluation methods is selecting the most important scenarios to evaluate the architecture. The number of possible scenarios can be very large for even small systems, which makes it impractical to check all scenarios. ScenarioML supports this task with its ontology that allows reuse of a single event type in several scenarios, or several times in a single scenario, resulting in fewer distinct events that may need to be covered.

A third challenge for scenario-based architectural evaluation methods is the difficulty of determining and expressing the non-functional requirements. Ideally, quality requirements are written completely and unambiguously in a requirements document prior to architecture design. Too often, however, quality requirements are not written or poorly written. Kazman *et al.* argue that quality attribute requirements for both existing and planned systems are often missing, vague, or incomplete [24]. Even if the quality attributes exist, they are limited to simple statements. For our approach, these quality attributes need to be described using scenarios, as in our previous work [30]. The scenarios need to describe specific examples (or counterexamples) of current and future uses of the system. Since these quality attributes need to be gathered for the most part from the stakeholders, designers need to work closely with stakeholders during requirements elicitation, specification, and analysis. Once identified, our approach facilitates their expression and management.

Traceability between requirements and architecture is a key condition for software maintainability with a reduced negative impact on software quality. Software evolves to meet users' new requirements, to correct defects, and to cope with changes to the environment in which it operates, among other reasons. Management of maintenance tasks demands some effort on the part of the developers, depending on the nature of the change and on available tool support. Tools that support requirements traceability (e.g. DOORS and Requisite Pro) manage source code and/or architecture versions [19], and supporting effective regression testing can alleviate the burden of software maintenance. When evolution of stakeholder requirements creates software maintenance tasks, traceability assists developers in locating other artifacts that also need modifications. Hence, traceability increases maintainability.

One benefit of our approach is the traceability links that are established between requirements and architecture, which ease maintenance involving these artifacts. Our approach explores ontology-based requirements-level scenarios to trace requirements to architecture. It explicitly maps event types in the ontology to components in the structural architectural description, and uses the ontology to simplify and minimize the mapping.

6   Related Work

Software architecture specifies the high-level structure, behavior, and characteristics of a system intended to satisfy software product requirements. Evaluating an architecture against requirements during architecture design is important because it is faster and cheaper to fix defects early. However, evaluating an architecture is also challenging because it is not possible to guarantee absolutely that the architecture meets its requirements [16]. So, evaluating an architecture can give only an estimate of the likelihood that it satisfies its requirements.

Scenarios have been proposed as a means for analyzing and evaluating architectures by many researchers. Barber and Holt proposed using a scenario space for evaluating architectures [5]. The scenario space is a directed graph that represents possible threads of execution composed of services in the software architecture, which provides a high level view of the architectural execution. This visualization helps evaluate whether executing the architecture will support the anticipated scenarios for the application domain. Kazman *et al.* also used scenarios to analyze architectures with the focus on achieving quality attributes in their method, Scenario-based Architecture Analysis Method (SAAM) [23]. A number of other scenario-based architecture analysis methods are also geared toward evaluating architectures against the desired quality attributes described using scenarios. These include Software Architecture Level Modifiability Analysis (ALMA) [7], Performance Assessment of Software Architecture (PASA) [15], Architecture Level Usability Assessment (SALUTA) [15], ART-SCENE [31], and Architecture Trade-off Analysis Method (ATAM) [4]. None of these methods use an ontology to improve the clarity and efficiency of scenarios, and to provide an effective mapping between requirements and architecture to facilitate architecture evaluation. We build on their work in the ways we use scenarios to evaluate an architecture.

Grunbacher *et al.* proposed the CBSP (Component-Bus-System-Property) approach for bridging requirements and architecture [18]. CBSP uses intermediate models to systematically reconcile requirements and architecture. Unlike our approach, CBSP is not intended for the evaluation of architecture, but instead is used in the design process. It helps designers develop architectures based directly on the requirements. Another method that aids the design of software architectures is the integrated decision-making framework [20]. The framework aids in systematically determining architecture alternatives from negotiated requirements among stakeholders. It facilitates requirements elicitation, architecture alternatives exploration, and reaching agreement. However, it does keep any mapping between requirements and architectures.

Ontologies have been proposed as way of representing knowledge on the Semantic Web [8]. An ontology is a data model representing a set of concepts within a domain and the relationships between those concepts. On the Semantic Web, ontologies facilitate interoperability and allow autonomous agent interaction. The idea of ontologies for knowledge representation that facilitates the sharing of information between agents has been used in traditional software development, in particular, in requirements engineering. Kaiya and Saeki developed a method for analyzing requirements based on ontologies [22]. In this method, an ontology is used as a semantic domain for detecting defects in requirements such as inconsistencies and incompleteness. The ontology is not used to express part of the requirements, as is the case in ScenarioML. Breitman *et al.* use ontologies to formalized services specifications in multi-agent systems [10]. The role of the ontologies in this work is to enhance the communication protocol to allow software agents to exchange meaningful information. Ontologies capture the semantics of the operations and services provided by agents, allowing interoperability and information exchange in a multi-agent systems. Again, the ontologies are not used to express the requirements. Breitman and Leite considered an ontology of a web application as a sub-product of the requirements engineering activity [11]. From this viewpoint, they proposed a requirements engineering based process for the construction of ontologies. The process is based on language extended lexicon (LEL) and provides a way to implement ontologies using the application lexicon. Our research builds on this work.

7 Summary

In this paper, we proposed an approach for evaluating software architectures against requirements-level scenarios. The approach comprises four steps: (1) user requirements specification in the form of scenarios using ScenarioML [1], (2) architectures design using an architectural description language, (3) mapping the requirements scenarios into the architecture components through an ontology, and (4) architectures evaluation against the original requirements scenarios. While ScenarioML constitutes the basis for specifying the requirements, any ADL that supports structural and behavioral specification of architectures can be used to specify the architecture. In this paper, we focused on xADL [12].

As a proof of concept, we applied our approach to two example applications, where we used xADL as the language for describing the architectures. We used the first example, PIMS, to illustrate how our approach checks the consistency of an architecture in regard to functional requirements. We used the second example to show that our approach can be used to check the fitness of an architecture in regard to non-functional requirements including dependability. Furthermore, the second example demonstrates the applicability of our approach to distributed and decentralized systems.

The next step in evaluating the effectiveness of our approach is to use our tool supporting the approach, currently under development. With the tool, we will be able to automatically check all the considered scenarios, which will lead to better results.

This approach differs from other scenario-based architectural evaluation methods in that it uses an ontology for the underlying connection between the requirements and the architecture. The ontology provides, among other benefits, clarity and consistency in the scenarios and a base for efficient mapping between requirements elements and architecture components. We believe these will allow the development of effective automatic tool support.

Another benefit of our approach is the traceability between requirements and architectures made possible by the mapping. By explicitly mapping event types in the ontology to components in the architectural description, requirements changes in the scenarios can be traced to the architecture and vice versa. As a consequence, requirements can evolve while the pre-established mapping assists developers in locating impacted components in the architecture.

8   Future Work

We are currently developing a tool called SOSAE (Scenario and Ontology-based Software Architecture Evaluation) to support this approach. SOSAE is an Eclipse plug-in tool that facilitates the mapping between the ontology elements of the requirements and components of the architecture. Furthermore, SOSAE provides the mechanism for automatically "executing" the scenarios on the architecture. For the description of the scenarios, we plan to integrate SOSAE with the Scenario Workbench, an Eclipse plug-in tool for editing and working with ScenarioML scenarios. In this way, the scenarios will be described in the Scenario Workbench and automatically loaded in SOSAE. For the description of the architecture, we will provide a means for integrating SOSAE with an appropriate architectural description language. The description of the architecture will be also automatically loaded in SOSAE. The first version of the tool is focusing on xADL.

We plan to generalize SOSAE to work with a range of ADLs. Our choice for supporting this is the generic ADL Acme [17], a simple ADL that can be used as a common interchange format for architecture design tools and/or as a foundation for developing new architectural design and analysis tools. Acme is also attractive in this context because it incorporates both structure and behavior description mechanisms. Our approach will then make use of AcmeStudio [26], an Eclipse plug-in tool that facilitates editing and visualization of software architectural designs based on the Acme architectural description language (ADL).

In Section 4 we applied our approach to two example systems as an illustration and proof of concept. We are planning a more detailed and convincing evaluation of our approach. An analogous evaluation using real-world systems would also require subject systems with both detailed requirements and detailed architectures. However, our earlier study [13] found that such real-world systems are hard to find, and in practice may not exist. After our SOSAE tool is completed, we plan a study in which we observe the use of our approach by an industrial partner in developing a real system.

We are strongly interested in connecting stakeholders into the architectural phase of development. The present work describes using scenarios to evaluate an architecture; we also envision using scenarios to communicate stakeholder goals and needs forward to software architects, and also using stakeholder-level scenarios from the architects to communicate the results of architectural analysis and evolution back to the stakeholders. These in turn could be used to derive implied scenarios from the combined stakeholder and architectural scenarios, using the approach of Uchitel et al. [29], in order to identify possibly undesired implied scenarios.

We will also explore the capability of an ontology to improve the efficiency of the mapping between requirements and architecture. Currently, our approach uses the domain ontology to define equivalent event types that can be reused when expressing the scenarios. The mapping is performed through event types to the architectural components, which results in a simpler mapping if event types are reused several times or in several scenarios. We hypothesize that the mapping can be further simplified, facilitated, and made more evolvable through use of other ontology features supported in ScenarioML: specialization/generalization among events, relationships among instances of an event type with different arguments, and references from events to domain classes and individuals. For example, the events that map to a specific component can be determined by the domain entities that appear in those events, rather than the actions the events describes. In such cases, defining the mapping links in terms of finer-grained elements such as domain classes shows promise to provide mappings that can adapt under evolution more naturally and efficiently, and thus (among other benefits) help the requirements and architecture to evolve coherently together.

Our future work also includes using the full potential of the domain ontology to further reduce the complexity of requirements to architecture mapping. The version of ScenarioML used here has it own domain ontology sublanguage. We are moving toward the use of the OWL web ontology language [6] in order to make use of existing OWL tools and reasoners.

Acknowledgments

The authors would like to thank the ROSATEA research group at the Donald Bren School of Information and Computer Science of the University of California, Irvine, and the anonymous reviewers of an earlier version of this paper, for their valued suggestions and insights.

References

1. Alspaugh, T.A.: Relationships between scenarios. Technical Report UCI-ISR-06-7, Institute for Software Research, University of California, Irvine (May 2006)
2. Alspaugh, T.A., Sim, S.E., Winbladh, K., Diallo, M., Ziv, H., Richardson, D.J.: The importance of clarity in usable requirements specification formats. In: 5th Intl. Wkp. on Comparative Evaluation in Requirements Engineering (CERE 2007) (2007)
3. Babar, M.A., Gorton, I.: Comparison of scenario-based software architecture evaluation methods. In: APSEC, pp. 600–607. IEEE Computer Society, Los Alamitos (2004)
4. Barbacci, M.R., Carriere, S.J., Feiler, P.H., Kazman, R., Klein, M.H., Lipson, H.F., Longstaff, T.A., Weinstock, C.B.: Steps in an architecture tradeoff analysis method: Quality attribute models and analysis. Technical Report CMU/SEI-97-TR-029, Software Eng. Inst. (1998)
5. Barber, K.S., Holt, J.: Software architecture correctness. IEEE Software 18(6), 64–65 (2001)
6. Bechhofer, S., Harmelen, F.v., Hendler, J., Horrocks, I., McGuinness, D.L., Patel-Schneider, P.F., Stein, L.A.: OWL web ontology language reference. Technical report, W3C (2004), http://www.w3.org/TR/2004/REC-owl-ref-20040210/

7. Bengtsson, P., Lassing, N., Bosch, J., van Vliet, H.: Architecture-level modifiability analysis (ALMA). J. Syst. Softw. 69(1-2), 129–147 (2004)
8. Berners-Lee, T., Hendler, J., Lassila, O.: The semantic web. Scientific American 284(5) (May 2001)
9. Bertolino, A.B.: A practical approach to UML-based derivation of integration tests. In: 4th International Software Quality Week Europe and International Internet Quality Week Europe (QWE 2000) (2000)
10. Breitman, K.K., Filho, A.H., Haeusler, E.H., von Staa, A.: Using ontologies to formalize services specifications in multi-agent systems. In: Hinchey, M.G., Rash, J.L., Truszkowski, W.F., Rouff, C.A. (eds.) FAABS 2004. LNCS (LNAI), vol. 3228, pp. 92–110. Springer, Heidelberg (2004)
11. Breitman, K.K., Leite, J.C.S.d.P.: Ontology as a requirements engineering product. In: 11th IEEE Joint International Conference on Requirements Engineering (RE 2003), pp. 309–319 (2003)
12. Dashofy, E.M., Hoek, A.v.d., Taylor, R.N.: A highly-extensible, XML-based architecture description language. In: Working IEEE/IFIP Conference on Software Architecture (WICSA 2001), p. 103 (2001)
13. Diallo, M.H., Sim, S.E., Alspaugh, T.A.: Case study, interrupted: The paucity of subject systems that span the requirements-architecture gap. In: First Workshop on Empirical Assessment of Software Engineering Languages and Technologies (WEASELTech 2007) (2007)
14. Dick, J.: Rich traceability. In: International Workshop on Traceability in Emerging Forms of Software Engineering, Edinburgh, UK (2002)
15. Folmer, E., Gurp, J.v., Bosch, J.: Scenario-based assessment of software architecture usability. In: ICSE Workshop on Bridging the Gaps Between Software Engineering and Human-Computer Interaction, pp. 61–68 (2003)
16. Fox, C.: Introduction to Software Engineering Design. Addison-Wesley, Reading (2007)
17. Garlan, D., Monroe, R.T., Wile, D.: Acme: An architecture description interchange language. In: CASCON 1997, pp. 169–183 (1997)
18. Grünbacher, P., Egyed, A., Medvidovic, N.: Reconciling software requirements and architectures with intermediate models. Software and System Modeling 3(3), 235–253 (2004)
19. Hoek, A.v.d., Rakic, M., Roshandel, R., Medvidovic, N.: Taming architectural evolution. In: Joint 8th European Software Engineering Conference (ESEC) and 9th ACM SIGSOFT Symposium on Foundations of Software Engineering (FSE) (2001)
20. In, H., Kazman, R., Olson, D.: From requirements negotiation to software architectural decisions. In: 1st Intl. Workshop on From Software Requirements to Architectures (2001)
21. Jalote, P.: An Integrated Approach to Software Engineering. Springer, Heidelberg (2006)
22. Kaiya, H., Saeki, M.: Ontology based requirements analysis: Lightweight semantic processing approach. In: 5th Int. Conf. on Quality Software (QSIC), pp. 223–230 (2005)
23. Kazman, R., Abowd, G.D., Bass, L.J., Clements, P.C.: Scenario-based analysis of software architecture. IEEE Software 13(6), 47–55 (1996)
24. Kazman, R., Klein, M., Clements, P.: ATAM: Method for architecture evaluation. Technical Report CMU/SEI-2000-TR-004, Soft. Eng. Institute (2000)
25. Naslavsky, L., Xu, L., Dias, M., Ziv, H., Richardson, D.J.: Extending xADL with statechart behavioral specification. In: Third Workshop on Architecting Dependable Systems (WADS), Edinburgh, Scotland, pp. 22–26 (May 2004)

26. Schmerl, B., Garlan, D.: AcmeStudio: Supporting style-centered architecture development. In: 26th Intl. Conf. on Softw. Eng (ICSE 2004), pp. 704–705 (2004)
27. Suryanarayana, G., Diallo, M.H., Erenkrantz, J.R., Taylor, R.N.: Architectural support for trust models in decentralized applications. In: 28th Intl. Conf. on Softw. Eng (ICSE 2006), pp. 52–61 (2006)
28. Taylor, R.N., Medvidovic, N., Anderson, K.M., Whitehead Jr., E.J., Robbins, J.E.: A component- and message-based architectural style for GUI software. In: 17th Intl. Conf. on Softw. Eng (ICSE 1995), pp. 295–304 (1995)
29. Uchitel, S., Kramer, J., Magee, J.: Detecting implied scenarios in message sequence chart specifications. In: Joint 8th European Software Engineering Conference (ESEC) and 9th ACM SIGSOFT Symposium on Foundations of Software Engineering (FSE), pp. 74–82 (September 2001)
30. Xu, L., Ziv, H., Alspaugh, T.A., Richardson, D.J.: An architectural pattern for nonfunctional dependability requirements. Journal of Systems and Software 79(10), 1370–1378 (2006)
31. Zhu, X., Maiden, N., Pavan, P.: Scenarios: Bringing requirements and architectures together. In: 2nd Intl. Workshop on Scenarios and State Machines: Models, Algorithms, and Tools (2003)

Combining Formal Verification and Testing for Correct Legacy Component Integration in Mechatronic UML*

Holger Giese[1], Stefan Henkler[2], and Martin Hirsch[2]

[1] Hasso Plattner Institute for Software Systems Engineering at the University of Potsdam,
Prof.-Dr.-Helmert-Str. 2-3, D-14482 Potsdam , Germany
[2] Software Engineering Group, University of Paderborn,
Warburger Str. 100, D-33098 Paderborn, Germany
holger.giese@hpi.uni-potsdam.de,
{shenkler-mahirsch}@uni-paderborn.de

Abstract. One of the main benefits of component-based architectures is their support for reuse. The port and interface definitions of architectural components facilitate the construction of complex functionality by composition of existing components. For such a composition means for a sufficient verification either by testing or formal verification are necessary. However, the overwhelming complexity of the interaction of distributed real-time components usually excludes that testing alone can provide the required coverage when integrating a legacy component. In this paper we present a scheme on how embedded legacy components can be tackled. For the embedded legacy components initially a behavioral model is derived from the interface description of the architectural model. This is in the subsequent steps enriched by an incremental synthesis using formal verification techniques for the systematic generation of component tests. The proposed scheme results in an effective combination of testing and formal verification. While verification is employed to tackle the inherently subtle interaction of the distributed real-time components which could not be covered by testing, local testing of the components guided by the verification results is employed to derive refined behavioral models. The approach further has two outstanding benefits. It can pin-point real failures without false negatives right from the beginning. It can also prove the correctness of the integration without learning the whole legacy component (using the restrictions of the integration context).

1 Introduction

The main benefits of the component-based architectures are their support for information hiding and reuse. The interface of a component is well defined by structural elements and collaboration protocols (cf. [7]). The dependencies between components are reduced to the knowledge of the known interfaces or ports. Thereby, a component can be exchanged if the specified port remains fulfilled. The port and interface definitions of

---

* This work was developed in the course of the Special Research Initiative 614 - Self-optimizing Concepts and Structures in Mechanical Engineering - University of Paderborn, and was published on its behalf and funded by the Deutsche Forschungsgemeinschaft.

R. de Lemos et al. (Eds.): Architecting Dependable Systems V, LNCS 5135, pp. 248–272, 2008.

architectural components therefore facilitate the construction of complex functionality by composition of existing components.

Especially in domains like automotive software where the development of new functions is an exception rather than the regular case (cf. [48]) component-based development can result in dramatic improvements. However, as long as an open and flexible software architecture which facilitate reuse is missing, many functions are nearly built from scratch for each new version (cf. [25]). Today, initiatives such as AUTOSAR[1] are a first step towards open and flexible software architectures for automotive systems. The definition of standard interfaces and an infrastructure for the software components ensures that components from different suppliers and vendors can technically interoperate. However, also a correct integration at the application level is needed.

In general, the proper composition of independently developed components in the software architecture of embedded real-time systems requires means for a sufficient verification of the integration step either by testing or formal verification. However, the overwhelming complexity of the interaction of distributed real-time components usually excludes that testing alone can provide the required coverage when integrating a legacy component.

Today, often a model-based development approach is employed to plan the decomposition of complex systems into components which are developed by different suppliers. The MECHATRONIC UML approach is one approach which permits to plan the decomposition of complex real-time systems upfront. It supports the description and compositional verification of the real-time coordination by means of components and patterns [24] and the integrated description and modular verification of discrete behavior and continuous control with components [9,21]. While it also supports for the generation of code for hard real-time processing [8,10] from further refined models in practice, seldom the whole system will be generated from the models. Besides the automatically derived components also either manually programmed or already existing components which fit more or less to the MECHATRONIC UML models will be employed. Thus an approach is required which permits to integrate these legacy components not only syntactically but also provide the required verification guarantees.

The overwhelming complexity of the interaction of distributed real-time components usually excludes that testing alone can provide the required coverage when integrating a legacy component. Thus formal verification techniques seem to be a valuable alternative. However, the required verification of the resulting system often becomes intractable as no abstract model of the reused components which can serve the verification purpose is available. A number of techniques which either use a black-box approach and automata learning [32] or a white-box approach which extracts the models from the code [39,15,31] exists. However none of them exploits the knowledge about the context and a component-based view to provide an approach which could in principle scale even for larger systems and which can help excluding besides false positives also false negatives after a feasible number of learning steps.

In this paper we present a scheme how embedded legacy components in a MECHATRONIC UML architecture can be tackled based on our approach presented in [29]. For the embedded legacy components initially a behavioral model is derived from the

---

[1] www.autosar.org

existing interface description which is a safe abstraction. This abstraction is then in subsequent steps enriched by an incremental synthesis procedure. This procedure uses the counterexample of a formal verification step to improve the accuracy of the behavioral model of the legacy component. We extend our previous work by supporting a (safe) over approximation and a rigorous formalization of the approach.

The formal verification step based on [21,24] is employed to cover the inherently subtle interaction of the distributed real-time components completely which could not be achieved by testing. Local testing of the legacy components using our model-based testing approach [23] and our approach for deterministic replay [22] guided by the verification results in the form of counterexamples is employed to derive refined behavioral models for the legacy component.

The approach therefore extends our former work [21,22,23,24,29] and has the benefit that it could pin-point real failures in the test step which are no false negatives right from the beginning. In addition, it can also prove the correctness of the integration for an abstract behavioral model of the legacy component without learning the whole legacy component by only checking possible integration problems for the explicit given context.

Application Example
As a concrete example for a complex mechatronic product, we use a simplified version of the software for the RailCab research project[2]. The vision of the RailCab project is a mechatronic rail system where autonomous shuttles apply the linear drive technology, used in the Transrapid, but travel on the existing passive track system of the standard railway. One particular problem, which has been previously described in [24], is to reduce the energy consumption due to air resistance by coordinating the autonomously operating shuttles in such a way that they form convoys whenever possible. Such convoys are created on-demand and require small distances between the shuttles in order to achieve significant energy savings. Coordination between the speed control units of the shuttles becomes a safety-critical aspect and results in a number of hard real-time constraints, which have to be addressed when building the control software of the shuttles. In [24] it has been solved for a simplified version of this shuttle coordination problem. In this example convoys consist of at most 2 shuttles.

The main requirement of the shuttle controller software is to ensure that no rear-end collision happens when the first shuttle has to brake suddenly e.g., in case of an emergency. If the shuttle is the head of a convoy it may brake only with reduced force, because another shuttle drives behind it with a reduced, minimal distance and therefore reacts with delay. Therefore the controlling software needs to ensure that the following situation will never occur: The rear shuttle is in *convoy* mode and therefore reduces the distance and the front shuttle is in mode *no-convoy* and brake with full strength in case of an emergency.

Modeling
Within our modeling and verification approach for the software of complex real-time systems [24], modeling is divided into modeling the interaction between components of the system by reusable *coordination patterns* and modeling the detailed behavior of the components by relating to the behavior of the applied patterns.

---

[2] http://www-nbp.upb.de/en/index.html

A pattern describes communication and therefore consists of multiple communication partners, called *roles*. Roles interact through ports which are linked by a connector. The communication behavior of a role is specified by a real-time statechart (RTSC) and is restricted by an invariant. The behavior of the connector is described by another real-time statechart that is used to model channel delay and reliability, which are of crucial importance for real-time systems. The overall behavior of a pattern is restricted by a pattern constraint, whereas the behavior of a role can be restricted by a role invariant. Altogether, we call the constraints, invariants, and known communication partners *context information*

Within the shuttle example, distance coordination between two shuttles is modeled as a pattern. This DistanceCoordination pattern consists of two roles, the frontRole and the rearRole and one connector that models the wireless radio link between the two shuttles. The pattern specifies the behavior needed to coordinate two successive shuttles. The main requirement of the pattern is to ensure that no rear-end collision happens when the first shuttle has to brake suddenly, e.g. in case of an emergency. If the shuttle is the head of a convoy, it is allowed to brake only with reduced force, to ensure that it cannot collide with the shuttle which drives behind it with a reduced, minimal distance. Otherwise, as the follower shuttle will react with a certain delay, a collision might happen. We thus require that the front shuttle must not brake with full power if it is in *convoy* mode. For the rear shuttle, we require that it does brake with full power. These two requirements are called role invariants. On the other hand, the overall pattern constraint forbids the rear role to be in mode *convoy* while frontRole is in mode *noConvoy*. The pattern constraint and role invariants can be annotated to the pattern respectively its roles using timed ACTL[3] formulas. The pattern with its annotated constraint and invariants is depicted in Figure 1.

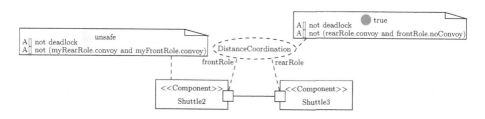

Fig. 1. The DistanceCoordination pattern

After the patterns have been specified, the concrete software components can be built. Components are designed by coordinating and refining each role RTSC of the involved patterns. The refinement has to respect the role RTSC (i.e. not add additional behavior or block guaranteed behavior) and additionally has to respect the guaranteed behavior of the roles in the form of their invariants. An additional internal RTSC for coordination is used to describe the required coordination of the refined roles. We further refer to the refined roles as component ports or ports in short.

---

[3] Timed ACTL is the subset of timed computation tree logic [13] which only contains **always** path operators.

In our example, the shuttle component must conform to the DistanceCoordination pattern and has to operate as both a rearRole and a frontRole as it may be follow, or be followed by, another shuttle as well as itself can follow another shuttle.

To complete the presented approach the outlined modeling capabilities are further extended by model checking and code generation. We prove that the given constraints hold for the system by using a model checker. Code generation on the other hand ensures that the constraints still hold for the code. However, in practice frequently not the whole system will be generated from the models. Instead several independent developed or already existing components that have been not automatically derived from MECHATRONIC UML models have to be integrated (cf. Figure 2).

Approach

Given a MECHATRONIC UML architecture which embeds a legacy component and behavioral models for all other components building the context of the legacy component, the basic question of correct legacy component integration is whether for the composition of the legacy component and its context all anomalies such as deadlocks are excluded or all additionally required properties hold. However, it is usually very expensive and risky to reverse-engineer an abstract model of the legacy component to verify whether the integration will work.

To overcome this problem we suggest employing some learning strategy via testing to derive a series of more detailed abstract models for the legacy component. The specific feature of our approach will be that we exploit the present abstract model of the context to only test relevant parts of the legacy component behavior. The approach depends only to a minimal extent on reverse engineering results.

We start with synthesizing a model of the legacy component behavior based on known structural interface description and a reverse engineered upper bound on the state size. Then, we check whether the context plus the model of legacy behavior exhibit any undesired behavior taking generic correctness criteria or additional required properties into account. If not, we use the resulting counterexample trace to test the legacy component. If the trace can be realized with the legacy component, a real error has been found. If not, we first enrich the trace with additional information using deterministic replay and then merge the enriched trace into the model of the legacy component behavior. We repeat the checks until either a real error has been found or all relevant cases have been covered.

Figure 2 illustrates our process with a summary of the overall approach. 1) Initially, we synthesize an initial behavior model for the legacy component based on known structural interface description and derive a behavioral model of the context from the existing MECHATRONIC UML models. 2) We check the combination of the two behavioral models and either get a) a counterexample or b) the checked properties are guaranteed. In the latter case we are done. 3) If we have a counterexample, we use this as test input for the legacy component. Deterministic replay enables us to enrich the observable behavior with state information by monitoring. If the tested faulty run is confirmed, we have found a real counterexample. If not, we can use the new observed behavior to refine the previously employed behavior model of the legacy component. We repeat steps 2) to 4) until one of the described exits occurs.

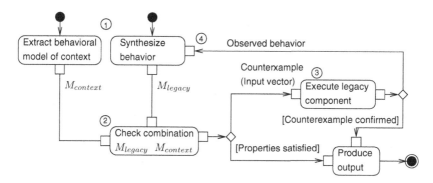

Fig. 2. Sketch of the approach

Overview

We first define in the next Section the prerequisite of our approach. We will introduce incomplete automata and chaotic automata which are required for learning the behavior. In Section 3 we describe the initial behavior synthesis and in Section 4 we describe the iterative process for behavioral synthesis. Based on the counterexamples from Section 4, we describe in Section 5 our testing approach. Section 6 compares our work to similar approaches and Section 7 presents the conclusion and future work.

2   Prerequisites

To provide a formal ground for our later employed MECHATRONIC UML concepts, we present a formal definition for the employed notion of automata, parallel composition, and refinement as well as the employed compositionality results for this formal model. The RTSC employed in MECHATRONIC UML are mapped to a finite state transition system in the form of extended Kripke structures (called I/O-interval structures [44]). We present here only a rather simplified version of this finite state transition model where discrete time is mapped to single states and transitions. This automata model is sufficient to permit the understanding of the underlying behavior model and to prove that the compositional verification combined with the testing and monitoring is correct. The simplification is justified by the following assumption which are valid for the considered domain: (1) the usual clock synchronization assumption which is common to many systems and means that time is progressing equally fast in any system component, and (2) a discrete time model suffices to model all time depending constraints, because the underlying infrastructure (hardware and possibly a real-time operating systems) does not react infinitely fast.

The simplified real-time automaton model and its real-time processing which corresponds to our employed notion of RTSC are defined as follows:

Definition 1. *An automaton is a 5-tuple $M = (S, I, O, T, Q)$ with a finite set S of states, input signals I, output signals O, a set of transitions $T \subseteq S \times \wp(I) \times \wp(O) \times S$ where $\wp(X)$ denotes the power-set of X, and the initial state set Q.*

The behavior is characterized by execution sequences called runs.

Definition 2. *A regular run is a sequence of states and I/O $\pi = s_1, A_1/B_1, s_2, \ldots,$ where for each $i \geq 1$ exists $(s_i, A_i, B_i, s_{i+1}) \in T$. We in addition have* deadlock runs *which are a sequence of states and I/O $\pi = s_1, A_1/B_1, s_2, \ldots s_n, A_n/B_n$, where for each $1 \leq i \leq n$ exists $(s_i, A_i, B_i, s_{i+1}) \in T$ and $\nexists s_{n+1}(s_n, A_n, B_n, s_{n+1}) \in T$. We write $[M]$ for the set of all regular and deadlock runs and use $\pi|_{I/O}$ to restrict a run to an observable* trace *and $\pi|_S$ to denote the related state sequence.*[4]

The time semantics of an automaton is simply that each transition takes exactly one time unit.

For convenience we use in the following S_i, I_i, O_i, T_i, and Q_i to denote the corresponding elements of M_i. Two automata M and M' with distinct input and output sets ($I \cap I' = \emptyset$ and $O \cap O' = \emptyset$) are further called *composable*. If also $I \cap O' = \emptyset$ and $O \cap I' = \emptyset$ holds, they are even *orthogonal* to each other.

2.1 Property Specification

Properties which should hold for a specific model are specified by using clocked CTL (CCTL) constraints (ϕ) and invariants (ψ). These formulas will be build using a shared set of atomic propositions P. An automaton M_i and any of its states $s \in S_i$ is annotated with all propositions in $P_i \subseteq P$ which they fulfill using a labeling function $L_i : S \rightarrow \wp(P_i)$. Thus an automaton $M_i = (S_i, I_i, O_i, T_i, Q_i)$ is accordingly extended to a 6-tuple $M_i = (S_i, I_i, O_i, T_i, L_i, Q_i)$. The label set $\mathcal{L}(M_i)$ denotes the set of all by the labeling considered propositions P_i. $\mathcal{L}(\phi)$ and $\mathcal{L}(\psi)$ denote the subsets of the basic proposition set P that is employed within the formulas.

Finally, for sake of simplification of the following formal definitions, we omit any syntactical details of CTL and CCTL and write $M \models \phi$ when an automaton M fulfills a constraint or invariant ϕ. The special symbol δ is used to denote that a *deadlock* (a state without any outgoing transition) can be reached. $M \models \neg \delta$ thus denotes that M does not contain any deadlocks.

2.2 Parallel Composition

In our application domain the composition of multiple components requires their parallel execution. As we model time explicitly and in a discrete manner, the required notion of parallel composition must result in the *synchronous execution* [13] of all systems running in parallel.

The communication is formalized by *synchronous communication* such that sending and receiving happens within the same time step. Consequently, the asynchronous event semantics of statecharts is modeled by explicitly defined event queues (channels) given in the form of additional automata. These explicit models of the event queues are required anyway to take the QoS characteristics of each connection into account.

To combine two composed automata we simply connect their input and output signals and consider their parallel execution.

---

[4] The concepts outlined here have some similarities with process algebra concepts. While regular runs reduced to the observable events are traces in CSP [30] or other process algebras, deadlock runs are related to ideas of failures in CSP or refusals. In contrast to the presented proposal, process algebra approaches abstract from states.

Definition 3. *For two automata* $M = (S, I, O, T, L, Q)$ *and* $M' = (S', I', O', T', L', Q')$ *which are composable to each other* ($I \cap I' = \emptyset$ *and* $O \cap O' = \emptyset$)*, we define their* parallel composition *denoted by* $M \| M'$ *as the automaton* $(S'', I'', O'', T'', L'', Q'')$ *with* $S'' = S \times S'$, $I'' = I \cup I'$, $O'' = O \cup O'$, $Q'' = Q \times Q'$, *and* $((s_1, s_1'), A'', B'', (s_2, s_2')) \in T''$ *iff* $(s_1, A, B, s_2) \in T$ *and* $(s_1', A', B', s_2') \in T'$ *exist with* $A'' = A \cup A'$ *and* $B'' = B \cup B'$. *Additionally*, $(A \cap O') = B'$ *and* $(A' \cap O) = B$ *must hold.* S'' *and* T'' *are further adjusted to exclude all non reachable state combinations and transitions. The labelling* L'' *for* $(s, s') \in S''$ *is easily derived as* $L''((s, s')) = L(s) \cup L'(s')$.

Informally, a transition in T'' is a combination of two transitions in each automaton iff all required local inputs by the other side are matching $((A \cap O') = B'$ and $(A' \cap O) = B)$ and the non local input and output signals are simply the union of both automata.

2.3 Automata Refinement

Our restricted notion of components means that they are derived by refining the role protocols from all the patterns they are participating in. Thus, we require an appropriate notion for refinement which is essentially a restricted version of simulation which additionally preserves reactivity. For two given automata we can define whether the first is a refinement of the second as follows.

Definition 4. *An automaton* $M = (S, I, O, T, L, Q)$ *is a* refinement *of automaton* $M' = (S', I', O', T', L', Q')$ ($M \sqsubseteq M'$) *iff hold:*

$$\forall \pi = \ldots s \in [M] \exists \pi' = \ldots s' \in [M'] : \pi|_{I/O} = \pi'|_{I'/O'} \wedge L(s) = L'(s') \quad (1)$$

$$\forall \pi = \ldots s, A/B \in [M] \exists \pi = \ldots s', A/B \in [M'] : \pi|_{I/O} = \pi'|_{I'/O'} \quad (2)$$

For each path in the refinement M equation 1 further ensures that a related path in M' exists. Equation 2 further ensures that every deadlock path of M is also a possible deadlock path for M'. Therefore, $\sqsubseteq$ implies simulation ($\preceq$).

2.4 Compositional Constraints

For our approach the interesting class of constraints is the constraints, which are preserved under refinement and composition with disjoint labeling.

Definition 5. *A constraint* ϕ *is compositional iff for any automaton* M_1, M_1', *and* M_2 *with* $\mathcal{L}(M_2) \cap \mathcal{L}(\phi) = \emptyset$ *holds*

$$(M_1 \models \phi) \Rightarrow ((M_1 \| M_2 \models \phi) \vee (M_1 \| M_2 \models \delta)) \text{ and} \quad (3)$$
$$((M_1 \sqsubseteq M_1') \wedge (M_1' \models \phi)) \Rightarrow (M_1 \models \phi) \quad (4)$$

CTL formulas are preserved by the bisimulation equivalence relation, while ACTL formulas are preserved by the simulation preorder ($\preceq$) [13]. The presented refinement implies simulation and thus preserves ACTL formulas also, but in contrast it additionally preserves deadlock freedom:

Lemma 1. *For automaton M and M' with $M \sqsubseteq M'$ holds $M' \models \neg \delta \Rightarrow M \models \neg \delta$.*

Proof. (sketch) Condition 1 ensures that for any $s \in S$ at least one related $s' \in S'$ exists with $(s, s') \in \Omega$. From M' deadlock free follows that s' will have at least one outgoing transition and due to condition 2 s also. Therefore, M is also deadlock free.

Invariants, upper and lower time-bounds, and ACTL formulas in general are constraints which refer only to all possible paths. Thus using the fact that a refinement or composition with disjoint labeling sets only reduces the possible sequences of states with identical labeling, they are compositional. That deadlock freedom is also compositional follows by construction for condition 3 and Lemma 1 for condition 4.

Compositionality can thus be established for the properties required so far during our studies such as deadlock freedom, upper bounds for the maximal delays of message transports, lower bounds for the minimal delays of message transports, and invariants. For example, the according CCTL formula with only A path quantifiers for a maximal delay is for d the maximal delay, p_1 the trigger condition, and p_2 the required condition: $AG(\neg p_1 \vee (AF_{[1,d]} p_2))$. In contrast, temporal logic formulas that demand explicitly that a specific state is eventually reached (abstracting from possible effects of non-determinism) are not preserved.

2.5 Parallel Composition and Refinement

We also require that parallel composition preserves refinement.

Lemma 2. *For any automaton M_1 and an automaton M_2 refining automaton M_2' ($M_2 \sqsubseteq M_2'$) holds $M_2 \sqsubseteq M_2' \Rightarrow (M_1 \| M_2 \sqsubseteq M_1 \| M_2')$.*

Proof. (sketch) For $M_1 \| M_2'$ we can form the construction of the parallel composition conclude that only path and deadlock path result which are also present in $M_1 \| M_2$. Therefore condition 1 and 2 must be fulfilled for $M_1 \| M_2$ and $M_1 \| M_2'$.

For a substitution of a restricted refinement that only adds disjoint I/O signals we further have to prove that compositional constraints and deadlock freedom are preserved.

Lemma 3. *For automaton M_1, M_2, and M_2' with $M_2 \sqsubseteq_{I/O} M_2'$, $I_1 \cap (O_2 - O_2') = \emptyset$, $O_1 \cap (I_2 - I_2') = \emptyset$, and $\mathcal{L}(M_1) \cap (\mathcal{L}(M_2) - \mathcal{L}(M_2')) = \emptyset$ and any compositional constraint ϕ holds*

$$(M_1 \| M_2' \models \phi \wedge \neg \delta) \Rightarrow (M_1 \| M_2 \models \phi \wedge \neg \delta) \tag{5}$$

Proof. Due to ϕ and $\neg \delta$ being compositional and Definition 5 we can for $M_2'' = M_2|_{I_2'/O_2'/\mathcal{L}(M_2')}$ conclude that $M_1 \| M_2'' \models \phi \wedge \neg \delta$ or $M_1 \| M_2'' \models \delta$. Due to Lemma 1 and 2 we even have $M_1 \| M_2'' \models \phi \wedge \neg \delta$. From $I_1 \cap (O_2 - O_2') = \emptyset$ and $O_1 \cap (I_2 - I_2') = \emptyset$ follows that M_2 adds to M_2'' only I/O that does not interfere with M_1 and thus $M_1 \| M_2$ has the same reachable state set and transitions and thus $M_1 \| M_2 \models \neg \delta$. As ϕ is only interpreted over states and the labeling is identical for $\mathcal{L}(\phi) \subseteq \mathcal{L}(M_2')$, ϕ must also hold and thus condition 5 is proven.

2.6 Incomplete Automata

When incrementally improving the accuracy of a behavioral model with respect to some original, we can use the concept of a incomplete automaton.

Definition 6. *An* incomplete automaton *is a 6-tuple* $M = (S, I, O, T, \overline{T}, Q)$ *with* $M = (S, I, O, T, Q)$ *an automaton and* $\overline{T} \subseteq S \times \wp(I) \times \wp(O)$ *denoting the known not supported interactions. To ensure that T and $\overline{T}$ are consistent we require that*

$$\neg(\exists s, A, B, s' : (s, A, B, s') \in T \wedge (s, A, B) \in \overline{T}).$$

The behavior is characterized by execution sequences called runs.

Definition 7. *A regular run* of an incomplete automaton *is a sequence of states and I/O* $\pi = s_1, A_1/B_1, s_2, \ldots,$ *where for each* $i \geq 1$ *exists* $(s_i, A_i, B_i, s_{i+1}) \in T$. *We in addition have* deadlock runs *which are a sequence of states and I/O* $\pi = s_1, A_1/B_1, s_2, \ldots s_n, A_n/B_n,$ *where for each* $1 \leq i \leq n$ *exists* $(s_i, A_i, B_i, s_{i+1}) \in T$ *and* $(s_n, A_n, B_n) \in \overline{T}$. *We write* $[M]$ *for the set of all regular and deadlock runs and use* $\pi|_{I/O}$ *to restrict a run to an observable trace and $\pi|_S$ to denote the related state sequence.*

The definition of the runs highlights the fact that in an incomplete automaton deadlock runs are only assumed when explicitly defined by $\overline{T}$ and not implicitly if no transition is present in T.

A concrete automaton is *deterministic* if for any s, A, and B holds that $|\{(s, A, B, s') \in T\}| \leq 1$. An incomplete automaton is *deterministic* if for any s, A, and B holds that $|\{(s, A, B, s') \in T\} \cup \{(s, A, B) \in \overline{T}\}| \leq 1$.

Given an incomplete automaton, we can then describe a completion step as any extension of S, T or $\overline{T}$ which again results in an incomplete automaton. In a final step an incomplete automata becomes *complete*, when for each possible interaction is either forbidden by $\overline{T}$ or present in T:

$$\forall s \in S, A \in \wp(I), B \in \wp(O) : (\exists s' \in S : (s, A, B, s') \in T \text{ xor } (s, A, B) \in \overline{T}).$$

2.7 Chaotic Automata and Closure

Taking the refinement notion of Definition 4, we can identify a maximal behavior (named chaotic automaton) which is an abstraction of every possible behavior as it might accept any sequence of inputs but may also deadlock for every possible interaction.

Definition 8. *For given input and output sets I and O, the* chaotic automaton $M_c = (S_c, I, O, T_c, Q_c)$ *is build as follows: The state set* $S_c = \{s_\delta, s_\forall\}$ *contains two distinct state, the transition set* $T_c = \{(s_\forall, A, B, s_\forall)|A \in \wp(I), B \in \wp(O)\} \cup \{(s_\forall, A, B, s_\delta)|A \in \wp(I), B \in \wp(O)\},$ *and* $Q_c = \{s_\delta, s_\forall\}$.

The chaotic automaton specified in Definition 8 is depicted in Figure 3[5]. We can see that both state $s_\forall$ and s_δ are possible initial states and that while s_δ will block any

---

[5] Note, we write in all figures and listings s_all and s_delta and not $s_\forall$ and s_δ as the mathematical notation is not supported by the used tool.

Fig. 3. Maximal chaotic behavior: the chaotic automaton

interaction, $s_\forall$ will support any possible interaction (all possible input and output combinations are referred to here by '*').

If also a number of properties are relevant, we have to further have states $s_\forall$ and s_δ for every possible proposition subset P' of P. However, it is much more efficient to instead label $s_\forall$ and s_δ with a new proposition p' and replace for all propositions $p \in P$ all occurrences of p by $(p \vee p')$ as well as occurrences of $\neg p$ by $(\neg p \vee p')$.

If we are interested in a safe abstraction, a special kind of completion is the chaotic completion where all defined behavior result in arbitrary chaotic behavior.

Definition 9. *Given an incomplete automaton* $M = (S, I, O, T, \overline{T}, Q)$ *we derive the* *related chaotic closure automaton* $M' = (S', I, O, T', Q')$ *as follows:*

1. *double the state set and include the chaotic automaton* $(S' = (S \times \{0\}) \uplus (S \times \{1\}) \uplus S_c)$ *and*
2. *adjust the transition set to the doubling such that all not specified interactions either are not supported or lead to the added chaotic automaton* $(T' = \{((s,0), A, B, (s',0)) | (s, A, B, s') \in T\} \uplus \{((s,0), A, B, (s',1)) | (s, A, B, s') \in T\} \uplus \{((s,1), A, B, (s',0)) | (s, A, B, s') \in T\} \uplus \{((s,1), A, B, (s',1)) | (s, A, B, s') \in T\} \uplus \{((s,1), A, B, s_\forall) | s \in S, a \in \wp(I), B \in \wp(O), (s, A, B) \notin \overline{T}\} \uplus \{((s,1), A, B, s_\delta) | s \in S, a \in \wp(I), B \in \wp(O), (s, A, B) \notin \overline{T}\} \uplus T_c.$

We denote the chaotic closure of M *as* $chaos(M)$.

In this construction $Q' = \{(s,0) | s \in Q\} \uplus \{(s,1) \in Q\}$. The states $(s,0)$ are those representing the case that no further extension is assumed which might thus result in a deadlock, while the states $(s,1)$ are those representing the case that all possible further extensions are assumed which therefore lead to chaos (which is represent by s_δ and $s_\forall$).

Note that this chaotic behavior is highly non-deterministic while the real legacy component behavior is required to be deterministic.

2.8   Observation Conformance and Refinement

Definition 10. *The incomplete automaton* M *is* observation conforming *concerning an* *automaton* M_r *iff* $[M] \subseteq [M_r]$.

Note that the defined notion of observation includes states in our case, while in a standard setting we would only consider the path.

Theorem 1. *If* M *is an observation conforming incomplete automaton concerning a* *concrete deterministic component implementation* M_r, *it holds that* $M_r \sqsubseteq chaos(M)$.

Proof. Condition 1 for refinement follows directly from $[M] \subseteq [M_r]$ as we let s_δ and $s_\forall$ fulfil all positive and negative propositions (by modifying the formulas accordingly). Condition 2 is fulfilled as the chaotic closure guarantees by construction only additional behavior which can always also result in a deadlock. □

3 Initial Behavior Synthesis

Given a concrete context M_r^c with abstract model M_a^c that refines the concrete context ($M_r^c \sqsubseteq M_a^c$) and a concrete component implementation M_r with hidden internal details (legacy component), the basic question we want to check is whether a given property ϕ as well as deadlock freedom ($\neg \delta$) holds. We are in particular interested in a guarantee that both properties hold or a counterexample witnessing that they do not hold. However, usually M_r cannot be employed to traverse the whole state space as the state space of the system $M_a^c \| M_r$ is too large to directly address this question.

To overcome this problem we suggest to build a series M_a^i of abstractions of M_r which are all safe when it comes to verification but become more and more accurate such that finally we can use them to conclude either that the integration works correctly or not.

$$M_r \sqsubseteq M_a^i \quad (\forall i \geq 0). \tag{6}$$

We thus start with synthesizing a model of the legacy component behavior based on the known structural interface description. While the interface description can be taken from the context or reverse-engineered straightforwardly from the legacy component, deriving an upper bound on the relevant legacy component states can become more complicated. The crucial criterion for a valid state abstraction is that for all possible inputs/outputs the state reached must be the same.

In a first step we simply build M_a^0 using the available information about the interface of M_r. We simply build an M_l^0 by determining the initial state s_0 of M_r and derive an automaton $M_l^0 = (\{s_0, I, I, \emptyset, \{s_0\})$. We can then use the chaotic closure to derive our first safe approximation: $M_a^0 = chaos(M_l^0)$. Due to Theorem 1 we then know that M_a^0 is a safe abstraction from M_r ($M_r \sqsubseteq M_a^0$).

Lemma 4. *For the initial model $M_a^0 = chaos(M_l^0)$ for M_l^0 build for the initial state s_0 of M_r as the automaton $M_l^0 = (\{s_0, I, I, \emptyset, \{s_0\})$ holds $M_r \sqsubseteq M_a^0$.*

Proof. Due to Theorem 1 we can conclude that M_a^0 is a safe abstraction from M_r as M_l^0 is observation conforming to M_r. □

In Figure 4(a) the initial trival automaton is depicted. The automaton consists of an initial state (depicted as a double circle) and the first state noConvoy::default which is connected via a transition with the initial state.

The automaton which results when the chaotic closure is applied to the trivial incomplete automaton depicted in Figure 4(a) which only captures the known initial state noConvoy::default is depicted in Figure 4(b). We can see how this initial state has been doubled and that one of these two states is connected via any possible interaction with both chaotic states $s_\forall$ and s_δ (all possible input and output combinations are referred to here by '*').

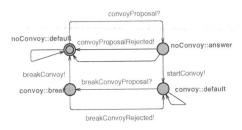

Fig. 4. Trivial initial implicit automaton encoding the known initial state (4(a)) and Initial behavior of a legacy component (4(b))

Fig. 5. Known behavior of context

In Figure 5 the known behavior of the context, the frontrole, is depicted. The automaton starts in the noConvoy state. The automaton remains in the state until the frontRole receives the convoyProposal message. Thereafter the automaton switches to the answer state. In this state, the automaton non-deterministically decides to reject the convoy (convoyProposalRejected) or to start the convoy (startConvoy). In the latter case the automaton switches to the convoy state and remains there until a breakConvoyProposal message is received. The automaton decides to reject or accept this message.

4 Iterative Behavior Synthesis

On the basis of the initial behavior synthesis, we describe in this section our approach of iterative behavior synthesis. First, we start with checking if the given properties hold for the initial synthesized behavior. If a counterexample exists, we proceed with testing based on that counterexample. While testing we monitor the legacy system. The monitored trace is used for learning the behavior. The new synthesized behavior is then the start point for the next iteration.

4.1 Formal Verification Step

The iterative behavior synthesis starts with checking for the abstraction derived from initial behavior synthesis (cf. Section 3), whether a counterexample for the required property ϕ exists. We therefore check for $i \geq 0$

$$M_a^c \| M_a^i \models \phi \wedge \neg \delta. \tag{7}$$

If the check succeeded, we have indeed proven that the property must also hold for $M_a^c \| M_r$ and $M_r^c \| M_r$.

Lemma 5. *Given a concrete context M_r^c with abstract model M_a^c and a concrete component implementation M_r with derived abstraction M_a^i such that the concrete context refines the abstract context ($M_r^c \sqsubseteq M_a^c$) and that the abstraction is valid ($M_r \sqsubseteq M_a^i$) it holds for any compositional property ϕ:*

$$M_a^c \| M_a^i \models \phi \quad \Rightarrow \quad M_r^c \| M_r \models \phi. \tag{8}$$

Proof. As refinement ($\sqsubseteq$) is a precongruence for parallel composition ($\|$) and $M_r^c \sqsubseteq M_a^c$, we can conclude that $M_r^c \| M_a^i \sqsubseteq M_a^c \| M_a^i$ must hold. Similarly, having $M_r \sqsubseteq M_a^i$ we thus have $M_r^c \| M_r \sqsubseteq M_r^c \| M_a^i$. As refinement preserves property ϕ, we thus can starting with $M_a^c \| M_a^i \models \phi$ conclude that $M_r^c \| M_r \models \phi$ must hold. □

If, however, the check did no succeed, we will have a counterexample in the form of a path π for $M_a^c \| M_a^i$ which is a witness that ϕ is not true for the abstraction. This counterexample restricted to M_a^i is then used to test the legacy component.

Listing 1.1. Initial counterexample

```
shuttle1.noConvoy, shuttle2.s_all,
shuttle2.convoyProposal!, shuttle1.convoyProposal?
shuttle1.answer, shuttle2.wait,
shuttle1.convoyProposalRejected!, shuttle2.convoyProposalRejected?
shuttle1.noConvoy, shuttle2.s_all
shuttle2.convoyProposal!, shuttle1.convoyProposal?
shuttle1.answer, shuttle2.wait
shuttle1.startConvoy!, shuttle2.startConvoy?
shuttle1.convoy, shuttle2.s_all
shuttle2.breakConvoyProposal!, shuttle1.breakConvoyProposal?
shuttle1.break, shuttle2.s_delta
```

In Listing 1.1 the counterexample of the first check is shown. The counterexample is a relatively long run. First, the closure sends a convoyProposal to the context. Afterwards, the context sends a convoyProposalReject. Then, the closure sends once again a convoyProposal and the context decides to build a convoy by sending a startConvoy. After building the convoy, the context tries to break the convoy but the closure goes in s_δ state and a deadlock is manifested.

4.2 Testing Step

If the test reveals that the path π is also possible in the concrete system, we can conclude that we have found a real integration problem.

Lemma 6. *Given a concrete context M_r^c with abstract model M_a^c and a concrete component implementation M_r with derived abstraction M_a^i such that the concrete context refines the abstract context ($M_r^c \sqsubseteq M_a^c$) and that the abstraction is valid ($M_r \sqsubseteq M_a^0$) it holds:*

$$\left(M_a^c \| M_a^i, \pi \not\models \phi \quad \wedge \quad \pi \in M_r^c \| M_r \right) \quad \Rightarrow \quad M_r^c \| M_r \not\models \phi \tag{9}$$

Proof. As π is a witness of $\neg\phi$ and ϕ is a run of $M_r^c \| M_r$ we can conclude that $M_r^c \| M_r \not\models \phi$ must hold. □

If we use our trick to weaken the properties rather than using a chaotic closure which distinguishes all possible subsets of the atomic properties P, it seems that we have to evaluate ϕ on $M_r^c \| M_r, \pi$ to check that the counterexample is a real one. As this could only happen when π visits states in the chaotic closure ($s_\forall$ or s_δ) it is guaranteed that in these cases π is not really a possible run of $M_r^c \| M_r$ as the concrete state will never include states of the chaotic closure. It is to be noted we assume that for runs the encoding (s, i) with $i \in \{0, 1\}$ is considered equivalent to s and therefore runs which are only visiting these states can be mapped to runs in the legacy component and therefore result in uncover real counterexamples.

If the run cannot be found when testing the legacy component, we can use the observed difference between π and the really observed behavior π' to derive an improved M_a^{i+1}.

In our example, if we test the legacy component based on the counterexample shown in the last Section with the techniques described in Section 5, we monitor the trace shown in Listing 1.2. As described in the next Section when testing the legacy component, we only monitor relevant events for deterministic replay. Hence, we monitor only the outgoing message convoyProposal at port rearRole and the incoming message convoyProposalRejected at the same port. If we look in more detail at the behavior while deterministically replay the legacy component with all relevant instrumentation for monitoring additionally the states and timing, the trace shows a conflict with expected behavior based on the initial counterexample (cf. Listing 1.3). In the next Section, we will shown, how conflict is manifested while checking the synthesized behavior based on the monitored traces.

Listing 1.2. Monitored relevant events for deterministic replay: blocking state

```
[Message] name="convoyProposal", portName="rearRole", type="outgoing"
[Message] name="convoyProposalRejected", portName="rearRole", type=incoming
```

Listing 1.3. Monitoring all relevant events: blocking state

```
[CurrentState] name="noConvoy"
[Message] name="convoyProposal", portName="rearRole", type="outgoing"
[Timing] count=1
[CurrentState] name="convoy",
[Message] name="convoyProposalRejected", portName="rearRole", type=incoming
```

4.3 Learning Step

In this learning step we employ the observed difference between π and the really observed behavior π' to derive an improved M_l^{i+1}. Then we derive M_a^{i+1} again as $chaos(M_l^{i+1})$ and have due to Theorem 1 by construction:

$$M_r \sqsubseteq M_a^{i+1}, \tag{10}$$

as π' is an observable behavior of M_r and all other behavior still present in M_l^{i+1} is already present in M_l^i.

For learning we have to distinguish two cases. First, a previously unobserved behavior π' has been recorded. We can then do the learning as follows:

Definition 11. *Given a deterministic incomplete automaton $M = (S, I, O, T, \overline{T}, Q)$ and a regular run π, we derive the deterministic incomplete automaton $M' = (S', I, O, T', \overline{T}, Q')$ which results from learning π (denoted by $learn(M, \pi)$) as follows: $S' = S \cup \{s \notin S | \pi = \ldots s \ldots \}$, $T' = T \cup \{(s, A, B, s') \notin T | \pi = \ldots s(A, B)s' \ldots \}$, and $Q' = Q \cup \{s \notin Q | \pi = s \ldots \}$.*

A second case is present, when the test was blocked. In this case we have a deadlock run π of the form $\ldots s(A, B)$ where (A, B) has been blocked in state s. Learning will then work as follows.

Definition 12. *Given a deterministic incomplete automaton $M = (S, I, O, T, \overline{T}, Q)$ and a deadlock run $\pi = \ldots s(A, B)$ where the last interaction was blocked, we derive the deterministic incomplete automaton $M' = (S, I, O, T, \overline{T}', Q)$ which results from learning π (denoted by $learn(M, \pi)$) as follows: $\overline{T}' = \overline{T} \cup \{(s, A, B)\}$.*

In both cases a learned behavior results in a safe abstraction, as shown in the following lemmata.

Lemma 7. *Given a concrete context M_r^c with abstract model M_a^c and a concrete component implementation M_r with derived abstraction M_a^i such that the concrete context refines the abstract context ($M_r^c \sqsubseteq M_a^c$) and that the behavior learned so far is valid (M_a^0 is observation conforming to M_r) holds for any possible run π of $M_r^c \| M_r$:*

$$M_r \sqsubseteq M_a^{i+1} \text{ for } M_a^{i+1} = chaos(learn(M_l^i, \pi)). \tag{11}$$

Proof. It follows form the construction that $learn(M_l^i, \pi)$ is like M_l^i observation conforming to M_r. Due to Theorem 1 refinement for $chaos(learn(M_l^i, \pi'))$ follows.   □

In order to be able to employ a trace to improve our abstraction, we only require that the implementation M_r is deterministic while M_a^i might include non-determinism. This is, however, no real limitation, as in the domain of safety-critical systems we will build components such that any non-determinism or pseudo non-determinism is excluded.

In our example, we have synthesized the automaton shown in Figure 6. First, the legacy component is in a noConvoy state. When sending the covnoyProposal message, the legacy component switches in state convoy.

4.4   Multiple Iterations

With the outlined procedure we can systematically derive a series of abstraction M_a^0, M_a^1, ..., M_a^n such that we stepwise improve our knowledge about the legacy component M_r. In contrast to other approaches for learning this series guarantees always refinement such that we can stop our efforts if a first n has been found with $M_a^c \| M_a^n \models \phi$

Fig. 6. Synthesized behavior: conflict with environment

as this implies that ϕ also holds for the real system ($M_r^c \| M_r \models \phi$). If in contrast we reach an n where the related counterexample π_n can also be detected in the real implementation $M_r^c \| M_r$ and thus the counterexample is also one for the implementation.

Theorem 2. *Given a concrete context M_r^c with abstract model M_a^c such that the concrete context refines the concrete context ($M_r^c \sqsubseteq M_a^c$) and a concrete component implementation M_r with derived series of abstractions $\{M_a^i | 0 \leq i \leq n\}$ constructed as outlined in Lemma 7, we can decide whether a property ϕ holds for $M_r^c \| M_r$ or continue the series.*

Proof. (sketch)
We can show that M_l^i is observation conforming to $M_r \forall 0 \leq i \leq n$ via induction. The first step of the induction is: Lemma 4 provides the guarantee that we will always at least have one first element M_l^0 in the series. Thus we can assume the condition for $n = 0$. In the induction step we show that if the series can be continued for i, Lemma 7 guarantees the condition also holds for $i + 1$.

If we cannot continue the series, we either have proven ϕ for $M_a^c \| M_a^n$ or the counterexample π_n is also present for $M_r^c \| M_r$. In the former case du to Lemma 5 we have proven the property ϕ for $M_r^c \| M_r$. In the latter, Lemma 6 allows us to conclude that the property ϕ is also violated by $M_r^c \| M_r$.

Thus, we can either continue the series or prove respectively disprove the property ϕ. $\square$

For finite state legacy components, we can even guarantee termination of this process. Assuming a finite number of states and transitions as well as deterministic behavior of the legacy component, every time where the counterexample could not be observed during testing, we will replace chaotic behavior by previously unknown states or transitions. Therefore, the number of not already captured states and transitions is strict monotonically decreasing with each iteration round. As it cannot fall below zero, the iterative process will thus terminate.

Based on the synthesized behavior shown in Figure 6, we build a closure and check it with the context. Listing 1.4 shows the counterexample. The property A[] not (rearRole.Convoy and frontRole.noConvoy) is violated. The trace shows, that the violation is only in the synthesized part of the model and therefore, we have a proof that the legacy component is in conflict with context! This example shows, that our approach supports a fast conflict detection.

Listing 1.4. Counterexample with conflict in synthesized behavior

```
shuttle1.noConvoy, shuttle2.noConvoy
shuttle2.convoyProposal!), shuttle1.convoyProposal?
shuttle1.answer, shuttle2.convoy
```

The approach supports besides possible fast conflict detection a systematic/automatic way of testing all relevant input combination of the context with respect to the specification (properties). The input for testing is the same as shown in the conflicting example (cf. Listing 1.1). The monitoring trace shows, that all interactions are performed by the legacy component with respect to the test input. The synthesized behavior, shown in Figure 7 confirm this observation. When checking the synthesized behavior containing the closure, a deadlock is manifested in the closure and not only in the synthesized part of the behavior. Hence, we will get a counterexample, which we can use as test input for the next step.

Listing 1.5. Succesful learning step: monitoring all relevant events

```
[CurrentState] name="noConvoy::default"
[Message] name="convoyProposal", portName="rearRole", type="outgoing"
[Timing] count=1
[CurrentState] name="noConvoy::wait"
[Message] name="convoyProposalRejected", portName="rearRole", type=incoming
[Timing] count=2
[CurrentState] name="noConvoy"
[Message] name="convoyProposal", portName="rearRole", type="outgoing"
[Timing] count=3
[CurrentState] name="noConvoy::wait"
[Message] name="startConvoy", portName="rearRole", type=incoming
[Timing] count=4
[CurrentState] name="convoy"
```

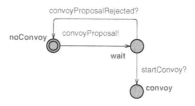

Fig. 7. Correct synthesized behavior w.r.t. context

5 Counterexample Based Testing

As shown in the previous sections, we can check via testing whether π is also a possible path for $M_r^c \| M_r$. If this is the case we have indeed found a witness that $M_r^c \| M_r \models \phi$ does not hold on the one hand and on the other hand we can use the π for extending our knowledge of the legacy component.

As proposed in [23], we can use a set of counterexamples of a model checker to generate test traces for our model. In general this is achieved by passing a constraint in the form of a temporal logic formula to the model checker that is known not to be satisfied by the model. The model checker returns an error trace leading to the part of the model that violates the constraint. This trace π is used to compute initial and final values for a test case. In our special case here, a specific counterexample is generated if the synthesized behavior is in conflict with the environment with respect to the properties of the environment or the interaction between the environment and the legacy system. Hence, we can take this counterexample to check whether π is also a possible path for $M_r^c \| M_r$.

The test case is directly derived from the counterexample. While executing the system with the test cases, we need to observe relevant events of the system to synthesize the behavior. Relevant information are the state, messages, and the time when a message is received/send or a state is changed (see Definition 1 and [34]). To observe these events, we need some white box information of the system.

In the case of software monitoring, instrumentation of the source code is needed to observe the relevant events. For safety critical systems, a hugh amount data is needed. This includes all timing, all external events (messages), and all scheduling events like thread switches. During the early development phases, where the software is executed on a host system, this is typically not a problem. During the later development phases, however, the lack of resources on a target system can result in severe problems. Due to this limitation probes for monitoring relevant events must often be removed or strictly limited for the later development phases. These different probes can then result in different operation times and timing and thus in different behavior. This effect is called the probe effect [42].

Because monitoring is often relevant during the whole life cycle of embedded systems, a popular technique is minimizing the relevant events and keeping the probes up during development and operation (cf. [16] and [19]).

We will use our platform independent deterministic replay approach [22] which minimizes the relevant events. In a first step, we (can) execute the system in the real environment and monitor only the relevant information for deterministic replay e.g, the incoming/outgoing messages and the period number when the messages were received/send (see Listing 1.2). In a second step, we reproduce the execution deterministically by the recorded data of the first step. We (can) add further instrumentation, which have no effects on the execution, to get the information of the relevant events for the behavior synthesize. These are especially the required state information (see Listing 1.3).

6   Related Work

Related to our approach are on the one hand side regular inference approaches and on the other hand model abstraction approaches for formal verification purposes. We first discuss the regular inference approaches.

Regular Inference

In regular inference systems are viewed as black boxes. It is assumed that the considered black box system can be modeled by a deterministic finite automaton (DFA). The problem is than, to identify the regular language $\mathcal{L}(M)$ of the black system $\mathcal{M}$. Learning algorithms are used to identify the regular language. A *Learner*, who initially knows only the alphabet Σ^* about $\mathcal{M}$, is trying to learn $\mathcal{L}(M)$ by asking queries to a *Teacher* and an *Oracle*. $\mathcal{L}(M)$ is learned by *membership queries* which asks the *Teacher* whether a string $w \in \Sigma^*$ is in $\mathcal{L}(M)$. Further, an *equivalence query* is required to ask the *Oracle* whether the hypothesized (learned) DFA $\mathcal{A}$ is correct ($\mathcal{L}(A) = \mathcal{L}(M)$). The *Oracle* answers yes if $\mathcal{A}$ is correct, or else supply an counterexample. Typically, the *Learner* asks a sequence of membership queries and build a hypothesized automaton using the observed answers. When the *Learner* determines that the hypothesized behavior is stable an equivalence query is used to find out whether the behavior is correct. If the query is successful the *Learner* has succeeded, otherwise the returned counterexample is used to revise $\mathcal{A}$ and perform further membership queries until deriving the next hypothesized automaton, and so forth.

Angluin's Algorithm. The most widely recognized regular inference algorithm is L^* developed by Angluin [1]. The algorithm organizes the information obtained from queries and answers in a so called observation table. The observation table regards each string as consisting of a prefix and a suffix. The prefixes are indices of rows and the suffixes indices of columns in the table. A prefix is a string which leads to a state in the system, and a suffix is used to distinguish prefixes that lead to different states from another. The complexity of the L^* algorithm is as follows. The upper bound on the number of equivalence queries is n (n is the number of states of $\mathcal{M}$). The upper bound on the number of membership queries is $\mathcal{O}(|\varSigma|n^2m)$.

Domain Specific Approaches. A number of approaches exist, which are based on Angluin's [1] learning algorithm. Some approaches, like [5], extend the algorithm of Angluin to get better runtime behavior in specific applications or domains. Other approaches use Angluin's algorithm and add technologies like testing or verification.

Hungar et al. [33,32,46,40,41] optimizes Angluin's algorithm by domain specific information, like the utilization of a deterministic system. They reduce the number of membership queries.

Li and Shahbaz et al. presents in [37,36,45] an approach which use testing to learn parameterized state machines. This approach is based on Angluin's algorithm. First a unit test for each component is executed. Then, the components are integrated. Based on the synthesized models tests are generated.

Berg et al. presents in [6] an approach which also tries to regular inference state machines with parameters. They have adopted Angluin's L^* algorithm to work more efficiently on a particular class of systems. They optimizes the approach in that they infer, for each state, a partitioning of input symbols into equivalence classes, under the hypothesis that all input symbols in an equivalence class have the same effect on the state machine.

The presented approaches in [2,14,20] are based on an automaton model of the system/component. Based on that model and a specification, they learn the required assumption to guarantee the specification.

A technique to model check a black box is presented by Peled et al. in [43] by combining regular inference and model checking. The idea of combining the two techniques is further elaborated to a method called adaptive model checking [27,28]. In [18] this approach is further extended to grey box checking. The authors assume that some parts of the system are known. These approaches have the possibility to find an error with respect to given properties while learning the model.

Grinchtein et al. presents in [26] an approach which extends the inference algorithm of Angluin and others to the setting of timed systems. More precisely they consider systems which can be described by a timed automaton.

Equivalence Check. In regular inference an equivalence oracle is required as introduced in this section. The oracle confirm that the suggested conjecture is correct or provide a counterexample. Two techniques provide an automatic approach for getting an counterexample, monitoring and conformance testing. The approaches based on monitoring affect the complexity of the regular inference algorithm negatively. As conformance testing provides a systematic way of achieving an answer to an equivalence query, it is mostly used [3]. Like [27] most conformance test approaches are based on Vasilevski and Chow [47,11]. According to Vasilevski, an upper bound for the total length of a test sequences suite is $\mathcal{O}(k^2 l |\Sigma|^{l-k+1})$. Hence, it is exponential in the difference between the number of states of the system and the hypothesis. A common assumption for conformance testing is that A has at most as many states as M [4].

Conclusion. In principle, all approaches based on Angluin require an equivalence check and the synthesized behavior is an under approximation of the legacy component. Also other learning approaches like [17] use an under approximation. Despite [27], most approaches rather try to synthesize the whole behavior and than finding conflicting situations. However, our approach considers especially the collaboration (context) between the environment and the legacy component. Thus, the whole behavior of the legacy system is not required but only the relevant part for the collaboration. As we have as starting point an over approximation, we did not require an equivalence check. Further, we check at every learning step the correctness of the model.

Abstraction
Abstraction is an important technique for handling the state explosion problem of model checking. Counterexamples are often used to refine an abstract model. The upper approximation is refined, if some behavior in the approximation which is not present in the original model is the cause of a counterexample. When this happens, it is necessary to refine the abstraction so that the behavior which caused the erroneous counterexample is eliminated. Based on white box knowledge like the program variables, the approach is to find a model of the system with a good abstraction to reduce verification efforts. First, it is started with an over-approximation of states (states are reduced to one). Then, the model is refined as long as erroneous counterexamples are eliminated. A number of approaches are investigating this problem, like [35,38,12].

These approaches are based on white box information. Hence, no tests are required and these approaches requires not to consider the possible alphabet of the system, which is the basis for an black box approach. An interaction to the environment of the system, e.g. in the form of a context, is not considered, too.

7   Conclusion and Future Work

In this paper we presented a scheme on how the correct embedding of legacy components can be tackled by a combination of compositional formal verification and testing. An initial behavioral model is derived from the existing interface description and minimal additional information about the possible states of a legacy component using reverse engineering. This behavioral model is subsequently improved using formal verification techniques to systematically generate test for the legacy component. The tests are then enriched using our deterministic replay capabilities for components such that they can be exploited to improve the behavioral model. While verification permits to completely cover the inherently subtle interaction of the distributed real-time components, local testing of the components guided by the verification results is employed to derive the refined behavioral models.

A serious limitation of the presented results is the limitation to a single legacy component. The approach can, however, be extended to multiple legacy components, by using the parallel combination of multiple behavioral models. The iterative synthesis will then improve all these models in parallel. While theoretically possible, we can currently provide no experience whether such a parallel learning is beneficial and useful for multiple legacy components. Our expectation that it depends on the degree in which the known context restricts their interaction which determines which benefits our approach may show also for this more advanced integration problems.

We also have to admit that the approach has currently been evaluated only for a very small example. We therefore plan to apply it at a larger scale. The employed learning strategy still provides several options for optimization. At first, the interplay between the formal verification and the test could be improved when a number of counterexample instead only single one could be derived from the model checker. Another improvement seems possible when specific strategies in model checkers to derive counterexamples (e.g., the shortest one) are considered.

References

1. Angluin, D.: Learning regular sets from queries and counterexamples. Inf. Comput. 75(2), 87–106 (1987)
2. Barringer, H., Pasareanu, C.S., Giannakopolou, D.: Proof rules for automated compositional verification through learning. In: International Workshop on Specification and Verification of Component Based Systems, Finland, pp. 14–21 (September 2003)
3. Berg, T.: Regular Inference for Reactive Systems. Licentiate thesis, it (April 2006)
4. Berg, T., Grinchtein, O., Jonsson, B., Leucker, M., Raffelt, H., Steffen, B.: On the correspondence between conformance testing and regular inference. In: Cerioli, M. (ed.) FASE 2005. LNCS, vol. 3442, pp. 175–189. Springer, Heidelberg (2005)
5. Berg, T., Jonsson, B., Leucker, M., Saksena, M.: Insights to Angluin's learning. In: Proceedings of the International Workshop on Software Verification and Validation (SVV 2003). Electronic Notes in Theoretical Computer Science, vol. 118, pp. 3–18 (December 2003)
6. Berg, T., Jonsson, B., Raffelt, H.: Regular inference for state machines with parameters. In: Baresi, L., Heckel, R. (eds.) FASE 2006. LNCS, vol. 3922, pp. 107–121. Springer, Heidelberg (2006)
7. Bosch, J., Szyperski, C.A., Weck, W.: Component-oriented programming. In: Malenfant, J., Moisan, S., Moreira, A.M.D. (eds.) ECOOP 2000 Workshops. LNCS, vol. 1964, pp. 55–64. Springer, Heidelberg (2000)
8. Burmester, S., Giese, H., Gambuzza, A., Oberschelp, O.: Partitioning and Modular Code Synthesis for Reconfigurable Mechatronic Software Components. In: Bobeanu, C. (ed.) Proc. of European Simulation and Modelling Conference (ESMc 2004), Paris, France, pp. 66–73. EOROSIS Publications (October 2004)
9. Burmester, S., Giese, H., Oberschelp, O.: Hybrid UML Components for the Design of Complex Self-optimizing Mechatronic Systems. In: Informatics in Control, Automation and Robotics. Springer, Heidelberg (2006)

10. Burmester, S., Giese, H., Schäfer, W.: Model-Driven Architecture for Hard Real-Time Systems: From Platform Independent Models to Code. In: Hartman, A., Kreische, D. (eds.) ECMDA-FA 2005. LNCS, vol. 3748, pp. 1–15. Springer, Heidelberg (2005)

11. Chow, T.S.: Testing software design modeled by finite-state machines. IEEE Trans. Softw. Eng. 4(3), 178–187 (1978)

12. Clarke, E., Grumberg, O., Jha, S., Lu, Y., Veith, H.: Counterexample-guided abstraction refinement for symbolic model checking. J. ACM 50(5), 752–794 (2003)

13. Clarke, E.M., Grumberg, O., Peled, D.: Model Checking. MIT Press, Cambridge (2000)

14. Cobleigh, J.M., Giannakopoulou, D., Psreanu, C.S.: Learning assumptions for compositional verification. In: Garavel, H., Hatcliff, J. (eds.) TACAS 2003. LNCS, vol. 2619, pp. 331–346. Springer, Heidelberg (2003)

15. Corbett, J.C., Dwyer, M.B., Hatcliff, J., Laubach, S., Păsăreanu, C.S., Robby, Zheng, H.: Bandera: extracting finite-state models from java source code. In: International Conference on Software Engineering, pp. 439–448 (2000)

16. Dodd, P.S., Ravishankar, C.V.: Monitoring and debugging distributed real-time programs. Softw. Pract. Exper. 22(10), 863–877 (1992)

17. Duarte, L.M., Kramer, J., Uchitel, S.: Model extraction using context information. In: Nierstrasz, O., Whittle, J., Harel, D., Reggio, G. (eds.) MoDELS 2006. LNCS, vol. 4199, pp. 380–394. Springer, Heidelberg (2006)

18. Elkind, E., Genest, B., Peled, D., H.Q.: Grey-box checking. In: Najm, E., Pradat-Peyre, J.-F., Donzeau-Gouge, V.V. (eds.) FORTE 2006. LNCS, vol. 4229, pp. 420–435. Springer, Heidelberg (2006)

19. Fidge, C.: Fundamentals of distributed system observation. IEEE Softw. 13(6), 77–83 (1996)

20. Giannakopoulou, D., Pasareanu, C.S.: Learning-based assume-guarantee verification (tool paper). In: Godefroid, P. (ed.) SPIN 2005. LNCS, vol. 3639, pp. 282–287. Springer, Heidelberg (2005)

21. Giese, H., Burmester, S., Schäfer, W., Oberschelp, O.: Modular Design and Verification of Component-Based Mechatronic Systems with Online-Reconfiguration. In: FSE 2004, pp. 179–188. ACM Press, New York (2004)

22. Giese, H., Henkler, S.: Architecture-driven platform independent deterministic replay for distributed hard real-time systems. In: Proceedings of the 2nd International Workshop on The Role of Software Architecture for Testing and Analysis (ROSATEA 2006), pp. 28–38. ACM Press, New York (2006)

23. Giese, H., Henkler, S., Hirsch, M., Priesterjahn, C.: Model-based testing of mechatronic systems. In: Geiger, L., Giese, H., Zündorf, A. (eds.) Proc. of the fifth International Fujaba Days 2007, Kassel, Germany. Technical Report, vol. tr-ri-07-285, pp. 51–55. University of Kassel (September 2007)

24. Giese, H., Tichy, M., Burmester, S., Schäfer, W., Flake, S.: Towards the Compositional Verification of Real-Time UML Designs. In: Proc. of the 9th European software engineering conference held jointly with 11th ACM SIGSOFT international symposium on Foundations of software engineering (ESEC/FSE-11), pp. 38–47. ACM Press, New York (2003)

25. Grimm, K.: Software technology in an automotive company: major challenges. In: ICSE 03: Proceedings of the 25th International Conference on Software Engineering, Washington, DC, USA, pp. 498–503. IEEE Computer Society, Los Alamitos (2003)

26. Grinchtein, O., Jonsson, B., Pettersson, P.: Inference of event-recording automata using timed decision trees. In: Baier, C., Hermanns, H. (eds.) CONCUR 2006. LNCS, vol. 4137, pp. 435–449. Springer, Heidelberg (2006)

27. Groce, A., Peled, D., Yannakakis, M.: Adaptive model checking. In: Katoen, J.-P., Stevens, P. (eds.) TACAS 2002. LNCS, vol. 2280, pp. 269–301. Springer, Heidelberg (2002)

28. Groce, A., Peled, D., Yannakakis, M.: Amc: An adaptive model checker. In: Brinksma, E., Larsen, K.G. (eds.) CAV 2002. LNCS, vol. 2404, pp. 521–525. Springer, Heidelberg (2002)

29. Henkler, S., Hirsch, M.: Compositional Validation of Distributed Real Time Systems. In: Preliminary Proc. of the 4th Workshop on Object-oriented Modeling of Embedded Real-Time Systems (OMER 4), Paderborn, Germany (October 2007)

30. Hoare, C.A.R.: Communicating Sequential Processes. Series in Computer Science. Prentice-Hall International, Englewood Cliffs (1985)

31. Holzmann, G.J., Smith, M.H.: A practical method for verifying event-driven software. In: ICSE 1999: Proceedings of the 21st international conference on Software engineering, pp. 597–607. IEEE Computer Society Press, Los Alamitos (1999)

32. Hungar, H., Niese, O., Steffen, B.: Domain-specific optimization in automata learning. In: Proc. 15 Int. Conf. on Computer Aided Verification (2003)

33. Hungar, H., Niese, O., Steffen, B.: Domain-specific optimization in automata learning. In: Hunt Jr., W.A., Somenzi, F. (eds.) CAV 2003. LNCS, vol. 2725, pp. 315–327. Springer, Heidelberg (2003)

34. Krichen, M., Tripakis, S.: Black-box conformance testing for real-time systems. In: Graf, S., Mounier, L. (eds.) SPIN 2004. LNCS, vol. 2989, pp. 109–126. Springer, Heidelberg (2004)

35. Kurshan, R.P.: Computer-aided verification of coordinating processes: the automata-theoretic approach. Princeton University Press, Princeton (1994)

36. Li, K., Groz, R., Shahbaz, M.: Integration testing of components guided by incremental state machine learning. In: TAIC-PART 2006: Proceedings of the Testing: Academic & Industrial Conference on Practice And Research Techniques, Washington, DC, USA, pp. 59–70. IEEE Computer Society, Los Alamitos (2006)

37. Li, K., Groz, R., Shahbaz, M.: Integration testing of distributed components based on learning parameterized i/o models. In: Najm, E., Pradat-Peyre, J.-F., Donzeau-Gouge, V.V. (eds.) FORTE 2006. LNCS, vol. 4229, pp. 436–450. Springer, Heidelberg (2006)

38. Lind-Nielsen, J., Andersen, H.R.: Stepwise ctl model checking of state/event systems. In: Halbwachs, N., Peled, D.A. (eds.) CAV 1999. LNCS, vol. 1633, pp. 316–327. Springer, Heidelberg (1999)

39. Lucio, D., Kramer, J., Uchitel, S.: Model extraction based on context information. In: ACM/IEEE 9th International Conference on Model Driven Engineering Languages and Systems. LNCS. Springer, Heidelberg (2006)

40. Margaria, T., Niese, O., Raffelt, H., Steffen, B.: Efficient test-based model generation for legacy reactive systems. In: HLDVT 2004: Proceedings of the High-Level Design Validation and Test Workshop, 2004. Ninth IEEE International, Washington, DC, USA, pp. 95–100. IEEE Computer Society Press, Los Alamitos (2004)

41. Margaria, T., Raffelt, H., Steffen, B., Leucker, M.: The learnlib in fmics-jeti. In: 2th International Conference on Engineering of Complex Computer Systems (ICECCS 2007), pp. 340–352. IEEE Computer Society, Los Alamitos (2007)

42. McDowell, C.E., Helmbold, D.P.: Debugging concurrent programs. ACM Comput. Surv. 21(4), 593–622 (1989)

43. Peled, D., Vardi, M.Y., Yannakakis, M.: Black box checking. In: FORTE XII / PSTV XIX '99: Proceedings of the IFIP TC6 WG6.1 Joint International Conference on Formal Description Techniques for Distributed Systems and Communication Protocols (FORTE XII) and Protocol Specification, Testing and Verification (PSTV XIX), Deventer, The Netherlands, The Netherlands, pp. 225–240. Kluwer, Dordrecht (1999)

44. Ruf, J.: RAVEN: Real-Time Analyzing and Verification Environment. Journal on Universal Computer Science (J.UCS) 7(1), 89–104 (2001)

45. Shahbaz, M., Li, K., Groz, R.: Learning parameterized state machine model for integration testing. In: COMPSAC 2007: Proceedings of the 31st Annual International Computer Software and Applications Conference, Washington, DC, USA, vol. 2- (COMPSAC 2007), pp. 755–760. IEEE Computer Society Press, Los Alamitos (2007)

46. Steffen, B., Hungar, H.: Behavior-based model construction. In: Zuck, L.D., Attie, P.C., Cortesi, A., Mukhopadhyay, S. (eds.) VMCAI 2003. LNCS, vol. 2575, pp. 5–19. Springer, Heidelberg (2002)
47. Vasilevskii, M.P.: Failure diagnosis of automata. Cybernetics and Systems Analysis 9(4), 653–665 (1973)
48. Weber, M., Weisbrod, J.: Requirements engineering in automotive development: Experiences and challenges. IEEE Software 20(1), 16–24 (2003)

Plug-and-Play Architectural Design and Verification

Shangzhu Wang, George S. Avrunin, and Lori A. Clarke

Department of Computer Science
University of Massachusetts Amherst, MA 01003, USA
{shangzhu,avrunin,clarke}@cs.umass.edu

Abstract. In software architecture, components represent the computational units of a system and connectors represent the interactions among those units. Making decisions about the semantics of these interactions is a key part of the design process. It is often difficult, however, to choose the appropriate interaction semantics due to the wide range of alternatives and the complexity of the system behavior affected by those choices. Techniques such as finite-state verification can be used to evaluate the impact of these design choices on the overall system behavior.

This paper presents the Plug-and-Play approach that allows designers to experiment with alternative design choices of component interactions in a plug-and-play manner. With this approach, connectors representing specific interaction semantics are composed from a library of predefined, reusable building blocks. In addition, standard interfaces for components are defined that reduce the impact of interaction changes on the components' computations. This approach facilitates design-time verification by improving the reusability of component models and by providing reusable formal models for the connector building blocks, thereby reducing model-construction time for finite-state verification.

1 Introduction

One of the distinguishing features of concurrent and distributed systems is the importance of defining how sequential components interact with each other. Consequently, software architecture description languages typically separate *components* that represent computations from *connectors* that represent interactions among these components [2, 21, 25, 27]. Connectors are considered first-class design entities since they often capture some of the most important yet subtle aspects of a system, such as non-determinism, interleavings of computations, synchronization, and so on. These are concerns that can be particularly difficult to fully comprehend in terms of their impact on the overall system behavior.

Adding to this difficulty is the wide variety of alternative choices for the interaction semantics. Choosing the appropriate interaction semantics for a connector often involves not only a choice from commonly used interaction paradigms, such as remote procedure call, message passing, and publish/subscribe, but also decisions about such details as the particular type and size of a message buffer

R. de Lemos et al. (Eds.): Architecting Dependable Systems V, LNCS 5135, pp. 273–297, 2008.

or whether a communication should be synchronous or asynchronous. As a result, it is often necessary to make frequent changes to the design of connectors in the course of experimenting with alternative interaction semantics. Design-time verification can be useful in helping designers evaluate their design choices. Typically, design-time verification uses finite-state verification techniques (e.g., SPIN [17], SMV [19], LTSA [22], FLAVERS [10]) to check whether certain properties of a system are satisfied. With design-time verification, designers can make sure that desirable properties of a system still hold when a connector or a component is modified. Usually several iterations involving proposing a design and then verifying that design are needed.

Although it is often necessary to make frequent changes to the semantics of the connectors while designing a system, in practice it can be difficult and costly to make these changes. Changing the specific semantics of a connector often requires nontrivial changes to the components as well. For example, a change from an asynchronous communication to a synchronous one may require changing the components so that a callback can be placed to explicitly notify the sender of the receipt of messages. This intertwined semantics of components and connectors also complicates design-time verification. When using finite-state verification techniques, for instance, it is necessary to build a formal model of the system that represents the computation of each component and the interactions between them. With the semantics of interactions intertwined with the semantics of computations, changes made to the interactions will often result in not only the re-construction of the connector models but also the component models. Although there are automated approaches for building these models, they still frequently require human intervention and insight. When the process of changing and re-verifying a design needs to be repeated frequently, the lack of reusability of the component and connector models could significantly increase the cost of design-time verification.

This paper describes the PnP (Plug-and-Play) approach that allows designers to experiment with alternative design choices of interaction semantics in a plug-and-play manner. This approach provides a library of pre-defined, reusable building blocks that can be composed in a number of different ways to provide a wide range of connectors with different interaction semantics. Modifying the specification of a connector can be easily achieved by adding, removing or replacing one or more of its building blocks. To minimize the impact on components of changes to connectors, the PnP approach also proposes a set of standard interfaces that allow components to communicate with each other through different connectors. The PnP approach not only improves the reusability of the designs of components and connectors, it also provides savings in model construction time during design-time verification. Specifically, pre-defined models are constructed for the library of building blocks, which can then be reused in the modeling of any system that uses these building blocks. In addition, since changes in the connectors often do not require changes in the components, the component models can often be reused, reducing the modeling cost when verification needs to be re-applied.

Section 2 describes how the PnP approach is supported at the design level. Section 3 shows how it could be supported for design-time verification. Section 4 illustrates the design and verification of a small system using the PnP approach. Section 5 describes related work, and Section 6 discusses the current status and future directions of our work.

2   The Plug-and-Play Design Approach

This section describes defines the standard component interfaces and describes the semantics of the building blocks. It also shows the protocols that are used between components and building blocks, and thus demonstrates how connectors can often be modified without requiring changes to the components.

From the implementation perspective, a component may correspond to a class, a thread, a process, or a composition of several threads or processes. In the PnP design approach, components are considered to be abstract units of computation that may have interfaces that define points of interactions to other components in the system. During design, it is up to the user to define the boundaries of components and their exposed interaction points (i.e., interfaces). Similarly, from the design perspective, connectors are abstract units representing the specified interaction semantics. The PnP approach currently provides two kinds of predefined building blocks for the construction of connectors: *ports* and *channels*. These building blocks are also considered abstract design units. For an implementation, one building block may correspond to a class, a component, or a function. Connectors may be implemented by composing the implementations of the building blocks that comprise the connector or, for efficiency reasons, could be implemented directly, depending on the services provided by the the the target programming language or operating system.

In the PnP approach, ports are responsible for hiding the semantic difference of the connectors from those components. Ports capture the synchronization aspects of interactions such as the conditions under which a component should be blocked or needs to wait for an acknowledgement after sending a message to another component. While such semantics can be easily embedded in a component's computation, with the PnP approach those aspects of the interaction semantics are captured in the ports, as part of the connector. Consequently, changes in the interaction semantics can often be made completely in the connector and, thus, independently of the components' computation. Channels are used to represent behavior of the storage medium associated with a connector. For example, a channel may represent a message buffer for message passing communication or an event service used in publish/subscribe systems.

The rest of this section presents the details of the PnP approach by showing how it could be supported for message passing, one of the most commonly used interaction mechanisms. Section 2.1 presents a set of example building blocks and illustrates how they could be used to construct connectors with different message passing semantics. Section 2.2 defines the standard interfaces that components may use to interact with each other through different connectors. It also shows

Send Port	**Asynchronous Nonblocking**	Waits for a message from the sender and sends a confirmation back immediately; the message may or may not be accepted and handled by the channel.
	Asynchronous Blocking	Waits for a message from the sender and sends a confirmation back AFTER the message has been accepted by the channel.
	Asynchronous Checking	Waits for a message from the sender and forwards it to the channel. If the message cannot be accepted by the channel, it returns and sends a notification to the sender. Otherwise, it blocks until the message is accepted and sends a confirmation back to the sender.
	Synchronous Blocking	Waits for a message from the sender and sends a confirmation back AFTER it is notified by the channel that the message has been received by the receiver.
	Synchronous Checking	Similar to "asynchronous checking send" except that when the message can be accepted by the channel, it blocks until the message is received by the receiver and then sends a confirmation back to the sender.
Receive Port	**Blocking (copy/remove)**	Waits for a "receive request" from the receiver and forwards it to the channel. It blocks until a desired message is retrieved from the channel and sends a confirmation to the receiver.
	Nonblocking (copy/remove)	Similar to "blocking receive" except that it returns immediately if no desired message can be retrieved currently. It then sends a notification along with an empty message to the receiver.
Channel	**1–slot buffer**	A buffer of size 1.
	FIFO queue	A FIFO queue of size N.
	Priority queue	A priority queue of size N.

Fig. 1. A set of message passing building blocks

how building blocks may be composed to yield specific interaction semantics by describing the protocols used between building blocks.

2.1 Message Passing Building Blocks

Many languages, such as CSP [16], Occam [9], and Linda [7] incorporate message passing facilities. There are also message passing libraries such as MPI [28] and PVM [14]. Although the fundamental message passing semantics come from two basic operations, send and receive, there are a surprising number of variations in their semantics. For example, a message may be sent synchronously or asynchronously and a component that receives messages may block or continue when a requested message is not available. Other aspects of message passing semantics also vary, such as how messages are stored in a buffer, how they are delivered, and what kinds of information regarding the status of message delivery are relayed to the sender or receiver components. Based on a study of the most commonly used message passing semantics, we have defined a set of building blocks for the construction of message passing connectors. This set of building blocks consists of different kinds of *send ports, receive ports,* and *channels* that together can be used to express a wide variety of message passing semantics. Figure 1 gives a few examples of these message passing building blocks.

Figure 2(a) shows an example of how one may specify an asynchronous message passing communication between a pair of sender and receiver components using these building blocks. The connector is composed of an asynchronous blocking send port, a blocking receive port, and a channel that buffers one message. Through this connector, the sender component sends a message without waiting

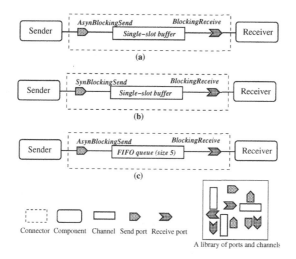

Fig. 2. Constructing message passing connectors

for an acknowledgement from the receiver but is blocked until the message is stored in the channel. The receiver component blocks until a message can be received. By replacing the asynchronous send port with a synchronous one from the library, the new connector in Figure 2(b) allows the sender to block not only until the message is stored in the channel but also until it has been delivered to the receiver. Similarly, channels can also be easily replaced. For example, the single-slot buffer can be replaced by a FIFO queue channel that holds up to five messages, when at most five messages need to be buffered (as shown in Figure 2(c)). Moreover, the replacement of channels can be done independently of the replacement of ports. This kind of "plug-and-play" development facilitates experimentation with alternative interaction semantics.

As we can see from the description of the building blocks in the figure above, channels are essentially message buffers that capture semantics such as the storage and delivery of messages. A send port is a mediator between a sender component and a channel. Different send ports provide different semantics by forwarding and interleaving the messages between the sender component and the channel in different ways. A similar notion applies to receive ports. To construct a message passing connector with specific semantics, one simply selects the appropriate channel to store and deliver messages and selects the appropriate ports from which components may send and receive messages. Section 3 gives a more formal definition of these building blocks in Promela, the modeling language of the SPIN model checker. While many other notations may be used for defining these building blocks (such as finite-state machines and labeled transition systems), in this paper, we have chosen Promela for its easy-to-understand, programming-language-like syntax and direct support for finite-state verification.

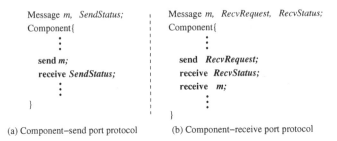

(a) Component–send port protocol   (b) Component–receive port protocol

Fig. 3. Standard component interfaces

2.2   Component Interfaces and Protocols among Building Blocks

The PnP approach supports a set of standard interfaces that components may use to interact with each other through different connectors. Such interfaces allow components to remain intact while the semantics of the connectors are changed through replacing ports and channels. In particular, the interfaces define how a component communicates to the port that is directly connected to the component. Figure 3 shows the standard interfaces for components to send and receive messages. In Figure 3(a), immediately after sending a message m a component blocks and waits for a *SendStatus* message from the connector. The content of the *SendStatus* message is a signal that indicates the status of the sent message. This interface is designed to work with connectors that implement different semantics for sending messages. For example, in the case of asynchronous message passing, the connector should immediately return the *SendStatus* message to the sender component, allowing the component to continue its execution. For synchronous message passing, however, the connector returns the *SendStatus* message after the sender's message has been delivered, thereby blocking the component until a message is received. This difference is supported via the appropriate choice for the send port between the component and the channel.

Similarly, in Figure 3(b), a component that wishes to receive a message first sends a receive request to the port and waits for feedback (the *RecvStatus* message) about whether the requested message has been successfully retrieved. It then waits for a message from the receive port, either a real message (when the receive is successful) or a null message (when the receive has failed). By always having the receive port send back an explicit status message to the receiver component, the same interface can be used for both blocking and nonblocking semantics. A blocking receive port does not send the status back to the component until a message has been successfully received from the channel and can be delivered to the component. A nonblocking receive port sends a failure status message immediately to the component when there is no message currently available in the channel, allowing the receiver component to continue its execution.

Using a notation similar to Message Sequence Charts, Figure 4 illustrates how a send port controls the interleaving of the messages between the component and the channel to support different interaction semantics. Figure 4(a) shows part of a scenario for an asynchronous blocking send. In this scenario, the

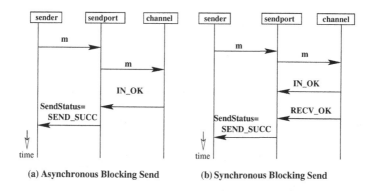

Fig. 4. Example scenarios of message passing interactions: asynchronous blocking send versus synchronous blocking send

SendStatus message SEND_SUCC is delivered to the component immediately after the message m is stored in the channel, indicated by the message IN_OK from the channel. In contrast, Figure 4(b) shows part of a scenario for a synchronous blocking send. In this scenario, the *SendStatus* message SEND_SUCC is not delivered to the component until after the message m has been stored in the channel and has been received by the receiver (indicated by the RECV_OK message from the channel). Notice that the same protocol is used between the sender component and the send port, and between the send port and the channel, for both synchronous and asynchronous message passing. Switching between asynchronous message passing and synchronous message passing can be achieved simply by substituting one kind of send port for the other kind.

With the standard interfaces described here, changes in such design decisions as the specific semantics for sending and receiving messages or the behavior of the message buffers can be accomplished by simply replacing the send or receive ports or the channels that are employed in the connector. So if verification reveals a problem in the behavior of the system due to inappropriate interactions between components, the designer can often modify the connectors without needing to change the components. Of course, certain kinds of changes in the connectors may require changes in the components. For example, a designer might replace an asynchronous blocking send port by an asynchronous checking send port that informs the sender when the channel is full. This change will only lead to more efficient execution if the sending component is redesigned to take advantage of the communication status information sent by the port.

Note that although the standard interfaces described here are with respect to message passing, they are actually more generally applicable. These interfaces can be used for other kinds of interactions such as RPC and publish/subscribe [34].

3 Verification Support for the Plug-and-Play Design Approach

In addition to providing a convenient and efficient way to specify and experiment with various interaction semantics, the PnP approach also supports design-time verification for checking behavioral properties of a system. For finite-state verification techniques such as model checking, formal models of the system need to be constructed before verification can be applied. In the PnP approach, we provide predefined and reusable formal models for the building blocks. Formal models for a particular connector are composed from the pre-defined models of the building blocks used to construct the connector. Connector models are composed at verification time with component models to form a system model that is then checked against the specified properties. Note that the designer is still responsible for providing the models of the components and specifying the properties.

Through verification, designers may find unexpected behaviors or errors in their system design. If the problems are caused by the interaction mechanisms, changes can be made by simply adjusting the building blocks of the connectors, perhaps without having to modify the components. In such cases, there is no need to recreate the component models. Moreover, predefined models for the building blocks can be used in most cases to represent the modified interaction mechanisms, also reducing the cost of model construction. This section describes how reusable models for the message passing building blocks can be defined, how they can be composed to form different connectors, and how the connector models are composed with component models using standard component interfaces.

For an initial evaluation of the PnP approach, we have chosen the widely used SPIN model checker as the verifier along with its input language Promela as the modeling language. We now give a short introduction to Promela describing some of its most important syntax and semantics that we will be using in our models. In Promela, communicating components are defined as processes using the keyword `proctype`. Communications between processes take place through channels that provide either buffered or synchronous message passing. A Promela channel can be declared using the keyword `chan`, the size of the buffer, and the data type for each field of the messages that can be accepted by the channel. The following Promela code shows an example of a typical channel declaration and the basic operations for sending and receiving messages.

With the send operation "!", the message is appended at the end of the channel when the channel is not full; otherwise, the sending process is blocked. With the receive operation "?", the first message in the channel is retrieved. When constants are used in one of the fields after "?", only messages with values that match the constants can be retrieved. The receiving process is blocked if the value of the first message in the channel does not match the constant specified. There are a number of variations for the send and receive operations supported by Promela. For example, with the receive operation "??", the first matching message in the channel will be retrieved, and thus the receiving process does not block as long as there is at least one matching message in the channel.

```
/* internal communication signals */
mtype = {SEND_SUCC, SEND_FAIL, IN_OK, IN_FAIL, OUT_OK,
         OUT_FAIL, RECV_OK, RECV_SUCC, RECV_FAIL};
typedef InternalMsg{
  mtype signal;
  byte port_pid;
}
typedef DataMsg{
  byte data;
}
typedef SynChan{
  chan signal = [0] of {InternalMsg};
  chan data = [0] of {DataMsg}
}
proctype SynBlSendPort(SynChan componentChan;
                       SynChan channelChan){
      DataMsg m;
      do
      :: componentChan.data?m;     /* receives m from the sending component */
         m.sender_id = _pid;
         do
         :: channelChan.data!m;    /* forwards m to the channel */
            if
            :: channelChan.signal?IN_OK,eval(_pid);/* receives IN_OK from the channel */
                                                   /* indicating that m is stored */
               break;
            :: channelChan.signal?IN_FAIL,eval(_pid);/* receives IN_FAIL from the channel */
                                                   /* this happens when the buffer is full */
            fi;
         od;
         channelChan.signal?RECV_OK,eval(_pid);/* waits for RECV_OK from the channel */
                                              /* indicating the receiving of m by a component*/
            componentChan.signal!SEND_SUCC,-1;  /* sends SEND_SUCC to the sending component */
      od;
}
```

Fig. 5. Example definitions of Promela channels

It is important to notice the difference between the Promela channels and the channels used as connector building blocks in our approach. Promela channels are used for sending and receiving messages between Promela processes. Promela channels can support only a limited number of simple message buffers, such as FIFO queues. On the other hand, our channels are architecture-level building blocks for connectors that can capture essentially arbitrary interaction semantics among components and are not necessarily message buffers. For example, a channel in a publish/subscribe connector may represent an event pool where delivery of events is based on subscription. Even when our channels are used as building blocks for message passing connectors, they can be much more complicated than simple message buffers. Such a channel may be able to handle messages based on their priorities, notify components of the current buffer status, or deliver messages to a group of interested components. In the following discussion, we always refer to the native channels in Promela as *Promela channels* to distinguish them from the architecture-level channels in the PnP approach. Here we model all the ports, channels, and components in a design as communicating processes in Promela. We use Promela channels to model the internal communications between components and ports and between ports and channels.

Note that the Promela models we create for the message passing building blocks are not necessarily the most efficient ones and there may be a number of different ways to model them in Promela. Instead of aiming for elegance or efficiency, our models are coded to clearly reflect the protocols that are used by the building blocks. These models can often be simplified and optimized for verification in a number of ways. We briefly discuss some possible optimizations in Section 6. Also note that the PnP approach is not tied to any particular model checker or modeling language. By using Promela and SPIN, we are only showing one possible way of modeling our building blocks and applying design-time verification. In fact, we have defined the same set of building blocks in the process algebra FSP and used LTSA (the Labeled Transition System Analyzer) [22] to verify the system designs. Somewhat different strategies may be appropriate when modeling the building blocks in a different modeling language.

3.1   Modeling Ports

Figure 6 shows the Promela model for a synchronous blocking send port. First a set of signals that are used to represent the status of sending and receiving a message are defined as the enumerated type mtype in Promela. The type SynChan defines two Promela channels that are used for communications between components and ports, and between ports and channels. The Promela channel signal is used to communicate message delivery status signals, and the Promela channel data is used to communicate application-specific data messages. The port is modeled as a Promela process (proctype) that takes two parameters of type SynChan, one of which represents the set of Promela channels for the communication with the component (component), and the other set of Promela channels for the communication with (channelChan).

The main part of the Promela code for the port is a loop in which the port accepts a message from the component and forwards it to the channel, and then, when the message has been accepted by the channel, forwards the appropriate status message back to the component. As we can see from the model in Figure 6, in Promela, a block of repeating statements is enclosed in a pair of do and od keywords. A number of statement blocks can be selectively executed when the loop is entered. The symbol : : is used to identify the beginning of a selective block. A block is executable when the first statement in the block is enabled. When more than one block is executable, one of them is selected arbitrarily. In our model for the send port, we only need one selective block, since the send port only has one thing to do, that is, to wait for a message m to be sent from the component and then deliver it to the channel. When the component is ready to send a message, the statement componentChan.data?m is enabled and therefore the rest of the statements can be executed.

As we can see from the model, after receiving a message from the component, the send port attaches its own process ID _pid to the message. Since one channel may be connected to multiple send ports, this _pid is sent along with the data message to the channel so that the channel can use it to notify the appropriate

```
/* internal communication signals */
mtype = {SEND_SUCC, SEND_FAIL, IN_OK, IN_FAIL, OUT_OK,
         OUT_FAIL, RECV_OK, RECV_SUCC, RECV_FAIL};
typedef InternalMsg{
  mtype signal;
  byte port_pid;
}
typedef DataMsg{
  byte data;
}
typedef SynChan{
  chan signal = [0] of {InternalMsg};
  chan data = [0] of {DataMsg}
}
proctype SynBlSendPort(SynChan componentChan;
                       SynChan channelChan){
     DataMsg m;
     do
     :: componentChan.data?m;    /* receives m from the sending component */
        m.sender_id = _pid;
        do
        :: channelChan.data!m;    /* forwards m to the channel */
           if
           :: channelChan.signal?IN_OK,eval(_pid);/* receives IN_OK from the channel */
                                                  /* indicating that m is stored */
              break;
           :: channelChan.signal?IN_FAIL,eval(_pid);/* receives IN_FAIL from the channel */
                                                  /* this happens when the buffer is full */
           fi;
        od;
        channelChan.signal?RECV_OK,eval(_pid);/* waits for RECV_OK from the channel */
                                             /* indicating the receiving of m by a component*/
           componentChan.signal!SEND_SUCC,-1;  /* sends SEND_SUCC to the sending component */
        od;
}
```

Fig. 6. Promela model for a synchronous blocking send port

port of the delivery status of the message. Each status signal that is addressed to this port will be tagged with its process ID number.

The send port then tries to forward the message m to the channel (channelChan.data!m). After that, it waits for a signal back from the channel that indicates whether the message can be properly stored in its buffer. Such a signal could either be IN_OK or IN_FAIL. To model this nondeterministic choice, we use the selective statement if...fi in Promela that allows a selective execution of one of its blocks. The semantics of how blocks are selected are the same as for the do...od statement described above. The send port makes sure that the signals from the channel are indeed addressed to it by matching its own process ID with the tag attached to the signal that is sent back. This is done by specifying its process ID as a constant that must match in a receive statement. For example, the receive statement channelChan.signal?IN_OK,eval(_pid) will only be executed when both constants IN_OK (an enumerated type in Promela) and eval(_pid) (eval(_pid) gives the constant value of _pid) match the values in a message that can be retrieved from the channel.

Since this is a synchronous blocking send, if the channel sends back an IN_FAIL signal, the port has to send the message to the channel again and keep trying until an IN_OK signal is received indicating that the message has been

```
proctype AsynNbSendPort(SynChan componentChan;
                        SynChan channelChan){
      DataMsg m;
      do
      :: channelChan.signal?_,eval(_pid);
      :: componentChan.data?m;                    /* receives m from the sending component */
         componentChan.signal!SEND_SUCC,-1;/* sends SEND_SUCC to the sending component */
         m.sender_id = _pid;
         channelChan.data!m                   /* forwards m to the channel */
      od
}
```

Fig. 7. Promela model for an asynchronous nonblocking send port

successfully stored in the channel. It then can break out of the loop and wait
for a RECV_OK signal from the channel which indicates that a receiver has successful received the message. Finally, after receiving both IN_OK and RECV_OK
signals from the channel, the synchronous blocking send port sends the send
status message (SEND_SUCC) back to the sender component. If for some reason
the message cannot be successfully delivered to the receiver, the channel will
issue a RECV_FAIL signal instead of a RECV_OK signal. In this case, the statement
channelChan.signal?RECV_OK,eval(_pid) will not be able to execute and the
port process is blocked. Since the port cannot send a SEND_SUCC signal to the
component, the component is also blocked. This is consistent with the semantics
of synchronous message passing where the component is blocked until the message is successfully delivered to the receiver. Notice that since the component
process does not care about the ID of the port, we simply send an invalid process
ID number -1 along with the SEND_SUCC signal.

As one may have guessed, the definition of an asynchronous blocking send
port is similar to its synchronous counterpart except that an asynchronous send
port immediately sends SEND_SUCC to the component after receiving IN_OK from
the channel. Similarly, for a nonblocking send port, SEND_SUCC may be sent to
the component before the message has been stored in the buffer by the channel.
Figure 7 shows the Promela model for an asynchronous nonblocking send port.
This port receives a message m from the component and immediately returns a
SEND_SUCC status signal to the sender component, regardless of whether message
m will be successfully stored in the channel or eventually received by the a
receiver component. In fact, the port ignores any signals sent from the channel
using a wildcard receive channelChan.signal?_,eval(_pid) (in Promela, _
can be matched with any value).

Figure 8 shows the Promela model for a blocking receive port. The receive port
starts by waiting for a recvRequest message from the component. When it arrives, it tries to send the request to the channel until the request is confirmed
by the channel (indicated by the OUT_OK signal). After the port successfully retrieves a message m from the channel (channelChan.data?m), it then sends a
RECV_SUCC confirmation to the receiver component followed by the message m delivered by the channel. A nonblocking receive port would send a RECV_FAIL signal
immediately to the component when the receive request is rejected by the channel
(indicated by signal OUT_FAIL). It then sends an empty message to the receiver

```
proctype BlRecvPort(SynChan componentChan;
                    SynChan channelChan){
    DataMsg recvRequest,m;
    do
    :: componentChan.data?recvRequest;  /* receies a receive request from the component */
       do
       :: channelChan.data!recvRequest; /* forwards the receive request to the channel */
          if
          :: channelChan.signal?OUT_OK,_; /* receives an OUT_OK signal from the channel */
             channelChan.data?m;          /* receives the message from the channel */
             break;
          :: channelChan.signal?OUT_FAIL,_; /* receives OUT_FAIL from the channel */
          fi;
       od;
       componentChan.signal!RECV_SUCC,-1;/* sends a REC_SUCC signal to the component */
       componentChan.data!m;             /* sends the requested message to the component */
    od;
}
```

Fig. 8. Promela model for a blocking receive port

```
typedef StatusMsg{
  mtype status;
}
proctype aSendComponent(SynChan sendPortChan){
    DataMsg myMsg;
    StatusMsg sendStatus;

      ...

    sendPortChan.data!myMsg;         /* sends a message to the port */
    sendPortChan.signal?sendStatus,_; /* receives the sendStatus message */
                                     /* with the value of  SEND_SUCC or SEND_FAIL */
      ...
}
```

Fig. 9. A sending component

component as a stub to accommodate the standard interface of the receiver component. Note that other variations of receive ports can be defined similarly. For example, a receive port (whether blocking or nonblocking) may ask the channel to keep the message (*copy receive*) that has been received in the buffer or to remove it (*remove receive*). A receive port may also support *selective receive* where a tag is used as the matching criteria to retrieve messages from a channel.

3.2   Modeling Component Interfaces

Figure 9 shows the component interface for sending messages through a send port. The component sends its message to the send port and immediately waits for a status signal back. Depending on the specific semantics of the send port the component is sending messages through, the status signal may be returned at different stages of message delivery and may indicate either a failure (SEND_FAIL) or success (SEND_SUCC). But no matter what kind of send ports the component is communicating with, the same interface can be used. As noted previously, this often allows the model of the port to be changed or replaced without having to change the model of the component.

```
proctype aRecvComponent(SynChan recvPortChan){
    DataMsg myMsg,recvRequest;
    StatusMsg recvStatus;

    ...

        recvPortChan.data!recvRequest;  /* sends a receive request to the port */
        recvPortChan.signal?recvStatus,_; /* waits for a recvStatus message */
                                        /* with value RECV_SUCC or RECV_FAIL */
        recvPortChan.data?myMsg;    /* receives a data message myMsg which */
                                    /* contains a valid message when recvStatus is RECV_SUCC */
                                    /* or contains data that should not be used */
                                    /* when recvStatus is RECV_FAIL */
    ...
}
```

Fig. 10. A receiving component

Similarly, Figure 10 shows the interface for receiving a message. In this model, a receiver component sends a receive request to the receive port and then tries to receive a status signal from the port, followed by a data message delivered by the channel. If recvStatus indicates RECV_SUCC, the message myMsg is the actual requested message delivered by the channel. If recvStatus indicates RECV_FAIL, the message myMsg is an empty message sent by the receive port as a stub and therefore, should not be used by the component. Such an interface for receiving messages makes it possible to support both blocking and nonblocking semantics.

3.3   Modeling Channels

For message passing, channels are essentially buffers that store and deliver messages. There are a number of different properties of a message buffer that may affect the overall correctness of the system. For example, some channels may notify the sender component when the buffer is full so that the component may choose to send at a different moment; other channels block the sender until space is available in the buffer; a third kind of channel may simply drop messages that are sent after its buffer becomes full without notifying the sender. Of course, channels may have buffers with different sizes and may implement different message delivery policies. We have defined the Promela models for a number of message passing channels that implement a variety of such semantics.

Figure 11 shows the model for a *single-slot-buffer* that only holds one message. The process model of a message passing channel takes two parameters of type SynChan. senderChan is used for the communication with the send ports that components are using to send messages to the channel. receiverChan is used for the communication with the receive ports that components are using to receive messages from the channel. The channel accepts a receive request from a receive port or a message forwarded by a send port, and handles them according to the current status of its buffer. In this particular implementation, the channel notifies the send port with an IN_FAIL signal when its message buffer is full, and notifies the receive port with an OUT_FAIL signal when no requested message is currently available in the buffer. This channel model can be easily composed

```
proctype single_slot_buffer (SynChan senderChan;
                             SynChan receiverChan){
  DataMsg recvRequest, m, buffer;
  bool buffer_empty = 1;
  do
  :: receiverChan.data?recvRequest;  /* receivs a recvRequest from a receive port */
     if
     :: (!buffer_empty && !recvRequest.selective)
                             /* if buffer is non-empty; it's not a selective receive */
        || (!buffer_empty && recvRequest.selective /* or buffer is not empty */
           && buffer.selectiveData          /* and the selective criteria matches */
              == recvRequest.selectiveData) ->
           receiverChan.signal!OUT_OK,-1;      /* sends an OUT_OK signal to the receive port */
           receiverChan.data!buffer;           /* stores the data message in the buffer */
           senderChan.signal!RECV_OK,buffer.sender_id;/* sends a RECV_OK signal to the send port */
           if                                  /* flushes the buffer if needed */
           :: recvRequest.remove ->
              buffer_empty = 1
           :: else
           fi
     :: else ->
           receiverChan.signal!OUT_FAIL,-1 /* sends OUT_FAIL to the receive port */
     fi
  :: senderChan.data?m; /* receives a message m from a send port */
     if
     :: buffer_empty ->
           senderChan.signal!IN_OK,-1;    /* sends an IN_OK signal to the send channel */
           buffer.data = m.data;          /* stores the message */
           buffer.sender_id = m.sender_id;
           buffer.selectiveData = m.selectiveData;
           buffer.selective = m.selective;
           buffer.remove = m.remove;
           buffer_empty = 0
     :: else ->
           senderChan.signal!IN_FAIL,-1 /* sends an IN_FAIL signal to the send channel */
     fi
  od
}
```

Fig. 11. Promela model for a single-slot buffer channel

with a number of send and receive ports by matching the Promela channels
channelChan used by the send ports and the channelChan used by the receive
ports with the senderChan and receiverChan used by the channel, respectively.

In addition to the single-slot buffer, we have defined the Promela models
for a variety of other types of channels, including one that stores and delivers
messages in a FIFO order and one that handles messages based on their priorities.
It is also possible to create a model for a channel that has a message buffer of
an arbitrary size. In this case, the Promela process of the channel takes an
additional parameter that specifies the size of the buffer. The models for these
channels can be instantiated with the size of the message buffer used in the
channel. This allows a range of similar message passing channels to be defined
by parameterizing the model.

3.4   Model Composition

As we have described above, ports and channels are modeled as communicating
Promela processes and they can be connected through specific Promela channels
that handle the communications between them. To construct the model for a
connector, we can simply compose the pre-defined Promela processes for its
building blocks by matching the specific Promela channels associated with them.

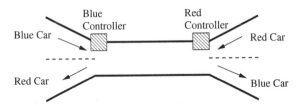

Fig. 12. A single-lane bridge with two controllers

Component models and connector models can be composed in a similar way. When design decisions about the semantics of a connector are changed and the system design needs to be re-verified, formal models of the system can be modified by replacing the Promela processes of the existing building blocks of the connector with those of the new ones. For example, when different semantics for sending messages are needed for a component, we can substitute a different send port for the existing one, and pass in the same Promela channels that allow the new send port process to communicate properly with the Promela process for the component. In Section 4, we give an example illustrating how system models can be constructed from the building block models and how they can be re-constructed when changes are made in the design of connectors.

4   The Single-Lane Bridge Example

This section presents an example to illustrate how designers may use the building blocks and the techniques we have described above in the design and verification of a small message passing system. In particular, we show how design-time verification may benefit from the PnP approach by saving on model construction time when repeated changes are made to the connectors in a software architecture.

As an example, consider a bridge that is only wide enough to let through a single lane of traffic at a time. An appropriate traffic control mechanism is necessary to prevent crashes on the bridge. For this example, we assume traffic control is managed by two controllers, one at each end of the bridge. Communication is allowed between two controllers as well as between cars and controllers. To make the discussion easier to follow, we refer to cars entering the bridge from one end as the blue cars and refer to that end's controller as the blue controller; similarly the cars and controller on the other end are referred to as the red cars and the red controller, respectively, as shown in Figure 12. Blue cars send enter requests to the blue controller when they try to enter the bridge and notify the red controller when they exit the bridge. A similar situation applies to red cars.

There are a number of possible ways to control the traffic on the bridge. For a simple version of the bridge example, which we refer to as "exactly-N-cars-per-turn", controllers may take turns to allow some fixed number (N) of cars from their side to enter the bridge. A more efficient single-lane bridge system, which we refer to as "at-most-N-cars-per-turn", may allow turns to be yielded immediately by one controller to the other if there are no cars waiting to cross the bridge from its side. No matter what traffic control mechanism is used, we want to make sure the bridge is safe, that is, no cars traveling in the opposite directions can be allowed on the bridge at the same time. Designing a bridge system that ensures this safety property requires a careful design of not only the components (cars and controllers) in the system, but also the specific semantics of the connectors used for the interactions between the components.

In particular, a designer may have to decide whether it is more appropriate to use message passing or event-based notification for the communication between components; whether the communication between cars and controllers needs to be synchronous or can be asynchronous; if message passing is chosen, what types of buffers should be used to store messages; what happens if a message gets dropped by a buffer, and so on. It is very easy to make mistakes on such matters when choosing the appropriate interaction semantics. Design-time verification can be very useful in evaluating the appropriateness of these design decisions.

For this example, message passing seems to be a natural choice for the communications between components, but we still have to make sure the appropriate message passing semantics are chosen for each connector. With our PnP approach, this can be achieved by selecting and composing a subset of the message passing building blocks from the library to define each connector, incorporating the component designs provided by the designer, and then using design-time verification to make sure that the resulting system design does not violate the safety properties of the bridge. Figure 13 shows an initial design of the "exactly-N-cars-per-turn" single-lane bridge example. In this design, asynchronous message passing is chosen for both the communication between the car and the controller on its entering side and the communication between the car and the controller on the other side. In this case, asynchronous blocking send ports are used for sending enter and exit request messages from the cars to the controllers. A FIFO queue channel is selected for buffering the enter request messages that are sent from different car components to the same controller, so that the requests are processed by the controller in a first-in-first-out order. A single-slot buffer channel may be used for exit request messages. Finally, blocking receive ports are used by each controller component to process enter and exit request messages. Notice that with this version of the bridge example, no communication is necessary between the two controllers.

To apply design-time verification using SPIN, the Promela model of the overall system design needs to be constructed. With the PnP approach, the system design is composed of components and various message passing building blocks. Therefore, a system model is simply a composition of all the Promela models for the message passing building blocks and components in the system. Specifically, models of the selected message passing building blocks are pre-defined and can be simply included in the system model at verification time. In general, the PnP approach expects designers to provide formal models for the components that employ the standard interfaces.

In principle, models of the components can be automatically derived from their designs if they are encoded in some suitable language. For the purpose of

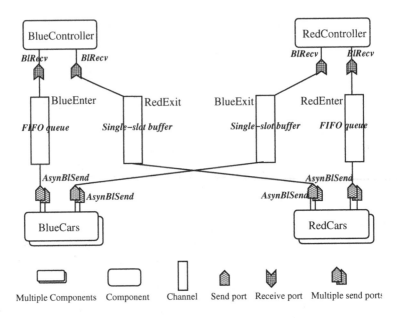

Fig. 13. An initial design of the "exactly-N-cars-per-turn" single-lane bridge example

this example, however, we constructed Promela models of the car and controller components manually. To allow the component models to be composed properly with the building block models, appropriate Promela channels are used to set up the connections between component processes and building block processes at the start of the Promela system. Due to space limitations, the complete Promela model for this version of the bridge example is presented in [34]. The safety property of the bridge example is described in LTL (Linear Temporal Logic), which can then be checked by SPIN against the Promela model of the system.

To make sure that our bridge system does not cause cars traveling from opposite directions to crash, we use finite-state verification to check our design. In this case, not surprisingly, verification reports a violation of the property. The cause of this violation is obviously that we have selected a wrong type of send port for sending enter request messages. Instead of using an asynchronous blocking send port, we should have used a synchronous blocking send port so that the car component waits for an acknowledgement from the controller before it tries to enter the bridge. With the PnP approach, the erroneous design can be easily corrected by replacing the asynchronous blocking send ports for sending enter requests with synchronous ones; no changes in the components are necessary. Verification needs to be applied again to confirm that the system now satisfies the property. With this approach, re-applying verification does not require the complete re-computation of the system model.

As we can see from this example, the pre-defined building block models can be easily composed with component models to create a system model. These pluggable models also make it easier to make changes in the model, especially

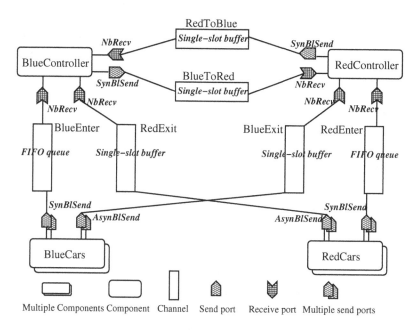

Fig. 14. The architecture design of the "at-most-N-cars-if-¿ waiting" single-lane bridge example

when such changes only involve the semantics of the connectors. Suppose that, in order to improve traffic flow, the designer wishes to change the "exactly-N-cars-per-turn" version of the bridge system into the "at-most-N-cars-per-turn" version. This requires the addition of new communication between the controllers and the modification of the controller components. Since this version of the system has additional functionality, it is not unreasonable to have to change the components to support this functionality. Still, however, we would like to limit the impact of these changes and reuse models of the components and connectors as much as possible. Figure 14 shows a possible design for the modified system, with two new connectors between the controllers, one for the blue controller to notify the red controller that no blue cars are waiting and one for the red controller to notify the blue controller that no red cars are waiting. In this case the designer chose synchronous blocking send, nonblocking receive, and a reliable single-slot buffer. Since the controllers poll for messages from cars and from the other controller, we must also change the connectors between the cars and controller to have nonblocking receive semantics. To verify that this new system still prevents crashes of cars traveling in opposite directions on the bridge, the component models need to be modified to reflect the new communications. Models of the new connectors, however, can be constructed from the library models of the building blocks.

From this single-lane bridge example illustrated above, we can see that the verification works in the same plug-and-play manner as the associated design approach. Having reusable models for building blocks of connectors and having the models of components stay relatively stable when only interactions are changed reduces the cost of repeated verification in an iterative design process. It therefore makes it easier and more efficient to experiment with alternative design choices for interaction semantics.

5 Related Work

The limitations and frustrations of component-based software development are well known (e.g., [11, 18]). Previous work, such as [2, 4, 15, 21, 25, 27], has proposed treating connectors as first-class entities in component-based development, although [15] in particular, has put the focus at a lower level of abstraction (programming level) than what we are interested in here.

There are a number of approaches that provide support for connectors and component composition. The Wright architecture description language [2], for example, uses the CSP process algebra to describe arbitrary connectors. The Architectural Interaction Diagrams (AIDs) approach [26] models connectors using process algebra. Constraint automata based approaches have also been proposed to specify and analyze the semantics of connectors composed from a set of primitive channels [3, 24]. In approaches like these, the burden is on the designer to construct a model of a connector with the right semantics from powerful, but low-level, primitives. Our PnP approach is aimed at providing a library of building blocks from which connectors representing a variety of interaction semantics can be easily constructed, offering "ready-to-use" pieces that hide from the user most of the details of how these pieces are actually constructed and modeled. As we noted above, however, the actual formal models of our building blocks used for verification could be built using any suitable formalisms with verification support, including CSP or AIDs. Another approach to support component composition is the *mediator* approach [31, 32] which defines mediators as special components that are used to modularize how other components interact with each other in terms of their behavioral relationship. While providing a way of reasoning about the connections, the mediator approach does not support the compositional specification of connectors as our approach does.

While our approach facilitates creating connectors from existing building blocks, the connector wrapper approach [29, 30] focuses on creating new connectors by incrementally transforming existing ones. The connector wrappers can be useful in reusing connector parts and supporting easy modification to connectors. Because of its restricted internal representation of operational semantics, however, this approach can only support connectors with limited kinds of interaction semantics. In contrast, our approach allows designers to explore a wide range of interaction semantics by providing a set of building blocks that can be expanded and that are not restricted to a specific formalism.

Although a similar notion of ports has been proposed in architectural description languages such as ACME [13] and ArchJava [1], in our approach, ports are used to explicitly capture some of the most important aspects of interaction semantics such as synchronization, and therefore are treated as parts of connectors.

Our definition of ports makes it possible to support standard component interfaces that allow connectors to be modified or replaced with minimal impact on the components. The term *building blocks* has been used in many different contexts. For example, in [33], building blocks are referred to as parts of software used to build a system. The building blocks in our approach are design-level elements used to construct connectors representing interactions.

There has been extensive work on applying verification to systems employing a specific type of component interactions. Our approach, however, is intended to provide a general framework that can support many kinds of mechanisms, rather than being restricted to a single type. Specific techniques have been used to model and reason about message passing systems. For example, in [5, 23] message passing systems are specified in sets of adapted message sequence charts (MSCs), and message channels are modeled as a finite-state automaton with inputs and outputs. A single automaton is constructed that accepts all linearizations of the MSCs that meet the specification of the channels. This automaton is then checked by standard techniques for emptiness to decide whether the system satisfies the specification of the channel.

Work has been done on verifying implicit invocation or publish/subscribe systems (e.g., [6, 12, 35]). In this work, the semantics of publish/subscribe systems are defined along several dimensions, which is very similar to what we have done for message passing. One of the limitations of the approach is its restriction to publish/subscribe systems: the user specifies choices on the dimensions, and a formal model, suitable for finite-state verification, is automatically constructed. In order to apply that approach to other interaction mechanisms, a suitable specification formalism and a model generation tool would have to be constructed. Our approach, on the other hand allows the verification of systems with different interaction mechanisms by supporting small, reusable formal models that can be used as building blocks to construct formal models representing different kinds of interactions. One advantage of their approach, however, is that both the formal models and the verifier may be optimized and refined specifically for publish/subscribe systems.

6   Conclusion and Future Work

Choosing appropriate interaction semantics for the connectors in a software architecture is often very difficult. In this paper, we present an approach that allows designers to easily experiment with alternative design choices of interaction semantics and to use design-time verification to evaluate their decisions based on the correctness of the overall system design. With this approach, components can interact with each other through different connectors using only a small set of standard interfaces. Because the interfaces usually do not need to change when changes are made to the connectors, the impact of such changes on the components is minimized. Our approach also provides a library of pre-defined building blocks to support the construction of a wide variety of different types of connectors. This plug-and-play approach provides savings in model construction time during design-time verification. With this approach, pre-defined models can be constructed for the library of building blocks, which can then be reused in the modeling of any system that uses these building blocks. In addition, since changes in the connectors do not often require changes in the components, the component models can often be reused, reducing the modeling cost when verification needs to be re-applied.

We are currently developing a prototype tool that supports plug-and-play design and verification. This tool is implemented as an extension of the ArchStudio architecture design environment [8]. With ArchStudio, designers can model, visualize and analyze system architectures. Our extension provides additional functionalities that allow designers to select specific interaction paradigms for component interactions, to specify connectors from pre-defined building blocks, and to use finite-state verification to evaluate the design. In addition to the prototype tool, we are also working on extending the current approach to support other kinds of interaction mechanisms such as publish/subscribe and remote procedure call. For evaluation, we are undertaking a case study to evaluate how well this approach supports the design and verification of microkernel-based embedded systems that are based on the CAmkES component model [20]. Specifically, we plan to show how the set of building blocks can represent a rich set of interaction semantics and how this approach can be useful in practice to help produce high-quality designs and implementation. As another collaboration with CAmkES, we are planning to investigate how the plug-and-play approach could be extended to the implementation level. Specifically, we want to explore the possibility of capturing implementation-specific information at the architecture level and mapping building blocks to implementation constructs such as classes, threads, processes, or functions. We would like to have our design approach combined with code generation so that code generation could also benefit from the plug-and-play of reusable building blocks.

We also plan to explore several important issues that are specific to the modeling and verification aspect of our approach. One of these is optimizing techniques to reduce the models created using our PnP approach to allow finite-state verification to be applied more efficiently. As we have mentioned previously, our current models for the library of building blocks are only intended for proof of concept and may not be the most efficient. These models often have unnecessary blocking statements or redundant data structures, which may unnecessarily increase the state space of the model. As an extreme example, consider our Promela model of a FIFO queue channel. Instead of implementing explicit data structures for buffering messages in FIFO order, we could simply use the native FIFO channel in Promela to handle the ordering of the messages.

We expect optimization to be extremely important since decomposing connectors into ports and channels that are modeled as separate processes introduces additional concurrency into the model, exacerbating the state explosion that limits finite-state verification. Without effective optimizations, our approach may be restricted to only small systems. Therefore, techniques that can reduce the size of the system model will be necessary to provide effective verification support. As an example of such a technique, commonly used connectors could be recognized and specially optimized models could be made available instead of directly composing from the building block models. Note that the techniques that are used for optimization may largely depend on the specific modeling language and verification tool that are used.

Another concern with our approach is the ability to provide meaningful counterexample traces when the verification fails. In finite-state verification, when a property violation is found, a counterexample trace is usually provided to give an example trace through the model that leads to the violation of the property. With our approach, tracing an error may require delving into the details of the models of the building blocks, which requires a low-level understanding of their semantics. It would be helpful if our approach could provide a more meaningful representation of the cause of a property violation. For example, it would be useful to indicate that a deadlock in a system may be due to the use of a message buffer that drops new messages when it is full. In this way, designers can focus on the building blocks that appear to be problematic in the system and experiment with alternative choices using the plug-and-play approach.

Acknowledgements

We are grateful to Prashant Shenoy for helpful conversations about this work.

This material is based upon work supported by the National Science Foundation under awards CCF-0427071, CCR-0205575, CCF-0541035, CCF-0733035, and by the U.S. Department of Defense/Army Research Office under award DAA-D19-01-1-0564 and award DAAD19-03-1-0133. Any opinions, findings, and conclusions or recommendations expressed in this publication are those of the authors and do not necessarily reflect the views of the National Science Foundation or the U. S. Department of Defense/Army Research Office.

References

1. Aldrich, J., Chambers, C., Notkin, D.: ArchJava: Connecting software architecture to implementation. In: Proc. 26th Intl. Conf. on Softw. Eng., Orlando, FL, USA, May 2002, pp. 187–197. ACM Press, New York (2002)
2. Allen, R., Garlan, D.: A formal basis for architectural connection. ACM Trans. on Softw. Eng. and Methodol., 140–165 (1997)
3. Arbab, F., Baier, C., Rutten, J.J.M.M., Sirjani, M.: Modeling component connectors in reo by constraint automata (extended abstract). Electr. Notes Theor. Comput. Sci. 97, 25–46 (2004)
4. Bálek, D., Plášil, F.: Software connectors and their role in component deployment. In: Proc. Third Intl. Working Conf. on New Developments in Distributed Applications and Interoperable Systems, Deventer, The Netherlands, pp. 69–84 (2001)
5. Bollig, B., Leucker, M.: Modeling, specifying, and verifying message passing systems. In: Proceedings of the Symposium on Temporal Representation and Reasoning (TIME 2001), pp. 240–248 (2001)

6. Bradbury, J.S., Dingel, J.: Evaluating and improving the automatic analysis of implicit invocation systems. In: Proc. 11th ACM Symp. on Found. of Softw. Eng., pp. 78–87 (September 2003)
7. Carriero, N., Gelernter, D.: Linda in context. Comm. ACM 32(4), 444–458 (1989)
8. Dashofy, E.M., van der Hoek, A., Taylor, R.N.: A comprehensive approach for the development of modular software architecture description languages. ACM Trans. Softw. Eng. Meth. 14(2), 199–245 (2005)
9. Day, M.: Occam. SIGPLAN Notices 18(4), 69–79 (1983)
10. Dwyer, M.B., Clarke, L.A., Cobleigh, J.M., Naumovich, G.: Flow analysis for verifying properties of concurrent software systems. ACM Trans. on Softw. Eng. and Methodol. 13(4), 359–430 (2004)
11. Garlan, D., Allen, R., Ockerbloom, J.: Architectural mismatch, or, why it's hard to build systems out of existing parts. In: Proc. 17th Intl. Conf. on Softw. Eng., Seattle, Washington, pp. 179–185 (April 1995)
12. Garlan, D., Khersonsky, S., Kim, J.S.: Model checking publish-subscribe systems. In: Ball, T., Rajamani, S.K. (eds.) SPIN 2003. LNCS, vol. 2648, pp. 166–180. Springer, Heidelberg (2003)
13. Garlan, D., Monroe, R.T., Wile, D.: Acme: Architectural description of component-based systems. In: Leavens, G.T., Sitaraman, M. (eds.) Foundations of Component-Based Systems, pp. 47–68. Cambridge University Press, Cambridge (2000)
14. Geist, A., Beguelin, A., Dongarra, J., Wiang, W., Manchek, R., Sunderam, V.: PVM: Parallel Virtual Machine, A User's Guide and Tutorial for Networked Parallel Computing. MIT Press, Cambridge (1994)
15. Gensler, T., Lowe, W.: Correct composition of distributed systems. In: Tech. of Object-Oriented Languages and Systems, pp. 296–305 (1999)
16. Hoare, C.A.R.: Communicating Sequential Processes. Prentice-Hall Intl., Englewood Cliffs (1985)
17. Holzmann, G.J.: The Spin Model Checker. Addison-Wesley, Boston (2004)
18. Inverardi, P., Wolf, A.L.: Uncovering architectural mismatch in component behavior. Science of Computer Programming 33(2), 101–131 (1999)
19. McMillan, K.L.: Symbolic Model Checking: An approach to the State Explosion Problem. Kluwer Academic, Dordrecht (1993)
20. Kuz, I., Liu, Y., Gorton, I., Heiser, G.: CAmkES: A component model for secure microkernel-based embedded systems. The Journal of Systems and Software (2006)
21. Magee, J., Dulay, N., Eisenbach, S., Kramer, J.: Specifying distributed software architectures. In: Proc. 5th European Softw. Eng. Conf., Sitges, Spain, pp. 137–153 (September 1995)
22. Magee, J., Kramer, J.: Concurrency State Models and Java Programs. John Wiley and Sons, Chichester (1999)
23. Meenakshi, B., Ramanujam, R.: Reasoning about message passing in finite state environments. In: Welzl, E., Montanari, U., Rolim, J. (eds.) ICALP 2000. LNCS, vol. 1853, pp. 487–498. Springer, Heidelberg (2000)
24. Mehta, N.R., Medvidovic, N., Sirjani, M., Arbab, F.: Modeling behavior in compositions of software architectural primitives. In: 19th IEEE Intl. Conf. on Automated Softw. Eng., pp. 371–374 (2004)
25. Perry, D.E., Wolf, A.L.: Foundations for the study of software architecture. SIGSOFT Softw. Eng. Notes 17(4), 40–52 (1992)
26. Ray, A., Cleaveland, R.: Architectural interaction diagrams: AIDs for system modeling. In: Proc. 25th Intl. Conf. on Softw. Eng., pp. 396–406 (2003)
27. Shaw, M., Garlan, D.: Softw. Architecture:Perspectives on an Emerging Discipline. Prentice-Hall, Englewood Cliffs (1996)

28. Snir, M., Otto, S., Huss-Lederman, S., Walker, D., Dongarra, J.: MPI: The Complete Reference. MIT Press, Cambridge (1996)

29. Spitznagel, B., Garlan, D.: A compositional approach for construct connector. In: Proc. Working IEEE/IFIP Conf. on Soft. Architecture (WICSA 2001), Royal Netherlands Academy of Arts and Sciences Amsterdam, The Netherlands, pp. 148–157 (August 2001)

30. Spitznagel, B., Garlan, D.: A compositional formalization of connector wrappers. In: Proc. 2003 Intl. Conf. on Softw. Eng., Portland, Oregon, pp. 374–384 (2003)

31. Sullivan, I.K., K.J., Notkin, D.: Evaluating the mediator method: Prism as a case study. In: IEEE Transactions on Software Engineering, vol. 22, pp. 563–579 (August 1996)

32. Sullivan, K.J., Notkin, D.: Reconciling environment integration and software evolution. ACM Trans. Softw. Eng. Methodol. 1(3), 229–268 (1992)

33. van der Linden, F.J., Müller, J.K.: Creating architectures with building blocks. IEEE Softw. 12(6), 51–60 (1995)

34. Wang, S., Avrunin, G.S., Clarke, L.A.: Architectural building blocks for plug-and-play system design. Technical Report UM-CS-2005-16, Dept. of Comp. Sci., Univ. of Massachusetts (2005)

35. Zhang, H., Bradbury, J.S., Cordy, J.R., Dingel, J.: Implementation and verification of implicit-invocation systems using source transformation. In: Proceedings of the Fifth International Workshop on Source Code Analysis and Manipulation. IEEE Computer Society, Los Alamitos (2005)

Data Flow-Based Validation of Web Services Compositions: Perspectives and Examples[*]

Cesare Bartolini[1], Antonia Bertolino[1], Eda Marchetti[1], and Ioannis Parissis[1,2]

[1] ISTI - CNR
Via Moruzzi 1 - 56124 Pisa
[2] Laboratoire d'Informatique de Grenoble
BP 53 - 38041 Grenoble Cedex 9
{cesare.bartolini,antonia.bertolino,eda.marchetti}@isti.cnr.it,
ioannis.parissis@imag.fr

Abstract. Composition of Web Services (WSs) is anticipated as the future standard way to dynamically build distributed applications, and hence their verification and validation is attracting great attention. The standardization of BPEL as a composition language and of WSDL as a WS interface definition language has led researchers to investigate verification and validation techniques mainly focusing on the sequence of events in the composition, while minor attention has been paid to the validation of the data flow exchange. In this chapter we study the potential of using data flow modelling for testing composite WSs. After an exhaustive exploration of the issues on testing based on data-related models, we schematically settle future research issues on the perspectives opened by data flow-based validation and present examples for some of them, illustrated on the case study of a composite WS that we have developed, the Virtual Scientific Book Store.

1 Introduction

The Service Oriented Architecture (SOA) is the emerging approach to develop and execute distributed applications. The SOA provides a flexible and cost-effective paradigm for complex system development, that facilitates the interaction among components developed by independent organizations. SOA applications can be built by integrating existing services into services compositions (or composite services). The reuse of existing software components is enabled by the adoption of standard interfaces and protocols, that also allow for the interaction between heterogeneous systems and technologies.

Compositionality is on the one side a highly promising feature of the SOA and on the other a tough challenge for developers. Unlike traditional component-based integration, which is carried on at assembly time, service composition can

---

[*] This research has been partially supported by ART DECO (Adaptive infRasTructure for DECentralized Organizations), an Italian FIRB (Fondo per gli Investimenti della Ricerca di Base) 2005 Project, and by TAROT (Training And Research On Testing), a Marie Curie Research Training Network.

R. de Lemos et al. (Eds.): Architecting Dependable Systems V, LNCS 5135, pp. 298–325, 2008.
© Springer-Verlag Berlin Heidelberg 2008

be performed at run time. Dynamic discovery and run-time integration hence form essential concepts of the SOA paradigm.

A concrete instantiation of the SOA are Web Services (WSs), which are implemented and composed by using established Web-based open standards, namely WSDL [36], UDDI [30], and SOAP [35]. We are concerned in this chapter with dependability insurance in the architecting of WS Compositions (WSCs). In particular our research addresses verification and validation (V&V) approaches in this new architectural standard, that raise several issues [6].

V&V of WSCs would correspond to the integration stage of the conventional testing process. The central problem is that the dynamic binding of services makes it impractical to test in advance all the concrete service combinations that can be involved in a workflow. Heuristics must be used to reduce the amount of test executions. A compelling research problem is then how to ensure the compliance of the composite services with the (functional and non-functional) requirements. One major issue is that the implementation of the WSs involved in the composition is generally unknown. Their interfaces are specified by the WSDL standard description language, but availability of behavioral specification cannot be assumed. Testing in the laboratory (off-line testing) can only be done under assumptions on this behavior, and to achieve more realistic verification, testing is often deferred to execution-time (on-line testing). Furthermore, testing a WSC might increase the workload of the involved services (that may be used at the same time in other compositions) and also the cost of testing (using the services may not be free of charges). The same kind of problems occurs for testing non-functional attributes of an architecture.

In recent years, several attempts have been made to adapt existing validation approaches to the validation of WSs and WSCs. In these, behavioral specifications have been mainly used that describe the foreseen sequences of events, as an input to formal verification. However, proving the behavioral correctness of the system may not be sufficient to guarantee that specific data properties are satisfied [23].

So far little attention has been paid to data validation or even data modelling for WSCs. Notwithstanding WSCs always entail operating and transforming persistent data, most of the times data flow requirements and data properties are expressed informally (in natural language), and consequently the application of rigorous data-flow based verification approaches is hardly feasible. We believe that data modeling represents an important aspect, which should be taken in consideration during both the implementation and the testing phase.

Of course the usage of data information for validation purposes is not a novelty. Several data flow oriented test adequacy criteria have been proposed in the past [8] for application to conventional software. The purpose of this chapter is to study how data flow-based test techniques should be adapted for validation of WSCs.

The chapter is structured in two main parts (corresponding to the "Perspectives" and "Examples" terms in the title): *i)* in Section 4 we overview all the ways in which data flow modelling and analysis may be used for the validation of WSCs: the contribution of this section stays in hinting future research directions; *ii)* in Section 5 we dig in a couple of outlined approaches, providing examples of application to a developed WSC case study: the Virtual Scientific Book Store (described in Section 3). Before that, in Section 2 we overview recent research work on validation of WSs and WSCs. Conclusions are finally drawn in Section 6.

2   Related Work

This section is a brief overview on recent investigations on WSs validation, first regardless of composition issues, then addressing specifically WSCs, and, finally, focusing on fault models for WSCs.

Validation of WSs. Validation of WSs has been mainly addressed by means of testing. Test data are selected either in order to show the conformance to a user-provided specification or according to their fault detection ability, assessed on fault models. For instance, the Coyote framework [29] requires the user to build test cases as MSCs [28]. A contract specification of the services under test is also necessary. The fault detection ability of the test data is assessed using mutation on contracts [16]. A simpler approach is proposed in [25] where mutations are defined on the WSDL language. But the mutation operations adopted in both approaches do not correspond to any widely accepted fault-model.

The approach proposed in [4, 3] focuses on testing the conformance of a WS instance to an access protocol described with a UML2.0 Protocol State Machine (PSM). This protocol defines how the service provided by a component can be accessed by a client through its ports and interfaces. The PSM is translated into a Symbolic Transition System (STS), on which existing formal testing theory and tools can be applied for conformance evaluation. For instance, in [13], STSs are used to specify the behavior of communicating WS ports and test data are generated to check the conformity of the effective implementation to such a specification. The advantage of this approach is that it uses a standard notation (UML 2.0 PSM) for the protocol specification.

The above approaches are summarized in Table 1.

Validation of WSCs. Validation of WSCs has been addressed by few authors suggesting to perform structural coverage testing of a WSC specification. For

Table 1. WSs validation techniques

Used models	V&V type	Ref.
WSDL	Mutation testing	[25]
WSDL + Protocol State Machines	Conformance testing	[4, 3]
WSDL + Symbolic Transition Systems	Conformance testing	[13]
WSDL + MSC	Conformance testing	[29]

instance, in [37, 40] it is considered that the WSC is provided in BPEL [21], the Business Process Execution Language, a de facto standard for programming WSCs. The BPEL description is abstracted as an extended control flow diagram; paths over this diagram can be used to guide test generation or to assess test coverage. An important issue in this approach comes from the parallelism in BPEL which results in a much more complex control flow and a very high number of paths. To cope with this problem, the above approaches make several simplifying assumptions on BPEL and apply only to a subset of the language. In [14], a transformation is proposed from BPEL to PROMELA (similarly to [7]). The resulting abstract model is used to generate tests guided by structural coverage criteria (e.g. transition coverage). Similar complexity explosion problems may be encountered in such methods, since the amount of states and transitions of the target model can be very high.

When a formal model of the WSC and of the required properties is provided, a formal proof can be carried out. For instance, Petri Nets can be built from workflows [20] or from BPEL processes [38] to verify properties such as reachability. In [12], the workflow is specified in BPEL and an additional functional specification is provided as a set of MSCs. These specifications are translated in the Finite State Processes (FSP) notation. Model-checking is performed to detect execution scenarios allowed in the MSC description and that are not executable in the workflow, and conversely. The complexity of the involved models and model-checking algorithms is the main concern making these approaches hardly applicable in real-world WSCs. Table 2 provides a classification of the above presented approaches.

Fault Models. The above investigations use models of the composition behavior and of properties or scenarios expressing the user expectations (MSCs or state based properties such as the absence of deadlock): faults manifest themselves as

Table 2. WSCs validation techniques

Original models	Transf. to	Other models	V&V type	Ref.
BPEL		None	Structural coverage	[37, 40]
BPEL	PROMELA	None	Structural coverage	[14]
Petri-nets		Properties	Formal verification	[20]
BPEL	Colored Petri-Nets			[38]
BPEL	FSP	MSC	Formal verification	[12]
BPEL to UML Activity Diag.	PROMELA	Properties	Formal verification	[7]

discrepancies between the system behavior and these expectations. An interesting characterization is proposed in [33,34] where failures of WSCs are considered as interactions between WSs, similarly to feature interactions in telecommunication services. Interactions are classified for instance as goal conflict or as resource contention.

The above fault models mainly focus on control. The verification of the data transformations involved in the WSC execution does not seem to have been explored so far. From the modeling point of view, this lack has been outlined in [18] where it is suggested to build a model representing the data transformations performed during the execution of a WSC. This model can be used together with behavioral specifications to automate the WSC process.

There is no literature on fault models based on data for WSCs. However, the proposition of data fault model for workflows by Sadiq and coauthors [23] could be applicable in the WS context. According to it, data can be *redundant* if they are not used by any activity. They can be *lost*, if the outputs of two concurrently executed activities are assigned to a single variable in a non deterministic order. Similarly, they can be *missing, mismatched, misdirected* or *insufficient*.

Although the above data fault model has not been designed specifically for WSCs, it can be of some interest in defining a data oriented validation strategy (see Section 4).

3 Case Study: The Virtual Scientific Book Store

We illustrate the concepts expressed in this chapter by means of an example of WSC implementing a *Virtual Scientific Book (VSB) Store*. VSB is a composite service which offers various functionalities related to scientific publications, including search of the ACM repository and visualization of the articles.

VSB has been realized from the composition of the three WSs described below: Pico, Google Citations, and ACM Search.

The Pico Service. Pico implements a database of scientific publications. Registered users can add, edit and remove the publications in the database, however its information is publicly available, therefore search results can be viewed by non-registered users. Moreover, to allow web developers to integrate information regarding their publications into their own pages, a SOAP-based web service (and its relative WSDL file) has been integrated in VSB. For sake of simplicity, although the service is composed of a high number of functions for different purposes, only three functions are presented here:

searchByAuthor performs a search of all the publications in the Pico database
   including a given name in their list of authors.
   − Inputs: author's name (type: string); research sector. If not specified,
      then all research sectors will be included in the search (type: string);
      year (type: string); publication type (journal, conference proceedings...).
      If not specified, then all publications from this author will be returned
      (type: string).

  – Outputs: a list of references. If no publication relative to the requested author were found a null element is returned (type: sequence of record elements, from a custom XML Schema Definition).

searchByTitle performs the search according to the requested title.

  – Inputs: publication title (type: string).
  – Outputs: a list of references identical to the previous function.

pdfGetter recovers the file containing the printable form of the publication and returns its URL. It is important to note that this function does not actually return a PDF file, but a publicly accessible URL, so the requestor has a greater flexibility in choosing how to recover the actual file.

  – Inputs: the name of the file (type: string).
  – Outputs: the full URL where the file can be retrieved, or a null value if it is not available (type: string).

The Google Citation Service. Google Scholar (`http://scholar.google.com`) is a freely-accessible website useful for publications search. One of its most interesting features is that it displays the (supposed) number of citations that a given publication has received (according to the Google database).

As Scholar does not provide any web service support, we have implemented a web service performing a research on Google Scholar and receiving a web page in return. It contains a single function:

citations retrieves a web page from Google Scholar and searches for the number of citations of the given publication.

  – Inputs: publication title (type: string).
  – Outputs: number of citations, 0 if there were no results from Google Scholar, or no results correctly matching the title were found (type: integer); URL of the page where the information was retrieved (type:string).

The ACM Search Service. Since the ACM scientific library does not provide any web service support, we have implemented a web service offering such a functionality. This service is composed of a single function:

pdfGetter queries the ACM repository with a search and receives a web page, which is then scanned to check whether the publication corresponding to the requested title is available on the repository. If so, this function returns a direct link to the PDF file, which can be used by the requestor. Note that this operation is not directly related to the operation of the Pico service with the same name; they are simply two operations which perform a similar function, but they are related to different WSDLs.

  – Inputs: the title of the publication to search (type: string); login credentials (type: sequence of two strings, username and password).
  – Outputs: the URL containing a direct link to the PDF file. It is a null value if the no results were returned by the ACM search, or if none of the results matches the requested title (type: string).

The Service Composition: VSB. The final VSB service provides a set of functionalities to easily access the aforementioned WSs. Its execution is divided into two distinct steps. In the first step, upon a user request, a search in the Pico database is executed and the list of publications corresponding to the search criteria is presented to the user; then, the user must select a publication reference and an operation to perform on it, and the service will execute the requested operation and return the resulting value to the user.

Initially, the service composition expects two possible inputs: an author's last name and/or a publication title. If none is provided, then an exception is raised. If either one is provided, then the composition will accordingly invoke the Pico *searchByAuthor* or *searchByTitle* function, and will return the resulting reference list. If both inputs are provided, then the composition will call both functions in parallel, and the result will be the merging of the reference lists returned by *searchByAuthor* and *searchByTitle*. The merging is obtained by means of an XSL stylesheet, which can be used thanks to a function (*doXslTransform*) provided by WS-BPEL as an XPath extension. The resulting reference list is then shown to the user in an easily-readable form.

In the second phase of the service composition, the user must select one reference from the reference list. The function provided by the service composition for this purpose is called *selection*. Last, the user requests one of two operations, namely "google" and "acm". The requested operation is then invoked. The former invokes the Google Citations service, allowing the user to know the number of citations. The latter first determines whether the document is contained in the Pico repository (information available in the reference). If so, the *pdfGetter* function of the Pico service is invoked; otherwise, the ACM Search service must be called. However, since the ACM repository requires authentication, the user's credentials are sent along with the request.

However, in the current implementation of the case study, credentials are not actually used (in a real working environment, their absence should throw a fault, but fault management is covered in another part of the example).

After the request and the credentials are sent to the ACM service, the result will be the same as the invocation of the Pico *pdfGetter* function, that is a direct link to the document. Therefore, the composition will retrieve the document and present it to the user as the final output.

4   Perspectives on Using Data Flow in Validating WSCs

A WSC implements a business process, i.e. a coordinated set of tasks, performed by humans or software, aimed at accomplishing a specific organizational goal [9]. Such a goal may be of the most varied nature, involving for example a supply-chain process, or a virtual travel agency, or an e-commerce transaction, and so on. Whichever its goal, a business process always entails the processing of persistent data, along a sequence of steps described into the process workflow specification. Clearly, a correct manipulation of the data is one crucial ingredient to guaranteeing the quality of the WSC. This is why we claim in this work that data flow based analysis can provide useful insights in V&V of WSCs and should complement currently proposed approaches, which are mostly centered around the process behavioral specification.

In this section we investigate data-based validation in a broad-wise perspective, attempting to identify the possible various usages of data-related information for validation purposes. In particular, in Section 4.1 we enumerate the data-based models of concern and their role in the development of the application, while in Section 4.2 we discuss issues on using these models for validation purposes.

4.1 Modelling WSCs Data

Data related information useful for testing purposes can be introduced at various stages during development of a WSC and can be of different nature. Depending on what information is available different kinds of models can be built and used, giving rise to a spectrum of opportunities for data-based validation. For instance, during the requirements specification stage, requirements might be expressed on the composition data flow, as suggested in [18]. Or, conversely, data flow related specifications can be extracted from the implementation of the composition. On the other hand, relations between input and output data can be expressed when the composition is specified and later on checked during testing. Finally, fault models focusing on data can be used and can be of general purpose or specific to some application domain.

The most basic and common descriptions for WS manipulated data are WSDL definitions, which provide the variables and operations used. WSCs are described on top of the WSDL definitions, by behavioral models provided as state or activity diagrams. They can be either built during the early stages of the development process or extracted from the implementation (typically, from BPEL [21] programs). There does not exist a standardized notation for a WSC model, and existing tools provide different visualizations.

Behavioral models focus mainly on the control flow. By modelling how the actions performed during the execution of the application can interleave, though, these models constitute an important source of information for data flow analysis as well, as they permit to analyse how data are passed between different invocations. These models could be augmented with data flow annotations. In Section 5.2 we discuss in detail how the BPEL process for the VSB case study can be annotated with definitions and uses of variables (see Table 5).

Annotated BPEL processes come however at a mature stage of development, when the WSC is implemented. As already said, data flow models could also be defined early in the life cycle, during the requirements specification of WSs. One already cited proposal of a notation for modeling data flow requirements comes from Marconi and coauthors [18]. Their notation provides a precise formal model which can be used for verification purposes. On the other hand, in many cases the derivation of technically sophisticated models already at the stage of requirement elicitation might be impractical. At early development stages developers might prefer the usage of abstract and more intuitive models, such as the Data Flow Diagrams (DFDs).

Fig. 1. DFD elements (D: data transformer; df: data flow; ds: data store; ep: external process)

DFDs were introduced in the 70's as part of structured analysis and design [39]. In this approach, a DFD represents a flow of data through a network of transforming processes (*data transformers*). The latter can also access *datastores*. The quite intuitive nature of this formalism is made further attractive for practitioners by a simple graphical notation. Commonly adopted symbols for the elements of DFD are shown in Figure 1. Although this kind of model is less used in the current state of the practice, we believe it can be useful since it highlights the goals of the composition from a data related point of view. Building a DFD forces developers to explicitly model their implicit knowledge on data handling, avoiding loss of information or misdirection of data flow, and helping to highlight the most critical data flow paths.

We draw a sketch of a DFD for the VSB case study in Figure 2. With reference to the DFD elements in Figure 1, the web services involved in the composition are represented as external processes (for the VSB these are RefFinder, Citation, PdfGet), whereas internal operations of the composition correspond to data transformers (e.g., ChooseRef).

Data fault models constitute another possible piece of information that could be useful for WSC validation purposes. One such model is supplied for instance by the already mentioned classification in [23]. We re-interpret that model in the context of WSCs as shown in Table 3. Fortunately, some of the problems identified in this classification do not apply when the standard languages BPEL and WSDL are used, since these languages ensure that the data exchanged between services conform to a mutual accepted specification.

Finally, in addition to the above mentioned models, the requirements specification may include properties focusing on data. Such properties may restrict the domain of the computed values (for instance if a year is specified in the *searchByAuthor* request, then all references returned by Pico must conform to that year) or express relations between them (for instance, the output references returned by *searchByTitle* must match the title provided in input). The set of these properties provide another model that could be used for validation (e.g. through applying model-checking techniques).

4.2   Model-Based Testing Issues

The models presented in the previous section can be used for testing purposes either individually or in a combined way. In this section we discuss how validation could be performed in presence of one or more of these models. A summary reference is provided in Table 4.

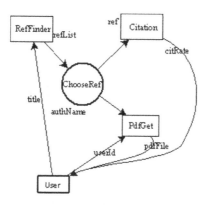

Fig. 2. DFD of the virtual bookstore

Using a Data Flow Model Built from the Requirements. The first row in Table 4 considers the case where a high level data flow model is built during the requirements specification, independently from any other specification of the composition or from the implementation. One example of DFD derived from the VSB service requirements is presented in Figure 2.

We hypothesize three situations, corresponding to the three columns of the table:

1. **Using a data flow model alone.** Even in the case the only available specification for the composition is an abstract data flow model (Table 4 Cell 1.1), this can be useful in two different ways for testing purposes:
   - **Measuring structural coverage.** Coverage criteria adapted to a data flow model can be defined. For instance, considering Figure 2, any path starting from the User input and returning back to him/her correspond to different data flows that should be covered. One path covers the operation of *RefFinder*, and passing through *ChooseRef* goes to *PdfGet*; another goes to *Citation* and returns directly to the User, and so on.
   - **Test data design.** Once established a coverage criterion, black-box testing strategies can be adopted to derive the appropriate test cases, i.e. demonstrating concrete executions involving the data flow model elements to cover.
2. **Using a data flow model together with a BPEL description:** We consider that both a data flow model and a specification of the WSC (BPEL) are available (Cell 1.2 in Table 4), although no formal relation between them is assumed. This information can be exploited for statically checking both if the defined BPEL composition conforms to the data flow requirements specified in the data flow model and if it properly implements all the data dependencies. In the VSB example, it could be checked that the citation score provided by the Google *Citation* service correctly refers the title provided by Pico.

Table 3. Data validation problems for WSs

Data validation problem	Relevance for WSC
Redundant data	Can occur when partners send messages (or parts) which are not used. Statically detected conformance between invocation of services and WSDL descriptions.
Lost data	Can occur when two data flows involving the same variable definition merge in a single flow: one of the values can be lost.
Missing data	Can occur when variables are used without having been instantiated, either manually or by a message. Can be statically detected by parsing the BPEL code.
Mismatched data	Cannot occur in BPEL. Type checking is enforced in the specification.
Inconsistent data	Can occur when a data flow involving a call to WS merges, after this call, with a data flow updating a variable containing a value coming from the WS; in other words, the BPEL program may incorrectly update this variable.
Misdirected data	No reinterpretation required for web services.
Insufficient data	Specification problem, not addressed in this work.

3. **Using a data flow model and a data fault model:** A data fault model could be defined mainly focusing on lost or inconsistent data. Once established, the data fault model can be used together with the data flow model (Cell 1.3 in Table 4) to seed faults into the latter (for instance, in *search-ByAuthor*, a future year reference could be provided). Fault coverage criteria can then be established on the data flow model and test data can be selected to detect the possible presence of these faults in the implementation.

Using a Data Flow Model Extracted from the BPEL Description of the Composition. We now assume that a BPEL description of the composition is available together with a WSDL definition for the involved services (Row 2 in Table 4). In this case, a more detailed data flow model could be (automatically) extracted from the process specification. The peculiarity of such a data flow model is that it provides another point of view of the composition, focusing on data interaction. The data flow model can be of course exploited as described above for the DFM alone (Row 1 in Table 4), but in this case the criteria, and consequently the derived test cases, can be applied at a more concrete level and could be aimed at checking the implementation (Cells 2.1, 2.3 in Table 4).

A more interesting possibility consists in exploiting the data flow model information to define coverage criteria for the BPEL process description (this case is studied in more depth in Section 5.2). In that case, data flow information can be combined with the control flow information to apply common data flow-based test coverage criteria, such as for instance *all-defs* or *all-uses* [8], either for measuring test adequacy or to guide test data generation (Cell 2.2 in Table 4).

Table 4. Data flow based validation issues

Reference model	Other available models		
	1 None	**2 BPEL**	**3 Data fault model**
1 DFM from Reqs	– Structural coverage of DFM – Black-box test generation 1.1	– Static verification (BPEL vs. DFM) 1.2	– Coverage of DFM/fault model – Black-box test generation 1.3
2 DFM from BPEL	– Structural coverage of DFM – Black-box test generation 2.1	– Define coverage criteria for BPEL – Guide test generation (to achieve BPEL coverage) 2.2	– Coverage of DFM/fault model – Black-box test generation 2.3
3 Data properties	– Common black box testing (category partition) 3.1	– Common data flow testing 3.2	– Coverage: Guide test generation 3.3

Using Data Property Specifications. Overall data properties differ from data flow modelling in the sense that they can express developer expectations on the composition results regardless of the data dependencies or the process execution flow. Such properties could state that the result of a query must belong in a given interval (for instance the publication years of the citation record), obey some formatting rules (for instance concerning the format of the string corresponding to a URL), or establish a relation between the computed data (e.g., the authors in the returned references must include the author name provided in input by the User).

As shown in Row 3 of Table 4, such properties could be used in several ways:

Black-box testing. If there is no information available on the WSC (Cell 3.1 in Table 4), black-box testing techniques, such as Category Partition [22], can be used taking into account the properties to select relevant test data.

Data flow testing. The specified set of properties can be used together with the BPEL specification (if available) to apply common data flow based testing techniques focusing on the data involved in the property expression (Cell 3.2 in Table 4).

Coverage criteria. The set of formal properties can be used in association with a data flow model or with a data fault model to define test criteria and related test strategies ensuring that any fault in the data flow model that has an impact on the property satisfaction can be detected with good probability (Cell 3.3 in Table 4).

5   Examples of Using Data Flow-Based Validation in the BPEL Process

In this section we discuss in more detail two possible approaches based on data flow modeling and analysis for the validation of WSCs. More precisely, Section 5.1 is concerned with using a data flow model derived from the requirement specifications (referring to Cell 1.1 in Table 4), while Section 5.2 focuses on a data flow model extracted from the BPEL description of the composition (Cell 2.2 in Table 4). The two examples are not necessarily related. The first relies on a high level data flow model derived from the specification, and can be completely independent from the subsequent WSC implementation. The second uses a data flow model derived from the BPEL code and is referred to for coverage testing.

5.1   Using a Data Flow Model Built from Requirements

A data flow model built from the requirements should include information on the expected dependencies between the data handled in the WSC.

Paths in a DFD correspond to dependencies between inputs and outputs of the WSC. For instance, the path *(title, refList, ref, citRate)* in Figure 2 means that *citRate* depends on the title provided by the user through the intermediate data *refList* and *ref*. Such dependencies make it possible to define test adequacy criteria based on the diagram structure, similarly to data flow adequacy criteria defined on control flow graphs (e.g. [8]).

Although the detailed design of such criteria is not in the scope of this chapter, we identify some issues that could help in their definition:

- Every path in the DFD starting at a WSC input A and ending at a WSC output B should be checked with at least one execution of the WSC resulting in the production of a new value of B corresponding to the actual value of A. In the example of Figure 2, this means, for instance, that VSB must be invoked with a publication title as input parameter; another invocation must be made with the author name, sector, year, type.
- A more thorough testing should require using different values for input to a given path, in order to check whether the path output value changes accordingly (for instance, if the *citRate* changes when *title* changes). So, an adequacy criterion could be defined, requiring every path to be exercised twice, with different input values.

— The above idea can be extended to all the successive pairs of edges in a path. For the path *(title, refList, ref, citRate)*:

- (title, refList) should be checked with different values of *title*;
- (refList, ref) should be checked with different reference list*s*;
- (ref, citRate) should be checked with different values of *ref*.

So, for an example, another criterion could be based on requiring to execute every path with a test set such that every arrow of the path takes at least two different values.

Other criteria could be defined to cover different *combinations* of events in the test paths. On the example of Figure 2, it is useful to check, for instance, that when the user provides a valid value for *userId* and a title corresponding to at least a valid reference, then a valid link to a pdf file is returned.

Another important issue in the definition of such data flow based adequacy criteria is related to *states*. Indeed, a difficult problem of WSCs validation arises when the involved Web services are stateful. Also in such cases the usage of data models is helpful, as a DFD may contain data stores modelling the internal state of the composition and that internal state could be exploited for the test path definition.

The interest of such adequacy criteria defined on a DFD is that they help test planning (and assessing the effort needed for testing) early in the development process, before the actual integration of the WSs involved in the composition. The assessment of these criteria could be automated, if they are formally defined on a DFD, even if this model is a quite abstract view of the effective implementation.

5.2   Extracting Data Flow Information from the BPEL

In this section we assume that the WSC is described in BPEL [21] and we study how common data flow based testing criteria [8] apply to this description (i.e., this section is concerned with Cell 2.2 of Table 4). To make the chapter self-contained, we present the main elements of the BPEL language, useful for understanding the testing methodology (we refer to [21] for a detailed description). A BPEL composition schema is a XML document conforming to a specific XML Schema format, which describes different aspects of a business process, such as:

— the roles involved in a message exchange;
— the port types to which the roles refer;
— the orchestration and specific aspects of the process organization;
— the correlation information which relates the messages with the correct composition instances.

A BPEL process is made of *activities*, which can be separated into *basic* activities, such as `receive`, `reply`, `invoke`, `assign`, `exit` and *structured* activities, such as `sequence`, `if`, `while`, `flow`, `pick`.

Various graphical representations are available for business processes, both involving BPEL [17] and other models. Such representations can either be general (UML2 Activity Diagrams [31], Business Process Modeling Notation [5], Event-Driven Process chain [24]) or specific to BPEL. Although the specification of WS-BPEL is standard, its integration with execution platforms is prevalently dependent on the development environment. Therefore, BPEL-specific notations are usually bound to some tool such as IBM WebSphere Business Model [15], Eclipse BPEL Project [11] or Active Endpoints' design tool ActiveBPEL Designer [1]. Without any loss of generality, we adopt the last one in the rest of the section.

Speaking in general, the BPEL process can be visualized by a directed graph $\mathcal{G}(\mathcal{N}, \mathcal{E})$, in which $\mathcal{N}$ is the set of nodes, and $\mathcal{E}$ the set of edges. Nodes can be associated with the individual activities, while edges represent the control flow between activity invocations. Data flow-based test adequacy criteria are conventionally defined on the control flow graph of a program, which is annotated with variable definitions and uses. In the case of BPEL this standard process of annotation needs to be adapted and made more effective by taking in consideration the specific features of this language.

Beyond the generic and idealistic scenario depicted above, we are aware that defining a suitable representation of BPEL control flow is a complex problem. BPEL includes activities allowing for parallel execution as well as for synchronous and asynchronous communication, which require to extend the conventional control flow graph. Different proposals have been presented (e.g., [37, 40,19]) and a general agreement has not been reached yet. The attitude we took in this work is to rely as much as possible on the well established ActiveBPEL graphical representation, extending it only for some activities of the BPEL process which are peculiar with respect to other common programming languages. Specifically, this means that: apart from invoke, each basic BPEL activity is represented as a node. A part from flow and pick, each structured BPEL activity is represented by branches and joins. Moreover special consideration is also taken for the constructs **correlation** and **scope** which are peculiar of BPEL language. More details are provided in the following.

Invoke Activity. The invoke basic activity is used to call the WSs offered by a service provider. It may include other activities ruled by a *fault handler* or a *compensation handler*, which can be executed in alternative to the main flow in case of invocation problems. When one of these handlers is invoked, an alternative flow is activated, canceling the previous request. If problems are encountered during the main invoke activity, the condition becomes true and the alternative invoke flow is executed.

Flow Activity and Parallel Processing. The flow construct groups a set of activities to be executed in parallel. It is considered completed only when all the included activities are completed. The Link construct allows for synchronization of parallel activities. A Link connects a source activity with a target activity. The source activity must be completed before the target activity starts.

source and target activities can be arbitrarily nested within a flow activity. Considering the control flow diagram derived by the ActiveBPEL, parallel activities are delimited by a rectangle, while synchronization links are represented by arrows. Figure 3) is an example of flow activity representation. In it, once the user has established the search keywords if both an author and a title have been requested, a flow activity is executed and two invoke activities start in parallel. This means that the searching by author and by title are executed in concurrency and their output values assigned to two different variables. When both invoke activities are completed the flow is completed as well and the assign is executed which will merge the two results into a single variable.

Another BPEL activity that introduces parallel processing is the construct foreach - it is similar to flow and not detailed here for simplicity. Moreover, *event handlers* can be executed in parallel with any other activity in their scope, when the associated event occurs.

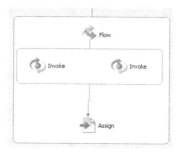

Fig. 3. flow derived graph

Pick Activity. The pick activity is associated with a set of events (messages or message part) and a set of activities. In particular, when it is executed, it blocks until one of its messages is received or one of its alarm goes off. Only a single message or alarm is executed and this causes all the other branches to go dead path. The subsequent flow of the BPEL process is therefore only conditioned by the type of message received and not by its content as in the standard if condition. From a testing point view, pick involves a set of variables each one different for the type of message associated. The selection of the variable to which a value will be assigned is established accordingly to the type of message received or to which timed event which has gone off. In other terms, pick represents a mutually exclusive conditional assignment of variables that influences the subsequent data flow. Figure 4 shows an example for the VSB: once the user has selected a record from the list of available publications the BPEL process awaits for an operation request. Depending on the message received either the variable representing the number of citations or that associated to the the URL of the pdf article will be assigned and successively queried for. Once defined the variable of interest, the left or the middle branches of Figure 4 will be executed. If no message is sent within 30 seconds, the alarm will expire and the right branch of Figure 4 will be executed.

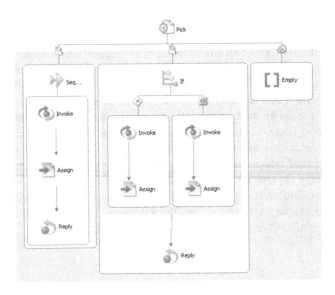

Fig. 4. pick derived graph

Correlation. Messages sent and received during a BPEL process need to be delivered not only to the correct destination server (port), but also to the proper instance of the business process provided by the server. For this, *correlation tokens* can be used, which provide the instance routing automatically [21]. This creates a dependence between received and sent messages inside a specific process and avoids mixing-up of data between concurrent instances of the same process. From a testing point of view, this means that different allocations of the same variable can coexist at the same time that have to be checked properly.

Scope. The last construct of relevance for data flow analysis is scope which is not properly an activity but rather a container. Its purpose is to restrict the execution of a certain part of the process to a self-contained environment. In particular a fault caught within a scope can be handled without affecting the rest of the process. A scope can define its own variables or handles. Thus, referring to the VSB, a scope has been introduced when the users select a specific record within the list of publications (see Figure 5). The assign activity in the left branch can issue a standard BPEL fault (*selection fault*) when the requested index is outside the range of publication in the list. The right branch can catch the selection fault and execute the activity contained in the handler; specifically an error message is created and sent to the user and the process is terminated. Alternatively, it is possible to resolve the faulty operation within the scope and continue the process execution.

From a testing point of view each alternative flows within a scope may allocate and manipulate different variables and influence the successive activities execution. However the management of exceptions and faults in BPEL is quite complex and would require a dedicated study. Here we only consider an example

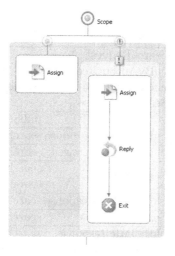

Fig. 5. scope derived graph

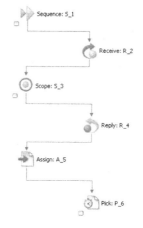

Fig. 6. Global control flow graph of the VSB example

of a fault handler as representative of possible alternate flows to be considered
for testing purposes.

Definitions and Usages of Variables Inside BPEL. The control flow graph
of the BPEL description relative to the VSB is shown in the Figures 6, 7, and 8
(the diagram has been split across more pages for readability). It includes a flow
activity, while there are no correlations or synchronization points.

Following the conventional data flow testing process [8], we annotate the control flow graph with the definitions and uses of each variable: the point in the
program where a value is produced is a *definition*, while the point where the
value may be accessed is a *use*. A use of a variable v in a node u and a definition

Table 5. Definitions and uses of the BPEL variables in the VSB case study

Node number	Var. defined	Var. used
1.1	pubSearchRequest	-
1.2	searchByAuthorRequest searchByTitleRequest pubSearchResponse	pubSearchRequest
1.3	-	pubSearchRequest
1.5	searchByAuthorResponse	searchByAuthorRequest
1.6	searchByTitleResponse	searchByTitleRequest
1.7	pubSearchResponse	searchByAuthorResponse searchByTitleResponse
1.8	searchByAuthorResponse	searchByAuthorRequest
1.9	pubSearchResponse	searchByAuthorResponse
1.10	searchByTitleResponse	searchByTitleRequest
1.11	pubSearchResponse	searchByTitleResponse
1.12	pubSearch_faultMsg	-
1.13	-	pubSearch_faultMsg
1.14	-	pubSearchResponse
2	-	selectionRequest
3.1	selectionResponse	pubSearchResponse selectionRequest
3.2	selection_faultMsg	-
3.3	-	selection_faultMsg
4	-	selectionResponse
5	googleCitationsRequest acmPdfRequest	selectionResponse
6	getCitationsRequest or getPdfRequest	getCitationsRequest or getPdfRequest
6.2	googleCitationsResponse	googleCitationsRequest
6.3	getCitationsResponse	googleCitationsResponse
6.4	-	getCitationsResponse
6.5	-	selectionResponse
6.6	pdfGetterResponse	pdfGetterRequest
6.7	getPdfResponse	pdfGetterResponse
6.8	acmPdfResponse	acmPdfRequest
6.9	getPdfResponse	acmPdfResponse
6.10	-	getPdfResponse

of v in a node d form a *definition-use pair* (or *du pair*), denoted (d, u), if and only if, the value of v defined in d can potentially be used in u.

The following examples illustrate definitions and uses for BPEL processes:

– for the elementary operation **from** with syntax

```
1  <from variable="BPELVariableName" part="NCName"?>
2    <query queryLanguage="anyURI"?>?
3      queryContent
4    </query>
5  </from>
```

the variables used are **BPELVariableName** and all the variables used in the
queryContent. The latter is usually an XPath expression [32] that may
involve other BPEL variables.

– for the elementary operation **to** with syntax

```
1  <to variable="BPELVariableName" part="NCName"?>
2    <query queryLanguage="anyURI"?>?
3      queryContent
4    </query>
5  </to>
```

the variable defined is **BPELVariableName**, while the variables used are all
the other variables accessed in the **queryContent**.

Table 6. Du-pairs of BPEL variables in the VSB case study

Variable name	DU pairs
pubSearchRequest	(1.1, 1.2), (1.1, 1.3)
pubSearchResponse	(1.2, 1.14), (1.2, 2), (1.7, 1.14), (1.7, 2), (1.9, 1.14), (1.9, 2), (1.11, 1.14), (1.11, 2)
searchByAuthorRequest	(1.2, 1.5), (1.2, 1.8)
searchByAuthorResponse	(1.5, 1.7), (1.8, 1.9)
searchByTitleRequest	(1.2, 1.6), (1.2, 1.10)
searchByTitleResponse	(1.6, 1.7), (1.10, 1.11)
pubSearch_faultMsg	(1.12, 1.13)
selectionRequest	(2, 3.1)
selectionResponse	(3.1, 4), (3.1, 5)
selection_faultMsg	(3.2, 3.3)
getCitationsRequest	(6, 6)
getCitationsResponse	(6.3, 6.4)
googleCitationsRequest	(5, 6.2)
googleCitationsResponse	(6.2, 6.3)
getPdfRequest	(6, 6)
getPdfResponse	(6.7, 6.10), (6.9, 6.10)
pdfGetterRequest	(5, 6.6)
pdfGetterResponse	(6.6, 6.7)
acmPdfRequest	(5, 6.8)
acmPdfResponse	(6.8, 6.9)

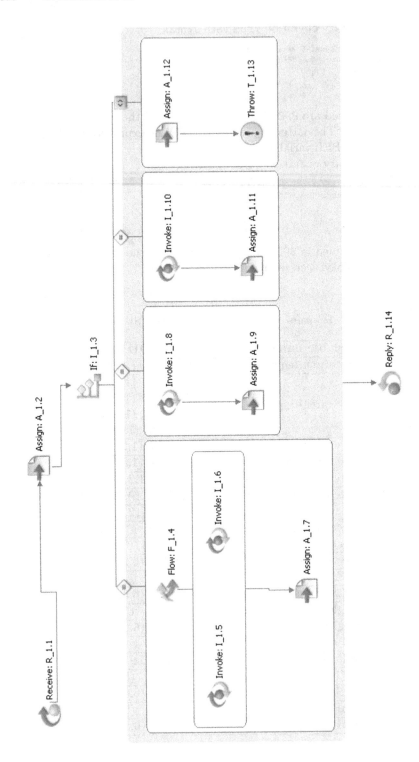

Fig. 7. Control flow graph of expanded Sequence: S_1 of Fig. 6

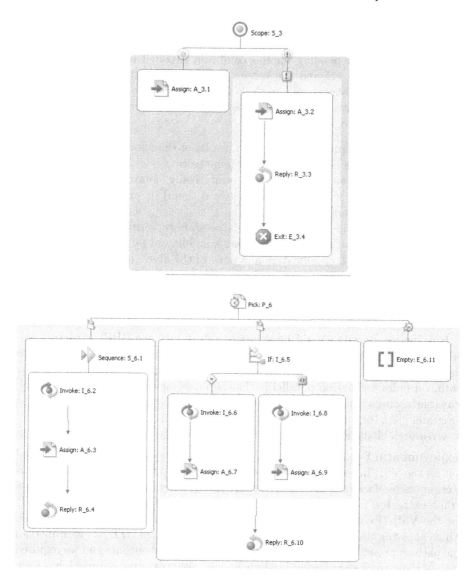

Fig. 8. Control flow graphs of expanded S_3 and P_6 of Fig. 6

Table 5 provides the variable definitions and uses of the VSB BPEL process (the numbers refer to the node numbers as reported in Figures 6, 7 and 8). With respect to node 6 an alternative between a variable definition or use is provided. This is due to the usage of pick activity. Depending on the type of data received by the user either the variable getCitationsRequest or getPdfRequest is first defined, and then used for deciding which flow must be successively executed among those provided by the pick activity.

In Table 6 we finally show the corresponding du pairs. Note that there are several du pairs for the variable `pubSearchResponse`, because it foresees various alternative actions depending on the condition satisfied in the `if`. Thus one definition is in node 1.2 and the others in one of 1.7, 1.9 or 1.11. Moreover due to the `pick` activity in node 6, the du pairs for `getCitationsRequest` and `getPdfRequest` involve only node 6. This is not a general case, but is specific to the `pick` implemented in the VSB.

Testing Purposes and Criteria. The results of the above data flow analysis can be used for static analysis or for coverage testing.

Typical suspicious situations that can be statically identified could be *dd* (two successive definitions without any use between them) or *-u* (data used without being previously defined) [27].

For instance, considering Table 5, it is possible to verify that each variable definition, a part from `pubSearchResponse`, is followed by at least a definition in a node of the BPEL specification and none of the above mentioned anomalies is detected. `pubSearchResponse` has two consecutive definitions, as explained in the previous section, but this is not a fault.

Concerning testing, classical data flow-based coverage criteria can be used such as *all-uses*, *c-uses* and *p-uses*, or *all-du-pairs* [8].

But specific criteria should be defined to deal with the BPEL structure, especially with parallelism and inter-process communication features. Indeed, to the du pairs formed between a variable definition and use on a same control flow path, du pairs defined on parallel paths should be added, as suggested in [19]. Possible testing criteria can be inherited for the data-flow testing of concurrent programs [26,10], but the peculiarity of the BPEL language makes this task a new research challenge and few proposal are currently available [37,40,19].

Experimental Feedback. Two different testing experiments have been carried out on the VSB implementation, reflecting the two approaches presented in this section: using data flow model built from the requirements and using data flow graph extracted from the BPEL specification. In the former, we used the DFD for the VSB (Figure 2) defined exploiting only the requirements specification. Thus, applying the path coverage as structural criterion of DFD, we identified all the paths representing dependencies between inputs and outputs and we required each of them to be exercised at least once. A black-box testing approach has been adopted for deriving the appropriate test cases. These have been finally executed on the available VSB BPEL implementation demonstrating that the concrete execution effectively satisfy the input/output requirements specification.

The second experimentation focused on the application of the all-du-pairs criterion on the data flow model extracted from the BPEL representation. Test cases have been derived for each du pair in VSB (see Table 6) and successfully executed (no failure).

In an additional experimentation, the composition has been exercised for experimenting its robustness in case of malicious data entry. Input data corresponding to such situations are derived from the requirements and from the associated DFD. Possible invalid data include:

- after the initial search has been carried out, a list of publications (possibly empty) is returned. The service then expects the user to send an index to select a publication. An index which is not numeric or out of the boundaries of the list is invalid and produces a fault (standard BPEL fault: `selectionFault`);
- in addition to the above-mentioned index, another required input after the search is the requested operation, which is expected in the form of an operation-specific message. A message which does not match any of the possible operations is considered an invalid input, but in this case does not produce any fault, since the `pick` activity simply ignores any message which does not match the expected ones;
- further, an invalid username in the ACM service invocation should not make possible to get a valid pdf file.

For each of the above categories of invalid inputs, we have derived a test case exercising it.

The execution of such derived invalid test cases resulted in a single failure, relative to du-pair (`username` (42,45)). In this case, although the username was not valid, the invocation of the ACM Search service returned a link to the pdf document. This problem was due to the fact that the machine executing VSB had an IP address within the IP ACM authenticated network, so each request provided by VSB to ACM Search service was considered as valid regardless of the username.

6 Conclusions

WSs are the most prominent example of the emerging SOA. In this chapter, we have discussed several ways in which, depending on the information available, the flow of data in WSCs could be usefully referred to for Verification and Validation purposes. Although the verification of WSCs assumes strategic value, from a survey of related work we realize that data centered models have not yet been exploited for their potential.

In a WSC several services are combined to obtain, from their interaction, a more complex functionality. By considering in explicit way a model of how data are expected to be exchanged between the combined services, we can then check whether desired properties are satisfied or also test whether the implemented WSC (which could also be dynamically bound) complies with that model.

In this chapter we have started with a first classification of perspectives in using data flow-based V&V approaches. The objective of this overview in Section 4 has been to lay down possible interesting research avenues in data-based analysis and testing of SOA. The emerging set of approaches has been classified in Table 4.

We have also outlined in Section 5 some examples of possible realizations of the outlined approaches. In particular, we have discussed in Section 5.1 how a DFD could provide guidance in data based validation, even in absence of other

WSC specifications. As we discuss, this is a high-level informal approach that can provide an early interesting feedback. We then also provided in Section 5.2 guidelines for the usage of a data flow model extracted from the BPEL code for testing purposes. In particular, we discussed in detail the BPEL peculiarities, such as parallel executions and specific BPEL constructs, which require to revise the conventional flowgraph representation.

The approach has been demonstrated on the VSB case study, which implements and composes several services. The case study has been used also to derive the data flow from the BPEL specification and based on it for checking the validity of the input/ouput interaction among VSB components. First results have been obtained and analyzed.

With this work, we have just started to scratch the surface of the great potential offered by data flow modelling and analysis for WSC validation. Our purpose was presenting an exhaustive exploration of the perspectives opened by data flow-based validation and present examples for some of them. There remains of course much to do in future work.

Strangely enough, there does not exist a commonly agreed notation for modelling the BPEL flowgraph. As explained in the chapter, there exist various graphical notations that are bound to this or that tool. While we have adopted here ActiveBPEL Designer [1] for illustration purposes, we are currently studying a suitable graphical representation of BPEL that can take in consideration all the peculiarities of this specific language, relative to both control and data flow. We are also in parallel formalizing the process of data flow annotation of ActiveBPEL flowgraphs, which has been here sketched.

In this chapter we have adapted the notions of a *definition* and of a *use* of a variable from conventional programs to the specific constructs of BPEL. To realize data-flow based testing of BPEL programs, we need also to formulate and evaluate suitable adequacy criteria to measure coverage over BPEL executions. In the experimentation reported here we have plainly adopted the standard all-du-pairs criterion. However, we believe that more peculiar and effective criteria could be devised. For instance, one could focus the coverage measure on specified categories of client-server interactions. The definition of novel data flow based criteria is an important future work direction that requires serious and effort-prone empirical analyses. Thus, we intend to continue experimentation to identify more useful test criteria for WSCs.

A crucial issue in testing of WSs is how to deal with side effects, in those cases in which a system that is being tested invokes at run-time some already deployed services. If the invoked services are stateless, the invocation can be done without great problems. This is for instance the case of the services invoked in VSB, that consists of accessing a data base and recovering information and data. However, if the invoked services are stateful, appropriate measures must be considered. In our group, we are developing a framework to automatically generate mock services that can substitute the real stateful services for testing purposes [2]. Such a framework could be fruitfully combined with the research presented here.

Finally, as a future task we also intend to investigate the combined use data flow based testing with behavioural techniques, such as in [13], to gain the highest effectiveness from the combination of the two complementary types of approach.

References

1. ActiveBPEL Community. ActiveBPEL community edition engine (2008), accessed 2008-03-12, http://www.activevos.com/community-open-source.php
2. Bertolino, A., De Angelis, G., Frantzen, L., Polini, A.: Symbolic execution techniques for test purpose definition. In: Suzuki, K., Higashino, T., Hasegawa, T., Ulrich, A. (eds.) TestCom/FATES 2008. LNCS, vol. 5047, pp. 266–282. Springer, Heidelberg (2008)
3. Bertolino, A., Frantzen, L., Polini, A., Tretmans, J.: Audition of web services for testing conformance to open specified protocols. In: Reussner, R., Stafford, J., Szyperski, C. (eds.) Architecting Systems with Trustworthy Components. LNCS, vol. 3938, pp. 1–25. Springer, Heidelberg (2006)
4. Bertolino, A., Polini, A.: The audition framework for testing web services interoperability. In: 31st EUROMICRO International Conference on Software Engineering and Advanced Applications, pp. 134–142 (2005)
5. BPMN. Business process modeling notation specification, Version 1.0 dtc/06-02-01 (2006)
6. Canfora, G., Penta, M.D.: Testing services and service-centric systems: challenges and opportunities. IEEE IT Professionnal 8(2), 10–17 (2006)
7. Cao, H., Ying, S., Du, D.: Towards model-based verification of BPEL with model checking. In: Sixth International Conference on Computer and Information Technology (CIT 2006), Seoul, Korea, September 20-22, 2006, pp. 190–194 (2006)
8. Clarke, L.A., Podgurski, A., Richardson, D.J., Zeil, S.J.: A formal evaluation of data flow path selection criteria. IEEE Trans. Software Eng. 15(11), 1318–1332 (1989)
9. Davenport, T.H., Short, J.E.: The new industrial engineering: Information technology and business process redesign. Sloan Management Review, 11–27 (1990)
10. Dwyer, M.B., Clarke, L.A.: Data flow analysis for verifying properties of concurrent programs. In: SIGSOFT FSE, pp. 62–75 (1994)
11. Eclipse Foundation. BPEL project, http://www.eclipse.org/bpel/
12. Foster, H., Uchitel, S., Magee, J., Kramer, J.: Model-based verification of web service compositions. In: ASE, pp. 152–163. IEEE Computer Society, Los Alamitos (2003)
13. Frantzen, L., Tretmans, J., Vries, R.d.: Towards model-based testing of web services. In: Polini, A. (ed.) International Workshop on Web Services - Modeling and Testing (WS-MaTe 2006), Palermo, Italy, June 9, 2006, pp. 67–82 (2006)
14. García-Fanjul, J., Tuya, J., de la Riva, C.: Generating test cases specifications for BPEL compositions of web services using SPIN. In: International Workshop on Web Services Modeling and Testing (WS-MaTe 2006) (2006)
15. IBM. IBM websphere business modeler, http://www-306.ibm.com/software/integration/wbimodeler/
16. Jiang, Y., Hou, S.-S., Shan, J.-H., Zhang, L., Xie, B.: Contract-based mutation for testing components. In: IEEE International Conference on Software Maintenance (2005)

17. Koehler, J., Vanhatalo, J.: Process anti-patterns: How to avoid the common traps of business process modeling. Research Report RZ-3678 (May 2007), http://www.zurich.ibm.com/~koe/papiere/rz3678.pdf

18. Marconi, A., Pistore, M., Traverso, P.: Specifying data-flow requirements for the automated composition of web services. In: Fourth IEEE International Conference on Software Engineering and Formal Methods (SEFM 2006), Pune, India, September 11-15, 2006, pp. 147–156 (2006)

19. Moser, S., Martens, A., Gorlach, K., Amme, W., Godlinski, A.: Advanced verification of distributed ws-bpel business processes incorporating cssa-based data flow analysis. In: IEEE SCC, pp. 98–105. IEEE Computer Society, Los Alamitos (2007)

20. Narayanan, S., McIlraith, S.: Analysis and simulation of web services. Computer Networks 42(5), 675–693 (2003)

21. OASIS WSBPEL Technical Committee. Web services business process execution language version 2.0 (2007), http://docs.oasis-open.org/wsbpel/2.0/wsbpel-v2.0.pdf

22. Ostrand, T.J., Balcer, M.J.: The category-partition method for specifying and generating fuctional tests. Commun. ACM 31(6), 676–686 (1988)

23. Sadiq, S.W., Orlowska, M.E., Sadiq, W., Foulger, C.: Data flow and validation in workflow modelling. In: Database Technologies 2004, Proceedings of the Fifteenth Australasian Database Conference, ADC 2004, Dunedin, New Zealand, January 18-22, 2004, pp. 207–214 (2004)

24. Scheer, A.W., Abolhassan, F., Jost, W., Kirchner, M. (eds.): Business Process Excellence - ARIS in Practice. Springer, Heidelberg (2002)

25. Siblini, R., Mansour, N.: Testing web services. In: ACS/IEEE International Conference on Computer Systems and Applications (2005)

26. Taylor, R., Levine, D., Kelly, C.: Structural testing of concurrent programs. IEEE Transactions on Software Engineering 18(3), 206–215 (1992)

27. Tsai, B.-Y., Stobart, S., Parrington, N.: Employing data flow testing on object-oriented classes. Software, IEE Proceedings 148(2), 56–64 (2001)

28. Tsai, W.T., Bai, X., Paul, R., Feng, K., Yu, L.: Scenario-Based Modeling and Its Applications. In: IEEE WORDS (2002)

29. Tsai, W.T., Paul, R., Song, W., Cao, Z.: Coyote: an XML-based framework for web services testing. In: 7th IEEE International Symp. High Assurance Systems Eng (HASE 2002) (2002)

30. UDDI Spec Technical Committee. UDDI OASIS standard version 3.0.2 (2004), http://www.oasisopen.org/committees/uddi-spec/doc/spec/v3/uddi-v3.0.220041019.htm

31. UML2.0. Object management group (OMG). Unified Modeling Language: Superstructure, Version 2.0 formal/05-07-04 (2005)

32. W3C. XML path language (XPath) version 1.0, http://www.w3.org/TR/xpath

33. Weiss, M., Esfandiari, B.: On feature interactions among web services. In: Proceedings of the IEEE International Conference on Web Services (ICWS 2004), San Diego, California, USA, June 6-9, 2004, pp. 88–95 (2004)

34. Weiss, M., Esfandiari, B., Luo, Y.: Towards a classification of web service feature interactions. Computer Networks 51(2), 359–381 (2007)

35. World Wide Web Consortium. SOAP version 1.2 (2007), http://www.w3.org/TR/soap/

36. World Wide Web Consortium. Web services description language (WSDL) version 2.0 (2007), http://www.w3.org/TR/wsdl20/

37. Yan, J., Li, Z., Yuan, Y., Sun, W., Zhang, J.: BPEL4WS unit testing: Test case generation using a concurrent path analysis approach. In: 17th International Symposium on Software Reliability Engineering (ISSRE 2006), Raleigh, North Carolina, USA, November 7-10, 2006, pp. 75–84 (2006)
38. Yang, Y., Tan, Q., Xiao, Y., Liu, F., Yu, J.: Transform BPEL workflow into hierarchical CP-Nets to make tool support for verification. In: APWeb 2006, pp. 275–284 (2006)
39. Yourdon, E., Constantine, L.: Structured Design. Yourdon Press (1975)
40. Yuan, Y., Li, Z., Sun, W.: A graph-search based approach to BPEL4WS test generation. In: Proceedings of the International Conference on Software Engineering Advances (ICSEA 2006), Papeete, Tahiti, French Polynesia, October 28 - November 2 (2006)

Using Architecture Analysis to Evolve Complex Industrial Systems

Tommy Kettu[1], Eckhard Kruse[2], Magnus Larsson[1,3], and Goran Mustapic[1]

Industrial Software Systems
[1]ABB, Corporate Research, Forskargränd 7, 72178 Västerås, Sweden
[2]ABB, Corporate Research, Wallstadter Str 59, 68526 Ladenburg, Germany
[3]Mälardalen University, Box 883, 72123 Västerås Sweden
{Tommy.Kettu,Magnus.Larsson,Goran.Mustapic}@se.abb.com,
Eckhard.Kruse@de.abb.com

Abstract. ABB is a large industrial company with a broad product portfolio that contains products that can be categorized as highly complex industrial systems. Software embedded in complex industrial systems must support rigid system dependability requirements. It is not only a challenge to design and implement these systems as dependable, but it is also difficult to maintain this important property over time. There are several factors that make software evolution a challenging task, such as: size of the software base is measured in order of MLOC, products are long-lived and extended to support new requirements over time longer than 10 years. Because of personnel turnover important knowledge is lost from time to time, and the only artifact that is really up-to-date is the implementation itself. Therefore, to obtain an up-to-date view of the system and prevent expensive mistakes during system evolution, it is beneficial to find practical ways to obtain an up-to-date view on an architectural level without having to read thousands of lines of source code. These activities should be seen as an important contribution for preventing the introduction of faults into software systems since they contribute to improve and maintain the overall system dependability. This experience paper provides practical advices on how to reconstruct the architecture of existing systems by combining the use of tools and the existing knowledge within the organization. The paper is based on experiences from two cases in different sub domains within industrial automation.

Keywords: D.2.11 Software Architectures; D.2.7.m Restructuring, reverse engineering, and reengineering.

1 Introduction

Once deployed in the field at customer sites, many industrial systems have a lifetime of ten years or more. To build a software intensive system that lasts for that time period is clearly a challenge, and to get it right from the beginning is even harder. Even if the software is flawlessly written the hardware will decay over time, leading to replacements and reinstallations of the software. One huge problem with replacing old outdated hardware with new hardware is that the software might not run on it. That

R. de Lemos et al. (Eds.): Architecting Dependable Systems V, LNCS 5135, pp. 326–341, 2008.

is,. the lack of hardware drivers in the old software will prevent execution of the old software on the new hardware. Furthermore: new development tools get introduced, some software components become obsolete over time [1], new versions of operating systems are used because the old ones are not supported any more, requirements on new functionality are added to the system, etc. To adhere to these requirements of change, the software system must be modified. Because the changes in the system environment over time are inevitable, regardless of how well the system is prepared and designed for evolution, it will have to be modified, which in some cases involves redesign of the whole system, or some of its parts.

One of the keys to supporting evolution of legacy software is the understanding of the software system in general and its software architecture in particular. Making a change to the legacy software should be based on rational decisions and with a clear understanding of the impact on most important properties of the system. Even for systems that are referred to as "dependable systems", it is recognized that many other properties are relevant, such as: functionality, usability, performance and cost [11]. Analysis of tradeoffs between all important system properties are first made on architectural level, which is one of the reasons why the software architecture should be well understood as a means to be able to reason about the impact of change. But, as the authors in [2] argue, even if architectural documentation for a system exists, we do not know if what was designed is what was actually built! This is especially true when we add the time aspect of 10 or 15 years. Therefore, to do the reasoning about the impact of change, an important task is first to rediscover the architectural information. With architecture reconstruction we mean: analyzing existing artifacts, such as code, to obtain a high-level view (architectural view) of the SW system and updating the documentation. In an industrial setting, a particularly interesting question that needs to be answered by architectural analysis is: what is the impact/risk of changing the system? This provides input to another analysis - costs vs. benefits of implementing certain change in the system. Architectural reconstruction for academic purposes may have rather different goals that do not involve economic aspects.

Our focus area is: how to reconstruct cost-effectively the architecture and how to follow up on architectural rules to prevent architectural degradation during system evolution?

To do a cost-effective, reliable and quick architecture reconstruction, it would be beneficial to automate the process and use software tools as much as possible. The particular question that we are interested within the scope of this paper is how these tools can be cost-effectively applied in a real industrial context, on millions of lines of code. The goal is also to find tools that could become an integral part of the development process and support the enforcement of architectural rules on system implementation during system evolution.

Related work has been done in the field of architecture reconstruction and reverse engineering of software. Binkley presents a thorough study of source code analysis and a road map of future challenges in the area [3]. This study is mainly focused on static source code analysis. The shortcomings of having only static analysis is pointed out by Riva and Rodriquez [4] with the following quote "In both the approaches (dynamic and static), multiple views obtained from different perspectives are necessary for describing and understanding software architectures". State of the art on software architecture reconstruction approaches is presented in [14].

The Corporate Research unit within ABB has been involved in software architecture reconstruction and evaluation in many different ABB business units. In this paper we present two such cases. For each case, we describe our experiences in architecture reconstruction for purpose of system evolution, assisted by using software tools.

The contributions of this paper are the experiences and lessons we have learned from using architecture analysis as a mean to evolve complex software systems. In particular, we show that:

- It is likely that off-the-shelf tools will not fit out of the box in the context of the system investigated and they will need to be customized.
- The quality of system analysis can be improved by combining the use of tools and the existing knowledge within the organization.
- Rather than static analysis of source code, in certain cases a more promising approach can be to base the analysis on binaries.

The rest of this paper is organized in the following way. Section two describes related approaches to architecture analysis and reconstruction and tools that we have used in our analysis. Section three and four describe two cases from the industry, approaching the topic from different angles. The first case study shows how architecture analysis interacts with ongoing development activities and how it can trigger actions even by using quite simple analysis methods. The second case study highlights some intricacies and solutions in real-life analysis work and thus shows that there is no simple 'standard approach' for doing architecture analysis in complex systems. The last section of this paper, section five, contains conclusions and recommendations on future work.

2   Approaches and Tools for Architecture Analysis and Reconstruction

Based on literature search and our experience we found that different approaches can be taken for analyzing software architecture. Three approaches that are well known are ATAM [5], Bosch [6] and CBAM [7]. The SEI's Architecture Tradeoff Analysis Method (ATAM) is probably the leading method in the area of software architecture evaluation. The, method is based on analysis of scenarios and architecture decisions with stakeholders, resulting in identification of risks, non-risks, sensitivity points, and tradeoff points in the architecture. Another approach is the one taken by Jan Bosch. He mentions the following four different types of architecture assessment: scenario based, simulation based, mathematical model based and experience based. These approaches do not consider economical issues. If this is a major concern then the Cost Benefit Analysis Method (CBAM) can be utilized. The CBAM analyzes architectural decisions from the perspectives of cost, benefit, schedule and risk.

A part of the architectural analysis in system evolution is the process of reconstructing the actual current architecture. Which architecture reconstruction approach should be taken depends on the context of the analysis. The analysis is performed with a task in mind, which we refer to as the *target question*. In most approaches the software itself, and in isolation from its development environment, is the subject of investigation. For this kind of analysis there are static and dynamic approaches. This is also the main line of most research in the area. However, working on the software alone is not always sufficient. A more general approach to software architecture analysis, which we refer to as *holistic*, involves other sources of information, as for example, documentation, developers, product managers or users. One such semi-automatic analysis method for reconstructing architectures based on the recognition of architectural patterns is presented in [13]. An interactive system called Dali that aids user in interpreting architectural information is presented in [2]. A state of the art on software architecture reconstruction approaches is presented in [14]. In summary, we see the following main lines of approaching the analysis and reconstruction, namely, static, dynamic and holistic.

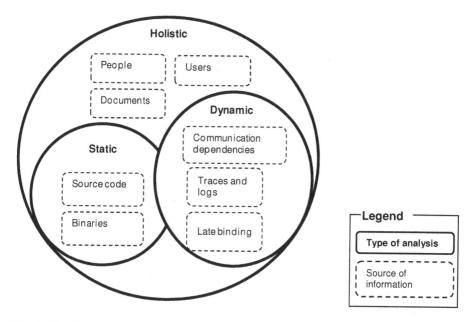

Fig. 1. The figure presents three types of software architecture analysis: static, dynamic and holistic. For each type some possible sources of information that is used to perform the analysis are shown.

These types of architectural analysis are also hierarchical to a certain degree (see figure 1). The basic type is the static approach where only code (compiled or not) is used as base of information. Another type is the dynamic approach, where for instance dynamic calls and late binding are monitored to draw conclusions. The top level type of approach is the holistic, where everything that can bring answers to the target question, not just software, is considered.

2.1 Static Analysis

The starting point for static analysis is the source code as base of information. Source code is well structured data, and can be parsed and analyzed by tools fairly easy.

Many vendors and researchers have realized that and build many tools for this analyzing purpose. Several of these tools target to create a dependency graph of all components in the software system. As this is useful information, such tools have been used in our case studies and the tools are described briefly below.

LXR – the Linux Cross Referencer. LXR is a versatile cross-referencing tool for relatively large code repositories, which LXR can index and hyperlink and give access to via a web-browser. It supports a number of programming languages out of the box, such as C/C++, Perl, Ruby, PHP, Pascal, and others. One main advantage of this tool is that it is an open source tool, allowing customization, which is a feature that we exploited in one of the case studies.

Understand C. This is a commercial tool that is very good at assisting developers when analyzing for example call chains and doing other tasks that are developer centric.

Hierarchical graph analyzer tool (HGAT). HGAT is a tool developed internally at ABB Corporate Research. It is mainly intended for visualization of components and their dependencies, in a hierarchical way. For example, a software system can be structured into subsystems, modules and components, and each layer is visualized, enriched with additional information such as size of the component in LOC represented with according bubble size. This tool does not do the code analysis itself, i.e., the raw data needs to be provided to it, e.g., in a database.

Lattix LDM [8]. It is a commercial tool based on design structured matrixes (DSM). It has a plug-in concept for language parsers, with a number of available plug-ins supporting various programming languages such as C/C++, Ada, C# and Java. The tool can parse and visualize dependencies spanning several programming languages and even relational databases.

In addition to architectural tools there are metrics tools that can be used to get a better understanding of the software. For example, lines of code (LOC), coupling and cohesion can be metrics of interest answering the target question.

2.2 Dynamic Analysis

Data from the execution of the analyzed software is considered during dynamic analysis. It is not possible to discover references between components or sub systems that are set up with late binding until the software executes. Examples of late binding are references that are resolved with names of components or dependencies through socket communication. The fact that communication between subsystems is often established at runtime points to the shortcomings of static analysis. As pointed out in [9] the problem of static analysis is that many false positives (connections that do not exist) are reported due to conservative over-approximations.

To utilize and extract dynamic data during execution tool support is needed, and it is important that as many dynamic dependencies as possible are discovered. A challenge doing the extraction is to have the right input data to the software to make the software execute all dependencies. As the case often is that not all execution paths can be exercised from test suites alone, dynamic analysis of this kind can not give 100% of all dependencies, however, those that are found can be trusted to be true, i.e., there are no false positives. When source code is available, typical tools used for dynamic analysis are well known debugging tools like the Microsoft Visual Studio debugger and the GNU debugger GDB.

Dynamic analysis should be seen as a complement to static analysis. The target question should be considered carefully before dynamic analysis is deployed, since setting up appropriate test suits and exercising the code can be time consuming. Naturally, already existing test suites or execution paths should be reused for the analysis to minimize the effort of getting dynamic dependency data.

Of course, dynamic analysis can be used for many other purposes beyond detection of component dependencies. Examples are the identification of dead code or frequently executed code, analysis of resource usage, such as, memory, execution times, etc. From an architectural reconstruction perspective as targeted in this paper, however, the component dependencies are of special interest.

2.3 Holistic Analysis

Many questions about the software can be answered by using static and dynamic analysis approach. However there are questions that require a broader approach. Typical questions of this kind that are relevant for evolution of the software are: Are there any organizational reasons why the software is structured to fit development on single site location? What is the reason why only developer Joe can maintain the software? Or what is the background and history of subsystem X and why can't it be substituted with COTS component Y? A broader approach to analyze the software system can then be taken and that is what we refer to as the holistic approach.

Holistic can be defined as looking at the whole system rather than just concentrating on individual components (software). The holistic approach of analyzing a software system includes more than just the software itself. For this kind of analysis it is appropriate to use any source of information that can help answering the target question, e.g., documentation, interviews and configuration management data.

Documentation that is up-to-date with the current implementation is a very valuable source of information during a holistic analysis of the software. However, sometimes the documentation is not aligned with the current implementation and in this case it has less value but can still be used. Even old or original documentation is valuable to get a view of the planned/designed architecture and can serve as a hypothesis of how the software was supposed to be implemented at the time of documentation. Such a planned view is often the architect's perception of the software architecture and is not always the same as the actual implementation. That is, the architect's perception of the overall architecture can be the same even if the implementation changes over time. The architect has the ambition to control the evolution of the software but it is the developers that do the implementation, and in cases of unclear communication of the architectural rules the developers might deviate from the rules, implicit or not. Thus, deviations between the planned view and the actual view should carefully be investigated. An example is the approach taken by Lindvall et al. who have used a planned view as a comparison with the discoveries from dynamic analysis [9].

Another source of information is *interviews* with the people knowing the code, such as developers, testers, designers and architects. People in these groups often know the reasons to why the software has evolved to the current state and interviews can be used to discover this. Dynamic and static analysis can be used to find out what the current state of the software is and a combination with knowing the reasons why the software is in a particular state can be very valuable information. Interviews can also be carried out after dynamic and static analysis has been performed to discuss the findings from the analysis to point out and catch anomalies in the software. Section 3 further elaborates on this topic.

Analyzing *configuration management data* and looking at what parts of the code that are most frequently changed can give valuable input. Parts that are often changed tend to be complex to understand and with high probability of mismatching the design documentation. These parts can have many dependencies and often play a central role in the software. Such components need to have special attention to prevent breaking the code during evolution of the software. In addition to discover vital components, configuration management data can be used to understand who of the developers is changing/modifying the different software components. This information can be used when planning who to talk to during the interviews, as described above.

3   Experiences from Analyzing a Large Client-Server System

In this case we accompanied the development and evolution of a very large (MLOC) distributed client-server software system in the area of industrial automation. The system has evolved significantly throughout various release cycles in a number of years. It is based on C/C++/Microsoft COM technology and has started to move towards C#/.NET technology, with still the major and core parts of the codebase remaining in old technologies. The system is hierarchically structured into several layers (subsystems, components, modules) with COM being used as communication infrastructure between the components.

The requirements on the system in terms of reliability, availability and overall performance/data throughput are very challenging, while at the same time the continuing further development of the system always poses the risk of breaking existing, well-running functionality.

The goal of the research project was to analyze the system architecture and to propose improvement measures, which can be fed into the ongoing development taking into account risk-benefit assessment for each activity.

3.1   Approach and Tools Used

This case study exemplifies the holistic approach mentioned above. The whole environment was considered, or, in business terms, the goal of efficiently developing a high quality, dependable product. Thus, before starting technical investigations, the current situation was analyzed and looked upon from different perspectives, such as:

- Status of the software: architecture, core design principles (and deviations), used technologies, implementation metrics etc.
- Challenges: known problem areas? What is stable/evolving? Specific dependability issues? What new requirements call for design/architecture change? External factors: new technologies/standards/regulations?

- Business and organization: product strategy, where is it in its lifecycle? Ongoing development activities, areas of focus, where is the money flowing? Who are the experts/architects and what do they think?

The answers helped to focus the static analysis and to avoid spending too much time on subsystems that were going to be substituted soon or which the development organization definitely did not want to touch anyhow.

The next step was to dig into the software architecture. There were different sources of information to get an overview such as design documentation, interviews with developers, and bug tracker databases. But then, the only un-biased, always up-to-date reality was of course the source code. Doing tool-based analysis of the code and reflecting the results with the other sources of information and discussing them with the developers resulted in some eye-openers – which in turn were the best way to stimulate subsequent measures.

The first source of information automatically collected from the system implementation was code metrics. Fig. 2. shows a histogram of modules with different sizes. The modules at the borders of the histogram deserve a more detailed look. The right-hand side outlier might be a module which originally was appropriately designed, but then was growing and growing as more functionality was added, without ever doing an appropriate refactoring or redesign. In our case, the most right-hand side outlier turned out to be very critical regarding the overall system dependability (and also regarding the performance).

The left-hand side outliers might be an indication that some minor new functionality had to be added and the developers did not know where to put it, so they just created more and more new small modules – so again, candidates for refactoring.

To find out in what areas the code was changed or growing most, we used LOC-metrics in combination with source code comparison tools. We applied them to the different versions of the product code base in the configuration management system.

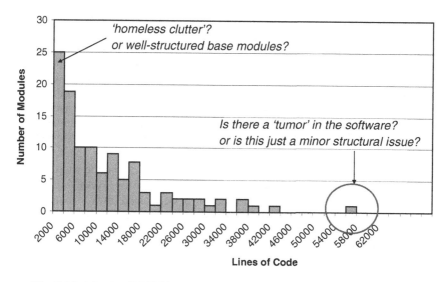

Fig. 2. Module size (LOC) histogram showing possible anomalies in the software

The next step was to understand dependencies between components. In this case COM-dependencies were analyzed by parsing the IDL-files. The extracted interface information was stored in a database, where it was enriched by further information, such as: the 'owning' component (which is not always the same as the components implementing an interface), number of functions per interface, internal/public tags, .NET compatibility issues, etc. Some manual work was needed, e.g., to explicitly specify callback interfaces. From a semantic perspective the component dependency/ownership is reversed in the case of callback interfaces because the definition is not 'owned' by the one or more components which have to implement it, but by the caller. Using the interface database it was easy to dig for further information:

- General statistics such as number of interfaces per subsystem/module/ component.
- Coupling, cohesion, complexity of software dependencies.
- Number of interfaces vs. functional coverage (e.g. some small modules had amazingly complex interfaces).
- Unexpected dependencies between 'independent' system parts.
- Prohibited usage of internal or obsolete interfaces.

To visualize the extracted information the Hierarchical Graphical Analysis Tool (HGAT) tool was used. The HGAT tool is, as its name suggests, a hierarchical analysis tool. It builds a hierarchical internal model of the code which is then shown in a graphical view. Its automated layout mechanisms helped to analyze the dependencies and the layering of the software. The tool assists in running what-if scenarios, e.g.,: if certain dependencies can be removed, is it possible to move system components between layers etc.? Fig. 3. shows how HGAT visualizes components (circles), dependencies (arrows start from the depending module) and potential layering (dashed horizontal lines). The sizes of the circles represent the components' LOC; components with the same shade of grey belong to the same subsystem.

Regarding the system's dependability, the middle layer is the most interesting one, because critical/unstable components in this layer may have system-wide impact. In contrast, the UI/application layer is nicely isolated as it has no incoming dependencies. The base layer is the foundation of the whole system, but its components are independent of the system on top, were typically very stable and could also be tested more easily. As the block arrows indicate, it is thus one goal to move code from the big middle layer where 'everything depends on everything' to the base layer or to the UI/application layer. It turned out, that some components resided in the middle layer even though there was no good architectural reason for that, but just because some dependencies were built into them, which should not be there.

The tool-assisted analysis has shown that already technically quite simple analysis approaches brought a lot of insight and stimulus for discussion. However, whether a finding from the analysis was really a problem to be tackled always required some judgment by the developers. And this judgment must not be limited to whether the design can be improved. It has to predict the actual benefits, e.g., in terms of maintainability and extensibility of the code and the required efforts/costs of the change and the risk of breaking something.

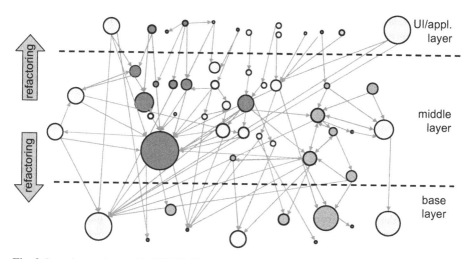

Fig. 3. Layering analysis with HGAT: Circles/colors/sizes represent components/subsystems/LOC, thin arrows represent dependencies

We sorted the proposed improvement measures into different categories:

- Implementation: remove dead code, refactor redundant code, etc., structure and naming of code in the file system.
- Design/architecture: improve layering, reduce component dependencies, break up or re-design components.
- Technology: .NET/COM interoperability.

In a second step, we categorized the improvement measures according to different criteria to evaluate and prioritize them. This was necessary to translate them into input for the required management decisions, which are about when to invest money and allocate people for what expected savings/added customer value and how this fits into the overall product development roadmap:

- Targeted software quality: maintainability, extensibility, reliability, understandability, etc.
- Size of change: from 'cosmetic' to 'rather rewrite from scratch'.
- Cost of fixing the problem vs. expected benefit.
- Timing: is there a hard deadline when it has to be fixed (e.g., .NET-COM migration)? When would be a good point in time? For example, module has to be reworked anyhow; the right developers are available, etc.

As final outcome a report of analysis results and the proposed improvement measures with an assessment of the above criteria was delivered to the development organization. In a joint discussion a subset of the measures has been identified as candidates for realization in the course of future development activities.

3.2 Lessons Learned

In this case we have shown that tool-based analysis can be very useful to gain insight into the software architecture and to get a fresh view on a system which has evolved over time, and to trigger discussions about improvement measures. However, the tools can only do part of the work. Some information had to be added (or corrected) manually based on an understanding of the system. Tool based analysis does not necessarily have to be very complex and sophisticated. The results are valuable as soon as they provide new information to the development team. Once the results of an analysis were derived and visualized the interpretation was discussed with the developers and resulted in deeper follow-up investigations. Finally, we came up with a set of improvement measures which also made economical sense, and could be taken into account when planning the further product development roadmap.

For the system in this case study, we came to the conclusion that this type of software architecture analysis should be performed as a regular activity accompanying the normal development work. As it is tool-based, especially the repetition of analyses can be done with quite low efforts but still requires some manual work. By doing that, unexpected deviations from the intended architecture can be detected early and counter-measures can be planned for.

From a cost-benefit perspective, the overall investigation was a small fraction compared to the yearly efforts of the regular development and maintenance of the product. Thus, by improving the development efficiency within a subsystem or by avoiding some later costly architectural restructuring, the efforts on the analysis are already very well spent.

4 Experiences from Analyzing a Large Real-Time system

The system analyzed in this case is a complex industrial control system. It is a real-time system with application logic implemented in C, C++ and script code. The application code consists of more than 2 MLOC. The system architecture is a layered architecture with object oriented design within the layers. The product line architecture approach is used in the control system design, so the common code base is reused across the product line. The common code base is used in a multi-OS and multi-node context. One of the challenges in implementation of product line architecture is the selection of techniques for implementing software variability [10]. In this case several variability implementation techniques are used, such as:

- Conditional defines in C/C++ code.
- Separate files for different configurations.
- Separate link-lists for different configurations, to exclude particular component that are not relevant for certain configurations.
- Separate scripts for different products in the product line.

Given this existing code base, we evaluated several tools for static analysis of code; searching for tools that can help system architects in analyzing dependencies in the system and helping them maintain the architectural integrity during the system evolution, ideally as an integrated part of the regular system integration builds. The tools should also be useful to software developers working with different subsystems of the system, to get accurate and up-to-date information about users/clients of the services that they provide. The main goal of doing the analysis in this case study was to increase the system modularity. The system dependability is also expected to increase as a consequence of this work, as the number and quality of the internal interfaces within the system will be scrutinized; the number of available interfaces will be decreased, and their quality improved as part of the expected refactoring work resulting from such an analysis.

4.1 Approach and Tools Used

The analysis started with a study of some basic metrics, like LOC, number of components and functions in the software, as well as, cyclomatic complexity, in order to get a first feeling of the size and complexity of the software. Some informal interviews were conducted with the software architect and key developers, and the available documentation on architectural level was retrieved and read before proceeding with the technical analysis. These initial steps gave a good insight of the main architectural decisions, e.g., the adoption of the product line concept and the variability techniques used.

Based on the positive feedback on the tool chain used in the previous case study a static analysis using the Linux cross-referencing software, LXR, and the HGAT tool was attempted as a first test also in this case. Several discoveries were made, mainly related to the fact that in this case we tried to analyze complex C code. The most important discovery was that LXR does not resolve dependencies correctly when the symbol names are not unique, but some of the problems were also related to the implementation of variability needed for a product line approach, namely, the usage of conditional defines. In a very large code base it is very likely that people use non-unique symbol names. The behavior of LXR with non-unique symbol names results in a high possibility for false positives, i.e., dependencies that are not true. This makes LXR less suitable for continuous, tool based, monitoring of architectural violations in the code base of this case.

Even though HGAT is very powerful one limitation of the tool is that it can only show one hierarchical level in a view, i.e., you only see a certain level of granularity at a time. Due to this a second analysis iteration was performed based on the combination of LXR and Lattix LDM. This proved to be partly successful, especially as Lattix includes a feature for defining dependency rules, but the basic problem with false positives remained.

One possible approach to overcome these difficulties is to analyze only one of the configurations at time. For a selected configuration, analysis is then performed on binaries rather than the source code. Some advantages of using binaries rather than source-level analysis are reported in [12]. Much of the information that is present in the source code is not present in the binaries, but the information essential for our purpose - dependency analysis - is still present. We simply let the compiler do the "hard work" of removing code that is not of interest for the particular configuration. For each of the binaries (partial results of product build process), it is possible to obtain a list of the symbols that it exports (defined by the module) and that it imports (unresolved references).

Based on this approach, a program named DependencyTool was developed that analyzes the dependencies between the binary object files. For each binary object file processed by the tool, it is possible to get a list of symbols (defined and undefined), as well as, symbol types (data, common data, functions) and scope (local, global). Binaries can be linked recursively, which means that one globally defined symbol can be found in more than one place. If a global symbol is defined in more than one binary, we assume that the binary with more global symbols includes the one with fewer global symbols. Otherwise, multiple definitions of the same symbols would cause a link error when the final system image is built. After the tool generates a hierarchy, it is possible to determine the architectural visibility scope for each binary. If all dependents are found within the same branch in the hierarchy the binary is "local" to the branch, otherwise it is global. A snapshot of the tool GUI is shown in Fig. 4.

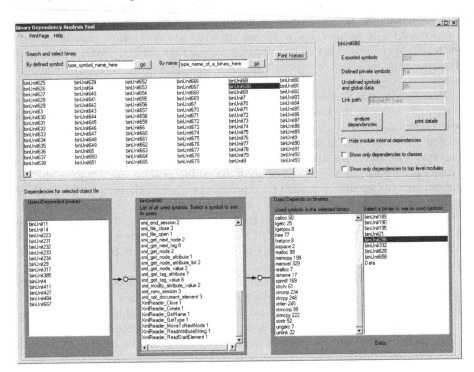

Fig. 4. A screen dump from the DependencyTool. A selected module is the dark grey box in the middle. The user interface shows which modules that use the selected module, and which symbols in that selected module that are used. The UI also shows which symbols in which modules are used by the selected module.

There is an additional advantage when working with binaries, rather than the source code. By doing simple regrouping of symbols defined by the tool configuration files, it is possible to separate a subset of API exposed by a module, from the rest of the symbols exposed by the same module. For example, it is possible to separate POSIX networking API from the VxWorks module to get a better overview of dependencies to this particular API.

Our analysis showed that the system architect's intentions had been honored, in the sense that the layered architecture was almost perfect, with only a very limited number of violations. Some erosion was however discovered, exposed as occasional usage of API functions that weren't public. These findings were conveyed to the development team subject to further analysis.

Besides the "interactive" use of the tool, it is also possible to use it "offline" as an integrated part of the daily build process. Using a simple configuration file that describes the layers of the layered architecture and the rules about allowed and disallowed dependencies, it is possible to monitor violations of the dependency rules.

4.2 Lessons Learned

Our experiences from C code analysis tests using tools like Understand C, that can analyze the source code, show that it is very easy to be dragged into low level code details and that an overview on architectural level is seldom achieved using such tools.

When using C source code as basis for the analysis we came to the conclusion that it is very difficult to get a full picture of the dependencies that is 100% correct, without any false dependencies due to e.g. duplicate symbol names, leading to time consuming validity checks, making this approach less suitable for regular, automated, monitoring of architectural violations in the software.

The analysis of the binaries provided a path for investigation. Such analysis could be integrated into the regular integration builds. This analysis is then fully automated, but must be implemented separately for each build configuration. Combined with a set of rules for allowed and disallowed dependencies, violations of the architectural rules in the software system implementation can continuously be monitored and kept under control.

The overviews these tools give of the software system are also very valuable for discussions within the organization about system evolution, as they give excellent, up-to-date information of the status of the implementation. Without continuous monitoring, ideally integrated into the integration builds, the architecture will slowly erode. The erosion will mainly affect the system modularity, but will also have impact on the system dependability.

5 Conclusion

Even though there are many tools and approaches for architecture analysis, when addressing the evolution of complex real-life software systems, there is no standard, 'out-of-the-shelf' solution. This is highlighted by the two case studies we present in this paper.

From the holistic perspective of architecture analysis, it is important to take the organizational environment into account. Thus, the investigations are guided by the business goals and cost-benefit considerations. Even technically simple analysis approaches can then be very valuable to provide new information and to trigger architecture refactoring activities.

On the other hand, also the selection of tools and technical approaches is not straightforward and depends very much on the specific software system and the problems to be addressed. Many of the existing tools are limited to static analysis, i.e., they work on the source code. This approach is limited since hidden dependencies, for instance, via sockets or other types of late binding, are not detected, even though they may be relevant for understanding the dependencies between software components in the system. Also for certain languages like C, ambiguities can appear in the resulting analysis since duplicate symbol names can be used at different places, referring to different functions or data. We have taken the approach in one of our cases to work on compiled code to eliminate the ambiguities of multiple symbols. The advantage is that we let the compiler and linker resolve the real dependencies in the code.

To prevent architectural degradation, static and dynamic analysis of the software can be performed as regular activities in the development process providing quick and possibly automatic feedback on the architectural issues. If degradation can be minimized, evolution of the software to meet new requirements in the future can be easier.

Performing holistic analysis of software requires buy-in from the organization - management should be willing to accept surprising or negative findings and provide the resources to act in time if required. Developers should see the tools as companion and help rather than as threat that they are blamed for design mistakes. To address these challenges, the development team has to be involved early in the analysis and be prepared that the outcome might give rise to some additional, unforeseen work – but also to the chance to improve the overall quality and dependability of their system!

Applying a reverse engineering tool is just a starting point - it gets more interesting when the output of the tool is discussed with the people involved in developing the system. We have seen in both our case studies that the discussions following architecture reconstruction have proven very useful when planning software evolution. The discussions also led to more questions and served as a base for further investigations with appropriate tools, and continued interaction with people knowing about the system.

In summary, analyzing a software system is more than just looking at the software itself, all sources of information available should be utilized to make the best possible plan for evolution of the software system.

References

1. Merola, L.: The COTS software obsolescence threat. In: Fifth International Conference on Commercial-off-the-Shelf (COTS)-Based Software Systems, 2006, p. 7 (2006)
2. Kazman, R., Carriere, S.J.: Playing detective: reconstructing software architecture from available evidence. Automated Software Engineering 6, 107–138 (1999)
3. Binkley, D.: Source Code Analysis: A Road Map. In: Future of Software Engineering, 2007. FOSE 2007, pp. 104–119 (2007)
4. Riva, C., Rodriguez, J.V.: Combining static and dynamic views for architecture reconstruction. In: Proceedings Sixth European Conference on Software Maintenance and Reengineering, 2002, pp. 47–55 (2002)
5. Clements, P., Kazman, R., Klein, M.: Evaluating Software Architectures: Methods and Case Studies. Addison-Wesley Professional, Reading (2001)
6. Bosch, J.: Design and Use of Software Architectures: Adopting and Evolving a Product-Line Approach. Addison-Wesley Professional, Reading (2000)
7. Kazman, R., Asundi, J., Klein, M.: Making Architecture Design Decisions: An Economic Approach. Pittsburgh (2002)

8. Sangal, N.: Lightweight Dependency Models for Product Lines. In: Software Product Line Conference, 2006 10th International, p. 228 (2006)
9. Lindvall, M., Ackermann, A., Stratton, W.C., Sibol, D.E., Ray, A., Yonkwa, L., Kresser, J., Godfrey, S., Knodel, J.: Using Sequence Diagrams to Detect Communication Problems between Systems. Fraunhofer Center for Experimental Software Engineering (2007)
10. Svahnberg, M.: A study on agreement between participants in an architecture assessment. In: 2003 International Symposium on Empirical Software Engineering, 2003. ISESE 2003, pp. 61–70 (2003)
11. Avizienis, A., Laprie, J.-C., Randell, B., Landwehr, C.: Basic Concepts and Taxonomy of Dependable and Secure Computing. IEEE Transactions on Dependable and Secure Computing 1(1), 11–33 (2004)
12. Balakrishnan, G., Reps, T., Melski, D., Teitelbaum, T.: WYSINWYX: What You See Is Not What You eXecute, IFIP Working Conference on Verified Software: Theories, Tools, Experiments, Zurich, Switzerland (2005)
13. Guo, G.Y., Atlee, J.M., Kazman, R.: A Software Architecture Reconstruction Method, WICSA1, San Antonio, Texas, USA (1999)
14. Damien, P., et al.: Towards A Process-Oriented Software Architecture Reconstruction Taxonomy. In: Proceedings of the 11th European Conference on Software Maintenance and Reengineering (2007)

Author Index

Lecture Notes in Computer Science

Sublibrary 2: Programming and Software Engineering

For information about Vols. 1– 4553
please contact your bookseller or Springer

Vol. 4909: I. Eusgeld, F.C. Freiling, R. Reussner (Eds.), Dependability Metrics. XI, 305 pages. 2008.

Vol. 4906: M. Cebulla (Ed.), Object-Oriented Technology. VIII, 204 pages. 2008.

Vol. 4902: P. Hudak, D.S. Warren (Eds.), Practical Aspects of Declarative Languages. X, 333 pages. 2007.

Vol. 4899: K. Yorav (Ed.), Hardware and Software: Verification and Testing. XII, 267 pages. 2008.

Vol. 4888: F. Kordon, O. Sokolsky (Eds.), Composition of Embedded Systems. XII, 221 pages. 2007.

Vol. 4880: S. Overhage, C.A. Szyperski, R. Reussner, J.A. Stafford (Eds.), Software Architectures, Components, and Applications. X, 249 pages. 2008.

Vol. 4849: M. Winckler, H. Johnson, P. Palanque (Eds.), Task Models and Diagrams for User Interface Design. XIII, 299 pages. 2007.

Vol. 4839: O. Sokolsky, S. Taşıran (Eds.), Runtime Verification. VI, 215 pages. 2007.

Vol. 4834: R. Cerqueira, R.H. Campbell (Eds.), Middleware 2007. XIII, 451 pages. 2007.

Vol. 4829: M. Lumpe, W. Vanderperren (Eds.), Software Composition. VIII, 281 pages. 2007.

Vol. 4824: A. Paschke, Y. Biletskiy (Eds.), Advances in Rule Interchange and Applications. XIII, 243 pages. 2007.

Vol. 4821: J. Bennedsen, M.E. Caspersen, M. Kölling (Eds.), Reflections on the Teaching of Programming. X, 261 pages. 2008.

Vol. 4807: Z. Shao (Ed.), Programming Languages and Systems. XI, 431 pages. 2007.

Vol. 4799: A. Holzinger (Ed.), HCI and Usability for Medicine and Health Care. XVI, 458 pages. 2007.

Vol. 4789: M. Butler, M.G. Hinchey, M.M. Larrondo-Petrie (Eds.), Formal Methods and Software Engineering. VIII, 387 pages. 2007.

Vol. 4767: F. Arbab, M. Sirjani (Eds.), International Symposium on Fundamentals of Software Engineering. XIII, 450 pages. 2007.

Vol. 4765: A. Moreira, J. Grundy (Eds.), Early Aspects: Current Challenges and Future Directions. X, 199 pages. 2007.

Vol. 4764: P. Abrahamsson, N. Baddoo, T. Margaria, R. Messnarz (Eds.), Software Process Improvement. XI, 225 pages. 2007.

Vol. 4762: K.S. Namjoshi, T. Yoneda, T. Higashino, Y. Okamura (Eds.), Automated Technology for Verification and Analysis. XIV, 566 pages. 2007.

Vol. 4758: F. Oquendo (Ed.), Software Architecture. XVI, 340 pages. 2007.

Vol. 4757: F. Cappello, T. Herault, J. Dongarra (Eds.), Recent Advances in Parallel Virtual Machine and Message Passing Interface. XVI, 396 pages. 2007.

Vol. 4753: E. Duval, R. Klamma, M. Wolpers (Eds.), Creating New Learning Experiences on a Global Scale. XII, 518 pages. 2007.

Vol. 4749: B.J. Krämer, K.-J. Lin, P. Narasimhan (Eds.), Service-Oriented Computing – ICSOC 2007. XIX, 629 pages. 2007.

Vol. 4748: K. Wolter (Ed.), Formal Methods and Stochastic Models for Performance Evaluation. X, 301 pages. 2007.

Vol. 4741: C. Bessière (Ed.), Principles and Practice of Constraint Programming – CP 2007. XV, 890 pages. 2007.

Vol. 4735: G. Engels, B. Opdyke, D.C. Schmidt, F. Weil (Eds.), Model Driven Engineering Languages and Systems. XV, 698 pages. 2007.

Vol. 4716: B. Meyer, M. Joseph (Eds.), Software Engineering Approaches for Offshore and Outsourced Development. X, 201 pages. 2007.

Vol. 4709: F.S. de Boer, M.M. Bonsangue, S. Graf, W.-P. de Roever (Eds.), Formal Methods for Components and Objects. VIII, 297 pages. 2007.

Vol. 4680: F. Saglietti, N. Oster (Eds.), Computer Safety, Reliability, and Security. XV, 548 pages. 2007.

Vol. 4670: V. Dahl, I. Niemelä (Eds.), Logic Programming. XII, 470 pages. 2007.

Vol. 4652: D. Georgakopoulos, N. Ritter, B. Benatallah, C. Zirpins, G. Feuerlicht, M. Schoenherr, H.R. Motahari-Nezhad (Eds.), Service-Oriented Computing ICSOC 2006. XVI, 201 pages. 2007.

Vol. 4640: A. Rashid, M. Aksit (Eds.), Transactions on Aspect-Oriented Software Development IV. IX, 191 pages. 2007.

Vol. 4634: H. Riis Nielson, G. Filé (Eds.), Static Analysis. XI, 469 pages. 2007.

Vol. 4620: A. Rashid, M. Aksit (Eds.), Transactions on Aspect-Oriented Software Development III. IX, 201 pages. 2007.

Vol. 4615: R. de Lemos, C. Gacek, A. Romanovsky (Eds.), Architecting Dependable Systems IV. XIV, 435 pages. 2007.

Vol. 4610: B. Xiao, L.T. Yang, J. Ma, C. Muller-Schloer, Y. Hua (Eds.), Autonomic and Trusted Computing. XVIII, 571 pages. 2007.

Vol. 4609: E. Ernst (Ed.), ECOOP 2007 – Object-Oriented Programming. XIII, 625 pages. 2007.

Vol. 4608: H.W. Schmidt, I. Crnković, G.T. Heineman, J.A. Stafford (Eds.), Component-Based Software Engineering. XII, 283 pages. 2007.

Vol. 4591: J. Davies, J. Gibbons (Eds.), Integrated Formal Methods. IX, 660 pages. 2007.

Vol. 4589: J. Münch, P. Abrahamsson (Eds.), Product-Focused Software Process Improvement. XII, 414 pages. 2007.

Vol. 4574: J. Derrick, J. Vain (Eds.), Formal Techniques for Networked and Distributed Systems – FORTE 2007. XI, 375 pages. 2007.

Vol. 4556: C. Stephanidis (Ed.), Universal Access in Human-Computer Interaction, Part III. XXII, 1020 pages. 2007.

Vol. 4555: C. Stephanidis (Ed.), Universal Access in Human-Computer Interaction, Part II. XXII, 1066 pages. 2007.

Vol. 4554: C. Stephanidis (Ed.), Universal Acess in Human Computer Interaction, Part I. XXII, 1054 pages. 2007.